GREAT BRITISH
PADDLING
ADVENTURES

ADLARD COLES
Bloomsbury Publishing Plc
50 Bedford Square, London, WC1B 3DP, UK
Bloomsbury Publishing Ireland Limited
29 Earlsfort Terrace, Dublin 2, D02 AY28, Ireland

BLOOMSBURY, ADLARD COLES and the Adlard Coles logo are trademarks of Bloomsbury Publishing Plc

First published in Great Britain 2025

Copyright © Richard Harpham and Ashley Kenlock, 2025

Richard Harpham and Ashley Kenlock have asserted their rights under the Copyright, Designs and Patents Act, 1988, to be identified as Author of this work

For legal purposes the Acknowledgements on p. 336 constitute an extension of this copyright page

All rights reserved. No part of this publication may be: i) reproduced or transmitted in any form, electronic or mechanical, including photocopying, recording or by means of any information storage or retrieval system without prior permission in writing from the publishers; or ii) used or reproduced in any way for the training, development or operation of artificial intelligence (AI) technologies, including generative AI technologies. The rights holders expressly reserve this publication from the text and data mining exception as per Article 4(3) of the Digital Single Market Directive (EU) 2019/790

A catalogue record for this book is available from the British Library

Library of Congress Cataloguing-in-Publication data has been applied for

ISBN: PB: 978-1-4729-8914-7; ePub: 978-1-4729-8913-0; ePDF: 978-1-4729-8912-3

10 9 8 7 6 5 4 3 2 1

Typeset in Barlow Semi Condensed
Designed by Austin Taylor
Printed and bound in India by Replika Press Pvt. Ltd.

To find out more about our authors and books visit: www.bloomsbury.com and sign up for our newsletters

For product safety related questions contact: productsafety@bloomsbury.com

IMPORTANT SAFETY NOTICE AND LEGAL DISCLAIMER

This book contains descriptions of paddling routes and locations around the UK. Undertaking any activity on or near water carries with it some risks that cannot be entirely eliminated, for example, you might get lost on a route or caught in bad weather. The information contained in this book should not be relied upon as a sole means of navigation. Users should consult all other relevant and available publications and information, such as the local Harbour Authority guidance or Waterway Authorities Navigation Notices. Users should also check local weather and water conditions with the appropriate authorities prior to departure.

The guidance contained in this book is based on the accumulated experience of the authors. Such guidance is generic and takes no account of users' own experience, advice from other paddlers, actual or forecast meteorological conditions, water conditions or other waterway users powered or otherwise.

All internet addresses given in this book were correct at the time of going to press. Bloomsbury Publishing Plc does not have any control over, or responsibility for, any third-party websites referred to or in this book.

The publishers and authors accept no responsibility for any errors or omissions, or for any accident, loss or damage arising from the misuse of information or guidance contained in this book.

GREAT BRITISH PADDLING ADVENTURES

More than 50 routes for kayak, canoe and paddleboard

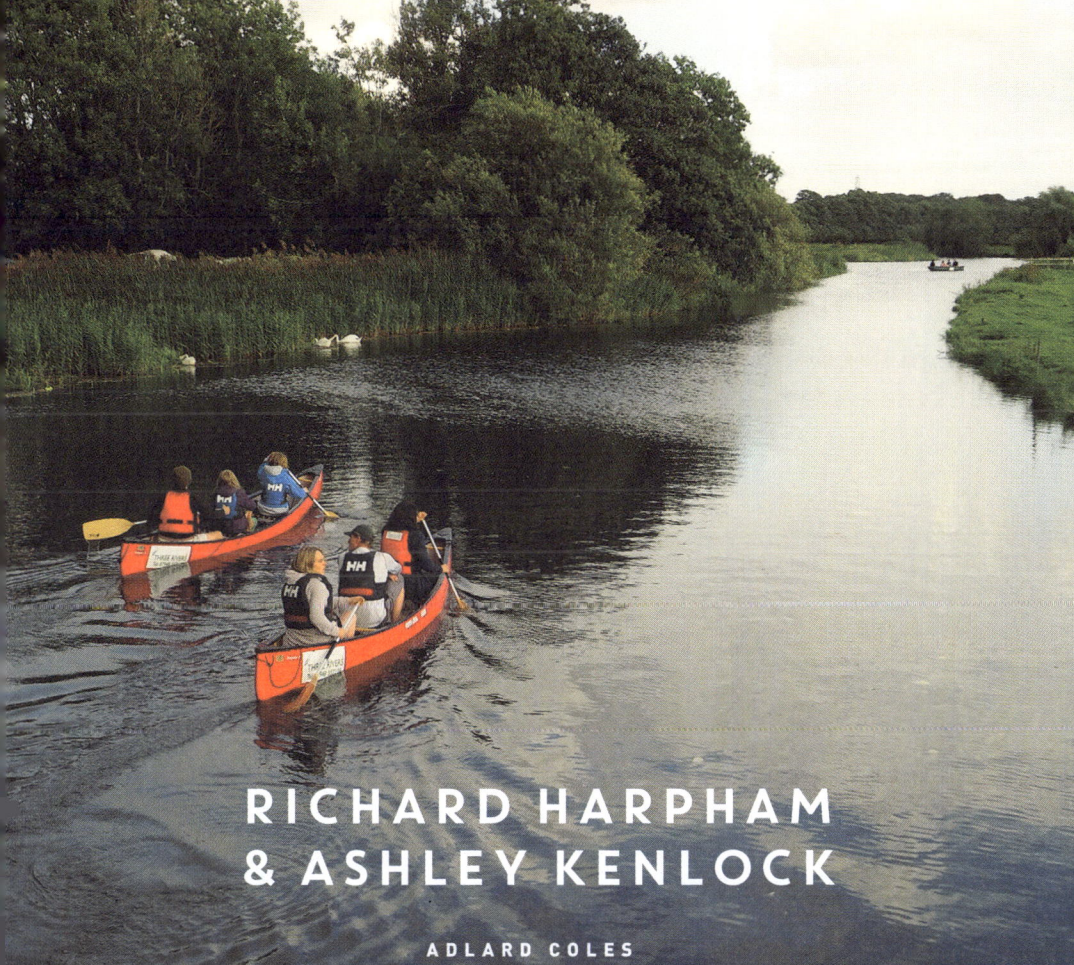

RICHARD HARPHAM
& ASHLEY KENLOCK

ADLARD COLES

CONTENTS

Introduction 6
Before you go 8

SOUTH WEST ENGLAND 20
1 Carrick Roads: Mylor to Flushing 20
2 Padstow 24
3 Fowey 30
4 Boscastle to Tintagel 35

SOUTH OF ENGLAND 40
5 Lulworth Cove and Durdle Door 40
6 Studland and Old Harry Rocks 45
7 Poole Harbour and Beyond 49

8 River Avon at Bradford-on-Avon 54
9 River Thames: Lechlade-on-Thames to Godstow, Oxford 59
10 Oxford's River Cherwell 68
11 River Rother and Bodiam Castle 74
12 River Great Stour, Canterbury 78
13 River Thames: Richmond 83

EAST OF ENGLAND 88
14 River Stour: Constable Country 88
15 River Waveney: Bungay Loop 96
16 River Bure and Salhouse Broad 103
17 Burnham Overy Staithe 111
18 River Nene 115
19 River Great Ouse 122
20 The Cambridge Backs 133

MIDLANDS 140

21 Grand Union Canal 140
22 River Wye: Kerne Bridge to Symonds Yat 147
23 Warwick Castle and the River Avon 153
24 Ironbridge Gorge and the River Severn 157
25 River Trent and the Staffordshire Canals 162
26 Caldon Canal: Leek Branch 171
27 River Derwent and Matlock Bath 175

NORTH OF ENGLAND 181

28 River Ribble 181
29 River Ouse, York and the River Ure 188
30 River Tees: Cotherstone to Barnard Castle 193
31 Windermere: the Lakeland Jewel 199
32 Lake District: Ullswater 206
33 Derwent Water and River 210
34 Lindisfarne – The Holy Island 217

SCOTLAND 223

35 River Tweed: Kelso to Berwick 223
36 Forth & Clyde Canal: The Kelpies to the Falkirk Wheel 231
37 Loch Lomond 238
38 River Teith (Eas Gobhain) 244
39 Loch Tay and River Tay 250
40 Loch Insh and the River Spey 259
41 River Spey: Aviemore to Boat of Garten 264
42 River Spey: Advie to Carron Bridge 268
43 Aigas Gorge and River Beauly 274
44 The Great Glen 278
45 Loch Ness & River Ness 288

WALES 296

46 Llyn Padarn 296
47 River Conwy 302
48 River Dee: Llangollen Canal and the Pontcysyllte Aqueduct 309
49 Lake Bala (Llyn Tegid) and the head of the River Dee (Afon Dyfrdwy) 321
50 River Usk (Afon Wysg) 327

About us 334
Acknowledgements 336

INTRODUCTION

We have been blessed to explore so many rivers, lakes, lochs, canals and the seascape together for a great many years. In the course of this, we have enjoyed extraordinary wildlife, connected with historical trails and sites, and generally embraced 'messing about on the water'. A strong passion for adventure has always coursed through our veins, locked into our DNA, and we hope that some of this will rub off on you. This book is intended to inspire, support and perhaps challenge everyone to explore our island nation more under paddle power.

A great number of friends, customers and coaches have helped shape our journey, providing new ideas, good techniques and top tips. From sharing a new stroke with one of our local customers to running a Paddle UK course, it remains a privilege and honour to share learning in the great outdoors. Our coaching chain, individuals who have trained us and honed skills, have been selfless and patient in equal measure. Thanks a million, team.

We have tried to include a wide variety of different trips, in all corners of the country, and of varying difficulty and duration. So there are gentle paddles as well as tougher challenges to test your steel if that's what you're interested in. Some even involve overnight camping. Most are suitable for all of paddleboards, kayaks and canoes, but we indicate clearly for each trip so you can be sure, safe, and can focus on enjoying your time out on the water.

Happy trails!

Ash and Rich

OPPOSITE Get ready for the natural highs of exciting adventures...

ABOVE ...as well as peaceful journeys through remote countryside.

BEFORE YOU GO

Not only do we want to inspire you to go out and explore the waterways, we want to make it as easy as possible to do so, safely and mindful of others. All the paddle adventures we've featured are rated for difficulty based on how much experience we think you need before you attempt them. For each route we have based the difficulty on the profile of a beginner to intermediate paddler in typical conditions.

Whatever level of experience you have, we've included something for you. If you're very new to paddling, however, we thought it sensible to cover important things for you to know before you begin your adventure.

CHOOSING YOUR CRAFT

Whilst paddling ability will of course affect your experience, so too do the conditions on the day (which you can't control) and your choice of craft (which you often can). For example, in moderate conditions, with bigger waves or stronger winds, a paddleboard would require more effort and skill than a kayak might.

In terms of strokes, most techniques and skills are transferable regardless of which type of craft you use, but each craft does have some unique elements, such as the type of rescues, which may be worth bearing in mind.

New customers regularly ask us whether a paddleboard, kayak or canoe is best for them. Ultimately, the type of paddling you wish to enjoy should dictate your choice. For example, an inflatable paddleboard is ideal for many short trips because it is easy to transport, inflate and deflate. For whitewaters, however, you might find a kayak more stable, easier to control, and less likely to be swept away from you!

So it depends whether it's bimbling along a river or racing against serious competitors that you're interested in. Also bear in mind that even along the same route, the view you're going to get from standing up on a paddleboard or sitting in a kayak could be very different.

BUYING YOUR OWN KIT

It is fair to say that you generally get what you pay for with a wide range of kit. Buying new means you get the benefit of the retailer's range, and should be offered the best option to suit your situation and intentions. The dealer should also provide a warranty backed up by the manufacturer.

If you buy secondhand it is important

> **TOP TIP**
>
> Join Paddle UK to receive *Paddler Magazine* featuring information on the different disciplines, paddling trips around the world to inspire you and news from the governing body.

BELOW Whether using a paddleboard, kayak or canoe, this book has something for you.

to gauge the condition of the craft beforehand. Pay close attention to: broken fittings; gravel rash; repaired holes; deep scratches. These shouldn't necessarily put you off buying. More cosmetic problems (i.e. normal wear and tear) may mean you can grab a bargain.

It is sometimes difficult to tell which will be the best shape and design of craft for you, regardless of whether you buy new or secondhand. A good way to determine its suitability is to try before you buy, but if you buy new, good dealers will usually have a demo fleet. Alternatively join a local club or visit your nearest paddling centre that hire out different craft so you can try theirs before spending your own cash.

Key things to consider before you buy your own:

SIZE – ensure it is comfortable for you, providing good connectivity between you and the craft so that your arm power is easily transferred to the paddle.
LENGTH – this affects the speed: the longer it is, the faster it will be.
WIDTH – this affects the stability: the wider it is, the more stable it will be.
SHAPE – the shape of the hull will impact how well it turns: those that have a more curved, banana-esque shape will be easier to turn.
MATERIAL – the new generation of paddleboards are inflatable, making them light and easy to store and transport. Plastic kayaks and canoes are very durable but heavier than their composite alternatives. Performance and competition craft, such as racing and slalom kayaks, are generally made of carbon or glass fibre.
WEIGHT – further to the above, craft such as carbon Kevlar racing kayaks and composite canoes are stiff and lighter, making them easy to carry. There is always a trade-off with durability, however.
FITTINGS – more technical outfitting includes adjustable foot pegs, air bags in canoes, keeling thwarts for soloing canoes, as well as hatches, handles and other extras.
SKEGS AND RUDDERS – some kayaks have skegs that drop down to help the craft go in a straight line, which can be helpful when you are learning, or going on a longer paddle.

PORTAGING

Many river trips will involve portaging – having to carry your kit overland to avoid locks, weirs and other obstacles. Depending on the craft, you may be able to carry it over your shoulder or under your arm (an inflatable paddleboard). Be careful dragging it on the ground in case sharp objects damage the hull. For heavier craft you may need a trolley. You can improvise rollers using flotsam or small logs if nothing else is available. As with many paddling skills and techniques, it is best to practice portaging on flat ground to assess your own capabilities before heading out.

WHAT TO WEAR

Another standard question we often get asked is to what to wear for paddling. There is a saying in the outdoor adventure world – 'there is no such thing as cold weather, just the wrong clothing'. The simple answer is to dress for the weather, which may mean a coat or a dry suit, but may also mean shorts and a sun hat.

FOOTWEAR – whilst you may see some paddleboarders going barefoot, flip flops and sandals are ideal for time on land. Footwear is important whatever the season, but on whitewater a solid sole with a good grip is essential.

HEADWEAR – at either end of the weather spectrum, headwear is important. In colder weather a woolly hat can take the edge off cold air and prevent heat loss. In warmer weather a cap or wide-brimmed hat can prevent sunburn to your eats and face. Remember the water can reflect sunlight.

CLOTHING – wearing layers is the best way to regulate body temperature, because you can add or remove them to suit your comfort level. On certain paddles, a dry suit or waterproof and windproof tops can make all the difference too.

BELOW Dress up warmly, wear safety equipment, and let the fun begin.

BELOW Doggy paddles off the south coast.

WHERE TO PADDLE

Though we will go into the specific things you need to know to paddle each location featured, there are also some general points to be aware of when considering where to paddle.

RIVERS – there is a grading system in place to help you determine the nature of the water:
Grade 1 – slow-moving flat water, maybe some ripples.
Grade 2 – small waves and little stoppers, but unlikely to cause a capsize.
Grade 3 – bigger waves and whitewater, requiring a specific route.
Grade 4 to 6 – whitewater, become increasingly more demanding in terms of the skill required to navigate.

Always bear in mind that rivers can change quickly and when in spate (flood) can be different from other times. This book contains rivers at the lower end of the scale, Grade 1 to 2 in typical conditions.

LAKES AND LOCHS – conditions can vary, from glass-like flat calm to 3ft waves in strong winds. Larger bodies of water can seem like the sea. The length of open water subject to fetch (wind sheer) and the depth of the water all has an impact. Staying close to shore is advisable. You should head to land at the first sign of gusting winds, storms or white caps. If venturing further from the shore, fit your kayak or canoe with buoyancy bags for additional flotation.

SEA AND COAST – with sheltered harbours, estuaries, coves and headlands, Britain is a sea kayaking paradise (we like to forage seaweed, mollusks and other edibles for a paella at the end of a trip!). However, sea kayaking and coastal paddling is not something you should attempt without adequate preparation. The sea and coast is an ever-changing three-dimensional environment, with waves, tides and the shape of the shore dynamics that will make every trip different, even along the same route. Storms, offshore winds and large waves can make this a challenging exercise. Always paddle within your limits, check the forecast before you go, and seek local advice.

TOP TIP

Visit UK Rivers Guide, Sea Kayak Guide, Open Canoe Association or Song of the Paddle for up to date information about rivers and waterways.

RULES FOR ACCESSING BRITISH WATERS

Depending on where you're paddling, there are different restrictions on where you can go, whether rivers, canals, the coastline, or open waters such as lakes and reservoirs. Scotland leads the way with 'right to roam' freedoms providing you behave responsibly.

In England and Wales, access is usually limited to where there is an established right of navigation. This includes many rivers and canals, but it's worth bearing in mind that in lots of places, the owner of the riverbank also owns half the riverbed and the water flowing. Paddle UK and open water swimming groups have been challenging this under the Clean Waters Clear Access campaign.

Paddle UK offers a national licence as part of membership. Other ways to get a licence include via the Canal and River Trust, though theirs is obviously limited to waters under their jurisdiction, or the Environment Agency, but theirs is regional so again limits access nationwide.

CHECKING THE WEATHER

We often say 'you'll never beat the weather – the best you will achieve is a score draw'. It is really important that you check the weather and environmental conditions for the places you paddle.

Become familiar with the Beaufort scale, paying close attention to the indicators for wind speed increasing. Also bear in mind the impact of wind direction, and possible changes, especially if you are using a paddleboard – you will effectively act like a sail. That's fun with the wind behind your back, but makes things more difficult if you're paddling against it.

There are a range of useful apps to choose from: Wind Finder, Windy, Magicseaweed/Surfline, Acuweather, Lightning Near Me, The Met Office

Check local maps, charts and a detailed weather forecast whilst planning your trip.

TOP TIP

A licence from Paddle UK will grant you permission to paddle most canals and waterways as well as some private waters, such as the Cambridge Backs. The licence is included with membership, but that also has additional benefits, such as insurance, member discounts, coaching and qualification opportunities, and much more.

ASSESSING THE WIDER ENVIRONMENT

The weather will probably be the factor that has the most impact on your paddle, but pay attention to other potential risks, whether temporary or permanent.

RIVER GRADE

1 – no rocks or hazards, little ripples and waves, but nothing too difficult for beginners.
2 – can have waves and small stoppers, but shouldn't prove too challenging for someone who has basic skills.
3 – more waves and stoppers, sometimes drops, and may have obstacles such as rocks that require you to paddle a certain route.
4 – can have big waves, stoppers, drops and obstacles that can impact the flow of the water, so you need to assess the route before you begin paddling (some rapids may be graded 4).
5 – strong currents, waves and stoppers can make these very difficult to paddle, so should only be attempted by those with plenty of experience.
6 – rivers that may seem impossible to paddle and should not be considered except by highly advanced paddlers.

TIDES

This is relevant for any coastal paddling, even if you are paddling in an estuary rather than on the sea. Check the UKHO EasyTide website to find out when high and low tides are for the precise time you plan to paddle. Paddling against the tide is harder than paddling with it (in the Skerries in Scotland the tides can race at 20 knots), but in areas with a wide tidal range (the Bristol Channel has the second widest in the world – 12 to 14 metres) this may impact where you get in and out of the water. Avoid wind against tide, which creates uncomfortable waters at stronger levels.

SEA STATE

It is important for anyone sea (or surf) kayaking to make a realistic assessment of whether their craft and their abilities are up to the task – not just how things look now, but if they were to get worse too.

On moving water the risks increase because of specific hazards such as strainers (trees and branches that allow water to pass through but trap kayaks, canoes and paddleboards), undercuts, siphons, and rocks where you may get stuck. Consider how exposed the location is (whether paddling through a canyon or around a headland or crossing a large bay).

We have flagged up things to be aware of for each of the routes, but you should be vigilant at all times to remain safe. When paddling in new waters, try to seek out information from paddlers who have experience of the area, such as an instructor or guide.

Ultimately the key thing to always bear in mind is how far from help you will be if you get into trouble.

> **TOP TIP**
>
> Download and use the River App to access both live and historical river data.

WATER QUALITY

In recent years there has been increased pressure on the water companies and local authorities to monitor and improve our water quality on rivers and coastal areas. During flood conditions water companies in some instances retain a licence to discharge

OPPOSITE The Kelpies in Scotland as seen from the water.

untreated effluent into our waters. It's important to check whether the water you may be swimming or practicing skills could be affected by outfalls or spillages.

NAVIGATION

In an increasingly digital world there is a risk that paper maps become obsolete and we become reliant on GPS. But paper maps can be an inspiration in themselves, and are probably a bit more likely to survive being dropped in the water.

It is a useful skill to have to be able to read the lie of the land, maintain a sense of direction and observe natural features. Taking compass bearings will help you orientate the map, as will logging your speed over time. Use a pencil to highlight key markers (hills with contours, locks, etc) on the map and note how long it takes you to travel between them. This will help you develop a sense of your own pace, and project how long it may take you to paddle other distances.

GPS can still be a back-up, however – we carry a Garmin inReach on expeditions and a TopoActive Etrex in more remote areas.

PREPARING FOR EMERGENCIES

Wherever you go, but especially if you haven't been there before, it is useful to have at least one location app on your phone, and a paper-based Ordnance Survey map as a back-up.

Sometimes the places you will want to go to paddle are not always readily accessible by emergency services, so being able to give an accurate location that they can access may be useful and save time in the event things don't go to plan.

Good apps include: What Three Words, Postcode Finder, OS Locate.

If it becomes necessary for you to abandon your craft, it can be very useful to have a 'ditch kit' with you, containing: additional clothes, a torch, a multi-tool (such as a Leatherman), gaffer tape, a first aid kit (in a waterproof bag).

You can read more about safety skills and practicing rescues below.

> **TOP TIP**
>
> Tell a friend or family member about your trip and anticipated return time, and paddle with experienced peers where possible.

LOOKING AFTER THE PLANET

Remember the rule of thumb: wherever you paddle, leave only bubbles, take only pictures and be considerate to other users.

As paddlers, there are lots of ways we can make a difference to improve the environment: collecting plastic and other litter; removing abandoned fishing line, hooks and lures; car sharing to reduce traffic and pollution; giving nesting birds and other wildlife space; being aware of invasive species and ensuring you don't contaminate the waterways; joining groups such as Surfers Against Sewage, Planet Patrol and the Marine Conservation Society.

> **TOP TIP**
>
> Carry some old gloves, a good knife and bag to collect rubbish while out paddling.

WHERE TO GET COACHING AND OTHER INFORMATION

If you're the kind of person who learns by doing, then joining your local club is a great way to find qualified coaches but also like-minded people with whom you can develop your skills.

Learning from books or watching videos online is great, but you may find the learning curve slower-paced than taking a proper course. Remember also that 'practice makes permanent' so you don't want to gain bad habits.

TOP TIP

Check out Paddle UK's website and new e-learning portal for how to find coaching near you. Drop Canoe Trail a line for coaching courses or whitewater skills trips.

Paddle UK introduced the Personal Paddling Awards (PPA), and there are several different levels:

Start Award – a taster session lasting perhaps a couple of hours or more designed to get you out on the water as quickly as possible.

Discover Award – typically a day spent covering the fundamentals of paddling: moving forward, steering, turning, plus some theory and basic self-rescue skills.

Explore Award – a two-day course covering rescues, developing personal paddling skills and more advanced strokes.

Craft-specific Awards – progress your skills on different craft in more moderate and challenging conditions.

They also offer dedicated rescue courses, from Paddle Safer up to the Paddlesports Safety and Rescue Course (PSRC), which cover both theory and practice to help you and others stay safe.

TOP TIP

See whether a coach runs any training in a swimming pool. Pool sessions make some skills, such as rolling in a kayak, more pleasant to learn.

TOP TIP

Wear a helmet for whitewater, rapids or rocky areas and particularly where the risk of a tumble or capsize is increased. It also keeps your head warm in cold weather.

BELOW Take a course to push your paddling to the next level.

ABOVE Rapids are exciting, but you need to know how to stay safe.

SAFETY AND RESCUE SKILLS

It's important to learn the basics of self-rescue, whatever the craft you are using. You need to be a confident enough swimmer to reach the bank if you lose your craft. It's better to lose your paddle than your craft, so stay with the latter if possible.

We recommend a hierarchy of rescue protocols:

Self - assess the risks and keep yourself safe first and foremost.
Team - ensure the rest of your group is safe next (if they are able, they will also be self-rescuing).
Casualty - if someone is in trouble, and you can safely assist them, shout to them and/or use a line or paddle.
Equipment - this should always be your last priority; don't put yourself at any risk to rescue lost equipment.

TOP TIP
Air bags or blocks in a kayak or canoe add buoyancy so can make rescues easier.

PADDLEBOARD SAFETY

Paddleboards are buoyant in themselves, but it is also recommended that you wear a buoyancy aid (and a wet suit, if possible) in case you get separated from your board.

If you opt for a leash, one attached to a waist belt is better than one attached to your ankle because it can be easier to reach and release quickly if it gets snagged. On sheltered waters with no wind such as bays and small rivers you might not feel like using a leash, but on any open water or in windy conditions it is essential.

If you fall off your paddleboard, kick like a seal on to the side of the board adjacent to the carry handle and pull yourself up. Alternatively, crawl up from the tail of the board, wriggling forward on your chest and then straddling it like a cowboy. Getting someone to hold and stabilize the board whilst you practice this can help.

TOP TIP
Wear a waist harness and read the latest advice about leashes on SUPs.

KAYAK SAFETY

It would be useful to practice a capsize or roll in a warm pool rather than in a river or open water. Don't worry, it's not as scary as it might look. To get out of the kayak after it turns over, reach out and release the spraydeck loop. With your hands by your hips, push against the cockpit. Make sure your legs are completely out before surfacing.

OPPOSITE Canoes are a great way to paddle with a partner.

To learn how to roll (staying in the kayak and avoiding the need to swim and get back in) you really need to be shown by a coach so you can practice safely.

You will also be able to practice the T rescue. This is where you position your kayak at 90 degrees to the upturned kayak, then drag it upside down on to your cockpit to allow the water to drain. Use a seesaw motion until it is empty, then flip the kayak back over and help the now-swimming paddler back into it. Rafting your kayaks side by side is the easiest way to do this.

> **TOP TIP**
>
> Develop your sense of balance on the water by moving around your kayak. A fun challenge is to exit the cockpit and try to put your nose on the nose of the kayak. Warning: practice this in calm sheltered water conditions – it may not work out as planned the first time.

CANOE SAFETY

Swim lines can be particularly useful with canoes. They are essentially floating ropes attached to the rope loops at the end of your canoe. In the event of a capsize they allow you to grab hold of the canoe on a long line, using yourself as anchor to stop the canoe blowing away on open water, or even shooting off without you in whitewater rapids.

To use a swim line effectively:
- Position the swim line on the bow and stern of the canoe.
- Make sure it is not too loose, where it could become a tangle hazard.
- If you capsize, grab the line and swim back to the bank.
- Swing the canoe around like a pendulum to bring it to the bank downstream of you.
- Don't try to stop it immediately – get a firm footing and lower your centre of gravity to stop it escaping.
- Practice makes permanent – handling a waterlogged craft is tricky so practice before you need it or sign up for a rescue course.

> **TOP TIP**
>
> Get a small builders muck bucket or large dustpan to use as a speedy bailer.

> **TOP TIP**
>
> Fit buoyancy to canoes and kayaks to make rescues easier and reduce the swamped craft effect.

As with kayaks, you can use a T rescue to help other paddlers. Lower your gunnel to allow the other canoe to slide on its side over your own, then carefully rotate it upside down so the water empties – being sure it goes into the river rather than your own canoe! Refloat the canoe and help the other paddler back into it.

> **TOP TIP**
>
> Let the water empty slowly from the craft to avoid lifting too much weight. Good manual handling is important to protect your back.
>
> When their canoe is still partially flooded, you could consider using a scoop rescue to get them out of the water faster. You use their waterlogged canoe to basically scoop them up, then they climb into your canoe and can help you empty theirs. This might be the right approach to take if you don't believe you have the strength to perform a T rescue on your own. If you attempt it, make sure you keep hold of your paddle so you don't lose it.

LEADING A GROUP

After you've been paddling a while, you will invariably have met plenty of others doing it, as well as those who want to try. Leading a group can be a lot of fun, but your number one priority is the safety of those you are leading. You need to make a careful plan of any route with plenty of extraction points in case the weather or other conditions change. Check the forecast but always be prepared for the unexpected.

We always bear the acronym CLAP in mind:

BELOW Under paddle-power you will see the country from a completely new angle.

Communication – give group members clear instructions, agreeing in advance verbal and visual signs, though nobody should be out of shouting range.
Line of sight – don't let any of the group get so far ahead or so far behind that you lose track of them.
Avoidance – researching and anticipating potential problems is better than having to improvise solutions after they happen.
Position of maximum usefulness – paddle where you can assist the group, for example by showing the group the best line along the river, or by staying closer to weaker paddlers.

This applies to open water and whitewater but also when simply practicing some skills.

TOP TIP

If you are leading a group, come prepared. Carry a knife, a saw (to cut thwarts in pinned canoes, for example), a repair kit, gaffer tape, map and anything else you have ever found yourself needing – whether you had it at the time or not.

Ideally learn with professional instructors or more experienced peers to develop your leadership and decision-making skills. If you want to take this hobby further, consider taking a Paddle UK qualification. One of the best things about paddling is getting to share it with others – as we ourselves have found out.

KEY TO SYMBOLS USED IN THIS BOOK

- tides/tidal flow
- moving water
- whitewater
- rapids
- open water
- waves
- wind / fetch

- offshore / strong winds
- rocks
- weirs / sluices
- dams
- locks
- shallow rivers
- tunnels
- trees
- fishermen

- fishing pitches
- portages
- rowers
- other craft
- ferries
- restricted access
- canoe
- kayak
- sup

KEY TO DIFFICULTY

 suitable for all, especially beginners

 intermediate, some experience required

 challenging, for experienced paddlers only

SOUTH WEST ENGLAND

1 CARRICK ROADS: MYLOR TO FLUSHING

Explore one of Britain's finest harbours, which has attracted swashbucklers and adventurers since the dawn of time. Enjoy the backdrop of this fine naval port with rolling hills and aquamarine waters to stir the soul. The area has narrow estuary shores with great pubs and cafes, castles defending these ancient waters and even small fishing villages. Though be aware that cargo ships visit the main port, so stay close to shore unless making a crossing.

The Lowdown

DIFFICULTY

DISTANCE 13km, with the opportunity to double or triple your mileage if the mood takes you by extending your range up the Carrick Roads and creeks to Truro.

You could also plan to go and out and back with the tides for a round trip.

DIRECTIONS Park at Mylor Bridge near the quay or alternatively, if you are starting further downstream, at Mylor Churchtown, where you'll park on the quay. Beware: it gets very busy in high season. The shuttle is 5km (about 10 minutes).

HAZARDS

CRAFT

ABOVE Launching early morning at Mylor Bridge.

BACKGROUND Britain's largest estuary, Carrick Roads, is a classic Cornish estuary and home to a wide range of incredible history, stunning wildlife and a host of activity. It's also known for deep water – down to depths of 34m – and is bustling with maritime history, naval presence, local fisheries and, of course, popular tourism.

The Carrick Roads lends itself to paddling in kayaks and SUPs in particular, with relatively sheltered waters and a choice of launch points offering A to B journeys and circular routes, allowing paddlers to choose the best location to avoid wind and waves.

A SLICE OF HISTORY There's plenty of maritime history among the centuries-old naval ports of Mylor and Falmouth, the latter of which was home to the packet ships, sail vessels carrying royal mail to and from the colonies after official appointment in

SUP'ERS NOTE

Be aware of conditions for the open water section. Large tankers and other big boats operate in the estuary and deeper water of Falmouth.

	LOCATION	GRID REFERENCE	POST CODE	WHAT3WORDS
START (1)	Mylor Bridge Quay	SW805360	TR11 5NE	barbarian.digesting.hopper.
START (2)	Mylor Church	SW820353	TR11 5UF	treble.deck.skid
CROSSING TO ST MAWES*	St Mawes	SW840327	TR2 5DE	crew.pegged.videos
FINISH	Flushing Quay	SW808337	TR11 5TZ	beast.casual.ties

*conditions permitting

ABOVE St Mawes Castle after crossing the Carrick Roads.

1688. The ports were a former base for the French resistance during the Second World War and the naval training ship HMS *Ganges* was moored in Mylor for over 30 years (there's a memorial in the church alongside a 5.2m-tall Celtic cross, uncovered during 19th-century restoration).

Just up the creek, the Pandora Inn boasts a rich history. Its former owner, Captain Edwards, a nasty piece of work by reputation, was dispatched to Tahiti to bring the HMS *Bounty* mutineers to justice. Around the headland, St Mawes Castle was built by Henry VIII as part of his artillery defences against the Spanish and French.

ROUTE Starting at the Mylor Bridge, up one of the spurs of the Carrick Roads, requires consultation with the tides to avoid mud flats and running aground. Just after high tide means a slow-moving conveyor of saline waters flowing out towards the estuary mouth. However, once you're paddling alongside the rolling green hills and flared oak trees, stunted by the conditions, you can relax. Perfect waterside properties and moorings populate these otherwise still waters. This creek opens up by Mylor Boatyard, church and, more importantly, the first watering hole, Mylor Café, awaits (it gets busy in the tourist season so pack a snack or be prepared to wait).

Heading left up into the wider estuary following the left shore, you leave behind more moorings and pontoons with cormorants and herons fishing. The Pandora Inn is a short paddle away and tucked further up into the creek, offering a great pit stop. You can continue further up the estuary for many miles to the city of Truro, but you'd need to use the tides to avoid a slog. Instead, heading back out towards the sea, retrace your route to Mylor Church and then follow the Trefusis headland on your right, around towards the charming village of Flushing. There's an option to explore further and paddle across to St Mawes Castle on the other side of the estuary (conditions permitting). Tankers and other bigger craft use the shipping lanes, so make a direct crossing to the opposite shore. Once there you can simply imagine you're storming the castle before heading round into the sleepy Cornish village.

Depending on conditions and other marine traffic, backtrack to the shortest direct crossing or cut the corner back to the Trefusis headlands, closer to Flushing. As you transit back to the opposite shore you get a unique view of Falmouth and Penryn.

WHERE'S THE MAGIC?

The Carrick Roads is the epitome of a Cornish getaway with fantastic pubs and cafés on the estuary and, of course, a rich maritime history. The defences and castles at St Mawes and Pendennis (on the opposite headland) provide the perfect backdrop to this paddle and a real sense of adventure.

There are usually plenty of navy ships and bigger craft moored below the backdrop of a colourful array of houses on the opposite hill.

There's still time to explore the little nooks and crannies of the Trefusis headlands before rounding the first quay at the Flushing Sailing Club and on to the main village quay close to the pub.

MY RICH ADVENTURE The Carrick Roads is a very special place for me, as I grew up in Flushing and it's here I learnt to swim in the sea, row a dinghy and sail with my uncle, who was a Cornish fisherman. Exploring these waters years later by kayak was a truly nostalgic experience, giving me a salty trip down memory lane.

My paddle involved a misty start, with warming rays clearing the foggy tendrils before I cruised to St Mawes via the Pandora Inn and made a pitstop in Mylor Church to visit the graves of some of my relatives buried there.

CALORIE CREDITS The Mylor Café has freshly prepared food at great prices (W: https://cafemylor.com). Further up the creek there's the iconic 13th-century Pandora Inn (W: www.pandorainn.com), or why not visit the Waterside seafood restaurant on Flushing Quay (W: thewatersideflushing.com).

WILDLIFE SAFARI Cormorants, kingfishers, herons, seals and jellyfish abound. Don't forget to check out the miniature kingdoms amid the rock pools.

OTHER ATTRACTIONS Visit the Eden Project to see the incredible vision and transformation of these former clay pits into magical ecosystems for flora and fauna (W: www.edenproject.com). Travel a bit further north to visit the Lost Gardens of Heligan, 200 acres of magical gardens (W: https://www.heligan.com).

Stop by the National Maritime Museum in Falmouth to unlock Britain's proud naval and maritime history (W: https://nmmc.co.uk), or escape the crowds by touring Cornwall's world-famous surfing beaches and seaside villages.

THE SHARED ECONOMY You can hire SUPs and sit-on-top kayaks at Mylor Quay in Falmouth (W: www.falmouthriverwatersports.co.uk).

BELOW Finishing our paddle trip at Flushing Quay.

2 PADSTOW

Find Cornish creeks, upmarket seaside towns and golden sands to while away the time on this easy paddle starting from Padstow's ever popular quayside. Following the ebb or flood of the tide you can reach Rock, opposite over the waters or up the Camel Estuary. Padstow is a gastronomic hot bed of eateries as well as ice cream and pasty rewards to ensure your trip is memorable. As you venture towards the estuary mouth the beaches become ever more golden and inviting for a sunbath and snooze.

The Lowdown

DIFFICULTY
An easy paddle assuming fair conditions, check wind, waves and tides to keep it simple.

DISTANCE Padstow Quay to beaches and mouth of Camel Estuary, including Rock: 4.5km.

DIRECTIONS You can launch at the harbour by the car park but you'll need to pay a launch fee. It's a 100m carry depending on your parking spot and space. We've also launched elsewhere in sea kayaks on previous trips and surfed the waves at the mouth of the estuary. Be aware of the tides and open expanse of water and if in doubt ask the locals.

If you want to allow time for beaches, exploring and grabbing some rays, include a day's paddling on the Camel Estuary and Padstow.

HAZARDS

CRAFT

	LOCATION	GRID REFERENCE	POST CODE	WHAT3WORDS
PARKING	Car park on quay	SW920753	PL28 8BN	defender.uses.complies
START/FINISH	Padstow Quay	SW920754	PL28 8BN	presented.crumples.workflow
LANDING	Rock	SW928757	PL27 6FD	inherits.importing.chess
ENTRANCE TO CAMEL ESTUARY	Mole End, Trebretherick	SW922781	PL27 6SA	suspect.broadens.imparting
CYCLE ROUTE	Above viaduct	SW924740	PL27 7QH	decanter.regarding.assorted

BELOW Matt and the team crossing from Padstow to Rock dodging ferries.

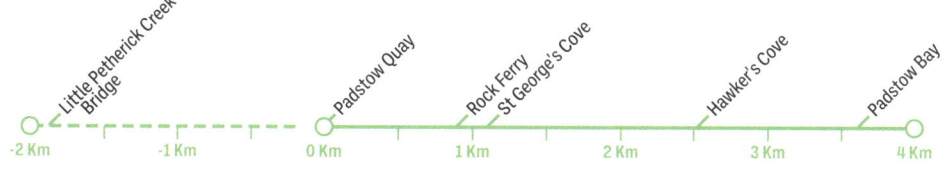

BACKGROUND
With long, golden beaches, a dramatic coastline, fine eateries galore and a ferry over the water to the upmarket seaside town of Rock, Padstow Quay, harbour and the Camel Estuary together form the quintessential place to enjoy a holiday on the British coast.

A SLICE OF HISTORY
Padstow has a long and interesting history. It was once a major port and stands on an ancient trading route between Brittany, France, and Ireland, believed to date from the Bronze Age. The name Padstow is thought to derive from Saint Petroc, who established a monastic settlement here in approximately AD 520.

Padstow is recorded in the *Domesday Book* (1086), when it was held by Bodmin Monastery and has a recorded population of 12 households. It became a busy and important fishing port during the Middle Ages.

From 1899 until 1967, Padstow railway station was the westernmost point of the former Southern Railway and was stopped under the Beeching railway cuts to now become the much-loved Camel Trail permissive cycle route (27.8km from Padstow to Wendford Bridge).

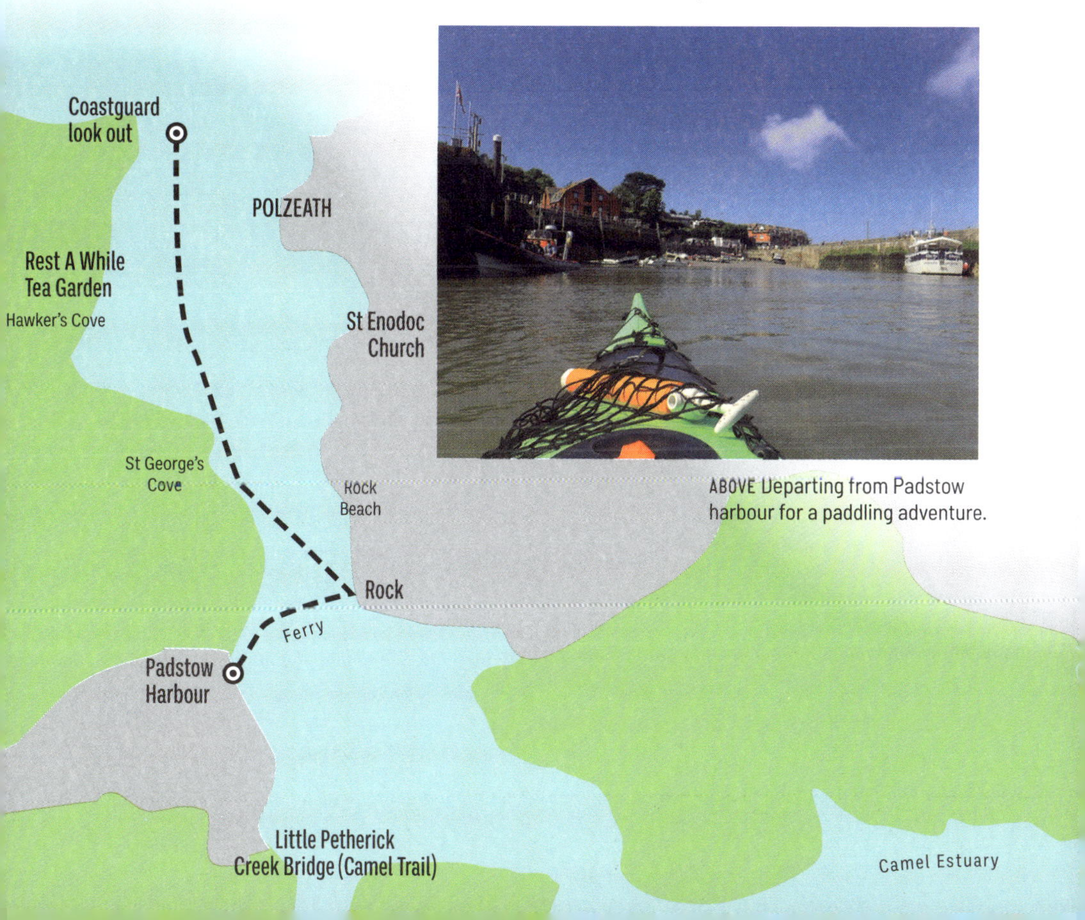

ABOVE Departing from Padstow harbour for a paddling adventure.

ABOVE Ash and William heading out from Padstow to explore the beaches.

ROUTE Once launched and depending on the tide (in or out) you can choose a variety of routes, from heading up the Camel Estuary river to exploring beaches and Rock, across the estuary on the north coast of Cornwall. From leaving the slipway you do need to stay alert for ferries and fishing boats heading across the waters. It can get a bit like the classic arcade game *Frogger*, but as long as you have clear line of sight and cross channels quickly and directly it is pretty straightforward.

Following the ferry across the water to Rock makes for a simple trip to bolt on to your paddle at Padstow, and from the slipway across is just over a kilometre. At lower tides this may involve some zigzag manoeuvres to avoid sandbanks.

If you head up the estuary out towards the Celtic Sea from the harbour, it's ~750m to St Saviour's Point war memorial on the hill on the left bank. This is opposite Rock Beach, which reveals itself further as the tide heads out. Half a kilometre past this is the bijou and compact St George's Cove, which follows around the small headland to the left to the bigger Harbour Cove. We had a combo of SUPs and kayaks on our last visit and spent ages playing here on the beach, joined by relatives who had followed along on the coastal track to meet us.

About 700m later at the end of the main beach is Hawker's Cove and the Rest A While Tea Garden, open from Easter to October and offering refreshments and a beachy vibe. From here it's a final kilometre to the mouth of the Camel Estuary, with Stepper Point Coastguard lookout on the cliffs to the left. To the right around the corner is the charming Polzeath, which usually has surf waves.

Set back on the far side of the bay is St Enodoc Church, almost lost to the surrounding dunes. You can land on the beach in Daymer Bay if you fancy stretching your legs.

Following the Camel Trail on the right bank as you head upstream, you'll pass the fishing boats of the fleet, the lobster hatchery and sea cadets as you head about 1.5km inland to reach the railway viaduct. The Little Petherick Creek Bridge (on the

Camel Trail) is a solid steel girder affair, and if you paddle under it and cycle over it during a single visit, we're pretty sure you're entitled to claim it.

Depending on tide levels and times you can paddle under the bridge and up almost 2km towards Petherick. When the tide's out you'll be greeted with stinky mud flats and banks.

EXTEND THE TRIP
You can extend the trip by going with the tide inland on the flood and out with the ebb as far as Wadebridge, ~7km past the viaduct bridge. Again, avoid tidal mud flats and check tides to stick to the main channels. On the right bank as you head inland is the Camel Trail, so it's possible to convert this paddle to an A to B route, starting or finishing at Wadebridge at high tide and using the ebb or flood to transport you to your destination.

BELOW Arafat and Foxy heading out to the estuary.

OUR RICH ADVENTURE
We've paddled our hearts out in Padstow, camped in the car parks, sea kayaked, SUP'd and generally had the best time. We've had great nights out with lovely food from local independents and wonderful beach picnics, leaving us with lots of fond memories of a place that feels like a second home to us. We've also swapped paddling kit for bikes and hired a tandem for the Camel Trail, which proved a step too far in our marriage! Our good friend Charlie Fish, fishmonger and all-around nice guy, was a member of the Life Boat crew here and owns a couple of static caravans in a local park, providing an adventure HQ.

On one of our many trips we followed the family around the estuary and over to Rock as they hopped on the ferry and we sea kayaked. Paddling up under the old bridge on the estuary or surfing the waves at the mouth of the river have left Padstow firmly etched in our hearts.

CALORIE CREDITS
Padstow is home to world-famous chef Rick Stein and his family, but equally importantly a huge range of independent local eateries, from gastro pubs to fine dining.

If you love fish and shellfish, as I do, then you can't go far wrong making a reservation at Mussel Box (W: www.musselbox.co.uk).

You can enjoy Stein's fish and chips on the quay, but be warned: there can be long queues on a summer day (W: https://rickstein.com/restaurants/steins-fish-and-chips/).

Shipwrights is a traditional Cornish pub offering good food done well (W: https://shipwrightspadstow.co.uk/).

You'll find a relaxing place to stop at the Rest A While Tea Garden (T: 01841 532919), while there are Cornish pasty shops, bakeries and ice cream opportunities around every corner, so make sure you paddle hard so you can enjoy the afters!

WILDLIFE SAFARI
Watching dolphins, seals and puffins is a must here, as is rock pooling for the coastal mini beasts.

BELOW Heading back up the estuary to Padstow.

WHERE'S THE MAGIC?
Padstow is one of those places that once in your heart will never leave. If you're a foodie, be warned: it will capture your gastronome heart, too. You can escape the hustle and bustle quickly with your own paddling craft to marvel at golden sand beaches and aquamarine waters. Tides also ensure this is an ever-changing playground, with estuaries, beaches, and nooks and crannies to keep you busy for hours. Kick back and find a secluded beach spot that equals any Caribbean deserted island on a warm, sunny day.

OTHER ATTRACTIONS
Hire a bike, tandem or electric Silver Dream Machine and explore the Camel Trail, a Sustrans-backed trail of nearly 30km. We discovered our limits by tandem and almost stacked it, but had the best day out following this former railway track (W: https://www.padstowcyclehire.com).

The National Lobster Hatchery may not sound like a standard day out, but this is Cornwall and fishing is in

the blood. Great for all the family (W: www.nationallobsterhatchery.co.uk).

Wave Hunters offers boat charters and sea safari trips to spot dolphins, puffins and seals, among other wildlife (W: www.wavehunters.co.uk/location/padstow).

St Enodoc Church stands amid the sand dunes at Daymer Bay. Former Poet Laureate Sir John Betjeman was particularly fond of it and he lies buried in the churchyard (W: www.northcornwallclusterofchurches.org.uk/our-churches/st-enodoc/).

Around the corner from Padstow is Polzeath, with its golden sands and regular waves making it a haven for surfers from the four corners. While studying at Plymouth University, we'd make the trip to surf there regularly.

THE SHARED ECONOMY Camel Ski School was established in 1977 and offers high-quality watersports and instruction, from waterskiing to wakeboarding, boat hire and SUPs galore. It even has an innovative floating party café called the Island! (W: www.camelskischool.com).

Operating from Padstow, Newquay and St Ives (and also in Scotland), Vertical Descents offers kayaking trips, coasteering and other outdoor activities (W: www.verticaldescents.com).

ABOVE Arafat and Foxy off the golden sandy beaches near Padstow.

BELOW Arafat SUP'ing across the bay.

3 FOWEY

Join the rich naval tradition of Fowey as you paddle among water craft of all shapes and sizes in this beautiful harbour and more remote estuary. There's plenty of wildlife, stunning boats and lots more to see, including the twin artillery forts of St Catherine's and Polruan, which defended this traditional Cornish port for centuries.

The Lowdown

DIFFICULTY
You'll need to judge the tides to make the going easy.

DISTANCE A simple 4-5 km paddle up to Golant or double the distance up and down the estuary past Cliff towards Lerryn which is 9km round trip. Heading down to the port will add a couple of kilometres to your trip.

DIRECTIONS Unload at Caffa Mill car park. You may be able to park there during the off season or drop off and park further afield, with a short walk back to the slipway.

HAZARDS

CRAFT

	LOCATION	GRID REFERENCE	POST CODE	WHAT3WORDS
START/FINISH	Fowey Custom House Quay Landing	SX127522	PL23 1AL	croaking.commands.grumble
	Rowing club, Castle Dore, Golant	SX123546	PL23 1LW	letter.matter.engraving
	Lerryn public house and village (high tide)	SX140571	PL22 0QD	plodding.masses.swung
	Pont Creek	SX143518	PL23 1LX	nervy.primed.education
HARBOUR ENTRANCE	St Catherine's Castle	SX119509	PL23 1JH	doghouse.salt.limo

BELOW Ash and the crew paddling up the estuary at Fowey.

BACKGROUND
Fowey was always a family favourite with us when we lived in Flushing opposite Falmouth, being a similar Cornish town with gig racing, sailing regattas and waterwide pubs and cafés. This is a fantastic paddling location, including the shelter of the natural harbour, majestic forts standing guard and lots of hidden creek and estuary spots to explore.

A SLICE OF HISTORY
Fowey is steeped in maritime history, but did you know that the Pont Pill estuary is thought by many local people to be part of the inspiration for Mole, Ratty, Toad and Badger's adventures in *The Wind in the Willows*? Author Kenneth Grahame loved to holiday in nearby Lerryn, and locals believe Grahame's time spent near the river may have inspired the bedtime stories he told to his son, and later developed into the famous children's book.

ROUTE
Launching from the slipway by Caffa Mill car park, you have a choice on whether to head inland or towards the harbour mouth, typically governed by the tide times if you want to reach the top of the estuary.

Turning left and heading up the estuary, the water winds in and out in a classic snake-like shape. The first left-hand bend passes Mixtow and the small marina there. Rounding the bend you come to a large-scale docks and industrial plant, with loading for heavy materials and barges. Around the corner the estuary settles into a large-scale moorings with craft of all shapes and sizes on show (we played our own version of *Supermarket Sweep* here, picking out our favourite of the traditional classic sailing craft moored there).

After 2.5km you'll reach the entrance to Penpol Creek ranging a further 2.3km inland past the historic St Cadix landmark, the site

BELOW Foxy enjoying the SUP action at Fowey.

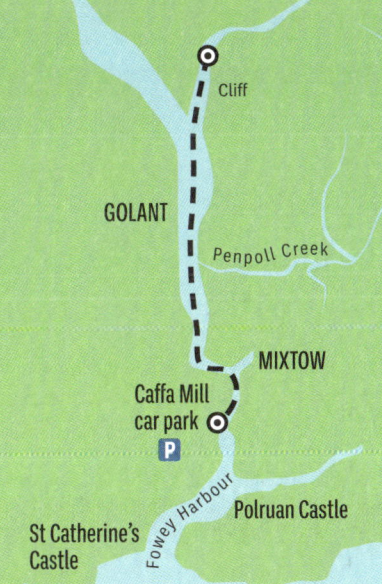

of an ancient Celtic prayer oratory. There are so many deserted places to enjoy a quiet family picnic or a swim on this paddle.

Further up the estuary is the picturesque village of Golant, with stone buildings and white-wash Cornish dwellings. Be aware that sand bars and shallows reveal themselves at low tide.

At 4km the estuary splits between the River Lerryn on the right, leading up to Lerryn village and its quiet backwaters and the Ship Inn, which is a further 2.3km on. The left-hand channel leads up to the small town St Winnow, which although compact, offers a campsite, historic church and a farm museum.

ABOVE Exploring the estuary.

The creek continues to narrow as it weaves past the Shirehall Moor local nature reserve on the left bank. The River Fowey now winds onwards up to Lostwithiel, which was beyond our reach on the day we paddled. Obviously, if you've paddled up this far you'll need to return back to the start, going with the flow to Fowey Harbour.

Once back at the slipway starting point you can paddle out towards the harbour entrance, which was lit up by the afternoon sun and looking its best when we were there. Sailing boats were hoisting sails

and gig crews were preparing to depart moorings as the water came to life. About 800m down towards the harbour mouth on the left is Pont Pill (Cornish: Pyll Por' Reun, meaning creek of seal cove). This is a tidal river and is only navigable at high water. It extends over 1.5km inland and was deserted on our visit.

Don't miss a visit to the harbour entrance, navigating past Polruan town to see the 'castles' (artillery forts) defending this ancient port. Readymoney Cove is nestled behind St Catherine's Castle on the right and there are a few bays around Combe Haven with small rock pools and rock gardens to explore. Now returning to the harbour, there's a real sense of satisfaction to have explored Fowey and its tendril waterways.

OUR RICH ADVENTURE

As a young man, I visited the area under sail in 23-foot sonatas and watched the gig racing. But my last visit to Fowey was a real family affair, with the older generations in tow, so we hired motorboats to ease the paddling load. We were soon racing against each other, putting the paddle to the metal! We swapped craft throughout the day, tried towing our kayaks and SUPs and even stopped for refuelling snacks at a local marina café with ice cream and yummy treats. It's easy to let the Cornish way of life seep into your psyche.

RIGHT Arafat and the team back on terra firma.

WHERE'S THE MAGIC?

This trip inspires you to explore Britain's incredible maritime heritage with castle defences, rare sailing craft, gigs and the chance to play pirates! The estuary has a fair tidal range so the character of the paddle changes from high to low. Fowey always seems to be bustling with maritime life and lots of energy with working boats to pleasure craft.

CALORIE CREDITS

This is a booming Cornish harbour town with no shortage of locations to grab an ice cream, cream tea or pasty. You can opt for more refuelling with a pub meal watching the water lap the quay at a number of waterside pubs. Fowey offers some classic eating locations with sea views or at the very least the sounds of Cornwall, with gulls hollering.

ABOVE The ferry at Fowey leading the way.

Across the water at Bodinnick is the quintessential Cornish inn, the Old Ferry Inn (W: www.theoldferryinn.co.uk), or the Lugger Inn in Polruan (T: 01726 870567). If you head up the creek, tide permitting, there are also watering holes at Golant and Lerryn.

WILDLIFE SAFARI Seals, gulls and lots of other birds bring your paddling adventure to life. Don't forget that stopping in smaller bays offers the chance for wildlife on a micro scale, with crabs, small fish and shellfish to be found in rock pools. You may also be able to forage seaweed and other edibles during your trip.

OTHER ATTRACTIONS Fowey River Hire offers white-knuckle adrenaline rides on RIBs (Rigid Inflatable Boats) out into the bays around Fowey, plus SUP and kayak hire as well as self-drive smaller boats to unlock your inner sea-faring tendencies (W: www.foweyriverhire.co.uk).

A few bays away is Lantic Bay, a National Trust site with cliff-top walks, hidden coves and plenty of locations to boost your fresh air miles (W: www.nationaltrust.org.uk/visit/cornwall/lantic-bay).

The Lost Gardens of Heligan are a short drive away, magical Victorian Gardens, woodland walks and farmland with, of course, a great tea room (W: www.heligan.com).

THE SHARED ECONOMY There's a kayak and SUP rental base at Golant further up the estuary, with Paddle Cornwall SUP and Encounter Cornwall offering great paddle vibes. You can find out more here (W: www.encountercornwall.com).

4 BOSCASTLE TO TINTAGEL

Spend a legendary day exploring King Arthur's realm from the water, including paddling Tintagel beach and Merlin's Cave. This is a delightful out-and-back paddle with 12km of caves, channels, islets and other rocky places to whet your appetite. Like all coastal paddles, check the forecast before venturing out along this rugged and exposed coastline.

The Lowdown

DIFFICULTY

DISTANCE Boscastle to Tintagel, out and back: 12km.

DIRECTIONS Unload kit at the harbour and park back up the hill to avoid high tides and potential embarrassment of your car being waterlogged and in Davey Jones' Locker.

Exiting at Tintagel means a serious climb up a steep hill, so this should be avoided.

HAZARDS

CRAFT

*caution needed for wind, wave and tide action

	LOCATION	GRID REFERENCE	POST CODE	WHAT3WORDS
START/FINISH	Slipway at Boscastle Harbour	SX096913	PL35 0HD	improvise.warm.dunk
HALFWAY POINT	Beach at Tintagel Castle	SX051890	PL34 0DQ	blacked.impeached.lunges

BACKGROUND The North Cornwall coast is spectacularly rugged and imposing with high cliffs and hidden coves dotting the land. It is synonymous with pirates and of course links to King Arthur and the Knights of the Round Table. Up and down the coastline there is great surfing in North Cornwall and Devon, and it is easy to fall in love with the sea here.

RIGHT Arafat hot dogging in Boscastle harbour.

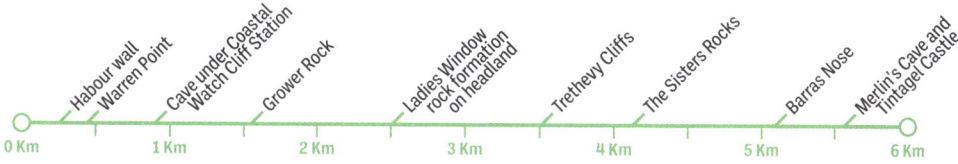

A SLICE OF HISTORY

The stunning Tintagel is famous for being the supposed birthplace of the legendary King Arthur, making it an iconic tourist destination.

The pretty Cornish village of Boscastle was first inhabited by the Bottreaux family around 1080. The name derives from Bottreaux Castle (pronounced 'Botro'), a 12th-century motte-and-bailey fortress, of which few remains survive. Since then it has been known as a fishing village and for its stonemasons.

Sadly, Boscastle, and the nearby villages of Crackington Haven and Rocky Haven, suffered devastating flooding in 2004 when an estimated 2 billion litres of water hit, leaving approximately 100 homes and business destroyed (although, thankfully, no lives were lost).

ROUTE

It is possible to unload vehicles at the quay at Boscastle on the slipway but do be aware that King Cnut couldn't turn back the tide either. Launching, you can't see out on to the open sea, but don't worry; it's sheltered until you pass the rock guarding the harbour entrance. Like all sea paddling it can be committing so it's worth scouting the sea for white caps before venturing out, asking a local and checking the forecast. Do also check the tides so you know whether it's manageable or it'll be a slog to get back.

The natural harbour offers a family-friendly paddling spot with ledges, gullies and small storm beaches before you head along the coastline. If you simply want to enjoy a splash about then you don't need to go any further. We spent an hour or two snorkelling and playing on SUPs and kayaks here after the journey out and back to Tintagel.

Once you leave the cove then it's a left turn between the islet called Meachard and the main cliffs, and almost immediately there is a cavernous hole at the foot of the cliff to test your skills and explore. There's always a choice of whether to follow the coastal corridor, cut across the bay or tuck in and follow the undulations of the coastline more precisely. The bay to your left is known as Western Blackapit, and has more small, rocky islets including the

ABOVE Approaching Tintagel to storm the castle.

ABOVE Leaving Boscastle natural harbour to head along the coast.

superbly named Grower Rock. Try as we might, after staring at it for some time it did not appear to change size!

We decided to cut across the bay to Short Island, and Long Island, which sits behind it. As you thread through the channel between these imposing lumps you round the corner and see another bay and Saddle Rocks. Again you can choose whether to cross the bay mouth or hug the coast. In the bay is Bossiney Haven (or Bossiney Cove). There are plenty of smaller tendrils eroded into the cliffs over millennia but be aware of swell refracting off the steeper walls.

There are more rock islands off the next headland, known as the Sisters, and you do get a sense of the majesty of this beautiful area, which has remained unchanged over generations. Threading around or behind the rocks you are at the penultimate bay, which leads on to Tintagel Haven and the castle. From the sea the cave and footbridge to the castle ruins are more visible.

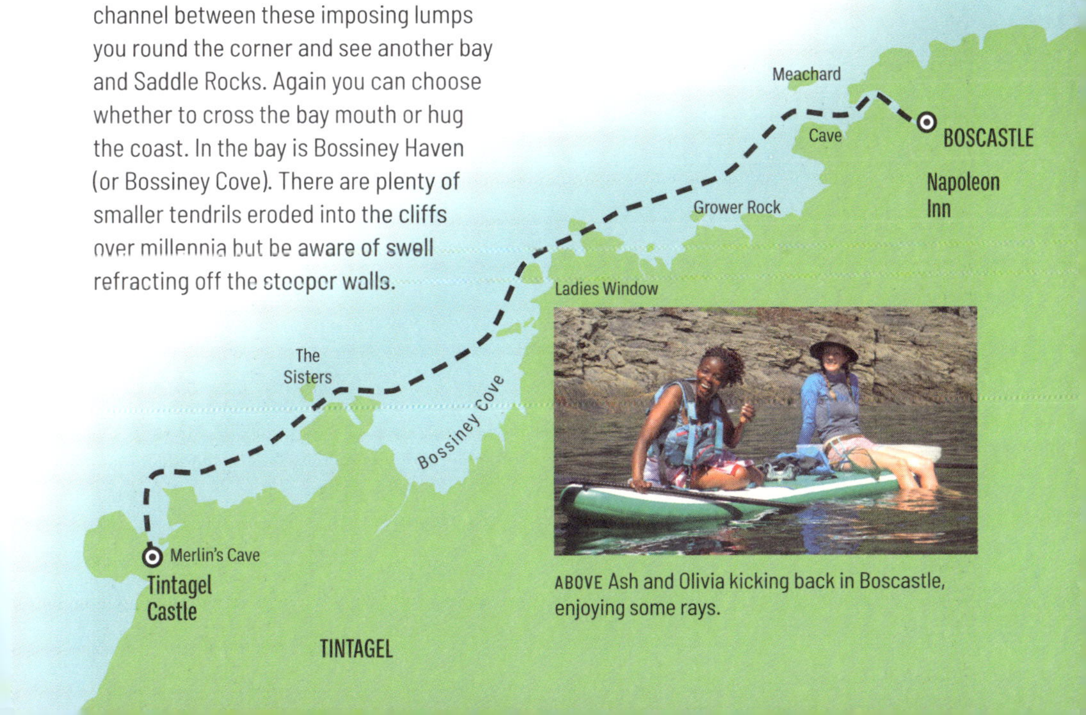

ABOVE Ash and Olivia kicking back in Boscastle, enjoying some rays.

Typically, your covert mission is no longer secret, as walkers patrol the headline, enjoying the views. Rounding into the last bay you'll see the impressive stairs up from Merlin's Cave to Castle Road and the car parks. There was a definite sense of achievement as we beached and became an instant tourist sensation ourselves – mission accomplished (albeit we still needed to paddle back!).

EXTEND THE TRIP Changing your trip from an A to B journey, rather than returning you could paddle on from Tintagel, 12km along the north Cornwall coast to Port Isaac, made famous in the blockbuster film *Fisherman's Friends*. This extended route passes by more caves and headlands and the wide mouth bay of Trebarwith Strand beach.

MY RICH ADVENTURE As one time residents of Cornwall, we have visited Tintagel many times over the years. More recently, a family holiday saw the extended tribe hire a farmhouse in the narrow lanes above Boscastle. We met family at Tintagel after a couple of hours exploring the caves and playing as waves surged through narrow gaps. At Boscastle we SUP'd, snorkelled and explored the caves. The perfect holiday adventure.

Storming the small beach and caves at Tintagel makes this trip worth every ounce of expended energy. The coves, caves and headlands typify our magnificent coastline and paddling on the sea. The Atlantic swell makes the paddle slightly more demanding but the warm water at least means it's altogether pleasant.

CALORIE CREDITS There are many fantastic café's and a huge variety of food on offer in Boscastle, catering for a wide range of tastes. Sample the welcoming pub culture at The Wellington (W: https://

BELOW Arafat exploring the mighty caves located just around the corner from Boscastle.

wellingtonhotelboscastle.com), or try The Good Stuff café down on the quay, which prides itself on its locally sourced delicacies (W: www.thegoodstuffcafe.co.uk). Grab goodies for your trip at the wonderful Boscastle Bakery (T: 01840 250205).

WILDLIFE SAFARI
Seals, gulls and cormorants are never far away. The rock pools and seaweed along this coastline are teeming with life under the spell of the tide.

> **WHERE'S THE MAGIC?**
>
> Steep, rocky cliffs, big caves, gorgeous swim spots and a historic castle enveloped in mystery and intrigue make this area a magical place to be. You can walk the cliff-top site searching for Excalibur and the Knights of the Round Table. Eventually you'll find *Gallos*, a 2.4m-tall bronze statue of the famed king, which stands guard over the promontory.

OTHER ATTRACTIONS
The jewel in the crown of this area is the incredible Tintagel, according to legend once home to King Arthur and now accessed via a jaw-dropping new suspension bridge (W: www.english-heritage.org.uk/visit/places/tintagel-castle).

If you're looking for more local myths and mysteries, the one-and-only Museum of Witchcraft and Magic in Boscastle runs events throughout the year, has 25 permanent displays and over 3,000 intriguing artefacts, and runs a regular blog (W: https://museumofwitchcraftandmagic.co.uk).

If you're keen on doing more outdoors, the South West Coast Path, England's longest waymarked long-distance footpath and a National Trail (630 miles from Minehead in Somerset to Poole Harbour in Dorset) weaves along the land's edge,

ABOVE Rock hopping our way from Boscastle to Tintagel, enjoying the rocky pinnacles.

offering the chance to truly clear cobwebs and marvel at the sea's power on stormy days.

Snorkelling remains one of the most accessible activities in the area, so become an aquanaut by diving below the surface of these aquamarine waters.

While in Cornwall, although a fair drive south, the Eden Project remains a unique and inspiring destination for all the family and is well worth a visit (W: www.edenproject.com). If it's culture you're after, check out the inspirational Minack Theatre, an open-air theatre perched on the cliffs in Penzance (W: www.minack.com).

THE SHARED ECONOMY
The nearest paddle sports location is Skern Lodge Activity Centre, in Appledore, North Devon, which has been offering paddling, surfing, climbing, archery and a wide range of activities since 1976 (W: www.skernlodge.co.uk).

Further north at Ilfracombe, OSKC Watersports offers SUPs, sit-on-top kayaks and a store (W: www.oskcwatersports.co.uk).

SOUTH OF ENGLAND

5 LULWORTH COVE AND DURDLE DOOR

Explore the land that time forgot on the world-famous Jurassic Coast, 150km of incredible landforms, beaches and fossils in the counties of Devon and Dorset. The geological wonders that are Lulworth Cove and Durdle Door form part of England's only natural World Heritage Site and paddling this coastal stretch in the right conditions is awe-inspiring, but you'll need to check tides, wind and weather conditions to avoid getting into difficulty - it's a long return walk along the cliff if you can't paddle back.

The Lowdown

DIFFICULTY
Check tide and conditions before setting off as they should not be underestimated.

DISTANCE Lulworth Cove to Bats Head: 7km, out and back.

DIRECTIONS It's a 300m walk from the car park at Lulworth Cove to the water's edge, so factor that into your plans. Head into the prevailing wind (usually easterlies when we've been there) to check your skills in current conditions.

HAZARDS

CRAFT

BACKGROUND

Lulworth Cove and Durdle Door form one of the most incredible geological sites in the world and are part of the reason why the Jurassic Coast was designated a UNESCO World Heritage Site in 2001. The South West Coast Path follows the coastline offering an elevated vantage point.

A SLICE OF HISTORY

The Jurassic Coast World Heritage Site was designated in 2001 with Man O'War beach, Durdle Door and Lulworth Cove some of the most visited coastal locations in the UK. The sedimentary rocks are 150 million years old and the fossils that can be found here offer glimpses of the ancient world. There are also tufas, which are bowl-shaped fossils where trees used to be and rotted away. Durdle Door is a limestone arch, 33m at its thickest but reduces to 5m at the top.

ABOVE Navigating the Bat's Head arch located off the superbly named Scratchy Bottom cliffs.

ROUTE

Launching in Lulworth Cove is a sensory overload, with folds of multicoloured rock filling your view. The cove itself is about 400m across to the opposite side and worth exploring to take in the incredible geology.

It's about 250m directly out of the cove to hit the high seas. The right side

	LOCATION	GRID REFERENCE	POST CODE	WHAT3WORDS
PARKING	Car park at Lulworth Cove	SY821800	BH20 5RJ	carriage.trendy.masterful
START (1)	Lulworth Cove	SY824799	BH20 5RQ	spend.founders.plodding
START (2)	Kimmeridge Bay car park	SY908790	BH20 5PE	library.decorate.puddings
FINISH	Bat's Head	SY795803	DT2 8DW	winds.pricing.unlimited

of the bay has a slight reef, so in certain conditions you do need to take a wider arc to avoid breaking waves and a possible early dip. Once out into the main sea corridor we recommend paddling into the prevailing wind first, usually from the east, to check you can handle the conditions.

Turning west to your right you'll follow the high cliffs along the coastline and 350m along you'll reach the Stair Hole cove and arches. Depending on conditions and your skills it is possible to paddle into here, but do check the wave patterns and paddle within your ability to avoid getting into difficulty.

Follow the rocky coastline and about 700m along you'll reach Dungy Head, the start of St Oswald's Bay, with its own beach set back into the cove. Just keep paddling and enjoying the scenery and 700m later you'll see the start of rocks in the water and the beginning of Man O'War beach, which is set back behind the rock reef. There's a gap in the middle of the reef, or you can hug the shoreline and sneak in behind to land on the beach.

The reef continues and rises up to form one of the most photographed natural arches in the world: the superbly named Durdle Door. The name Durdle is derived from the Old English *thirl*, meaning 'to pierce' (as in 'nostril'). As with all coastal paddling make sure you check the wave patterns through the arch, remembering that typically the fifth and sixth waves are biggest. A top tip is to just keep paddling to provide support as you travel under the arch.

Landing on the beach can be tricky here; it's quite steep, so be prepared for a scramble. The corner behind the arch can be calmer, allowing you to exit with style and grace. Be aware that the stretch of beach between Durdle Door and Bat's Head (about 1km) is well used and you may want to head further down towards Bat's Head for something a little more off the beaten track. Look out for skinny dippers here (the hill behind the beach is appropriately named Scratchy Bottom!). At higher tides you can paddle through the Bat's Hole (the cave

BELOW Sunset, the magic hour for all paddlers.

through the headland) and out to the other side and back. At lower tides this may not be possible.

This is a natural wonder and a place to enjoy and be in the moment – no rushing off anywhere. Once you have refuelled your spirit with the joys of life, make your way back along the coastline to Lulworth Cove to load up on snacks at the seaside.

EXTEND THE TRIP You can start this paddle further eastwards, paddling from Kimmeridge to Lulworth Cove (park at Kimmeridge Bay car park), which adds an extra 8.5km to the trip. Cross the main bays or hug the coastline to explore Kimmeridge, Brandy Bay, Worbarrow Bay and Mupe Bay. Be sure to check the prevailing wind and tides to ensure you have favourable passage.

ABOVE Passing through Durdle Door to enter a mythical dimension.

OUR RICH ADVENTURE This part of the Jurassic Coast has been a favourite of ours for well over a decade and never fails to deliver, whether paddling in kayaks, sea kayaks or SUPs.

One of our favourite paddles took place on an autumn day, when we rounded Durdle Door to pass through the main arch and stumbled across a Bollywood movie being shot there. The heroine and protagonist were in the waves depicting an argument with a discernible slap to the man, just as four-five sea kayaks paddled into shot. And cut!

Just when you imagine things couldn't get more sublime (or ridiculous, depending on how you look at it), on another occasion we paddled down towards Bat's Hole and passed by the rocky outcrop to a cacophony of shrieks and screams as an embarrassed group of skinny dippers ran for cover.

CALORIE CREDITS Lulworth Cove is a seaside destination with cafés, fish and chips and ice cream galore, and you'll be more than ready to stock up on yummy treats by the end of your paddle. Worth a mention are Finleys Café (W: http://

finleyscafe.co.uk) and the Lulworth Cove Inn (W: www.lulworth-coveinn.co.uk).

WILDLIFE SAFARI
Surprisingly rare butterflies grace the locality including the Lulworth skipper and Ardonis blue. There are plenty of gulls, wading birds and other wildlife to capture your heart – even beavers, which have recently made a return to Dorset for the first time in 400 years due to the excellent work of the Dorset Wildlife Trust.

WHERE'S THE MAGIC?

Folds and layers of rock capturing millions of years in geological time, incredible arches and the circular Lulworth Bay make this a top-drawer paddle.

ABOVE Exploring the arches and cliffs from Lulworth Cove to Durdle Door.

OTHER ATTRACTIONS
Visit Lulworth Castle for woodland walks, a children's playground and tea in the café. This 17th-century castle and hunting lodge is run in partnership with English Heritage. The estate includes Lulworth Cove and Durdle Door coastline (W: https://lulworth.com).

Monkey World ape rescue centre has over 250 primates that have been rescued from around the world (W: https://monkeyworld.org).

THE SHARED ECONOMY
Canoe Trail's Sea Kayaking the Jurassic Coast expedition features this trip and also explores Old Harry, Poole Harbour, The Needles and Durdle Door (W: www.canoetrail.co.uk/canoe-camp/expeditions/sea-kayaking-the-jurassic-coast).

There's also stress-free kayak and SUP hire from Lulworth Activities (W: https://lulworth-activities.co.uk).

6 STUDLAND AND OLD HARRY ROCKS

Scout Old Harry's giant stacks, arches and pillars. These crumbling white towers and bridges, which could almost be made of cheese, provide an excellent playground for your paddling adventure. The swell makes threading through the pillars a little more challenging, but you can paddle along the cliffs towards Swanage, keeping your eyes peeled for the resident peregrine falcons. There are small secluded stone beaches to stop and break up your paddle.

The Lowdown

DIFFICULTY

Check tides and conditions to ensure this paddle is with the tide out to Old Harry and back, or pushing you around to Swanage.

DISTANCE South Beach, out and back: 6km. South Beach to Swanage, A to B: 6.5km.

DIRECTIONS Old Harry can be tackled as a short out-and-back paddle starting on South Beach, or further along at Knoll Beach, or alternatively you can go with the tides and paddle along and round to Swanage, enjoying an A to B with a 15-minute shuttle back (7.2km) to collect vehicles.

HAZARDS

CRAFT

	LOCATION	GRID REFERENCE	POST CODE	WHAT3WORDS
PARKING	South Beach car park, Studland	SZ037825	BH19 3AU	prop.early.permanent
START/FINISH (1)	Beach launch	SZ040825	BH19 3AL	sharpens.scorch.fools
MIDPOINT (1)	Old Harry Rocks	SZ056825	BH19 3AN	exist.resonates.balconies
FINISH (2)	Swanage	SZ034786	BH19 2FH	debut.extreme.indicated

BELOW Ash and William enjoying a blue sky day in winter at Old Harry.

ABOVE Stunning chalk cliffs when sea kayaking from Old Harry to Swanage.

BACKGROUND The three massive chalk formations that make up Old Harry Rocks are located at Handfast Point on the Isle of Purbeck at the southern end of Studland Bay in Dorset. These famous natural landmarks mark the most easterly point of the Jurassic Coast, a UNESCO World Heritage Site (see Route 5, page 40).

A SLICE OF HISTORY Anvil Point Lighthouse, just past Swanage, is a beautiful example of a 19th-century lighthouse, while Swanage Pier is a classic Victorian seaside pier, offering a café and beautiful promenade into the bay.

The Jurassic Coast UNESCO World Heritage Site was designated in 2001 and stretches 150km between Old Harry Rocks at Studland, and Orcombe Point at Exmouth in East Devon. It is one of only two natural World Heritage Sites in the UK and was designated by UNESCO for the outstanding universal value of its rock, fossils and landforms, which date back some 185 million years.

ROUTE Launch from South Beach near Joe's Café or park at the Knoll Beach car park and paddle down, which adds an extra 1.25km each way to the paddle. Hug the beach on your right to ease your way towards the towers and pillars of Old Harry. Like all good magic tricks, the reveal changes with your position and location, and you'll discover more impressive arches and channels to explore.

It's a little over 1.5km out from the South Beach launch point to round Old Harry and view the different towers. As you round

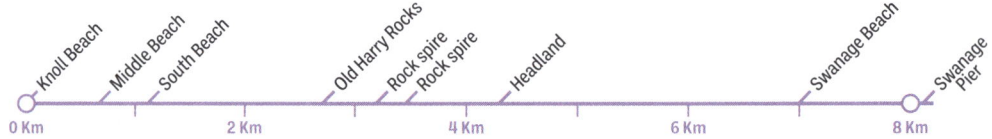

6 • STUDLAND AND OLD HARRY ROCKS

the A to B option down to Swanage, continue following the beach on your right. Swanage is a long beach, so be prepared for about 3km along and down towards the town.

EXTEND THE TRIP The Jurassic Coast is an incredible geological time capsule of our nation's coastline, with impressive formations and features to explore from the water, providing you with a true sense of adventure.

You could extend beyond Swanage by adding a further 6km out and back, returning to Swanage. Durston Castle and park, Swanage Pier and Anvil Point Lighthouse lighten up the paddle. If you continue onwards in a westerly direction beyond Anvil Point Lighthouse, it becomes more remote and less accessible for pick-up.

OUR RICH ADVENTURE We've paddled Old Harry by sea kayak, kayak and SUP, starting when we first trained for a charity challenge we called Big 5 Kayak Challenge, which involved sea kayaking around the Isle of Wight, the Channel, and Land's End to the Isles of Scilly, among others. On one training session, we paddled around to Swanage and finished in darkness, which was interesting trying to determine the first columns, squeeze through the different channels, depending on conditions and tides. It may involve some watching of the wave sets to determine the biggest ones (usually fifth and sixth wave) and ensure there is water over the rocks and any reefs.

Once around the back of Old Harry the viewpoint is some contrast to previous views, with Studland Beach hidden from sight. Above the towers and pillars is the green, green grass of the Studland headland and usually an audience of walkers watching your every move.

Heading westwards there are various smaller bays cut into the cliffs and other towers and features to explore. It is well worth taking your time to enjoy the geology and stacks, taking plenty of photos along the route. About 700m after the main Old Harry stacks the cliffs become more uniform with fewer features. About 750m beyond the last stack the coastline heads in, bending away to the right as you reach Swanage Bay beach.

If you're heading back around to Studland then the top end of the beach is a good turn-around point. If you're doing

WHERE'S THE MAGIC?

It's like a scene from *The Goonies*, with windows in the rock strata, pillars and arches and something mesmerising about the white cliffs and watery backdrop. In the distance, past Bournemouth, you can see the Isle of Wight and the Needles, and you truly feel like you're exploring the high seas of our proud island nation.

lights for landing in the correct place! Subsequent trips with the Canoe Trail Jurassic Sea Kayak Expedition have seen novice paddlers enjoy this stunning chunk of coastline.

CALORIE CREDITS Joe's Café on South Beach is a cheery oasis of food and snacks (W: https://joescafesouthbeach.godaddysites.com/), or visit the Bankes Arms Inn in Studland for great access to South Beach, the cliff path walks, roaring fires and good food (W: www.bankesarms.com/). The Blue Pool Nature Reserve and Tearooms is a slight drive, but worth the effort (W: https://bluepooltearooms.co.uk).

WILDLIFE SAFARI Seals pop up along the coastline and peregrines dive from the chalky cliffs and towers of Old Harry. Don't forget to investigate the rock pools for the tiny creatures living there!

OTHER ATTRACTIONS If you enjoy diving, the drift dives along the Jurassic Coast are simply world class. Contact https://skindeepdiving.co.uk/ to book a trip. Don't forget snorkelling offers a shorter time underwater but the same benefits.

Durlston Country Park and NNR includes a fascinating rock room, which houses samples of rocks collected over time from the Jurassic Coast (W: www.durlston.co.uk/). Or walk the Studland to Swanage coast path (7.7km, A to B) above Old Harry – it's amazing and, randomly, a great place to practise cartwheels. While you're in the area, check out Durdle Door and Lulworth Cove and the Poole Harbour paddles (Route 7, page 49) featured in this book. Finally, Swanage Pier is well worth exploring (W: www.swanagepiertrust.com).

THE SHARED ECONOMY Canoe Trail's Sea Kayaking the Jurassic Coast expedition (W: www.canoetrail.co.uk/canoe-camp/expeditions/sea-kayaking-the-jurassic-coast) features this trip and explores Old Harry and the surrounding cliffs, Durdle Door and Lulworth Cove.

Studland Water Sports at Knoll Beach hires out SUPs, bodyboards and kayaks, and runs guided tours to explore this magical stretch of coast. They also offer waterskiing and banana boat rides (W: http://studlandwatersports.co.uk).

BELOW Surfing between the pillars at Old Harry.

7 POOLE HARBOUR AND BEYOND

This is a magical trip around Europe's largest natural harbour, where you'll have the chance to experience the bustle of Poole Quay and old maritime haunts such as the Poole Arms, dating back to the 17th century. The Harbour has huge expanses of nature reserves as well as the fantastic Brownsea Island, credited with the creation of the Scouting movement.

The Lowdown

DIFFICULTY
Check the tides and conditions to ensure you paddle with the ebbing tide out to Shell Bay.

DISTANCE Wareham to Shell Bay: ~22km (assuming you paddle the 6km around Brownsea Island).

DIRECTIONS Arrange to drop off your craft near Wareham Bridge to launch on the high tide ebbing out into Poole Harbour to ensure the perfect conditions for a conveyor belt ride around one of Britain's wilder estuary and harbour spaces.

In terms of vehicle shuttle, Wareham Bridge to Shell Bay Beach car park is about 19km/25 minutes. In peak holiday season it may take longer.

HAZARDS

CRAFT

	LOCATION	GRID REFERENCE	POST CODE	WHAT3WORDS
START	Wareham Bridge	SY923871	BH20 4LR	reinstate.currently.emporium
FINISH (1)	Shell Bay	SZ035865	BH19 3BA	looked.ended.corner
FINISH (2)	Heather Walk, Studland	SZ037864	BH19 3BA	fantastic.tester.funded

BACKGROUND Poole Harbour is a Mecca for boating whether in a canoe, kayak or SUP. It is a large expanse of open water, so be sure to check the conditions for tide, wind and weather. It can feel quite remote, with limited exit points, although you can seek shelter on a beach or behind a headland for lunch if need be. Closer to the harbour mouth is the chain ferry and more boating life with over a dozen marinas and yacht clubs close to Sandbanks and Poole.

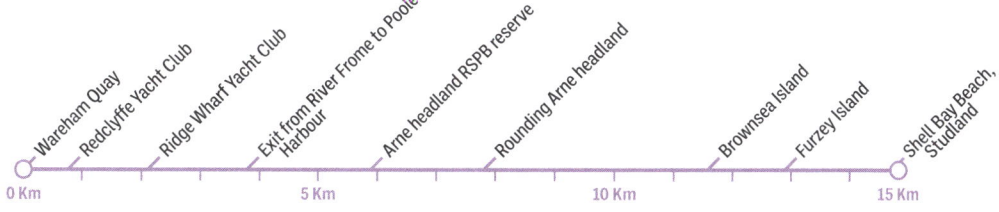

ABOVE Meandering down from Wareham out into Poole Harbour.

A SLICE OF HISTORY

In the centre of Poole Harbour lies Brownsea Island, famous as a launchpad for the Scout and Guide movement in 1878. There's also the chain ferry traversing between the Isle of Purbeck and Sandbanks.

Poole Harbour played a key role in practising landings and mustering the smaller ships used in the D-Day landings. Since then the Special Boat Service (SBS) have used Poole for their fast boat training.

Corfe Castle is over a thousand years old and was built by William the Conqueror. Now run by the National Trust, it is well worth a visit for its majestic ruins and picturesque walks around the wider site.

ROUTE

Launch from Wareham Quay adjacent to the bridge and head down the estuary, following the moorings and day boats as you move towards the wider expanses of Poole Harbour. You are on the River Frome, which snakes back and forth for the first 2–3km. There are campsites alongside the river (at Redcliffe Farm and Ridge Farm Camping & Caravan Park), perfectly placed if you're planning to explore the area over a few days.

You can also launch at Ridge Wharf Yacht Centre, but this would incur launch fees and miss out the initial 2km of this beautiful trip. As you approach the open water make sure you follow the channel, as if the tide is already racing out you can end up getting a little stuck on sand and mudbanks.

After 4km of paddling you'll enter the open water sections of Poole Harbour with headlands, small islands and bays. Having a paper map can be useful for navigation.

RIGHT The open expanses of Poole Harbour.

On your right is the Arne Reedbeds NNR. Ahead to the right is the main Arne headland, which you can traverse around as a marker. If conditions are in your favour you can cross over to the Arne headland on a downwind paddle with some small wave surfing.

Cutting across the bay is about 2km of paddling, allowing a break on the Arne peninsula for a snack or a brew. By keeping the peninsula on your right side you can hug the shore and paddle another 2.5km around the headland until you begin to turn sharp right. The water opens up and you will see Poole Ferry Terminal and Brownsea Island, which is now visible about 3km away to the south-east.

As a former Scout I am always excited to visit Brownsea Island, run by the National Trust. Depending on your timings and weather conditions, you can opt to circumnavigate the island (~6km), seeing the castle on the south-east tip. There are, of course, plenty of smaller islands to investigate, including Furzey Island and Green Island.

You can finish your trip landing on Shell Bay Beach, which is close to the National Trust car park or you can opt for Bramble Bush Bay and carry to the car. Depending on conditions and the tides (aim for slack water) then it is possible to paddle out of the harbour, dodging the car ferry at Sandbanks. Be warned: this can be very lumpy on spring tides racing at high speed and with waves up to 3ft. I can remember one client distinctly saying he had reached his Everest and we should go back in!

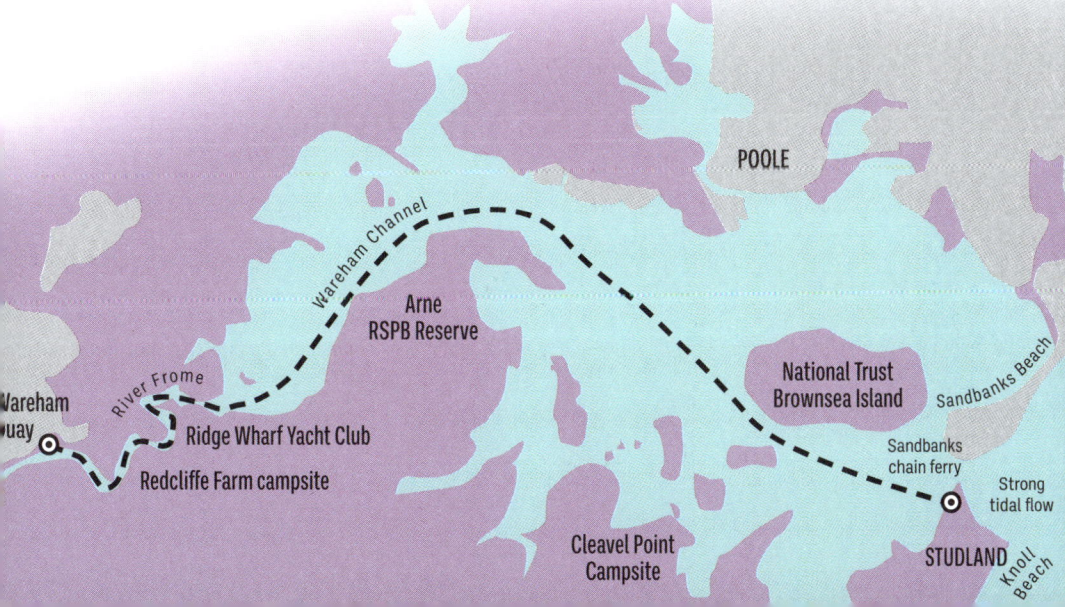

EXTEND THE TRIP You can extend this trip for a full day of adventure launching from within Poole Harbour and heading out to Old Harry Rocks following Studland Bay around. This adds another 6km just to get to Old Harry, so we've listed it as a separate route (Route 6, page 45). The National Trust, which owns the island, has introduced launching and finishing at the middle car park for commercial operators if you choose to launch there.

OUR RICH ADVENTURE We first made this paddle during training for crossing the English Channel as well as circumnavigating the Isle of Wight. Since then it has become a firm favourite with friends and clients alike. Our last trip prior to going to press truly had a sting in the tail, with winds gusting over 45mph. It was a day for surfing downwind and avoiding any unwanted action broadside.

On a previous trip, heading out past the chain ferry as Poole Harbour blasted out on the ebb tide was the deep end for some of our friends. If in doubt, paddle it on the slack tide or portage over the spit to avoid the potentially rough conditions of the tide racing out from the harbour.

CALORIE CREDITS Pack a picnic and snacks for the main trip, as there are no real watering holes en route. However, Joe's Café at South Beach is a cheery oasis of food and snacks (W: https://joescafesouthbeach.godaddysites.com/). Or visit the Bankes Arms Inn in Studland for great access to the beach, cliff-path walks, roaring fires and good food (W: www.bankesarms.com).

Visit the 17th Century Poole Arms on Poole Quay after your paddle (W: www.poolearms.co.uk).

BELOW Weaving through the high banks of the Poole Harbour estuary.

7 • POOLE HARBOUR AND BEYOND 53

ABOVE The magic of Corfe Castle.

WILDLIFE SAFARI Seals pop up along the coastline here and peregrines dive from the chalky cliffs and towers of Old Harry. There are plenty of wading birds, too, so look out for little egrets and even the puffins that nest here each season. Over 250 red squirrels live on Brownsea Island!

WHERE'S THE MAGIC?

Poole Harbour is Europe's largest natural harbour and is a wonderland of wetlands and woodlands teeming with bird and wildlife of all shapes and sizes.

OTHER ATTRACTIONS Stay at the Norden Farm Campsite, with great facilities for multiple paddling days and activities in the area (W: https://nordenfarm.com).

Visit the off-the-beaten track Blue Pool Nature Reserve and Tearooms, a hidden gem since 1935 (W: https://bluepooltearooms.co.uk). For something a little different, embrace your inner Stig of the Dump with the mud trail and water park at Dorset Adventure Park (W: www.dorsetadventurepark.com).

Take time, as always, to explore the National Trust landmarks in the area including Corfe Castle and Brownsea Island (W: www.nationaltrust.org.uk/visit/dorset/corfe-castle).

Finally, the Jurassic Coast offers world-class diving. Contact https://skindeepdiving.co.uk/ to book a trip.

THE SHARED ECONOMY Canoe Trail's Sea Kayaking the Jurassic Coast expedition features this trip along with paddling Poole Harbour (W: www.canoetrail.co.uk/). The Watersports Academy at Sandbanks (W: https://thewatersportsacademy.com/activities) offers SUPs, wakeboarding, yachting and powerboating.

BELOW Corfe Castle ruins are well worth a visit.

8 RIVER AVON AT BRADFORD-ON-AVON

This is a mellow paddle with a nice change of scenery. It flows from the old tithe barns and stone of Bradford-on-Avon downstream to charming narrow and quintessentially English river banks before weaving alongside the canal with its aqueducts and bridges. Be aware of the large weirs, which need to be portaged, and loop back to the start on the canal super highway. This is a compact paddling journey that really does feel like a time travelling journey through the ages.

The Lowdown

DIFFICULTY
Lovely paddle with some portages and a return loop by canal Grade 1 moving water.

DISTANCE Loop: 13km.
Bradford-on-Avon to Dundas Aqueduct, A to B: 6.5km.

DIRECTIONS Park in the car park by the tithe barn at Barton Country Park. Start by Barton Bridge and paddle back on the Kennet and Avon Canal to make a loop. You'll need to exit the canal at the Tithe Barn and carry down to the car park.

HAZARDS

CRAFT
*watch for shallows and hazards

BACKGROUND The River Avon (Bristol) is located in the southwest and is 85 miles long. It is one of five Avons in the UK and it is believed the name derives from the Welsh word for 'river', Afon. At Bradford-on-Avon the river is unusual as it meets rail, road and canal in the same location.

The canal links to the Kennet and Avon Canal and passes under two impressive aqueducts at Dundas and Avoncliffe. The river winds down towards Bath and Bristol and continues to pass historic bridges, pumping stations and weirs. Bradford on Avon's McKeever Bridge was named after champion kayaker Ed McKeever, who came from the town and won gold at London 2012.

A SLICE OF HISTORY The Town Bridge Chapel, a Grade I listed building, has served as a chapel and even town gaol during its history. It was originally a pack horse bridge, and Bradford-on-Avon likely received its name as it was a place to ford the river ('broad ford').

The 14th-century Saxon tithe barn is an impressive structure and our proposed parking and launch site to the river behind the site at the bridge. It is part of Barton Farm Country Park and preserved by English Heritage.

In 1724 the River Kennet was made navigable from Reading to Newbury, and by 1727 boats could reach as far as Bath. For

8 • RIVER AVON AT BRADFORD-ON-AVON

	LOCATION	GRID REFERENCE	POST CODE	WHAT3WORDS
PARKING	Car park, tithe barn	ST823604	BA15 1LF	parading.upstarts.cookie
START	Barton Bridge	ST822605	BA15 1LF	converter.polka.trailing
TOWN BRIDGE		ST826609	BA15 1LJ	committee.pebbles.them
AVONCLIFF WEIR	By Guns Cross (portage)	ST805600	BA15 2HA	things.economics.jigsaw
THE INN AT FRESHFORD	On the Frome	ST791600	BA2 7WG	highs.arrow.gross
LIMPLEY STOKE WEIR	Portage on right bank	ST782610	BA2 7FX	singer.crowned.part
RETURN POINT	Dundas Aqueduct	ST784625	BA2 7BL	stews.audit.claps

hundreds of years before this people had talked about linking the Kennet with the Avon, but it was not until 1794 that a route was fixed via Devizes and an Act was passed. The resulting canal was completed in 1810.

Caen Hill on the Kennet and Avon Canal is one of the longest continuous flights of locks in the country – a total of 29 locks with a rise of 72m over 3.2km and a 1 in 44 gradient, for anyone who's counting.

Further downstream, the River Avon bisects the city of Bath, a UNESCO World Heritage Centre. Here you'll find the Pulteney Bridge, built in 1774, its iconic arches spanning the flow, and the adjacent Pulteney Weir with its horseshoe shape.

ROUTE Unload in the car park near the tithe barn and head over to the pool by the Barton Bridge, which would not look out of place in a knight's tale or a fantasy film. From here you can explore upstream, or downstream and return using the conveniently located canal (such foresight!). On the opposite bank is Bradford-on-Avon Rowing Club.

It's a short paddle to the town centre 200m upstream where you paddle under the railway bridge and the McKeever Bridge before reaching the older, stone Town Bridge, with its handy 'lock up' for

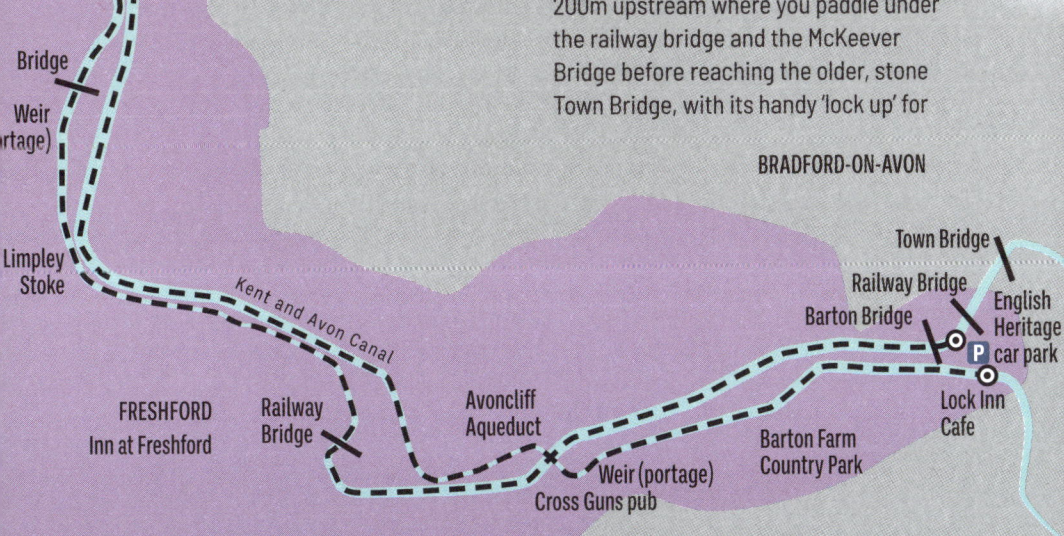

ABOVE Ash with Foxy and Bambi paddling over the Avon on the Avoncliff Aqueduct.

misbehaving crew mates. The town has decent food and drink establishments, including Timbrell's Yard (W: https://timbrellsyard.com/find-us) next to St Margaret's car park, where we ended our day.

Downstream from the put on and it feels like another classic English touring river, with clear waters, treelined banks and slow-moving currents. The river is pretty straight heading westwards following the adjacent railway lines and then bends left as it passes the Barton Farm Country Park. About 1.9km downstream at Avoncliff the river drops over a large, lumpy weir, which you need to avoid since there are no lines or buoys preventing a rapid descent. Instead, portage on the left-hand side up on to the canal towpath, just upstream of the weir. As you portage around the weir you'll be pleased to see the Cross Guns pub, with tables, benches and lawns alongside the lapping waters. Just after the pub is the Avoncliff Aqueduct.

You can relaunch under the bridge on the grass bank and continue downstream for another kilometre to what looks like a river T-junction, where the River Frome joins the Avon. Stick your nose 500m up the Frome here to reach the village of Freshford and its lovely inn. The Avon heads right into an S-bend and passes under the railway line 150m on. The Kennet & Avon Canal runs parallel to the river and offers the return loop back to Bradford-on-Avon, as and when you need it.

Once around the bend the river straightens and continues towards Limpley Stoke, running parallel to the canal. Around 1.8km downstream, avoid another large weir with a nasty vertical face by portaging in the large meadow on the right-hand side back to the canal or around the weir.

The river flows onwards for 250m or so

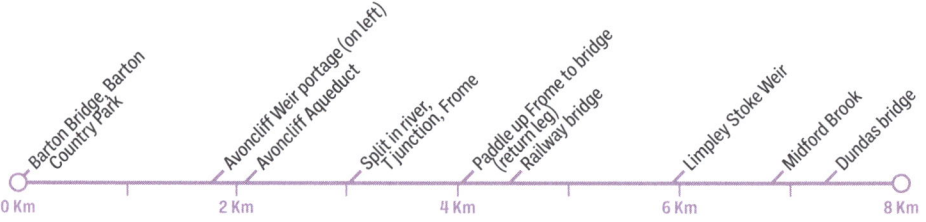

until it squeezes under Stokeford Bridge and the B3108, where it speeds up and drops a little with a ledge. Around 900m later as you cruise onwards, truly in the swing of things, you'll see the Dundas Aqueduct 450m ahead – an impressive sight as it seems to fly over the river. Milford Brook joins the Avon from the left here.

Pull up on the right-hand side and exit the river. Be warned: it's a steep climb up steps to the canal above, but a lovely paddle awaits for the return to Bradford-on-Avon after scouting the route you've just conquered.

EXTEND THE TRIP Explore the Kennet & Avon Canal by paddling east or west to take in the unmissable rolling English countryside (great motivation when paddling the Devizes to Westminster Race!). We thoroughly recommend you explore the villages and towns linked by this historic waterway.

Or why not paddle on to Bath from the Dundas Aqueduct, which is another 15km looping around the city? Arrange a shuttle to complete the journey.

OUR RICH ADVENTURE This section of the River Avon was entirely new to us when we arrived to paddle, but we knew straight away this was going to be a good one. We had our dogs and Bambi, a large rescue foster dog, to cram into the canoe. Fun family times.

Launching near the old tithe barn and carrying through the courtyard from the car park, one could definitely feel like a lord, lady or squire ('Bring me my canoe, the Golden One!'), as we carried our yellow craft. We paddled up and downstream, around the old bridge, up to the town, and then downstream to the weirs and aqueducts that light up this river and canal journey.

BELOW A highlight of one of the loveliest canals in the country.

ABOVE On the River Avon below the Aqueduct by the Cross Guns pub.

WILDLIFE SAFARI Kingfishers, moorhens, coots and lots of other smaller wildlife inhabit this slow-moving waterway.

> **WHERE'S THE MAGIC?**
>
> This ever-changing journey, with so much action condensed into such a short distance, makes this a trip worth repeating. The river itself feels inviting, and there are ample opportunities for wild swimming.

CALORIE CREDITS The award-winning Bridge Tea Rooms offer lunches, light meals and, of course, the quintessential afternoon tea (W: www.thebridgetearooms.co.uk), or right by the Avoncliff Aqueduct is the No.10 Tea Garden (W: https://avonclifftea.com).

You pass the Cross Guns on your paddle, so it would be rude not to stop (W: https://crossgunsavoncliff.com), or turn left up the River Frome to visit the Inn at Freshford (W: https://theinnatfreshford.com).

The Barge Inn is conveniently positioned on the canal, overlooking Bradford-on-Avon (W: https://thebargeinn.org).

OTHER ATTRACTIONS The Kennet & Avon Canal is one of the loveliest in the country and an area both Ash and Rich know well, with Rich having raced the Devizes to Westminster International Canoe Race on several occasions. While in the area, visit the Caen Hill Locks, a serious feat of engineering, and enjoy all the canal has to offer.

If you're after something a little more exotic, take a trip to Wolves of Wiltshire & The Little Zoo (W: www.thelittlezoo.co.uk), a small animal sanctuary that houses over 100 rescued exotic animals and a Eurasian wolf pack.

There's so much to do in the historic city of Bath, including, of course, the world-famous Roman baths, which have been refurbished (W: www.romanbaths.co.uk).

THE SHARED ECONOMY Connect with LiveFree Adventures, which offers canoe, kayak and SUP hire by Dundas Aqueduct (W: https://livefreeadventures.co.uk).

9 RIVER THAMES: LECHLADE-ON-THAMES TO GODSTOW, OXFORD

This is a delightful, secluded paddle along Old Father Thames. You can tweak the distances and destinations to suit your plans, from a shorter out-and-back trip to multi-day paddles with overnights at B&Bs or riverside wild camping. There are plenty of old bridges, follies and much more to see on this paddling adventure.

The Lowdown

DIFFICULTY
A classic touring river, easy Grade 1 with some lock portages.

DISTANCE Lechlade to Ye Old Swan at Radcot Bridge (day paddle): 10.54km.
Lechlade to Maybush Pub at Newbridge (2 days with camp): 26.41km.
Lechlade to Godstow Bridge (2-3 days with camp): 44.08km.

BELOW Rich on the mighty River Thames near Lechslade.

DIRECTIONS Park up at Lechlade Riverside car park, almost opposite the Bridge House Campsite. From there it is a medium-sized carry of ~150-200m, depending on parking spaces. Cross over the Thames Path and launch upstream of the Half Penny Bridge Tollhouse. The 40km shuttle from Godstow back to Lechlade takes about 40 minutes.

HAZARDS

CRAFT

	LOCATION	GRID REFERENCE	POST CODE	WHAT3WORDS
START	Lechlade Riverside car park	SU211989	GL7 3AQ	scorched.enlarge.harnessed
START OF RIVER	River Thames	SU210992	GL7 3AL	delay.betrayal.dividers
PORTAGE POINT	St John's Lock	SU221990	GL7 3HA	dishing.emulating.lamp
PORTAGE POINT	Buscot Lock	SU229980	SN7 8DE	nuzzled.corrects.dilute
PORTAGE POINT	Grafton Lock	SU271992	GL7 3HD	raven.defended.icon
	Swan Hotel, Radcot	SU286995	OX18 2SX	elevator.surging.compiler
PORTAGE POINT	Radcot Lock	SP296002	SN7 8JT	stove.rebel.otherwise
	Old Man's Bridge	SP299001	SN7 8JT	event.boils.rephrase
PORTAGE POINT	Rushey Lock	SP322000	SN7 8PS	wakes.cocktail.hikes
	The Trout Inn, Tadpole Bridge	SP334003	SN7 8RF	conductor.succeed.visitors
PORTAGE POINT	Shifford Lock	SP370010	OX18 2EJ	than.says.proofread
	Newbridge	SP403014	OX29 7QD	hound.mimics.profiled
PORTAGE POINT	Northmoor Lock	SP431021	OX13 5JP	quilting.tablets.credible
PORTAGE POINT	Pinkhill Lock	SP440071	OX29 4JH	mailboxes.reflected.foreheads
PORTAGE POINT	Eynsham Lock	SP445086	OX29 4BY	coconut.hinted.losing
PORTAGE POINT	King's Lock	SP479102	OX2 8PY	boring.empty.rates
FINISH POINT	The Trout Inn, Godstow near Wolvercote	SP484092	OX2 8PN	pack.entire.activism

BACKGROUND The River Thames is famous the world over as a major arterial river crossing England from west to east with the flow rising above Cricklade and flowing down to the Thames Estuary. This part of the river is delightful boating country, with cruisers and riverside pubs flanking your route. It is quintessential middle England with gentle flows in normal conditions.

A SLICE OF HISTORY The origins of Father Thames are something of a mystery, laid down in folklore. It's likely that people have always paid obeisance to the river in one form or another as the lifeblood of the capital's trade and prosperity. London's most impressive representation of the river god can be found in Trinity Square, near The Tower, perching high on the former

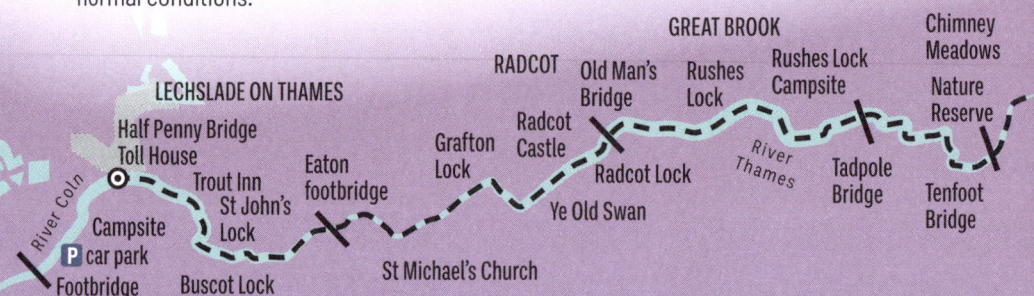

Port of London Authority building.

The old wooden bridge over the Thames at Lechlade was replaced by a stone one in 1220, and you get a good view of it as you paddle underneath. The workmen entrusted with building it were housed in an almshouse dedicated to St John the Baptist, which was founded by Peter Fitzherbert. The main priory was dissolved by Edward IV In 1472. The almshouse continued as an inn known as Ye Sygne of St John Baptist Head until 1704. After this it was renamed to The Trout Inn.

There are plenty of old pill boxes and Second World War defences along the length of the River Thames, so keep looking for them.

Godstow Abbey is an enticing finale to your paddle. Visitors can hike around the picturesque remains of this 12th-century nunnery with stone walls.

Over 800 years ago, the Magna Carta was sealed at Runnymede, marking an important moment in the history of British law and liberty. It was significant to paddlers and wild swimmers, too, as it gave us common folk access to the river land.

ROUTE Once onto the river after the warm-up portage from the car park, there's an opportunity to explore upstream (see notes below). From the start point, head downstream 350m towards the Half Penny Bridge Tollhouse and cruise under the bridge with not a care in the world. The Thames imitates a winding race track, with elongated chicanes as you zig and zag a kilometre down to St John's Lock and the first portage. Don't worry: these pedestrian interludes will become second nature to you and your crew – or expect a mutiny! All the weirs on the Thames should be avoided and are guarded by signs, buoys and other barriers to restrict access.

Paddle under the A417 road bridge and carry on for 200m, to where the river splits around the lock island and then rejoins so

the river feels whole again. Tucked behind the island spit is the lovely and ancient Trout Inn, with riverbank gardens and a welcoming spirit. Shortly after the lock you pass under a footbridge, or the Thames Path crosses the Thames to run along the left bank – however you want to see it.

The river resumes its winding course and you'll be forgiven for feeling that forward progress is slow, but in truth most people are happy to relax and go with the flow. This part of the Thames is decked in willows along its banks and feels tranquil and secluded. A kilometre downstream, you'll paddle past Buscot Old Parsonage, run by the National Trust. Around 500m later and it's time to stretch your legs at the Buscot Lock next to the boat hire centre. The weir channel is to the left and the lock is straight ahead by the lock keeper's cottage.

There's not much to report for the next kilometre (but that's the very beauty of it) until you reach the Eaton Footbridge next to the small moorings. The river continues to buck and twist and passes the village of Kelmscott, and then heads south to run past St Michael and All Angels church. Just over a kilometre on through lush green fields you arrive at Grafton Lock for your next leg stretch.

The route loops south-east now for 700m after the lock, before turning back on a north-easterly course towards Radcot, where the river splits around a couple of larger islands. Ye Old Swan Pub and campsite are located here, making for a good place to overnight or re-energise, depending on your destination, plans and pace. You're now 10.54 winding kilometres from Lechlade. The river returns to a sense of rural landscape, with leafy banks, fields and meadows before you reach Radcot Lock to portage.

We remember these traditional locks during our 183km non-stop paddle (minus two short sleep breaks) as sanctuaries, where we defrosted during blizzards and enjoyed a snack break. Many of them are quintessentially English chocolate box houses with well-kept lawns, borders and flower beds. At Radcot, you'll find Old Man's Bridge about 250m past the lock, which historically was important for connecting communities along the waterway.

The next section of the river looks like an untamed worm looping back and forth from north to south but always heading eastwards. It is a lovely stretch to shut

BELOW Second World War pillboxes guard your route on this Thames paddle.

your eyes, float and dream of sunny days, whatever the weather. After just over 3km you'll arrive at the Rushey Lock Campsite, another picturesque riverbank campsite. After portaging the lock the river continues its meanders until you reach The Trout Inn at Tadpole Bridge, just over a kilometre later.

Tenfoot Bridge comes next, about 2.8km after winding around Chimney Meadows NNR, and heads north-east 1.7km to where the river splits into a small loop. Around 400m on is a footbridge and shortly after that is Shifford Lock. The fields around the river here, still weaving slowly eastwards, form a patchwork quilt from an aerial perspective. The river course completes a northern loop past Shifford and then passes by a network

ABOVE The Trout Inn Riverside Pub at Godstow, a worthy watering hole at the portage around the sluices.

of lakes. About 4km from the lock you'll reach Newbridge.

Newbridge is a microcosm of Thames life, with a couple of pubs and the confluence with the River Windrush, which comes in on river left by the A415 viaduct. On the right bank is the lovely Maybush pub, which serves locally sourced food. The Rose Revived, on the left northern bank, has a cosy bar and log fires in winter. Weir Footbridge is just under 2km on from the road bridge. The scenery remains quintessentially English in its nature, so

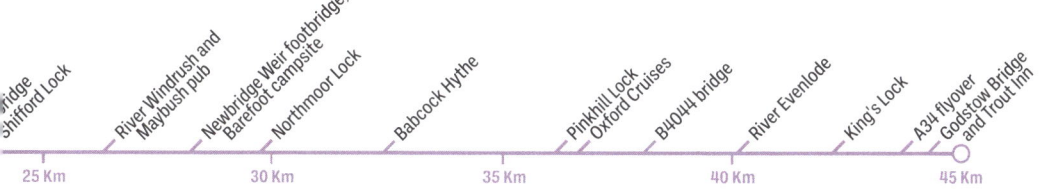

LEFT Godstow Abbey, adjacent to the lock at Godstow.

are almost full, do not fear: you're nearly there! Summon up the energy for the last stretch. Just after the lock the superbly named Wharf Stream and Chill Brook join the Thames, just before you pass a larger woodland. The River Evenlode also joins from the left bank, as the river now runs parallel with the much larger A40 bypass.

picnics are a must if you haven't stopped to eat at one of the aforementioned pubs.

Northmoor Lock is about 1.5km north with the rustic Bare Foot Campsite across the field from the lock. It will not disappoint. The river runs straight and true for the next kilometre and then winds and kicks northwards. After about 2.5km you'll reach Bablock Hythe and its giant riverside caravan park (you won't fail to miss it). The river begins to skirt around the Farmoor Reservoir, home to Oxford Sailing Club, and you'll pass Buckthorn Meadow and Shrike Meadow on its western shores.

Roughly 4km from the start of Bablock Hythe Caravan Park and after plenty of treelined paddling, you'll reach Pinkhill Lock in Witney, the place for tent-only camping (T: 01865 881452). You're closing in on Oxford now, signalling the end of your journey. After the lock you pass Oxford Cruisers, with its many berths behind Stroud Copse. Another kilometre and a half and you reach the B4044 flyover and the Eynsham Lock, which requires another portage. It too has toilets and a campsite area (T: 01865 811324).

If arms feel tired and fresh air miles

You have one more portage to navigate around King's Lock and its adjacent island leading to the weir. Once round the weir the river turns south for 1.5km, where it then runs under the A34 flyover. You've done it! You can now celebrate your 40km odyssey through middle England at Godstow Bridge and another Trout Inn (one of several on this route). While drivers shuttle back to collect vehicles, stretch your legs at Godstow Abbey or Wolvercote Community Orchard, which is set just back from the river.

EXTEND THE TRIP If you fancy a short paddle upstream there's plenty to witness from the comfort of your craft. About 1km from the bank start you reach the confluence with the River Colne and almost on the corner of this is St John the Baptist at Inglesham. According to the maps there's an old canal here but we've not explored it. Paddling down from Cricklade is a challenge, as it's often overgrown after autumn and winter with trees down, and can be very shallow in low conditions. This part of the river also looks like a dot-to-dot set of squiggles.

Our recommended route is on to the Trout Inn, but if you want to continue, the Thames cuts an arc through Oxford before heading down to Wallingford and Goring with its gap and many renowned locations for wild swimming, rowing and other watersports. Continue eastwards and the Thames connects incredible sporting venues on its course including Bisham Abbey (run by Sport England), Eton College Dorney Lake and Hurley, made famous for freestyle kayaking. Or you could choose the historic sites along this route, including Windsor Castle and Runnymede, where the Magna Carta was signed in 1215.

Heading on down the Thames there is much to see, although lots of locks to continue the whole-body workout (Route 13, page 83, offers a Richmond trip). Once in central London there are, of course, restrictions: you'll need craft licences, VHF radios and more advanced skills, as well as permission to paddle from Teddington to the Thames Estuary from the Vessel Traffic Services (VTS). SUPs are banned on this length of the river.

OUR RICH ADVENTURE

The Thames has been a true constant in our paddling lives, and we simply couldn't publish a book on paddling without giving it full mention.

In 2009 we paddled the length of the River Thames, from a snowy beach near its source in Cricklade to the QE2 Bridge/Dartford Crossing – 295km in 33 hours. It was our second challenge of the original Big 5 Kayak Challenge, which Rich created. We swapped between K2 racing kayaks and sea kayaks to navigate the narrow, overgrown headwaters.

Some years later we did a similar trip with our friend Graham Dandy for charity, with a team that included double gold medallist rower Steve Williams MBE. This was trickier, as the river was very low.

Since paddling two Devizes to

ABOVE Rich in calm waters near Lechslade.

ABOVE Godstow Lock – get ready for a portage around.

Westminster races (one in a canoe and one in a double kayak), we have frequently paddled the lower elements of the Thames. We also did Devizes to Tower Bridge with our good friend Andy Reid MBE, a triple amputee.

CALORIE CREDITS Stop in at the family-run Trout Inn by St John's Lock for food and drink or even a spot of theatre, which runs at different times throughout the year (W: www.thetroutinn.biz).

Ye Olde Swan is a stone-built retreat on the banks of the Thames and offers wild camping, glamping, events and great food (W: www.yeoldeswan.co.uk/).

Heading westwards, you are closer to Oxford and have moved into a new county. Stop at another Trout Inn at Tadpole Bridge for food and good ales (W: https://butcombe.com/the-trout-at-tadpole-bridge-oxfordshire) or The Maybush, for dog-friendly riverbank dining serving locally sourced food at Newbridge (W: www.themaybushnewbridge.co.uk/). The Trout Inn is an upscale country gastropub with Thames views from a beer garden, plus roaming families of peacocks (W: www.thetroutoxford.co.uk/#/).

Just off the river at Kelmscott, the Plough does food and accommodation (W: www.theploughinnkelmscott.com).

WILDLIFE SAFARI The River Thames is alive and kicking with all manner of wildlife. The upper reaches of the Thames are quieter with more kingfishers, herons, and swimming grass snakes, and, of course, swans, cormorants and geese. At dusk, bats and owls patrol the meadows while otters and water voles splash in the river.

9 • RIVER THAMES: LECHLADE-ON-THAMES TO GODSTOW, OXFORD

WHERE'S THE MAGIC?

There's a simple pleasure to be had from paddling across England, starting in our capital city and heading east to the Cotswolds. This trip gives you the opportunity to slow down and enjoy peaceful, often iconic landscapes with your fellow paddlers.

OTHER ATTRACTIONS Camp at the start of your trip at Bridge House Campsite on the riverbanks (W: www.bridgehousecampsite.co.uk).

Cotswold Boat Hire, which has been providing day boats and boat hire for 30 years, is at Buscot Lock (W: www.cotswoldboat.co.uk).

Ye Olde Swan at Radcot Bridge offers wild camping and glamping on the banks of the Thames (W: www.yeoldeswan.co.uk), or camp at the Rushey Lock campsite (T: 01367 870218) or Northmoor Lock, which has composting toilets, campfires (W: www.barefootcampsites.co.uk).

THE SHARED ECONOMY Check out Cotswold Canoe Hire on the banks for the River Thames by the Half Penny Bridge in Lechlade (W: www.cotswoldcanoehire.co.uk).

BELOW Bigger weirs await further down the Thames.

10 OXFORD'S RIVER CHERWELL

Oxford's winding narrow waterways, historic buildings and the chance to spy a spire or two make this short but ultimately rewarding paddle a favourite with our team. The start point is on the outskirts of rural life at Cutteslowe and flows gently into the city centre and then on to the River Thames. At almost every corner there is a folly, university hall, bridges and punts to capture your imagination. Make a short break of it and visit the museums while you're there.

The Lowdown

DIFFICULTY

A charming paddle with a few hazards, including rollers and an adjacent weir drop that needs to be portaged.

DISTANCE Paddle down from Willowbrook, Cutteslowe to Meadow Lane, Donnington, A to B, a distance of 7.35km. It's gentle flows so you could opt for an out and back from the start.

Paddle further with a Thames River extension on further to Sandford Lock: +3.5km.

DIRECTIONS Park up near Willow Brook car park or a nearby residential street and carry across to the Cherwell, which is about 150m. Or speak to the lovely people at the Victoria Arms to park there, ensuring you put money behind the bar.

HAZARDS
*and rollers

CRAFT
*kneel down as necessary

	LOCATION	GRID REFERENCE	POST CODE	WHAT3WORDS
PARKING	Willowbrook car park, Cutteslowe	SP511098	OX2 7PG	tells.guitar.snow
START (1)	Cherwell riverbank launch	SP512098	OX2 7PG	panel.become.method
START (2)	Victoria Arms pub	SP520089	OX3 0PZ	logs.stem.placed
	Boat rollers slide	SP521071	OX1 3UQ	owner.brings.down
	Left fork	SP525064	OX4 1BD	finely.cabin.hungry
	Magdalen Bridge	SP521061	OX1 4AU	test.post.fell
	Thames confluence	SP520050	OX4 1TL	snail.spoon.event
FINISH (1)	Exit to Meadow Lane, Donnington	SP524044	OX4 4AZ	ducks.filed.closet
PORTAGE POINT	Iffley Lock	SP525036	OX4 4EJ	perky.influencing.sulk
FINISH (2)	Exit at King's Arms, Sandford Lock, Sandford-on-Thames	SP531013	OX4 4YE	lofts.faces.pigs

BACKGROUND Oxford is one of the most famous university cities in the world reknown for punting, academic studies, tourism and historic buildings.

A SLICE OF HISTORY The River Thames around these parts is known as the Isis, from its source in the Cotswolds until it is joined by the Thame at Dorchester in Oxfordshire. It is derived from the old English name for the Thames, *Tamesis*. During the Middle Ages it was believed to be a combination of the rivers 'Thame' and 'Isis', hence its unique name.

On your route, you'll pass Holywell Mill House. A mill has stood at this location since at least 1200 and today it is owned by the University of Oxford's Magdalen College.

There is a bench on your paddling route in memory of JRR Tolkien (1892–1973), celebrated author of *The Hobbit* and *The Lord of the Rings* trilogy, and a professor at Pembroke College.

ABOVE Punts nestled under Magdalen Bridge, Oxford.

ROUTE Launching from Willowbrook near Sunnymead Park in Cutteslowe, it's a short paddle down of about 1.3km to the second start location, the Victoria Arms at Old Marston. The river runs gently south, bending left and right and then running along a long, narrow, treelined straight. It is totally relaxing, with limited distractions to detract from the perfect day's paddle.

The river bends right and on the bend is the delightful Victoria Arms, which is right on the river itself with

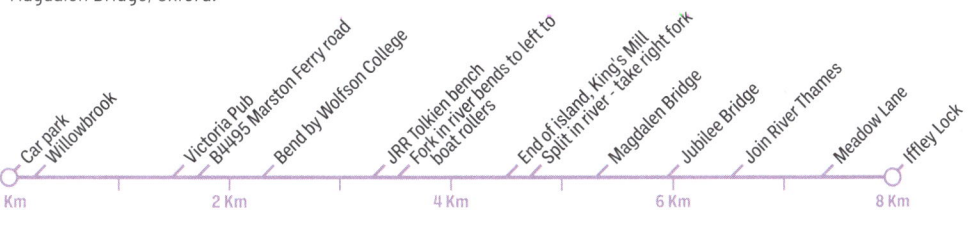

punts and lush green lawns. Another 170m downstream you'll pass under the B4495 Marston Ferry Road. Then 500m on you'll turn right into an S-bend, with Wolfson College dead ahead and a small boating lagoon on the bend. As the river straightens you'll pass under a small footbridge and continue on your way, looking out for the occasional troll...

ABOVE Craig Saffing kayaking the backwaters of the Cherwell on a sunny winter's day.

Oxford's spires are now coming into view as you float gently on, hopefully with snacks and a picnic on board. There are plenty of willows and other trees here, making the route seem more hidden as you paddle on. Sports pitches and cricket squares occupy the right bank and green meadows the left.

The paddle continues past Lady Margaret Hall and St Edmunds Hall, and under a small footbridge before passing a plaque and bench dedicated to the fantasy novelist JRR Tolkien, and you'll be forgiven for thinking you may be paddling into Middle Earth. About 200m on the river kinks left to Parson's Pleasure, a circular pool set into the river for male-only nude bathing. It closed in 1991 and now forms part of the Oxford Parks.

On the corner of the bend on the right are some boat slide rollers, which allow you to descend to the lower channel. Since

ABOVE Paddling the boat rollers in higher flows on the Cherwell.

ABOVE Gideon and Adam from our team enjoying a great day out on the Cherwell, finishing on the River Thames.

it was in flood when we took this trip, we paddled down them. The river then passes the bottom of the weir, dropping water from the upper left-hand channel above. You'll paddle under several smaller pedestrian bridges, including the Marston cycle path, where you'll feel the channel is pinched even narrower.

You're passing New College and St Catherine's College on your magical mystery tour with the Mesopotamia Walkway on your left side, separating the two channels, which widens on to a small island at Magdalen Fellows College Garden. You'll pass by King's Mill, which originally worked the left-hand channel (the one you didn't paddle). The river splits again into multiple channels – you'll take the right fork after passing Magdalen College Fellows Garden on the left and paddle around the front of Bat Willow Meadow and on to the island surrounded by the Cherwell, called the Water Meadow.

The river splits again and we took the left fork 700m down to Magdalen Bridge, where you'll find the Magdalen Bridge Boathouse and punt station. We turned back upstream on the narrow back channel up to Holywell Ford and mill, which is impressively old. When we went the sunshine was making the buildings, bridges and pretty much anything else take on an impressive warm glow. Once under the bridge on the central arch the river winds through more sports grounds.

After winding past more meadows you'll reach the more modern Jubilee Bridge spanning the Cherwell 400m downstream from Magdalen Bridge. You're now in striking distance of the River Thames and a contrasting wide river. Be aware: rowers and bigger boats frequent this stretch, so do stay more focused than you were on the Cherwell.

On to the Thames, turn left downstream towards London and enjoy the change of scenery. Head downstream for about 800m to Meadow Lane, under the shadow of the B4495 flyover, Donnington Bridge, and exit the river there. The backwaters of the Cherwell will have removed stresses and infused you with a sense of calm. Organise your shuttle back to the start or turn around and paddle back upstream, reversing your route.

EXTEND THE TRIP Once in the mood, you can of course extend your paddling route lock by lock along the length of the River Thames. In 2009 we paddled the river from Cricklade down to the Dartford Crossing, a total of 295km, in 33 hours.

The next lock is Iffley Lock, which is 730m from the bridge and by which stage you'll be into the swing of things on the Thames. The Oxford Mathematical Bridge at Iffley is one to admire. Then, about 500m on, you'll pass under the A423 ring road and then pass Hinksey Stream and the railway bridge. Sandford Lock is 1.75km on, which offers convenient exits.

OUR RICH ADVENTURE We've paddled Oxford's winding waterways on many occasions, enjoying hidden treasures and vantage points. On one of our winter trips the flows were a little bit higher than usual, which resulted in one of our team (with shameless giggles at their expense) taking an impromptu swim in the cool waters.

Rich also explored the city *par terre*, enjoying some of the same sights as he took part in the Oxford half marathon. It was a love-hate event, as he completed the course for charity while carrying a tumble dryer on his back alongside Martin Realey, of SSNaP (Supporting Sick Newborns and their Parents), who carried a washing machine.

CALORIE CREDITS Launch from the Victoria Arms, a riverside pub on the site of a former ferry crossing, with a mooring area for punts and a modern European menu (W: https://butcombe.com/the-victoria-arms-oxfordshire/food-drink). Or eat in style at the Cherwell Boathouse (W: https://cherwellboathouse.co.uk).

The Old Kitchen Bar at Magdalen College is on one of the backwater stretches of the River Cherwell (W: www.magd.ox.ac.uk/venue-hire), while the Isis River Farmhouse is a lively riverside pub with food and live music upstream of Sandford Lock (W: www.theisisfarmhouse.co.uk).

BELOW Destination River Thames as we make it to our egress point.

ABOVE Exploring Oxford's history on the quiet backwaters.

WILDLIFE SAFARI There is a surprising amount of wildlife on the Cherwell, including kingfishers and herons using the many willows as cover. Otters also live on the Cherwell, so keep your eyes peeled.

> **WHERE'S THE MAGIC?**
>
> With its small channels, historic bridges and hidden backwaters, Oxford's Cherwell is one of the UK's best little rivers to paddle, while the spires and towers of the universities and halls that make the city so famous are a sight to behold. One minute you can be on a tiny channel and the next, a busy waterway similar to a Venetian canal, before exiting on to the mighty River Thames.

OTHER ATTRACTIONS Visit the Pitt Rivers Museum (W: www.prm.ox.ac.uk), one of the best of its kind with over 500,000 artefacts from around the world and throughout history. It's also free to enter.

If you're up for more time on the water, try punting when you've finished your paddling trip. There are many punting companies available along this route, including Oxford Punting (W: www.oxfordpunting.co.uk).

In 2021 the Oxford Botanic Garden & Arboretum (W: www.obga.ox.ac.uk/visit-garden) turned 400, making it the oldest botanic garden in the UK. Today it contains over 5,000 different plant species from around the world.

THE SHARED ECONOMY Hire a canoe, kayak or SUP or even a hydrobike at Thrupp Canoe & Kayak Hire, just north of Oxford (W: https://tckh.co.uk).

Visit Moi's SUP School for paddling on the River Cherwell and other locations (W: www.moisupschool.co.uk/our-locations).

11 RIVER ROTHER AND BODIAM CASTLE

Paddle the gently flowing River Rother from Bodiam Bridge to Newenden, or extend your range and head to the Sussex coast with its abundance of wildlife. Along the way you'll explore living history, revisit our medieval heritage via castles that formed historic defences for our island nation, and follow in the footsteps of two icons of the screen, Monty Python and Doctor Who!

The Lowdown

DIFFICULTY
A gentle touring river with plenty to see at Bodiam Bridge and Castle or cut loose and paddle to Newenden.

DISTANCE 6km, A to B or paddle a loop to suit your time and energy levels.

DIRECTIONS At Newenden Bridge, you can use the railway car park or the laybys alongside for parking and loading.

HAZARD

CRAFT

	LOCATION	GRID REFERENCE	POST CODE	WHAT3WORDS
START	Bodiam Bridge, Robertsbridge	TQ784253	TN32 5UG	major.knee.responded
FINISH	Newenden Bridge, Northiam	TQ835270	TN31 6FE	vented.tadpoles.written

ABOVE Bodiam Castle, used in the filming of Monty Python, standing proud over the River Rother.

11 • RIVER ROTHER AND BODIAM CASTLE

ABOVE Rich canoeing on the River Rother by Bodiam Castle.

BACKGROUND Nestled on the banks of the River Rother and surrounded by a moat of some stature, Bodiam Castle near Robertsbridge dates back to the 14th century and is now maintained by the National Trust. Built around 1385 by Sir Edward Dallingridge, the castle and moat would be a major engineering project today, never mind centuries ago.

A SLICE OF HISTORY A stunning example of a 14th-century moated castle provides the backdrop to the start of this paddle. One of Britain's most romantic and picturesque castles, Bodiam was built in 1385 by Sir Edward Dallingridge, a former knight of King Edward III, who built it to defend the area against French invasion during the Hundred Years' War.

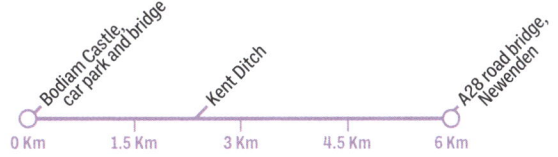

ROUTE Launching from the bank alongside the iconic Bodiam Castle and moat simply puts a smile on your face. As a warm-up you can weave in and out of the Bodiam Bridge arches or explore upstream towards Quarry Farm, which has family camping pods and glamping with the Original Hut Company, and offers a good base.

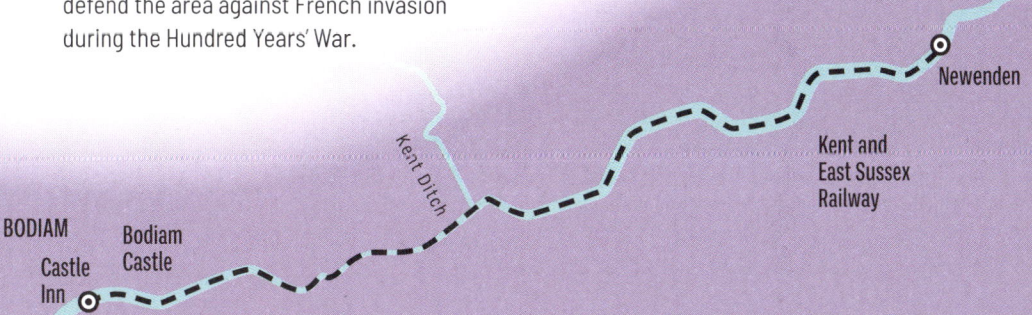

Now heading downstream, it is easy paddling all the way and the slightly raised banks offer some protection from the wind. However, in the event of funnelling easterly winds, which make for a difficult paddle, you may decide to reverse the paddle, leaving the castle reveal until the end.

The River Rother is edged by quiet fields and unspoilt countryside, making it the perfect spot for a family picnic paddle. It is also ideal for a wild swimming escape on a hot day. The river naturally bends and winds its way towards the sea and if you view it on a map it is the perfect snake shape.

Running parallel to the river are a series of drainage ditches bisecting fields and providing water for trees lining the banks and a patchwork quilt of irrigation waterways for the surrounding crop fields. After 2km the Kent Ditch joins the Rother on the left side. You're now a third of the way from the bridge at Bodiam to your destination.

Keep paddling towards Newenden, 6km downstream from the castle, where you can exit the river by the bridge. Just past the bridge is Bodiam Boating Station (see below).

EXTEND THE TRIP You can extend your paddle beyond Newenden towards the coast and all the way to Rye. You'll travel mainly through rural farming land, giving the sense of an escape to the countryside. Keep paddling along the raised banks heading east with plenty of zigs and zags. After about 5km you'll see another flow joining from the left bank. Another 7km on and Lock Rye Cottage is on the left, running parallel to the military road. The flow is now south, heading for the coast, and you should be able to smell the sea air.

Around 2km further and you'll reach the tidal flow with a tidal sluice. It is now a short paddle to the sea with Rye to your west and Camber Sands to the east. This final, 7km stretch is more built-up, leaving you yearning for the quieter waters. The **wonderful Rye Harbour Nature Reserve is**

BELOW Heading off to paddle the Rother for a quiet day out.

on the right bank before hitting the sea. Be sure to check tides and be aware that any mud flats and sandy beaches can make for a long walk.

OUR RICH ADVENTURE The castle with its flooded moat grabs your attention from the start, allowing visitors to imagine knights of old. The river was also flooded here, leaving limited headroom below the bridge arches. We parked up our camper van and took to the water to enjoy the excellent paddle down to Newenden. We'd arranged a taxi shuttle back to the van and arrived ready to cook up a romantic meal. Strange… we couldn't find the meat we'd left to defrost? It didn't take long to find the culprit – our lurcher foster dog had fancied it for herself, and with her long legs had removed it from the sink and gobbled down the evidence!

CALORIE CREDITS The Hub at Quarry Farm is a family-run café and shop stocked with locally sourced and ethical products (W: https://thehubquarryfarm.co.uk). Sedlescombe Organic Vineyard is also worth a visit. You can pair a tour of the vineyard with afternoon tea or a ploughman's lunch (W: www.sedlescombeorganic.com/). Or why not try the Castle Inn pub in Robertsbridge, which serves homemade food with a vintage vibe (W: www.castleinnbodiam.co.uk/)?

WILDLIFE SAFARI Like so many of our rivers, this area is teeming with bird life. Keep an eye out for kestrels and buzzards hunting over the fields. The High Weald surrounding Bodiam is also designated an AONB (W: https://highweald.org).

Run by Sussex Wildlife Trust, the Rye Harbour Nature Reserve protects important coastal and wetland habitat and is home to thousands of species of birds, plants and other wildlife. You'll find a café, toilets and shop at the new Discovery Centre, which also includes excellent interactive displays and information about the area and its history.

> **WHERE'S THE MAGIC?**
>
> The imposing fortress of Bodiam Castle starred as Castle Swampy in the iconic film *Monty Python and The Holy Grail* (1975), as well as appearing in an episode of the TV series *Doctor Who*.

OTHER ATTRACTIONS Hitch a ride on the Kent and East Sussex Steam Railway, which runs from Bodiam Station to Northiam Station near Newenden (W: https://kesr.org.uk). It's not daily, so you'll need to plan ahead and book in advance. SUPs can be deflated and carried on the train.

The Original Hut Company offers glamping in shepherd's huts and bell tents, with open campfires and private wash huts (W: https://original-huts.co.uk), while at Northam you'll find the Rother Valley Caravan & Camping Park (W: https://rothervalleypark.co.uk) and the Rother Valley Brewing Company (W: www.rothervalleybrewery.co.uk).

THE SHARED ECONOMY Rent a kayak or SUP at Bodiam Castle through Epic Life. They also offer team building activities, holiday clubs and other events for young people and families on holiday (W: www.epiclife.co.uk).

You can also hire a craft from Bodiam Boating Station, which has a choice of rowing boats, canoes, kayaks, SUPs and even motorboats, charter or self-hire (W: https://bodiamboatingstation.co.uk).

12 RIVER GREAT STOUR, CANTERBURY

The Great Stour is a simple but rewarding paddle skirting marshlands and lakes with a wide array of bird life and wildlife in their natural habitats. Make time to pass by Westbere Marshes and Stodmarsh National Nature Reserve. The Great Stour offers a charming A to B option or a loop out and back from the picnic site at Grove Ferry. There are plenty of great watering holes on this route so you can reward your efforts.

The Lowdown

DIFFICULTY
Gentle river flows with easy access and egress.

DISTANCE Fordwich to Grove Ferry: 7.1km.
Grove Ferry loop: 10km.
Grove Ferry to Plucks Gutter: 12.9km.

DIRECTIONS Launch from the George and Dragon pub at Fordwich, Britain's smallest town, and head downstream to finish at Grove Ferry. Or you could do a loop out and back from Grove Ferry, or paddle down to Plucks Gutter for an A to B trip.

HAZARDS

CRAFT

	LOCATION	GRID REFERENCE	POST CODE	WHAT3WORDS
START	Fordwich Bridge	TR179597	CT2 0BX	unlisted.alleyway.remit
FINISH (1)	Grove Ferry	TR236631	CT3 4BP	kingpin.forwarded.fermented
FINISH (2)	Plucks Gutter	TR269633	CT3 1JB	massive.unpacked.moved

BACKGROUND Kent's Great Stour splits Canterbury, giving it a Venice like quality, with channels and waterways flowing between historic buildings and monuments alike. The Cathedral was founded in 597AD and is the headquarters of the Church of England. The city itself has been the site of pilgrimages and was occupied by the Romans, who built its ancient walls. The Great Stour flows beyond Canterbury and becomes distinctly rural in its navigation, with beautiful parkland and nature reserves to explore.

RIGHT The Little Stour at Fordwich is a great place to start your paddle downstream.

A SLICE OF HISTORY

Situated amid the East Kent marshes, Richborough Roman Fort is perhaps the most symbolically important of all Roman sites in Britain, as it witnessed both the beginning and almost the end of Roman rule. Explore the huge stone walls that mark the site of this Saxon Shore fortress, the rolling defensive ditches and the impressive foundations showing the scale of this once bustling Roman settlement.

During the First World War, a secret 'Q' port was built on the banks of the River Stour in order to ferry troops and munitions across the channel. Camps were occupied by thousands of soldiers ready to cross to France and Flanders, as well as those working in the port. It later became a prison for soldiers who had broken the rules.

ABOVE Canterbury's historic architecture.

ABOVE Canterbury is like an English Venice, with waterways braiding through the city.

ROUTE Launch your craft from the riverbanks adjacent to the small bridge and car park of the George and Dragon pub. Float downstream under the bridge and let your adventure begin. The first 200–300m winds through the 'chocolate box' village of Fordwich, and you'll pass the Fordwich Arms and the Church of St Mary on the right bank. On the left bank is the launch site for the lovely folk at Canoe Wild (see below).

Leaving Fordwich you are immediately in the wilds of Kent, with wooded riverbanks and large lakes and bodies of water on either side of the river. Around 500m of straight river later you'll enter the Westbere Marshes and the river relaxes into an ongoing snake-like route with bends galore for the next 2km. You'll then arrive at the tidal lake, where the Great Stour skirts the outside right-hand edge and continues eastwards. Feel free to explore the lake if you have time.

Back on the river, the undulating nature of its winding route returns and remains unspoilt and rural, avoiding urban landscapes or civilisation. The river passes Hersden, which is set back and not on the river. The railway follows straight and true along the general path of the river on the right bank. You are now in the Stodmarsh NNR.

About 3.5km later you'll emerge from the rural escape to more facilities as you reach Grove Ferry Picnic Site, the Grove Ferry Inn, moorings and a marina, and Canoe Wild's second base. Grove Ferry itself is a country park run by Kent Council so parking and facilities are good. Around 400m of paddling after the bridge signals the end of the moorings and the river reclaims its wilder nature.

About 500m on the river kicks left at a sharper apex band, where you'll find more moorings and a boat house on the bend. The river becomes more winding, bending north-east for about 2km before looping around and heading more southeast towards the superbly named hamlet Plucks Gutter. About 1km after this change in direction the River Wantsum joins with a sluice. The Little Stour tributary meets the Great Stour just upstream of the bridge. Plucks Gutter is an obvious place to exit the river if you're doing an A to B route. (This is 13km from the start, although you could return back to Grove Ferry.) Plucks Gutter has moorings and a marina and the Spitfire Boat Club, but more importantly the Dog and Duck Inn, which offers food and drink to reward paddling prowess, or most likely for currency of some sort.

Once replenished, turn around and paddle back against the gentle flow or shuttle back to the start.

EXTEND THE TRIP Beyond Plucks Gutter it is 20km to the sea and Pegwell Bay. The river loops and winds all the points of the compass to make the journey more interesting and loops around Sandwich. The A256 viaduct at Sandwich is 10km on from Plucks Gutter and even though you are close as the crow flies to the coast, it is still another 10km through the port and docks to the Pegwell, which is just across from Ramsgate.

OUR RICH ADVENTURE We explored the wonderful city of Canterbury during a winter off-season and met the lovely folk at Canoe Wild, who run a hire and coaching company on the river. We subsequently attended a British Canoeing (now Paddle UK) conference together where it was great to share our paddling stories with like-minded people.

Paddling on the Great Stour was a real treat, as we were in no hurry. We slowed things right down, floated and operated at a pace slower than usual. It was heavenly, and perhaps there is something in these waters and this welcoming countryside that calls for a slower, more relaxed experience.

CALORIE CREDITS The George and Dragon at Fordwich offers decent grub and staff are very friendly (W: www.georgeanddragon.pub/menus). Alternatively, The Dog at Wingham is a great place to stay over and reward paddling endeavours (W: https://www.thedog.co.uk). It goes without saying they have dog-friendly rooms! Further downriver, the Grove Ferry Inn exudes a warm welcome with its décor and friendly staff and, being right on the river, is an obvious place to refuel (W: www.groveferryinn.co.uk).

WILDLIFE SAFARI The reedbeds at Stodmarsh NNR are like so many UK waters a sanctuary for migrating birds, such as swallows and house martins in the

BELOW Rich paddling the Little Stour, heading towards the nature reserves.

summer and starlings in the winter. The reedbeds are also home to bittern, marsh harrier, kingfisher, great crested grebe, coot, moorhen, reed bunting and bearded reedling, which can all be seen here through the seasons. As well as rare plants, Stodmarsh also supports a large variety of invertebrates such as dragonflies and moths. With its softer bank edges it also has a large population of water voles.

OTHER ATTRACTIONS Stay a few days in Canterbury like we did and see a show at The Marlowe Theatre (W: https://marlowetheatre.com). Or for more outdoor adventures, White Mills Lake offers wakeboarding, open water swimming and an aquapark (W: www.whitemillswake.co.uk/). Splash and dash all the way! Or for something more relaxing, head to Sandwich Lakes, a prime fishing location where you can unlock your inner angler (W: www.sandwichlakes.co.uk).

Just outside the city, the family-friendly Nethergong Camping is set in 26 acres of woodland and meadows with great facilities (W: www.nethergongcamping.co.uk).

THE SHARED ECONOMY Visit Canoe Wild for personal yet expert advice on all things paddling hire (W: www.canoewild.co.uk). The super friendly folk there offer courses, parties and of course paddling on canoes, kayaks and SUPs.

ABOVE Getting back to nature on the quiet waters of the Little Stour.

> **WHERE'S THE MAGIC?**
>
> Canterbury sets the tone for historic buildings and hidden water channels within city boundaries. We parked up our van for a few days and explored the city including live comedy at the theatre. As you launch downstream from Fordwich or Grove Ferry, you literally go with the flow. Kent seems to have that effect on people.

13 RIVER THAMES: RICHMOND

The heartbeat of our proud nation, the River Thames has shaped Britain's trade, political and social history and is one of the world's most famous rivers. This paddle might be at the quieter end of this busy waterway, but it is still literally buzzing with energy and action at every turn, with rowers, paddlers, boaters of all shapes and sizes forming an eclectic and loose flotilla. The wider vista of the Richmond Hill and historic buildings provide a nice backdrop to your trip.

The Lowdown

DIFFICULTY
Check the tides before heading out, and tidal flows.

DISTANCE Kew Bridge to Teddington, finishing at River Lane, Richmond, loop (full day): 18km.

DIRECTIONS This section of the River Thames is alive with fantastic pubs, rowing and kayaking clubs and all manner of people walking, jogging and messing about on the water. You can start and finish at River Lane in Richmond, paddling a circular route and choosing a course on the outside of any islands, or opt for a one-way trip with a shuttle depending on flows, tides and the section. Be sure to check tides and plan accordingly.

HAZARDS

CRAFT

	LOCATION	GRID REFERENCE	POST CODE	WHAT3WORDS
START OR FINISH	River Lane, Richmond	TQ178735	TW10 7AQ	vase.itself.ruled
	Kew Bridge	TQ190778	TW9 3AW	tapes.sage.forces
	Putney Bridge	TQ242757	SW15 1SN	begun.pirate.began
ROLLERS	Teddington Lock	TQ166715	TW11 9NH	pound.tender.raced

BELOW Ash and Rich pootling in a racing canoe on the Thames near Richmond Canoe Club.

SOUTH OF ENGLAND

ABOVE Thames rollers at portages further up the River Thames with Olympic medallist Steve Williams and Graham Dandy.

BACKGROUND
The River Thames is one of the most famous arterial trading routes in history. It flows from beyond Cricklade in Wiltshire down to the Thames Estuary and out to sea. It links our capital city to the world and has more historic buildings and locations along its route than any other river we have paddled. At 355km, it is Britain's second-longest river and over the years we have paddled almost all of it, including 292km of it in 33 hours during the blizzards of 2009.

A SLICE OF HISTORY
The name 'Thames' stems from the Latin *Tamesis*, itself stemming from the old Celtic name for the river, *Tamesas*, which is thought to have meant 'dark'. Each of the bridges along the river is a combination of endeavour, hard graft and beauty. Such is their renown that in 1968 the City of London sold London Bridge, further downstream, to Arizona-based entrepreneur Robert Paxton McCulloch, who apparently believed he was purchasing Tower Bridge.

Richmond itself has extensive royal connections. Erected in 1501 by Henry VII, former Earl of Richmond, Richmond Palace was a royal residence during the 16th and 17th centuries, although only remnants of this former grand palace survive today.

Richmond Park, an area of some 2,360 acres of wild heath and woodland originally enclosed for hunting, now forms London's largest royal park. The park is an NNR, SSSI and SAC, and is Grade I listed.

ROUTE
Arrive at River Lane early to beat the crowds. The beach area is perfect for launching a kayak, canoe or SUP. You are now on the Thames, England's major arterial river. This is all tidal, with London downstream to your right and the source of the Thames to the left via many miles and many locks. Teddington Lock is a few miles upstream and represents the top of the tidal section.

Just downstream is an island and if you stay river right you pass adjacent to the common land before the start of Richmond's quaint waterfront, with some gorgeous places to eat. On your right-hand side you'll pass by Richmond Canoe Club's pontoons and clubhouse doors, where you can greet fellow paddlers. You'll now see Richmond Bridge – pass under it with more islands on the left, the largest of which is Corporation Island.

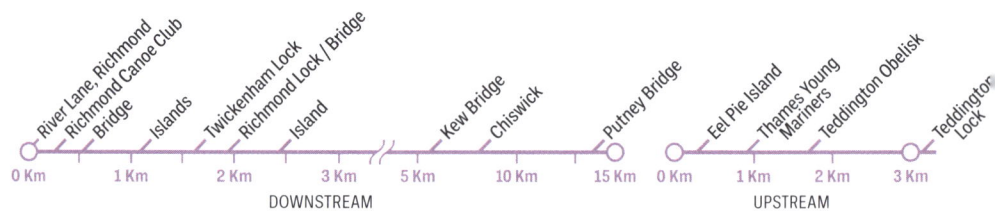

13 • RIVER THAMES: RICHMOND

After the islands and some moorings come two bridges in quick successes, one of which is Twickenham Bridge, 1.7km downstream from your starting point. The tidal locks are 300m on – these can be portaged on the left but do be aware it can be slippery when wet. It feels like a James Bond scene as you portage over this giant concrete structure.

Another 400m downstream you reach the larger island of Isleworth Ait (over 500m long), where the main flow is to the right, although you can sneak around the left side and explore the backwater. The river bends right at this point as you head towards Kew. The banks are transformed to green spaces and 2km after the Isleworth you reach Kew Palace on the right, opposite Lot's Ait and Brentford Ait Islands. Here there are more back channels to explore and make your own. Just after the island comes Kew Bridge, a good place to turn and head back towards your launch site. If you time the tides correctly around slack water it should be straightforward, or stick to the edges and inside of bends to avoid the faster flows.

ABOVE Ash and Rich used a racing canoe but this paddle is suited to normal canoes, kayaks and SUP.

Upstream from River Lane you'll see some of London's most desirable waterside property with small boat houses, docks and lovely waterfronts. Paddle upstream on the right-hand side, past urban waterside palaces towards Teddington Lock.

Here you'll see Eel Pie Island after 1km upstream, which you can circumnavigate river right upstream or downstream, offering a glimpse into the vibrant waterside community that call it home. Around 500m upstream from the start of the island you'll pass under Eel Pie Bridge before the river bends slowly around to the left.

Another 700m upstream and you'll pass Thames Young Mariners base, where you may see plenty of activity on the water and on the lagoon located just off the river. Shortly after this is the Teddington Obelisk, which is compact and smaller than you might imagine, tucked back behind the willows. Around 700m upstream from the Mariners base is Teddington Lock with moorings, footbridge and a big weir, which should be avoided. You can land at the rollers located between the lock and the island and portage to the non-tidal river towards Molesey Lock 7.75km away, and 4.5km beyond to Sunbury and Shepperton, which is a further 5km past Sunbury. Obviously, if you want to go with the flow, start further up at one of these Thames locks and paddle back to River Lane with the current.

EXTEND THE TRIP Paddle further downstream towards our capital city, taking in Fulham, Putney and as far as Chiswick. Putney Bridge is 15km downstream, but with the tide out and back this is not as far as it sounds. If you're going further, remember to take account of the tides so that you go out on the ebb and return on the flood tide. For SUP'ers, paddle out and deflate your SUP before returning by public transport.

Upstream you can portage at Teddington Lock by the rollers and head away from the capital, with locks galore.

OUR RICH ADVENTURE There are so many paddling adventures on the River Thames that condensing them into a few short paragraphs is tricky. This part of the Thames never gets boring and we've paddled it many times training, both during races and just out for a bimble. We also filmed with BBC News at Water Lane for our London to Marrakesh adventure, which started in central London at Tower Bridge.

Rich has also twice competed in the Devizes to Westminster International Canoe Race, once in a double racing canoe and the other time in a double racing kayak. At 200km and 77 portages nonstop, the race sees plenty of famous competitors taking part. Known as 'the Everest of kayaking', this route takes no prisoners and doesn't respect previous accomplishments!

On previous trips we have also taken Canoe Trail customers into central London to see iconic landmarks including the London Eye, Tower Bridge, Greenwich and the Houses of Parliament. Beware that due to heavy traffic, this route requires experienced leaders and permissions and

> **WHERE'S THE MAGIC?**
>
> The Thames is something of a paradox; for such a busy stretch of water it's surprising to see just how charming and calming it can be. We believe this has something to do with the shared energy of people enjoying this arterial river. The stately homes, incredible real estate, boat houses, follies and other monuments on show add to the feel-good factor.

SUPs are not permitted.

Also worth a mention is our Thames Estuary trip out to the Second World War Maunsell Forts, a committing 20-mile sea kayak paddle alongside major shipping lanes and windfarms.

CALORIE CREDITS
There are plenty of riverside pubs along the route and places to stock up or stop off for a picnic. Below Richmond Bridge you are spoilt for choice, with Peggy Jean at Riverside Green (W: www.daisygreenfood.com/location-peggy) and the White Cross (W: www.thewhitecrossrichmond.com), a favourite with the Twickenham faithful on match days. Tide Tables Café (W: www.tidetablescafe.co.uk) is just upstream of the bridge under the arches.

WILDLIFE SAFARI
Bird life is plentiful, including cormorants and swans. On one occasion we spotted something strange in the water, which turned out to be a neoprene-clad swimmer as opposed to the seal we imagined. There are, of course, deer in Richmond and cows on the common land, so keep your eyes peeled.

OTHER ATTRACTIONS
Kew Gardens is a national treasure and definitely worth a visit while you're in the area (W: www.kew.org/). A designated UNESCO World Heritage Site, the gardens boast over 50,000 plants.

Head to the other side of London to explore the Windsor Great Walk, a historic 3-mile avenue from Windsor Castle to the Copper Horse Statue. You may even catch a glimpse of the deer herd among the ancient oaks (W: www.windsorgreatpark.co.uk).

THE SHARED ECONOMY
Check out Back of Beyond, which offers SUP, kayak and canoe trips from Richmond (W: https://backofbeyonduk.com).

BELOW A bit of a jostle for space with the geese at Richmond tidal lock.

EAST OF ENGLAND

14 RIVER STOUR: CONSTABLE COUNTRY

Travel back in time on the River Stour, a classic English river that leaves Sudbury for the coast and winds through Constable Country in Suffolk. It seems there is a mill around every corner and even some flumes to paddle down. There are various small fish weirs as the river narrows with tight bends. There are a couple of campsites, one near the start and one closer to halfway, making this a perfect two-day paddling trip if you want to take your time.

The Lowdown

DIFFICULTY
Weirs, portages and small rapids at Langham Flumes.

DISTANCE Sudbury to Henny Swan, loop: 7km.
Sudbury to Cattawade, A to B:
Day 1 Sudbury to Rushbanks (camp overnight): 17.2km.
Day 2 Rushbanks to Cattawade (picnic site): 21.4km.
Total distance from Sudbury to Cattawade: 38.6km.

DIRECTIONS If you're doing the A to B option, there's a 29km shuttle back to the start, which takes about 35 minutes. For the return loop, park at Sudbury Theatre Trust.

HAZARDS

CRAFT

BACKGROUND The River Stour, Hay Wain's and Flatford Mill have been captured over time by one of Britain's most revered and famous painters, John Constable. Constable was born in East Bergholt in 1776 and enjoyed life on or around the river. The river is 76km long and forms the boundary between Suffolk to the north and Essex to the south. Dedham Vale at the eastern end of the River is an Area of Outstanding Natural Beauty (AONB).

ABOVE The backwaters of Constable's Stour looking radiant.

A SLICE OF HISTORY A chalk hill carving of the legendary Bures dragon sits above the town and was created as part of the Queen's Diamond Jubilee celebrations, measuring 75m x 95m with the perimeter extending to nearly half a mile. Legend has it that the villagers went out to slay the beast, but its skin and spines were so tough they failed to kill it. However, the dragon fled, never to return ... at least not yet!

There are so many Second World War pill boxes along the River Stour they become a bit like buses! However, remembering

	LOCATION	GRID REFERENCE	POST CODE	WHAT3WORDS
PARKING	Car parks at Sudbury Theatre Trust	TL871407	CO10 2BE	canyons.firework.hilltop
START (FINISH IF DOING LOOP)	Sudbury	TL872407	CO10 2BE	dwell.shrub.cable
END DAY 1 (A TO B)	Rushbanks Campsite	TL950333	CO6 4NA	achieving.goodbyes.hushed
	Flatford Mill and lock	TM077332	CO7 6UJ	unzipped.factory.procures
END DAY 2 (A TO B)	Cattawade picnic site	TM100330	CO11 1RG	sensitive.alley.static

why they're there will bring a sombre and worthwhile debt of gratitude.

Take a moment to appreciate Boxted Bridge as you pass beneath it. The bridge, which was built in 1901 by George Double and lies in the centre of the Dedham Vale AONB on the Essex–Suffolk border, was almost removed, but was saved through community pressure.

Flatford Mill is a Grade I listed watermill on the River Stour at Flatford in Suffolk's East Bergholt. According to the date-stone, the mill was built in 1733, but some of the structure may be even older. Attached to the mill is a 17th-century miller's cottage, which is also Grade I listed.

ROUTE Park at the Sudbury Theatre Trust car park, walk down to the small backwaters of the Stour and you'll be paddling within a matter of minutes. Once on the main river take the left channel at the spur and paddle the lush, clear waters, with Friars Meadow on either side. In summer the river has blankets of weed on this section. The first of many Second World War pill boxes along the Stour is opposite the meadow.

About 500m from the start and the river bends into a woodland with rough treeline on each bank as you pass Lady Island. Around 750m downstream the river reaches the first lock, requiring a short portage around the structure. Approaching the lock you'll see the spire of St Andrew's Church in Great Cornard. Green lands and sheltering trees provide cover for the next 700m and the river then kinks left, straightens and then right.

The river runs true and straight for 300m

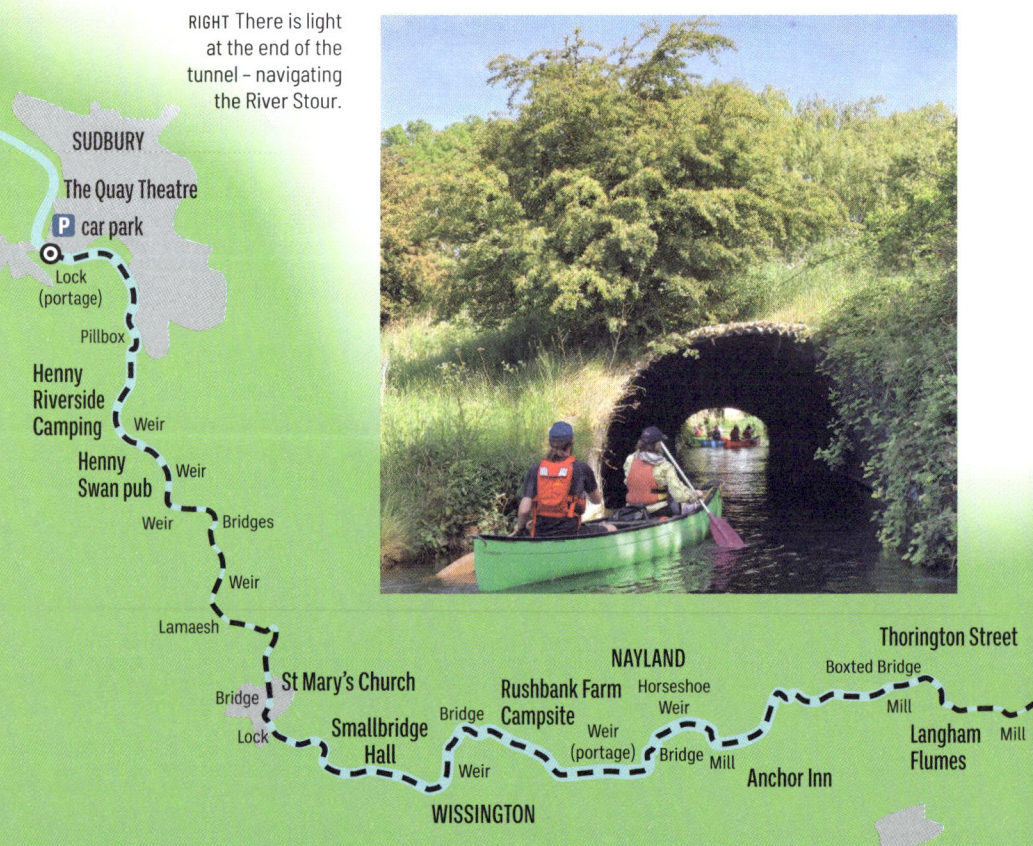

RIGHT There is light at the end of the tunnel – navigating the River Stour.

ABOVE Playing hide and seek under the troll bridge on the Stour.

before taking on an ever winding nature for the next few kilometres, with small loops and twists to keep you interested. About 2km from the last lock you'll reach the riverside pub of Henny Swan on Henny Road, with Henny Campsite next door. The river splits around an island and pool with a small weir, which you can shoot or portage around by Shalford Meadow. A bridge follows and 500m later there's a small weir with a portage on the left bank.

The river extends south for 2km with new tree plantations on the left bank, and a pill box on a bend before a weir, which you can portage or shoot carefully depending on your craft and experience (canoe or kayak only). Overhead power lines provide a good locator for the weir. Below the weir the river loops behind a small island. There's a small footbridge to the island crossing the flow. A few hundred metres later the river passes under the railway bridge.

Around 2km downstream, after much zigging and zagging, the river pours over a small drop weir close to the village of Lamarsh. You'll have seen the low spire of the Holy Innocents Church from the bank. The weir can be portaged or run again if you have the right craft and skills. The river bends round to the left with a long, slow, exaggerated curve for several hundred metres until you reach a small farm bridge.

The river bends round to the right and then heads mostly south, running into the town of Bures. You'll see the church spire for St Marys and the bridge as you arrive. The river loops around Bures until you pass the cricket club and a small bridge. It passes Nether Hall about 1km downstream, where you need to portage the lock. The pool below is extremely beautiful and you can imagine river nymphs residing here.

The river continues to create a random

course through these beautiful lands with tree-lined banks, kingfishers and other wildlife following your route. About 2km downstream the Stour straightens up as it flows gently past Smallbridge Hall, before rounding a bend with a small island. Just past the island is the bridge for Mill Hill Road, making this a potential exit point if your plans do not survive contact (as the military would put it). The river winds in a large arc north and then south for about 2.5km, with plenty of twists and turns until you reach Rushbanks Farm Caravan and Camping Site, just before the village of Wissington in Suffolk. We've used the campsite for our Canoe Trail trips and it's lovely to pitch up on the banks of the Stour and make camp.

Around 500m after the campsite the river passes St Mary the Virgin Church at Wissington, which is set behind a small, wooded area and passes under a footbridge. The river continues eastwards for about 1.2km and then reaches Wiston Mill, where it splits around a large island. The portage is on the right-hand side, taking you around a stepped weir that is not runnable. You can paddle up to the mill to get some picture-postcard photos before portaging, which is a short carry.

The river soon arrives at the picturesque Suffolk town of Nayland, with a pretty loop paddling past plenty of historic buildings. Around 1.5km from Wiston Mill you'll paddle under the A134 road bridge, having taken the left fork where the river split. You can take the shorter right fork, but you'd miss Nayland. About 500m on you'll reach the Horseshoe Weir, with a portage on the right-hand side.

BELOW Portaging one of the weirs on the top section near Sudbury.

Good news: 300m on you pass under another road bridge with the Anchor Inn on your left bank, offering refreshments for your endeavours. The river remains narrow here and in summer can feel tight with weed and rush from the banks. The next 5km is tranquil as you paddle towards Dedham Vale, with very little to spoil the rural countryside, and willows and kingfishers galore. The next landmark is Boxted Bridge, which is over 100 years old and was at one point under threat of replacement. Luckily, community power won the day. There's road access here on Wick Road for shuttles.

Once past Boxted Bridge and the small hamlet on the banks, it's back to winding riverbanks for about a kilometre until you reach the much famed Langham Flumes, where the flow channels and drops between concrete barriers create a flow and wave train. In high levels this can be dangerous, but you can portage on the right-hand side.

SUP'ERS NOTE

Only paddle the Langham Flumes in low-river conditions if you're experienced; our last customer trip there saw a couple of capsizes on the flumes.

Around 300m downstream the river splits around an island and the left channel is bigger, before passing under a bridge. Another 500m downstream the River Box joins the Stour and the magic carpet ride continues towards the coast. Higham St Mary's Church comes into view on the top bend as another tributary joins, before 700m downstream the river passes by a couple of lakes at Black Barn Nature Reserve.

The river arrives at Stratford St Mary and waves between islands with small bridges and landing places as well as the very welcoming Swan Inn on the riverbank. After the wild paddling a refreshment may be welcome! Around 1.5km on you'll paddle under the twin bridges of 'The St' and then the much larger A12 as you head into the Dedham Vale AONB. Around 500m on and you'll reach the picturesque Dedham Mill, lock and pond. John Constable's painting of the area now hangs in London in the Tate.

ABOVE Rob Campbell leaving the tunnel on the Stour.

After the lock you'll quickly see the road bridge for the B1029, which is another access/egress point for this historic waterway. Behind the bridge is the Dedham Boatyard restaurant and a rowing boat hire, so expect this section to be busy on warm summer days. A kilometre downstream after more snaking riverbanks you'll reach the Fen Bridge. There are plenty of smaller streams and splits to the river but staying on the main flow you are close to Flatford Mill, made famous in another Constable painting, as well as Willy Lott's Cottage. About a kilometre down you'll paddle under Flatford Bridge and then the river widens for the mill, lock and various bygone buildings. There's also a hostel here.

Once you've explored, portage to continue your journey. The river continues

ABOVE Second World War pillbox on the Stour.

to split into smaller channels as you near the coast and Cattawade, your destination, only a couple of kilometres from here. Around 500m from the mill you'll reach a sluice weir with a split in the Stour where you'll take the left-hand channel, which provides a direct paddle to the egress at Cattawade. The final sting in the tail is plenty of winding turns, but you should be able to smell the sea air and dream of seaside fish and chips.

There's a glamping site at Constable Water Park at Cattawade, which is 2.5km after the sluices where the Stour splits. A few hundred metres after that is the Cattawade picnic site next to the A137 bridge. That's it: another great paddling adventure crammed with great watering holes and serious history in the bag!

OUR RICH ADVENTURE The River Stour is an excellent place to unwind on days off in peak season. Rob Campbell and I used it as a training river for the Yukon River Quest, bashing out the miles over a short timescale. It rained many cats and dogs that day, and we had to use the canoe as a rain hat as we were soaked! We now run an annual trip to the Stour, to share this enchanting destination with our clients.

CALORIE CREDITS Visit the riverside Henny Swan pub, with its fantastic beer garden and a French-influenced menu (W: www.thehennyswan.co.uk) while

WHERE'S THE MAGIC?

The River Stour is such a movable feast for paddlers, from its narrow waterways, to fun weirs to point and shoot through, tidal sections and of course the Langham Flumes. However, it is the paintings of John Constable that capture the true beauty of this enchanting waterway, and you'll soon realise that things haven't really changed that much since he walked these riverbanks.

The Anchor Inn is a gorgeous pub adjacent to the river (W: www.anchornayland.co.uk). Or why not try The Boatyard Eatery, which offers snacks, platters and drinks on the banks of the Stour at Dedham (W: https://theboatyarddedham.co.uk), or The Swan at Stratford St Mary with rustic food and world-class beers and wines (W: www.stratfordswan.com)?

The first campsite on the banks of the River Stour is Henny's Riverside Camping (W: www.hennyriversidecamping.co.uk) with camping and glamping options. Rushbanks is another great campsite located usefully downstream to split the journey (W: https://rushbankscampsite.co.uk). If you prefer four walls, the FSC Hostel (W: https://fsc.inn.fan) located at Flatford Mill is a perfect stop on the way to the coast.

WILDLIFE SAFARI Kingfishers and swan families have captured our hearts on our various trips on the Stour.

OTHER ATTRACTIONS Visit the River Stour Trust Visitor Centre on the banks at Great Cornard Lock (W: www.riverstourtrust.org/our-venues/visitor-education-centre), or you could try out some other watersports at Alton Water Park (W: https://anglianwaterparks.co.uk/alton-water).

THE SHARED ECONOMY Check out Canoe Trail's River Stour Paddling Trip (W: www.canoetrail.co.uk). Alternatively, the family-run Paddle Company (W: www.thepaddlecompany.co.uk) offers hire and guided tours, while the Constable Park leisure park (W: www.constablepark.co.uk/) offers kayaking, SUP and glamping.

BELOW A welcome pub stop on the Stour.

15 RIVER WAVENEY: BUNGAY LOOP

Loop your way through England's green and pleasant lands on this quiet paddle down the River Waveney near Bungay. The Waveney can be extended from a short half day trip on the Bungay Loop to a two-day camping trip from Bungay via the Three Rivers Campsite down to Beccles on an A to B route. There are lovely campsites, places to hire kit and some great pubs along the way.

The Lowdown

DIFFICULTY
A quiet waterway with great facilities to spice up your paddle.

DISTANCE Bungay Loop (half day trip): 11km. Three Lochs and Beccles, A to B (multiday paddle): 24.4km.

DIRECTIONS For the Bungay Loop half day trip, launch from the lock by the Waveney Valley Canoe Club at the Riverside Centre and paddle upstream past Outney Meadow Caravan Park to the top of the loop. Or extend the trip for a multiday paddle downstream from Bungay Down to Beccles, finishing near Old Bridge Street. The 10km shuttle back to the Riverside Centre takes about 15 minutes.

HAZARDS

CRAFT

BACKGROUND Bungay is a historic market town in the Suffolk Borders on the edge of the Broads. It is a stunning paddling destination with local hire companies, riverside camping and a river that is the heartbeat of the town. There are castles, great food and a thriving canoe club all a stone's throw from the water's edge. Further down, Beccles is a thriving water metropolis with marinas and boating to the fore and a lido to add to the available activities.

A SLICE OF HISTORY The Bigod Castle standing in the middle of Bungay was originally a Norman castle built by the fabulously named Roger Bigod in about 1100 to take advantage of the natural protection provided by a curve in the River Waveney. The family danced a fine line with revolt and were on the losing side in the Great Revolt of 1173–75 when the castle was besieged and sacked by Henry II's forces.

Further down the river is Mettingham

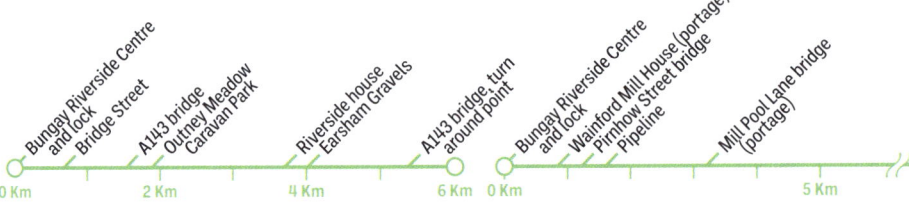

15 • RIVER WAVENEY: BUNGAY LOOP

	LOCATION	GRID REFERENCE	POST CODE	WHAT3WORDS
START/FINISH	Waveney Valley Canoe Club, Riverside Centre	TM340897	NR35 1BF	career.recruited.cornfield
RETURN POINT FOR LOOP	Top of Bungay Loop	TM329899	NR35 1DZ	appraised.square.tracking
	The Locks Inn Community Pub, Geldeston	TM390908	NR34 0HW	texted.thrashing.tumblers
	Three Rivers Pitch & Paddle campsite, Geldeston	TM388917	NR34 0LY	varieties.warmers.dynasties
MULTIDAY FINISH	Old Bridge Street	TM420911	NR34 9BA	passport.tonality.exclaim

Castle, a fortified manor house built in 1342. Only the gateway and a part of the wall remain, while the house was demolished in the 18th century.

ABOVE Foxy enjoying her morning paddle to Beccles for a look around.

One of my favourite adventure films growing up was *King Solomon's Mines*. I was excited to discover that the daughter of Sir Henry Rider Haggard, author of nearly 70 works of fact and fiction, including the novel on which the film was based, *She* and *Allan Quatermain*, lived in Cold Bath House, which you'll paddle past on this trip. Cold Bath House is located at the Vineyard Hills facing across the river to Outney Common. The House was first developed in 1734 as a spa by John King, a Bungay apothecary who identified a natural spring of water there, which he promoted as a cure for many ailments.

ROUTE For the perfect half day trip, launch from the Riverside Centre and Waveney Valley Canoe Club adjacent to the lock and paddle upstream, skirting the riverside town. Around 200m upstream you'll pass under the Bridge Street or Ditchingham

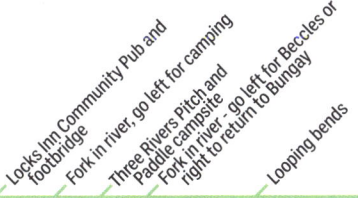

Dam road bridge, and 600m further on under the main A143 bridge.

Outney Meadow Caravan Park is on the left bank and you can hire canoes from here if need be. Take the right-hand fork, the main river drag, and you'll quickly leave behind any traces of urban life. We were there on a sunny day with blue skies – happy paddling memories.

The Bungay river loop encircles the Bath Hills Nature Reserve, which is managed by the Broads Authority.

The slow-moving river leaves you paddling subconsciously, requiring minimal exertion and leaving you to relax and escape the usual busy thought patterns. This is a great restorative place to tune in to nature and enjoy some quiet time. The banks are lush green, and reed mace and a selection of trees keep you company as you head generally north-west. The river was teeming with dragonflies while we were there, so keep your eyes peeled. They should be able to see you, as they have

ABOVE Canoeists at Shipmeadow Lock.

five eyes, the largest of which have 30,000 facets each. Bath Hills is laced with small ditches and channels, and the main river has intricate bends at random places, one of which became our swimming spot.

After about 1.8km you'll reach the top part of the loop and begin to turn south. Around 300m later you'll pass Cold Bath House, which had me reminiscing about the Allan Quatermain adventure stories. After another 600m you'll pass the end of the golf course and then 300m later begin to turn south on the western end of your paddling

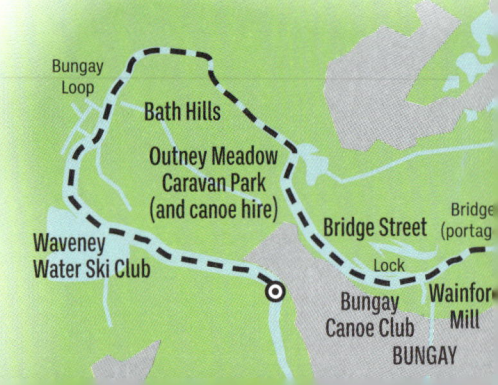

journey. We stopped for our picnic here in grassy meadows.

From the western end of the circuit you'll pass the gravel works excavations after 300m, adjacent to the waterski lake, presumably a former aggregate works. From here it's a kilometre or so to the A143 viaduct, which is the recommended turn around for this loop, as the river becomes smaller and more overgrown from this point. Retrace your route – about 5.4km to return to the start.

If you've planned to do the multiday paddle to Beccles, launch from the Riverside Centre and head east downstream, away from Bungay. You'll exit the town and paddle through lush green farming land and about a kilometre later, after several small bends, you'll arrive at Wainford Mill House, where you need to portage the weir. You can refuel here at the Silo coffee shop.

Back on the river (don't be tempted to stop for too long!) you'll pass under a footbridge and are flanked once again by open fields, with farms and silos visible. The Waveney winds on towards Ellingham Mill for about 2km and you'll see the church spire at St Marys from a distance. At Ellingham there's a weir under Mill Pool Lane which you'll need to portage. About 1.3km downstream and the gentle bends are replaced by S-bends, where you loop backwards and forwards.

About 2km downstream you'll reach The Locks Inn Community Pub at Geldeston, which serves great food on the riverbank and is nearly always surrounded by groups of paddlers and walkers. Make sure you support this locally run traditional pub. There's a footbridge over the river and 200m past this turn, back into the inlet to access the pub gardens and moorings.

After refreshments continue downstream for about 700m, where the river splits. The left fork heads to the Three Rivers Pitch & Paddle campsite at Geldeston. It's about 700m upstream to the large campsite and another charming village pub, The Wherry Inn (you'll have to pace yourself, though – we're not recommending a pub crawl!) You may decide to overnight at this campsite on the riverbank, and continue on towards Beccles and beyond the next day.

Return back to the river and paddle back to the river fork, taking the left fork (originally your right) and heading around the long bend for a kilometre as you approach the outskirts of Gillingham village (which is not on the river). You'll pass plenty of wooded riverbanks and small spinneys. Continue on for another 2km of wiggles and squiggles of riverbank meanders as you coast into Beccles.

Beccles is delightful, with small, private boat houses linked to riverside houses and moorings on the last few hundred metres. On the right bank on the first bend of urban civilisation after the wilds of the Suffolk-Norfolk border you'll

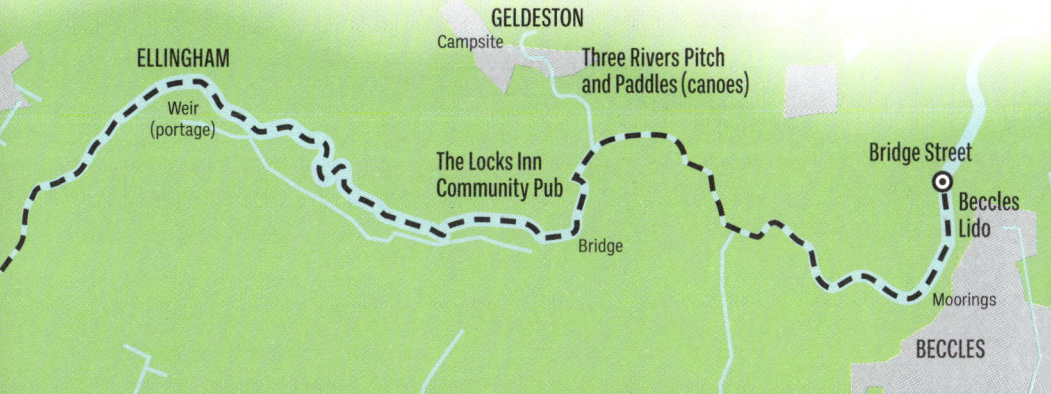

pass the Beccles Lido. After the left-hand bend the river straightens through the town (we paddled this section from both directions, staying downstream in a holiday cottage). A kilometre more of Beccles waterfront and you'll reach the main Norwich A146 road, having passed under the older Bridge Street roadway and Hippersons Boatyard. There are moorings throughout and places to exit the river.

EXTEND THE TRIP
The Waveney flows on eastwards towards the coast at Lowestoft and a maze of rivers. The river past Beccles snakes up and down, with woodland breaking up the countryside. Around 500m after the bridge you reach the sailing club and there are moorings along from the club.

From here the river extends for another 10.5km to the Waveney River Centre and holiday park, where you could opt for a caravan stay. The river passes nature reserves and Carlton Marshes so there's plenty of wildlife to see. You'll see the church spire of St Mary the Virgin at Burgh St Peter, and there's yet another watering hole, the Waveney Inn. You are now about 3.5km from Oulton Broad and close to Lowestoft. Scout an exit point such as Oulton Broad Watersports, where you may need to pay a landing fee.

OUR RICH ADVENTURE
We spent a week with family in Norfolk enjoying some decompression time from the pace of modern life. The house we rented was right on the River Waveney (well, several hundred metres down a lane) and we were able to paddle and swim most days.

We struck out to find waters new upstream and visit the Waveney Loop, which had been on our bucket list for many years. We hired a canoe from Outney Meadow campsite and launched from their site adjacent the A143 road bridge. Once on the water we headed upstream on this peaceful waterway with huge green willows stationed on the banks. The water was crystal clear and inviting us to take the plunge. We did, having found a large circular swing above a deep pool. Game on. Exploring downstream brought more fantastic paddling away from crowds and noise, bringing a fantastic holiday to a close.

CALORIE CREDITS
Make time to visit The Locks Inn Community Pub on the banks of the river near Geldeston. Although busy when we visited and enjoyed lunch, food was delicious and served promptly. It's a hub for paddle boarders and

LEFT William enjoying the Bungay Loop.

OPPOSITE Ash exploring the Bath Hill Nature Reserve on the Bungay Loop.

ABOVE SUP'ing into the heart of Beccles.

paddlers alike (W: www.thelocksinn.com).

There are plenty of places to eat well and be happy in Bungay, and several pubs within walking distance of the river, while The Wherry Inn at Geldeston (W: www.wherryinn.co.uk) is easily accessible from the Three Rivers Pitch & Paddle campsite (see below). The stunning Wainford Mill House has a riverside sauna, accommodation and The Silo coffee house (W: https://wainford.co.uk).

WILDLIFE SAFARI

Around 150ha of wetland surrounds the River Waveney, containing a dazzling array of wildlife, including teal, marsh harriers, kestrels and hobbies.

> **WHERE'S THE MAGIC?**
>
> The River Waveney feels like the purest spring water, with clear waters and reflections that would capture the attention of any photographer. Combined with great places to eat and drink and a stunning campsite, it is pretty hard to beat. Go see for yourself.

At ground level the observant might catch a glimpse of a grass snake, fen raft spiders, otters and even Chinese water deer.

OTHER ATTRACTIONS

Visit the rare collection of aviation history at the Norfolk and Suffolk Aviation Museum with artifacts and planes from Second World War bomber groups, air sea rescue and more (W: www.aviationmuseum.net).

THE SHARED ECONOMY

Book a canoe to explore these crystal clear waters via Outney Meadow Caravan Park (W: www.outneymeadow.co.uk/canoeing), or check in further downstream at the renowned Three Rivers Pitch & Paddle campsite, where you can hire sit-on-top kayaks, SUPs and canoes (W: https://threeriverspitchandpaddle.co.uk).

Visit Oulton Broad Water Sports Centre for sailing and paddling courses, SUP and kayak hire (W: https://oultonbroadwatersportscentre.co.uk).

16 RIVER BURE AND SALHOUSE BROAD

The Norfolk Broads is renowned for its quiet waterways and secluded channels, making this the perfect place to escape to and relax. The River Bure offers a unique mix of river scape interlinking hidden water expanses with tree lined pools and hidden broads. You paddle from secluded areas with plenty of wildlife such as Salhouse Broad to more bustling water metropolis towns like Horning and Wroxham with boating holiday activity and marinas.

The Lowdown

DIFFICULTY
Gentle paddle through river and broad sections.

DISTANCE Horstead Mill to Wroxham Broad car park: 11.9km.
Horstead Mill to Salhouse Broad: 13.5km.
Salhouse to The Weirs, South Walsham Broad: 12km.
Horstead Mill to Acle Bridge Inn: 30.7km.

DIRECTIONS The shuttle back from Acle Bridge to Horstead Mill is about 25 mins and 27km.

HAZARDS

CRAFT

	LOCATION	GRID REFERENCE	POST CODE	WHAT3WORDS
PARKING/POSSIBLE END POINT	Wroxham Broad car park	TG307165	NR12 8TS	music.heap.propelled
START (1)	Horstead Mill	TG267193	NR12 7AT	removing.fuse.positions
START (2)	The Rising Sun pub	TG277197	NR12 7AQ	awesome.outdoor.muted
CAMPSITE	Salhouse Broad	TG319155	NR13 6HE	strategy.sample.quote
SHORTER FINISH	Kingfisher car park South Walsham Broad	TG372139	NR13 6EB	abundance.football.scoping
FINISH	Acle Bridge Inn	TG414116	NR13 3AS	atlas.follow.deep

BELOW Launching at the green near the Rising Sun pub, Coltishall.

BACKGROUND The Broads National Park covers 303 square kilometres, most of which is in Norfolk. It has over 200km of navigable waterways, including seven rivers and 63 broads. The Norfolk Broads, one of our 15 national parks, has introduced a Paddlers Code of Conduct available from their website. There is a toll fee (7 day, 14 day or annual) for paddling which Paddle UK Members are exempt from. See here https://www.broads-authority.gov.uk/

A SLICE OF HISTORY The Broads formed on 10,000-year-old alluvial deposits of peat and silt, set down in ~8000 BC. But they're not a natural phenomenon. In the 1950s, a young botanist named Joyce Lambert deduced that the Broads were human made, formed by workers digging peat in the region. This finding transformed our understanding of the Broads and our knowledge of the region's economy during the Middle Ages.

Wherry men of the broads were not adverse to a little smuggling. In one famous case, a wherry man was sentenced to four years' hard labour and the confiscation of his craft. However, his friends were quicker than the law and took the wherry and sank it in a broad. When the owner was eventually released from prison, they raised it to find the cargo still intact!

St Benet's Abbey, which is the only Norfolk abbey founded in the Anglo-Saxon period, is thought to have been constructed in 1019. King Cnut (on the throne 1016–35) was an important benefactor, and this land may have been a royal estate (W: www.norfarchtrust.org.uk/project/st-benets-abbey).

The Broads have always attracted holidaymakers. For a glimpse into the past, head online and check out the British Pathé News film *Broads Holiday*, shot in 1962.

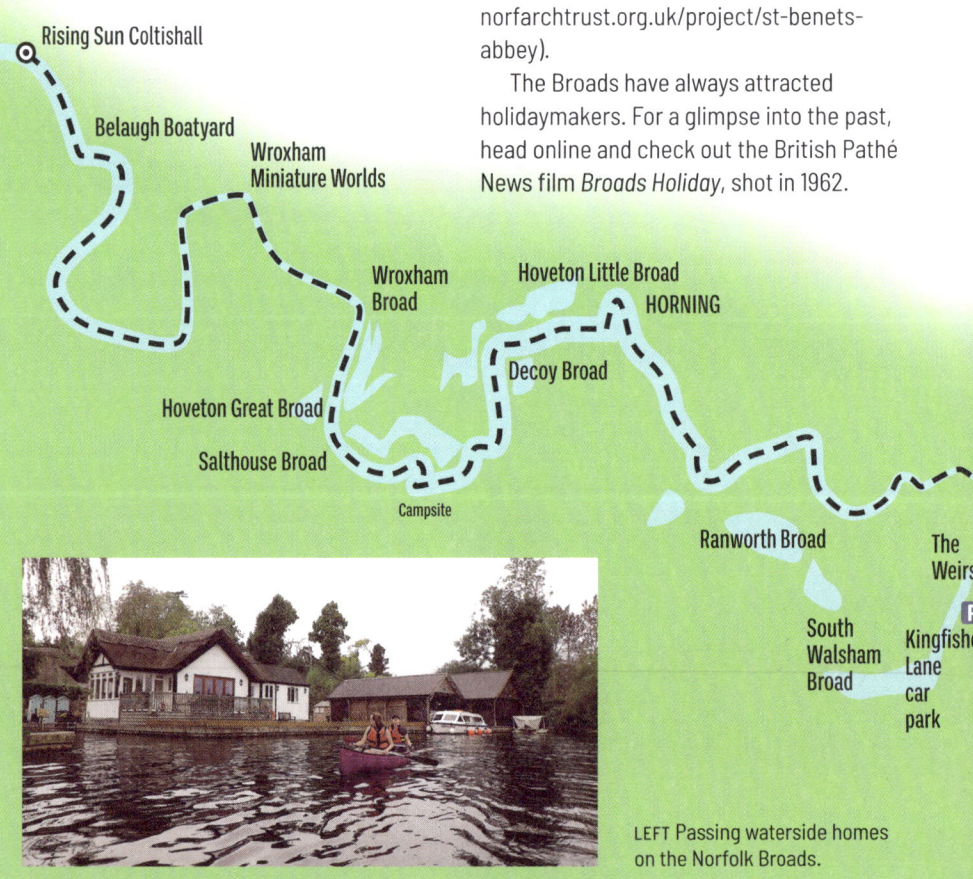

LEFT Passing waterside homes on the Norfolk Broads.

ABOVE Exploring the Broads on a Canoe Trail paddling expedition.

ROUTE Leaving from the lovely Horstead Bridge close to the mill of the same name, you'll be forgiven for stopping to enjoy the start, where there's often a flow by the bridge in which you can play. About 400m downstream the flows meet after the millstream and join up with the River Bure. There's a maze of little back channels before the river kinks left and right and gently flows on, passing the outskirts of Coltishall.

Another 800m on from the marriage of the two river flows the river bends around close to The Rising Sun pub, from where you can also launch. The pub car park gives easy access to a manicured riverbank. From the off, be prepared to share the waterway with motor cruisers and other paddlers of all shapes and sizes.

After the pub, the riverbank is open grass meadow before about 300–400m later on the left you pass by a variety of houses and old buildings. The river completes a large loop around moorings called the Anchor Moorings (you can choose your next gin palace or cruiser as you paddle by). The next section becomes more green and rural, with treelined banks and gentle bends. A kilometre on, you'll pass a water abstraction point and the river then bends around to the right before reaching an inlet channel with moorings.

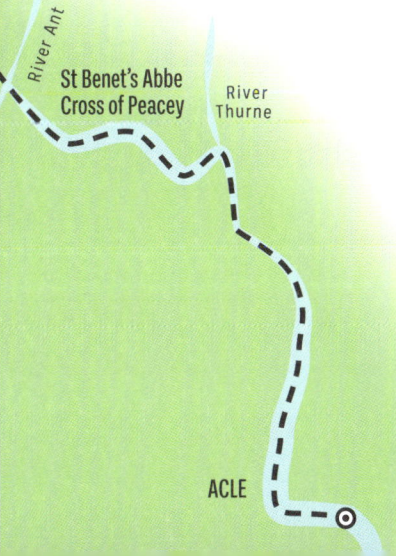

ABOVE Paddling past prime real estate on the Broads.

The river bends southwards and passes Belaugh Boatyard and then the tower of St Peter, Belaugh. The opposite bank is heavily wooded, with plenty of tree cover. Take time to admire the scenery and beautiful surroundings. Simply breathe it in and relax. After 1.75km of slow pace paddling you'll pass the confluence with the River Hor. The smaller Belaugh Broad is tucked away on the left after another 2km.

The river now turns north as it approaches the quaint town of Wroxham. The banks remain wooded with a feeling of quiet backwaters. Another 2km on and the Bure splits around an island and you can pick your route – the high road, perhaps. The right-hand channel is in fact a small broad called Bridge Broad. Around 500m later you'll pass under the railway bridge and into Wroxham, which has been a holiday destination for decades. You're now in marina and boat central. A second bridge, the A1151 Norwich Road, follows as you paddle through the town (there are plenty of pubs and restaurants in the town if you need to grab a bite). This section feels like an English Venice, with its many channels and backwaters. There are, of course, numerous holiday lets and accommodation options if you want to extend the trip.

The mosaic of waterways weave through the town for about 1.2km, and then its ~500m until the entrance to Wroxham Broad, on your right side, which has a

RIGHT St Peter, Belaugh.

sailing club and car park on the far shore if you wish to end your trip here. It's roughly a kilometre across the broad, depending on your exact route, and you can re-join the Bure at the south-west corner.

As the Bure heads eastwards you are again enveloped in magical treelined corridors of riverbanks and after about 800m you'll reach the entrance to Hoveton Great Broad on the left-hand side. This is part of a wetlands rehabilitation project and is not generally accessible to boats (although there is a canoe landing stage), so take only pictures and leave no trace. There's a smaller inlet/backwater just after Hoveton on the right. Around 700m past this you'll arrive at Salhouse Broad (W: www.salhousebroad.org.uk), one of our favourite paddling locations, with the channel on the right to enter. Spend a night at the campsite here, ready to continue this magical paddle on the Broads the following day. Note, there's road access here but it's a fair carry from the car park.

Back on the Broads, after a night under twinkly stars (fingers crossed), you'll head north once back on the Bure and after about 500m pass by Woodbastwick Hall, set back in the treeline. The river passes the exit from Hoveton Great Broad and does a few wiggles before straightening by Decoy Broad and Parson's Dyke. The Bure remains on a northerly course, completing a giant loop around Bure Marshes NNR.

Your route passes Hoveton Little Broad on your left as you head towards Horning, which is about 700m past the broad. Riverside houses and marinas return to your vista and the river turns southwards with a sharp right-hand bend. Horning is another pretty Broads town and another bustling water world, with marinas and places to eat and restock. You will be left in absolute awe of some of Britain's finest houses in the land with thatched boat houses, traditional carpentry and the occasional modern design that has slipped through the net.

After Horning there's a narrow entrance to Cockshoot Broad NNR on the right bank.

The river returns to a looping course after Horning for several kilometres,

passing St Benedict's Church, and 2km later you'll come to the more secluded Malthouse Broad, which you can explore with the entrance on the right bank. There's a Wildlife Conservation Trust centre here and The Maltsters pub to motivate you. Another 1.8 km on you'll reach the confluence with the River Ant, another Broads river you can paddle if you're extending your time in the area.

Around 500m past the meeting point with the Ant, the river passes St Benet's Abbey and, shortly after, the Cross of Peace, both of which are on the left bank. A shorter shuttle and equally lovely paddle is to turn right at St Benet's Abbey and head down the remaining 2km to "the Weirs " just before South Walsham Broad and stop in the corner to access Kingfisher Car Park and a shorter paddle and shuttle.

Staying on the longer route the river winds on for a few more kilometres until it meets the River Thurne at Thurne village at a giant T-junction. The Thurne Windmill is a few paddle strokes up the Thurne. Turn right and head south for 4km on the homeward straight to end your trip at the Acle Bridge Inn, where you can reward yourselves on a job well done.

EXTEND THE TRIP Paddle the River Ant to explore more of Norfolk's backwaters, or continue on the Bure to the coast at Great Yarmouth. After 3km you'll reach the village of Stokesby, and if you're making this a pub crawl, The Ferry Inn is worth a stop here. It's then another 18km to Great Yarmouth and the coast, where you'll meet the River Yare, and about 4km after that you could try and turn back the sea like Cnut did.

ABOVE Enjoying a great paddling day out with the pups.

ABOVE The Rising Sun, Coltishall.

Alternatively, there's Breydon Water and the mouth of the Yare to explore. Enjoy!

Explore further into South Walsham Broad to the weirs. The River Bure loops south from St Benet's Abbey with a horseshoe shape on the map. The paddle from Salhouse to here is 12km, making a lovely day paddle option or a longer day for those wanting to push the pace. This narrow winding route finishes by Kingfisher Lane where there is a handy car park, Kingfisher Car Park.

OUR RICH ADVENTURE Over the years we have explored many different bits of the Broads, finding joy in both the tiny creek-like waterways and bigger expanses of water alike. We've hired cruisers, paddled and swum these waters. However, the Bure was an obvious choice for the book, as we've paddled the river multiple times over the years and have fallen in love with Salhouse Broad and Canoe Trails now offers an expedition here. We reckon you could paddle the Broads for a lifetime and still never cover it all.

CALORIE CREDITS Grab food and drinks from the beautiful riverside pub The Rising Sun (W: www.risingsuncoltishall.co.uk), or visit the Staithe 'N' Willow café/bistro in Horning (T: 01692 630915) for a light bite, having explored much of the Bure and its Broads to get this far.

The Ferry Pub Inn is at the end of the main strip through Horning, just before you leave its busy waterways (W: https://horningferry.co.uk). You could then finish your trip at the Acle Bridge Inn and moor alongside bigger boats to take your place at the table (W: www.aclebridge.co.uk).

WILDLIFE SAFARI We spotted plenty of kingfishers on our trip as well as swans and herons. Birds are in particular abundance, including teal, wigeon, reed and sedge warblers. The marsh harrier has made a comeback and bittern numbers have also increased in recent years. The Norfolk Broads is also home to more than 250 different plants, including the nationally protected fen orchid and the rare crested buckler-fern.

WHERE'S THE MAGIC?

Literally all of it. Enter the Broads and you enter another world of treelined corridors, stunning wildlife and relaxing waterways. Don't rush it; take time to enjoy every hidden gem.

OTHER ATTRACTIONS Neatishead Radar Museum houses 20 rooms of radar features and displays covering the Second World War and the Cold War. There's a Grade II-listed radar building and a café, making it perfect for a family visit (W: www.radarmuseum.co.uk).

Re-wild yourselves with BeWILDerwood Norfolk, a family-friendly, treehouse-themed amusement park (W: https://norfolk.bewilderwood.co.uk).

Clippesby Hall (W: www.clippesbyhall.com) is an independent family-run and multi award winning camping park with glamping pods, shepherd's huts and caravan camping. It holds the AA 5 Pennant Premier Touring Park Award.

THE SHARED ECONOMY Check out Canoe Trail's Paddle & Camp the Norfolk Broads Trip (W: www.canoetrail.co.uk/canoe-camp/expeditions/canoe-camp-the-norfolk-broads).

Book into the Salhouse Broad Campsite, which does canoe hire too (W: www.salhousebroad.org.uk).

LEFT Sharing the water with wherries at Salhouse Broad.

17 BURNHAM OVERY STAITHE

Paddle to golden sands and get a taste of tropical paradise with sand dunes and narrow marshlands. The parking and harbour area make access easy and there is coastal track if you misjudge the tides for the return leg. Pack a picnic, sun hat and Hawaiian shirt to maximise beach blanket culture. Just down the road are some fantastic Norfolk Estates, cafes and restaurants to tantalise your taste buds.

The Lowdown

DIFFICULTY

DISTANCE ~7km, out and back, relax and make it a day with sunbathing and picnics.

DIRECTIONS Park in the car park next to the quay. Check the tide times, as you don't want to find your car under water at spring high tides.

It's free to park. If for some peculiar reason you don't fancy the estuary paddle then you can walk along the coastal track starting to the right of the car park.

HAZARDS

CRAFT

	LOCATION	GRID REFERENCE	POST CODE	WHAT3WORDS
START/FINISH	Burnham Overy Staithe	TF844443	PE31 8JE	pokers.scratch.yell
	Sand dunes	TF846457	N/A	otherwise.adjust.dripped

BACKGROUND Norfolk county belongs to Horatio Nelson – the signs tell you so, and Burnham, where we start our paddle, is a mile or so from his birthplace. Norfolk is also known as the place where the 'sea meets the sky', and it certainly lives up to its name through stunning sunsets and vistas.

A SLICE OF HISTORY Visit the impressive ruins of Creake Abbey, set slightly south from the coast and now cared for by English Heritage. Creake Abbey probably had its origins in 1206 when Sir Robert and Lady Alice de Nerford established the small chapel of St Mary of the Meadows at

BELOW Julien, Arafat and Ash paddling back to the quay at Burnham Overy Staithe.

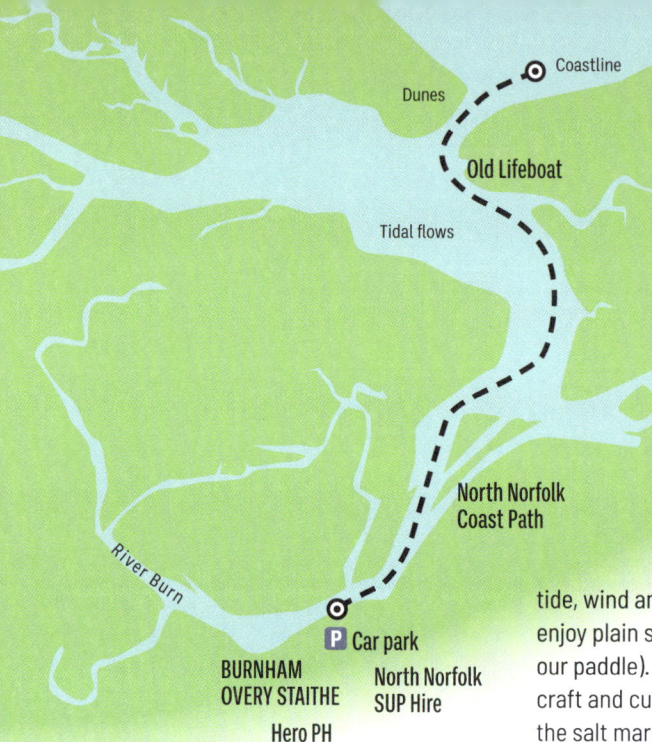

Lingerescroft, bordering the tiny River Burn, which still flows through the farm and past the abbey today. In 1217 they founded the Hospital of St Bartholomew there.

Or since we're close to the sea here, breathe in the maritime history of the area with its old boats, barges, cottages and buildings dating back centuries to a time without electricity and the engines of today.

ROUTE Setting off from the car park straight onto the water you are faced with two choices (easy or tricky), depending on the tide, wind and conditions. Paddlers can enjoy plain sailing or a battle (as we had on our paddle). There's an option to carry your craft and cut corners and muddy bends on the salt marshes, the alternative to digging in and paddling hard. There's also a coastal pathway for the inflatable crew, but it would be a long carry.

Turn right from the quay and follow the snaking and winding estuary towards the sea. The coastal path is on your right-hand side. Often families wade across the water and follow tracks across the marshes.

As you reach the apex of a large left-hand bend you'll round the corner and start to see the old grey lifeboat beached up near the high dunes. It signals that you're getting closer to the last bend to the right, with a beautiful natural swimming lagoon.

Above this iconic wild swimming spot are the bigger dunes, which make the perfect picnic spot.

It is still a 500m paddle to the sea. Before you head out onto the open sea, make sure you've followed the safety advice in the front of this book and check weather, tides and local knowledge. You can paddle left or right on the sea, conditions permitting, and traverse the endless miles of Holkham Beach and NNR.

EXTEND THE TRIP You can paddle into the back channels and thread into the marshes or if conditions allow paddle on the sea along to beaches to the east or west.

OUR RICH ADVENTURE Emerging from the strange times of lockdown, we headed to Norfolk, a favourite escape of ours, to find half the world had the same idea. Not being one for crowds, we abandoned Holkham and drove the leafy hedgerows a few miles to Burnham. This paddle makes you work for it, depending on the tides, with a meandering estuary out to the sea. But as

ABOVE Ash and Foxy chilling on the dunes at the estuary mouth.

BELOW Burnham Overy Staithe looking inviting at low tide.

they say, the 'juice is worth the squeeze', and you're rewarded with stunning dunes, great swimming spots and open beaches.

If you're really lucky you'll see the occasional seal and maybe even the Queen's Household Calvary, who take their regiment

and horses on their annual break to gallop these beaches. In a former life, Ash took riders and their horses on beach rides. We still return with our shires and cobs to ride on the beaches here and, of course, go paddling. We have also paddled out to Blakeney Point with our friends Jamie and Amie Queen to view the seal colony from a distance, which we did on a particularly icy winter's day.

CALORIE CREDITS The local pub is called The Hero, in honour of local legend Nelson, and of course fish and chips and ice cream are never far away (W: www.theheroburnhamovery.co.uk).

At nearby Wells you'll find *The Albatros* (T: 07979 087228), a Dutch barge with a café onboard serving Dutch pancakes and other yummy treats, available on deck or down below, and another favourite haunt of ours.

Drive a ways down to Thorham to The Lifeboat Inn – we love the menu and have eaten many times here (W: www.lifeboatinnthornham.com).

WILDLIFE SAFARI Seals, gulls (be careful of your picnic) and cormorants are abundant hiding in dunes and narrow watery channels.

WHERE'S THE MAGIC?

Sand nestling between the toes, stunning skies and lovely dunes to explore. The connection to Norfolk's rich maritime history is not to be missed.

OTHER ATTRACTIONS Try a bit of coastal foraging to grab samphire from the salt marshes (goes well with local fish), or have a go at crabbing – perfect for kids and adults of all ages!

Nearby is Blakeney Point NNR, run by the National Trust (W: www.nationaltrust.org.uk/visit/norfolk/blakeney-national-nature-reserve), where you can also visit the seals via a boat trip (W: www.blakeneypointsealtrips.co.uk). Or why not check out the RSPB at Titchwell Marshes (W: www.rspb.org.uk/reserves-and-events/reserves-a-z/titchwell-marsh/)?

THE SHARED ECONOMY You can hire kayaks from Burnham Overy Boathouse, a local traditional boat repair and kayak hire venue based in the old stone building adjacent to the car park (W: www.burnhamoveryboathouse.co.uk/hiring-kajaks).

LEFT A SUP'er's paradise, with warm waters, dunes and tunes.

18 RIVER NENE

Paddle into the heart of England on a classic touring river. The River Nene runs through Northamptonshire and Cambridgeshire to the Wash after joining the River Great Ouse. Upstream the River Nene connects to the North-South-running Grand Union Canal. The River Nene runs almost like a dot to dot of major towns and cities, including Northampton and Peterborough, and more rural destinations, including Wellingborough, Oundle, Fotheringhay and Alwalton. There are great pubs along the route too, so you can punctuate your journey with plenty of rewards.

The Lowdown

DIFFICULTY
An easy paddle, assuming fair conditions (check for head winds and shorten to different locations as required).

DISTANCE River Mill Tavern to Oundle Mill (longer full day): 20.5km.
Ringstead to Wadenhoe (full day out): 15km.
Ringstead to Islip (half-day leisurely trip): 7km.

DIRECTIONS The shuttle from Ringstead to Oundle Mill is 16km and takes about 20 minutes, depending on the time of day and traffic.

Launching at The River Mill tavern there are a couple of parking options: the top car park at the marina (seek permission) or drop off and park further towards Denford Village. Launch on the downstream side of the mill and lock, and paddle past moorings and marinas full of boats. Finish downstream at Wadenhoe moorings near the Village Hall or at Oundle Mill.

HAZARDS
*near Oundle

CRAFT

	LOCATION	GRID REFERENCE	POST CODE	WHAT3WORDS
PARKING	Near Watermill tea room, Ringstead	SP972752	NN14 4DU	incurring.string. sentences
LAUNCH AT LOCK	By the Lock at Ringstead	SP974752	NN14 4DU	fakes.topped. steepest
PICK-UP (1)	Islip Quay/Bridge	SP990785	NN14 3JU	summaries lamplight.developer
PICK-UP (2)	Village hall car park, Wadenhoe moorings	TL010833	PE8 5ST	applauded.splashes. input
FINISH	Oundle Mill	TL038868	PE8 5PB	brink.traps.witless

BELOW SUP ahoy – out for a bimble on the River Nene.

A SLICE OF HISTORY The spelling of River Nene has altered over time; it was previously called the "Nenn" or "Nyn" by draughtsmen George Cole and John Roper in an 1810 engraving. The Ordnance Survey of 1885 used Nene, which has become the norm.

Northampton was the location of England's first water-powered cotton spinning mill, on the Nene. It was constructed at a former corn mill, to the south-west of the town centre, in 1742. It is now used as a source of water for Carlsberg, who are the large brewer in the town and sponsors of the premiership rugby club, Northampton Saints RUFC.

Fotheringhay village on the River Nene has a rich history, including being the location of the birth of Richard III in 1542, and the site of Mary, Queen of Scots'

ABOVE Craig and Gideon with Foxy on the bow on a winter's paddle on the River Nene.

(1542–67) final imprisonment and beheading.

Hardwater Mill, Great Doddington is almost 1,000 years old and was used as a hiding place by the Archbishop of Canterbury during the 12th century.

ROUTE Launch downstream of the Water Mill Team Room and Lower Ringstead lock, which spans Ringstead Road close to Willy Watt Marina. You are quickly onto the water and heading away past a small mooring and marina. The river gently weaves and bends about 700m as you thread between lakes on either side used for fisheries. It then bends left at a right-angle and passes under the old railway line (now a cycleway and walking route).

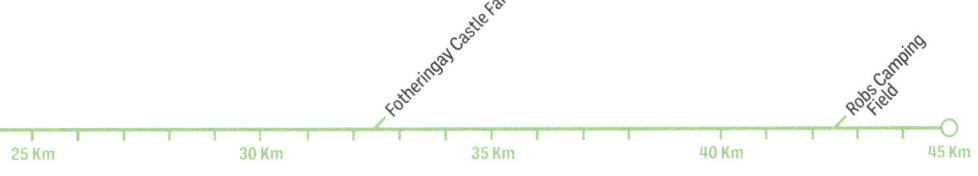

ABOVE Meandering river bends with churches providing excellent navigation aids.

The river now stretches around in a huge loop back on itself over a few kilometres as you pass by Woodford. You'll paddle past Woodford Riverside Marina and several moorings. Woodford is a pretty riverside village and you'll see St Mary the Virgin Church's spire as you pass. Rounding the bend about 600m later on the right, you'll pass a gravity overflow weir to a flood channel on your right.

The river bends left and then back to the right and you are now about 400m from Woodford Lock, requiring an 80m portage. Back on the water, you'll pass under the old railway again, so keep an eye out for cyclists and walkers waiting to cheer you on. A few hundred metres later and you'll hit a left-hand bend as the river reaches Denford, where again a church spire, Holy Trinity Church, signals your arrival.

About 400m from the bend the river splits into different channels. The left-hand channel leads on to the lock at Denford. The portage point for the weir and lock is on the front of the central island, which you'll reach by following left towards the lock. You can also paddle, taking the right channel closer to Denford, but this is a bit more choked and requires a portage at the north end of Denford.

From the left-hand lock it's ~900m of paddling until you pass under the giant viaduct of the A14 dual carriageway. After the A14 you'll pass under another bridge as Thrapston occupies the right bank and you re-join the other channels of the Nene. Just under a kilometre from the A14 bridge you'll reach the more impressive Nine Arch Bridge, bisecting Islip on the left bank from Thrapston on the right. If you double back on yourself just before the bridge there's a village green, which you can walk across to The Woolpack Inn.

Around 500m on, the river splits again with the old river mill, and the portage is on the central channel of the lock with a 50–60m carry. Back on the river you reach a small bridge and then the moorings on the right-hand side, behind which is the Middle Nene Sailing Club on the lake adjacent to the river and Thrapston Gravel Pit. The river follows and winds around the outer parameter of the gravel pits for another 2km, generally heading north-east. It then bends slightly south again, passing Heronry Lake and Aldwincle Lake as you approach Titchmarsh.

A kilometre of paddling beyond the lakes you'll reach Titchmarsh Mill and lock, with the portage route on the left side, lakes galore and open water around. There are moorings here, signalling the Middle Nene Cruising Club and marina. Keep going and weave left and right following the river for a kilometre or so until you pass under the road bridge at Thorpe Waterville. The river bends gently around to the left and after a kilometre reaches a small, triangular-shaped island.

After the island the river completes another huge looping S-bend back on itself as you skim past the edge of Wadenhoe village, circling around for 2km after the island. The lock is around to the right, but if you pull up to the moorings on the left side you can walk across the lawns to The Kings Head pub. There's a Scout campsite off the river at Wadenhoe, a potential stopping point if you want to reduce your paddling distance.

The lock portage at Wadenhoe is about 60m but is not the easiest, as a steep set of steps at the put in add to the workload. Once back on the water this section of the Nene continues to be tree lined and feels a little more off the beaten track. The next lock is 1.7km onwards and a 60m carry. You'll pass Lilford village and hall, and under the road bridge here.

The river runs north-east now for a kilometre or so before you reach Lilford Marina and lakes on the right side. A few hundred metres on you'll reach Oundle Rowing Club, at the least informing you that the homeward straight towards the finish is within reach. About 750m later and you'll reach the lock at Oundle Mill, signalling the end of this 20.5km paddle.

BELOW A portage at one of the islands.

ABOVE Sunset over the Nene near Oundle after a perfect day on the river.

EXTEND THE TRIP You can opt for multiday trips along the River Nene with plenty of local campsites and B&B options depending on whether you want to paddle continuously or break it up into day trips.

Heading past Oundle, which is another looping swirl around the riverside town, the route continues north and slightly east, passing more locks, and their portages, as well as quaint riverside villages like Cotterstock and Tansor and more lakes, until you reach the rural Fotheringhay Castle Farm campsite, which also has a farm guest house and accommodation at the local pub (www.fotheringhaycastlefarm.co.uk). It's about 12km including the portages, so if you want to create a multiday trip you either need to push the pace, start early or consider starting closer to the campsite. We use the Fotheringhay campsite for our Duke of Edinburgh trips and can recommend it. From Fotheringhay it's another 10km paddle to Robs Camping Field (T: 07514 771688), which is a little more remote and basic in terms of facilities but brilliant as a riverside campsite. From there you are within striking distance of the end of the trip. The river turns east at Peterborough, allowing you to paddle through the city towards Flag Fen Archaeological Park and the Fens in general.

OUR RICH ADVENTURE We've paddled canoes, kayaks and SUPs on the River Nene for many decades, and we use the river for coaching students through their Bronze and

Silver Duke of Edinburgh wards. We also use it for rest and relaxation, with our Canoe Trail team paddling at the Nene Whitewater Centre course at Northampton. It's one of our favourite local places to escape to.

CALORIE CREDITS

Our good friends Ben and Iona Straw have run The River Mill tavern at Ringstead, which serves delicious food, tea and cake, for a number of years (W: www.therivermillpub.co.uk/). It's a great excuse to escape from everyday life and go for a paddle or wild swim in this lovely stretch of the River Nene.

Further along your journey you'll pass close to The Woolpack Inn at Islip (W: www.thewoolpackinnislip.co.uk/), where you can grab great food at reasonable prices, while The Kings Head at Wadenhoe is a traditional village pub with good food and great reviews (W: www.kingsheadwadenhoe.com) and the Tap and Kitchen at Oundle is well worth a visit as a reward for a day's paddle or more (W: www.tapandkitchen.com/).

WILDLIFE SAFARI

The network of lakes and backwaters on this stretch of the River Nene valley leads to a huge range of bird life. Common species include wigeon, gadwall, teal, greylag goose and moorhen. If you look hard you may also see redshank, kingfishers and little egret.

OTHER ATTRACTIONS

If you're up for more paddling, try the rapids and whitewater at the Nene Whitewater Centre (W: https://northamptonactive.com).

Stanwick Lakes is a unique 300ha countryside attraction and nature reserve located in the heart of the Nene Valley with play areas, open spaces and paths that are perfect for families, walkers, cyclists and nature lovers (W: www.stanwicklakes.org.uk).

The Nene Way follows the route of the river valley for most of its length. Close to the area are other, more random activities, including the Nene Valley Railway (W: www.nvr.org.uk/) made famous by James Bond in *Octopussy*, or test your own inner James Bond at Skydiving Peterborough (W: www.ukskydivingadventures.com/locations/skydiving-peterborough-cambridgeshire).

THE SHARED ECONOMY

Explore the River Nene and Rushden Lakes with Canoe2 (W: www.canoe2.co.uk/), or visit the lovely folks at PaddleDays based at Denford, which has a range of hire options including SUP safaris and inflatable kayak tours (W: https://paddledays.co.uk).

Contact Canoe Trail for Duke of Edinburgh and school camping options on the River Nene (W: www.canoetrail.co.uk).

> ### WHERE'S THE MAGIC?
>
> The River Nene is as much a community of river types, 'water babies' and those choosing to mess about on the water as it is a river. There's the adrenaline filled Nene Whitewater Centre in Northampton, simple paddle hire options via local providers and of course a wide range of boating traffic, as the river feeds from the Northampton branch of the Grand Union Canal and flows into the Wash via the Great Ouse.

19 RIVER GREAT OUSE

Explore one of Britain's most popular touring rivers, packed with unspoilt wildlife habitats and a range of campsites, from woodland magic with open fires to riverside sites with great facilities. In between is miles of countryside and quaint English river towns. Choose from a range of hour to half day paddles from different start locations or plan a multiday trip.

The Lowdown

DIFFICULTY
A gentle river paddle, the epitome of an English touring river.

DISTANCE Kempston to Bedford Embankment: 6km.
Kempston to Matchstick Wood: 13km.
Bedford to Great Barford: 10km.
Matchstick Wood to St Neots campsite: 14km.
St Neots to Houghton Mill campsite: 22km.

DIRECTIONS Choose from a short half-day paddle up to 3-4 days down to Huntington and beyond. Start in Kempston or Bedford and do a return loop, or opt for an A to B journey to one of a number of locations and shuttle back by car or taxi.

HAZARDS

CRAFT

	LOCATION	GRID REFERENCE	POST CODE	WHAT3WORDS
PARKING/START	Car park, Kempston Mill Lane	TL023476	MK42 7FB	shunts.earl.megawatt
OUTDOOR CENTRE	Hillgrounds Road, Bedford (hire only)	TL026479	MK42 8PU	clips.feasts.skate
PORTAGE POSSIBLE START AND FINISH POINT	Bedford Embankment Butterfly Bridge	TL059494	MK40 3QF	scrap.events.basin
PORTAGE LOCK (CAN START AND FINISH HERE)	Cardington Lock – car park here as well	TL078489	MK44 3JZ	shots.cares.folds
PORTAGE (CAN START AND FINISH HERE)	Great Barford On road parking	TL134516	MK44 3LF	stops.attending.return
PORTAGE	Eaton Socon Riverside pub	TL174587	PE19 8GX	reason.skinny.trappings
CAFÉ AND POSSIBLE START AND FINISH POINT	Car park and cafe	TL180602	PE19 2AP	beaker.vibrate.numeral
PORTAGE POSSIBLE START AND FINISH POINT	Houghton Mill Lock Campsite and mill	TL282719	PE28 2BA	hissing.rudder.bulbs
FINISH	St Ives Bridge	TL312711	PE27 5UW	handbags.officers.couriers

ABOVE Rougher waters on the Duckmill known as the Etiennne Stott White Water Arena after Bedford's Olympic champion.

BACKGROUND At 229km, the River Great Ouse is the fourth-longest river in Britain. It winds its way through agricultural lands starting near Buckingham in the west, through stunning villages to Bedford and then on eastwards to the Wash. It ranges from gorgeous river towns like St Neots and Bedford or charming rural backwaters with willow line riverbanks, reed mace and lots of wildlife.

Bedford's iconic Victorian Embankment is a jewel in the crown, with beautiful tree-lined promenades and an energy and magic rarely surpassed. The best launch site is upstream from Water Lane in Kempston to explore islands, old bridges and the Embankment. You can extend your route from a few hours to a full day's paddling down to Great Barford or overnight using Canoe Trail's private woodland campsite (voted by Lonely Planet among the Top 52 Things to Do in the World for Families and featured in multiple publications) to paddle onwards on the second day down to St Neots.

There are camping options at St Neots at the Camping and Caravan Club site on the riverbank, 14.5km from Canoe Trail's Matchstick Wood. The third campsite on the river, at Houghton Mill, is 21.4km from St Neots campsite. Of course, you can break the journey into day-long paddles and stay within four walls.

A SLICE OF HISTORY The River Great Ouse is one of the oldest trading rivers in Britain with evidence of Viking trade, Domesday Book settlements and lots of unusual history. The castle was besieged in 1224 by King Henry III (1216–72), while elsewhere Bedford boasts a blue plaque on the river celebrating the spot where John Bunyan, author of *The Pilgrim's Progress*, was baptised in 1658 and a lock (Cardington) designed by John Smeaton, the father of civil engineering who made his name designing lighthouses.

ABOVE A group coaching course at Longholme Island on Bedford's Victorian Embankment.

ROUTE There are plenty of easy access points to vary your paddling trip in and around Bedford and beyond. Starting at Mill Lane in Kempston, unload in the small car park adjacent to the pedestrian footbridge and access the river here or via a new landing stage. The river is slightly quicker on this stretch with a shallower gravel bed.

Almost immediately you're into reed banks and leafy green trees on both the left and right. You'll pass a small island, Kempston Outdoor Centre, home of Canoe Trail, as you round a bend onwards towards Bedford. A long, straight, more open section follows before winding sections of river flanked by green meadows on the right side. Another straight emerges before you arrive at Honey Hill islands, where the river splits into several routes depending on debris and flow. River right is always passable whereas the left-hand channel can be an adventure of undergrowth and shallow waters.

You'll soon arrive at another wooden footbridge signalling Queens Park and Bedford's Eagle Brewery (sometimes you can smell hops). The railway bridge (large metal structure spanning the river) signals the start of Bedford's Embankment. Rowers train up and down this stretch.

You'll pass many bridges, pedestrian and road, along this part of the route. There's also a new cinema and food complex, Riverside North, alongside Viking

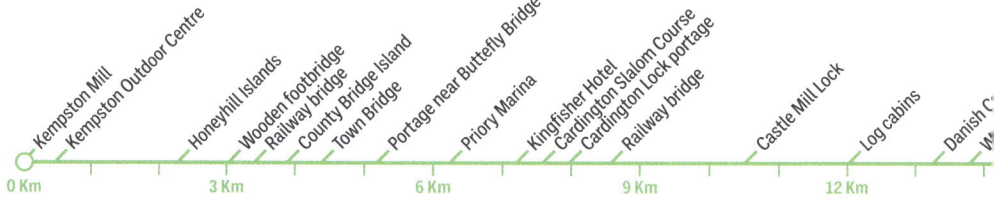

Kayak Club and Star Rowing Club. Make sure you say hello to fellow paddlers. Bedford Bridge is where John Bunyan was imprisoned around 1672. A stone set in the bridge marks the prison's location. The Embankment area is simply stunning and one of a few remaining in the country.

You can portage on to the lower river in a number of different locations, the first being Duckmill, renamed the Etienne Stott Whitewater Arena after the Bedford canoeist, who won gold, along with his partner Tim Bailey, in the C2 Canoe Slalom at the London 2012 Olympics. You can portage over the bank or there's a weir pass installed with yellow markers where canoes and kayaks can shoot the weir. Beware of the sluices to the right: if they're open you'll see waves and whitewater on the right of the pool at the bottom (these open for whitewater training or during flood conditions).

Alternatively, you can portage across the islands further down, either by Bedford Lock or the Butterfly Bridge adjacent to Longholme Café and boating lake. It's a 50m carry here, with the option of tea and cake from the café down the side of the boat house. Relaunch by the Canoe Trail portage sign and paddle on, turning left. You'll pass under a disused railway bridge and head towards Priory Marina, Priory Lake and the Priory Country Park, which is hidden behind trees.

The energy and activity of Bedford town centre is quickly left behind for a more rustic and tranquil river section with wildlife, willows and the occasional craft. The river turns left at the bottom of a long

ABOVE The narrow brook entrance to Canoe Trail's wild campsite.

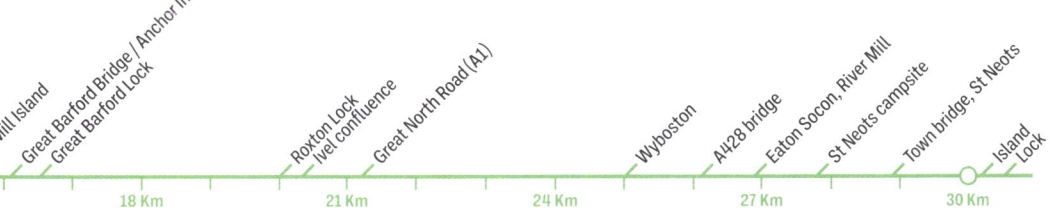

LEFT Paddlers using Castle Mill Lock – normally a place to portage around!

straight following the leafy green banks of the country park. You pass the Old Barns hotel, now called the Kingfisher, where you can grab a bite to eat. Opposite this is Cardington Artificial Slalom Course, the first of its kind in the country, where many of Britain's top athletes have competed over the years. At the end of this stretch is Cardington Lock with a portage point located just before it.

Avoid carrying your craft around the lock and opt to walk 25–30 minutes over the grass towards the small overgrown brook. Relaunch there and paddle 40m or so, and you'll neatly arrive at the downstream side of the lock. The back of the country park continues for another 1km or so until the old railway bridge, Allen's Bridge, crosses, which is part of the Route 51 National Cycle Route, formerly a rail route connecting Cambridge to Oxford and known as the 'brain line'. The river noticeably widens after this point to about 25m and also straightens out a bit.

There's still plenty of wildlife if you keep your eyes peeled and after 2.75km you arrive at Castle Mill Lock, which is a longer portage (130m) from a small wooden stage and a great place to stop and grab a picnic. Follow the tarmac to the landing stage and then walk down the plank to the launch point. Look back and you'll see a 2m-wide curtain of water over the drop weir. The river then continues under the Castle Mill Viaduct and the Bedford bypass, and then reverts to a series of snaking bends as you enter the Grange Estate.

You round a couple more bends, the left bank of which is tastefully developed with every size of log cabin you would aspire to own. It's 3.4km from Castle Mill to Willington Lock, with Matchstick Wood campsite (run by Canoe Trail) and the Danish Camp just before the lock, a great place to grab a brew, ice cream or something more substantial.

Willington Lock is a similar portage distance to the previous lock, with a 125m carry before paddling on a possible exit point or destination at Great Barford. In low flows during summer (with small waves of less than 1ft) it is possible to shoot the weir here.

Continue travelling with larger tree-lined banks and a superb wider pool listed in wild swimming guides. The river bends back around to the left with a brick wall entrance to a disused lock entrance. Despite the no entry signs it is possible to weave a clandestine course through this less-travelled backwater. This is an old mill and just as you exit this route you'll see a Great Ouse Boating Association (GOBA) mooring.

Two more bends or so and you'll reach the red brick multi-span bridge at Great Barford, a possible end point for your journey. If you've booked an overnight with Canoe Trail, the woodland campsite is ~2km from here, so portage the weir at Great Barford, a 130m carry on the right. This stretch of river is quintessentially English with gravel beds and long reeds billowing in the underwater currents.

Downstream from Great Barford you follow miles of willow lined riverbanks with lush green cover for kingfishers, cormorants and herons. Higher banks on the left side as you pass by a small rise indicate that Roxton Lock is not far away, about 3.6km from Great Barford. The lock is a short portage of 75m involving a kissing gate on the right side of the river adjacent to the confluence with the River Ivel, an old trading river with some great whitewater features. The weir can be paddled in low levels (less than 0.3m-high waves in the centre of the weir).

At this point the river is only 50m from the Great North Road, otherwise known as the A1, and about 1km downstream you'll pass under the stone bridges of the road heading to Scotland and see Kelpie Marine Boat Yard located between the bridges. 4km on from this you'll pass by the back

BELOW Quiet waterways weaving across the countryside.

of Wyboston Lakes and our friends at Ride Leisure, who offer wakeboarding, a fantastic aquapark and various watersports and team-building activities. The river passes under another road bridge, the A428 to Cambridge before arriving at the next portage point at Eaton Socon Lock (6.8km from Great Barford) and the impressive River Mill Tavern.

There is road access to Eaton Socon at the River Mill, offering a great watering hole on your journey. The portage is a little bit more demanding for paddlers as you need to climb on to a metre-high jetty and carry through a small gate adjacent the lock, but it's only a 50m effort. The river here is usually a hive of activity, as you're now close to St Neots, a traditional river town with rowing, dragon boating and boats galore. Around 800m downstream on the right bank is the St Neots Camping and Caravanning Club Site. Be sure to book in for riverbank camping with facilities in advance, allowing your trip across England's heartland to range over several days and nights.

Less than a kilometre after leaving the campsite you enter the main town of St Neots, with rowing clubs, waterside cafés and moorings. Look for the large dragonfly mural on the main town bridge, the signal for hopping out river left to explore the market town and grabbing a drink at Ambience Café. The car park at Ambience allows vehicle access about 100m from the riverside. Around 1.4km on you arrive at an island near a small marina. The River Great Ouse forks here and you'll head left, skirting converted riverside flats about 400m down to Little Paxton Lock with its 90m portage crossing a small road.

The river skirts the left side of an island before re-joining the other flow after 800m and returning to the familiar tree-lined, slow-moving river. After about 6km of rural

BELOW SUP safaris on the river with Canoe Trail.

ABOVE Paddling under the iconic bridge at Great Barford next to the Anchor Pub and lock.

tranquillity the route passes St Peter's Church at Offord D'Arcy on the right and then splits, with another sluice and lock ahead. Bear left and follow the river around 400m to the landing stage on the right-hand side, adjacent to the lock (7km from Little Paxton). The 134m portage is fairly random, involving crossing Station Lane, which is a blind bend, and then heading down a track to another dock.

The impressive Buckden Marina is on river left with a wide range of facilities for boaters. About 1.2 km after the portage point you pass under the main A14 road bridge. Brampton Lock is 2.4km after this with a simple portage of 70m highlighting your expert skills by this stage of your journey. The Brampton Mill gastropub is just a few hundred metres on, so you can reward your hard work here. The river tracks under the mainline railway with twin bridges 2km from the last portage. Godmanchester Lock is on the left-hand side of the island.

The old town of Huntington is now only a kilometre away, where you will pass former warehouses now converted to flats and housing, as well as the George Hotel, which dates to the 15th century and was home to the Cromwells. The river passes under the A1307 main road and then on to the footbridge and older town bridge. Skirting Huntington, the right bank is meadows and open spaces, the left bank the town. The river bends slowly to the right with small backwaters and tributaries such as Cooks Backwater and Fishers Dyke on the right surrounding Godmanchester Nature Reserve, which has multiple lakes and walks.

Roughly 4km from Huntington is the National Trust-run Houghton Mill, which includes glamping pods, a café and a campsite. You'll pass flood relief channels with overflow flood weirs opposite Wyton Marina before getting to Houghton Mill. There's a boat slide portage to access Houghton – it is possible to take the right channel around the island and miss it and the Mill campsite (as some of our Duke of

Edinburgh groups did). If you do portage via the lock then turn immediately left and paddle behind the island to the Mill – it's worth it.

After another iconic campsite you have various options to finish your paddle at any number of suitable watering holes with good vehicular access. St Ives (not to be confused with the Cornish fishing village of the same name) is 4.5km away with Tom's Bakery and old stone-work bridges and buildings. It has often been a destination on days off for short paddles, wild swimming and enjoying this ancient river port that dates to the 1100s and was developed by the monks of Ramsey Abbey. St Ives Bridge, which dates to the 1500s, is one of only four in the country with a chapel in situ.

EXTEND THE TRIP If you have the desire you can continue onwards and exit at Holywell to visit The Old Ferry Boat Inn, which is 9km from Houghton Mill, or stop at The Pike & Eel Hotel and Marina at 12km. Or just keep on paddling – it's 80km to King's Lynn and the beach at Bull Dog Sands.

WHERE'S THE MAGIC?

Bedford's tree-lined Embankment remains the heartbeat of this market town, while St Ives is a window into a bygone era with its ancient bridge and quaint layout. It also has a local seal population, which startled us during one wild swimming session!

OUR RICH ADVENTURE

We grew up paddling on the River Great Ouse. Rich joined Viking Kayak Club in Bedford, home to Olympic Champion Etienne Stott, as a youngster and paddling became our lives. We've enjoyed playing on the moving water of Duckmill (sluices with controllable flows), kayaking local rapids and weirs and competing at Cardington Artificial Slalom Course (one of the first slalom courses in the country).

Over the years we've paddled from the source upstream of Buckingham back to Bedford, and Bedford to King's Lynn on a couple of occasions. We often paddle stretches downstream with Duke of Edinburgh groups doing their Bronze and Silver Awards.

CALORIE CREDITS

There are so many places to choose from in the bigger towns that are good enough to warrant a trip irrespective of the paddling. Some of our favourites in Bedford include the Foxy Wings (W: www.foxywings.co.uk) as you enter the town and the Embankment and Swan hotels just after the town bridge. The Longholme Café (W: https://thelongholme.com) has great food and ambience.

Between Bedford and Cardington Lock is the Kingfisher Hotel with its listed barn (W: https://thekingfisherbedford.co.uk). Or visit the Danish Camp with riverside dining, just upstream of Willington Lock

BELOW Willow-lined riverbanks and tranquil waters make the Great Ouse one of Britain's best touring rivers.

(W: https://danishcamp.co.uk). The River Mill is a lovely pub at Eaton Socon Lock (W: www.therivermillpub.co.uk).

In St Neots, the Ambience Café offers great food on the riverside (T: 01480 219999), or visit the café at Houghton Mill and Waterclose Meadows (www.nationaltrust.org.uk).

WILDLIFE SAFARI

The River Great Ouse has escaped overdevelopment along the majority of its tree-lined banks and consequently is a wildlife corridor for a wide range of species. Otters are commonplace along the secluded waterways along with kingfishers, terns, dippers, coots and moorhens. We've even had seals venture up from downstream!

BELOW Happy paddlers taking a SUP course on the Ouse.

OTHER ACTIVITIES

Ride Leisure at Wyboston offers wakeboarding and an aquapark as well as corporate team-building with a 4x4 driving course, airguns, assault course and hovercrafts (W: https://rideleisure.co.uk). Box End Park also offers wakeboarding, great food, an aquapark and lakeside action (W: www.boxendpark.com).

Lazy Days Boat Hire at Huntington offers small motorboat and craft rentals from the marina (T: 07951 785305), while if you fancy a bit of clay shooting in a lovely rural setting check out Sporting Targets (W: www.sportingtargets.co.uk).

THE SHARED ECONOMY

Contact Canoe Trail (W: www.canoetrail.co.uk) to hire canoes, kayaks or SUPs for a half day, full day or multiday camp. Houghton Boats, adjacent to the Mill, offers punts and rowing boats (W: https://houghtonboats.com).

20 THE CAMBRIDGE BACKS

Cambridge is steeped in tradition, with historic colleges and buildings making up the impressive city skyline. The River Cam winds around the city colleges, ancient bridges and architecture, making it a gem. On a sunny summer day you will be centre stage with plenty of tourists punting past you. Heading in the other direction to Orchard Tea Rooms you enjoy willow-lined banks, green fields and the wilder side of the Cam. (Note: you need to hold a Paddle UK licence to paddle on The Backs and through Cambridge city centre.)

The Lowdown

DIFFICULTY
A slow drift through one of our most famous university cities.

DISTANCE The paddle to Stourbridge Common is 10.6km return, leading you through the historic cityscape or shorten it with a shuttle. Heading to the iconic Orchard Tea Rooms is 5.2km return in the opposite direction.

DIRECTIONS Unload at the Driftway car park at the Lammas Common Land (note there's a 1.98m height barrier). Then it's a short walk to the water's edge.

HAZARDS

CRAFT

	LOCATION	GRID REFERENCE	POST CODE	WHAT3WORDS
START	Driftway car park	TL446573	CB3 9PA	moved.sleep.repair
FINISH (1)	The Orchard Tea Garden, Grantchester	TL436553	CB3 9NE	lasts.grit.shady
FINISH (2)	Goldie Boathouse	TL456591	CB4 1JA	plus.solid.report

BACKGROUND Cambridge is a must-visit destination for domestic and overseas visitors as one of the most famous university cities in the world. The River Cam is equally renowned for punting, bridges of beauty and sandy coloured stone buildings adorning its banks. The Cam is blessed with a youthful energy exemplified by the excitement of tourists and students alike, cyclists in droves and lots of visitor attractions. The museums, cafes, bars and quirky shops will capture your heart.

A SLICE OF HISTORY Cambridge is of course brimming with history and is most famous for its university, which was founded in 1209. Further afield on your paddle, the Orchard Tea Garden has been a Cambridge hotspot for more than 125 years and a regular haunt of famous people, including the economist John Maynard Keynes and novelist Virginia Woolf. The place was like a second home to wartime poet Rupert Brooke, who wrote 'The Soldier' after returning from Antwerp in the last months of 1914.

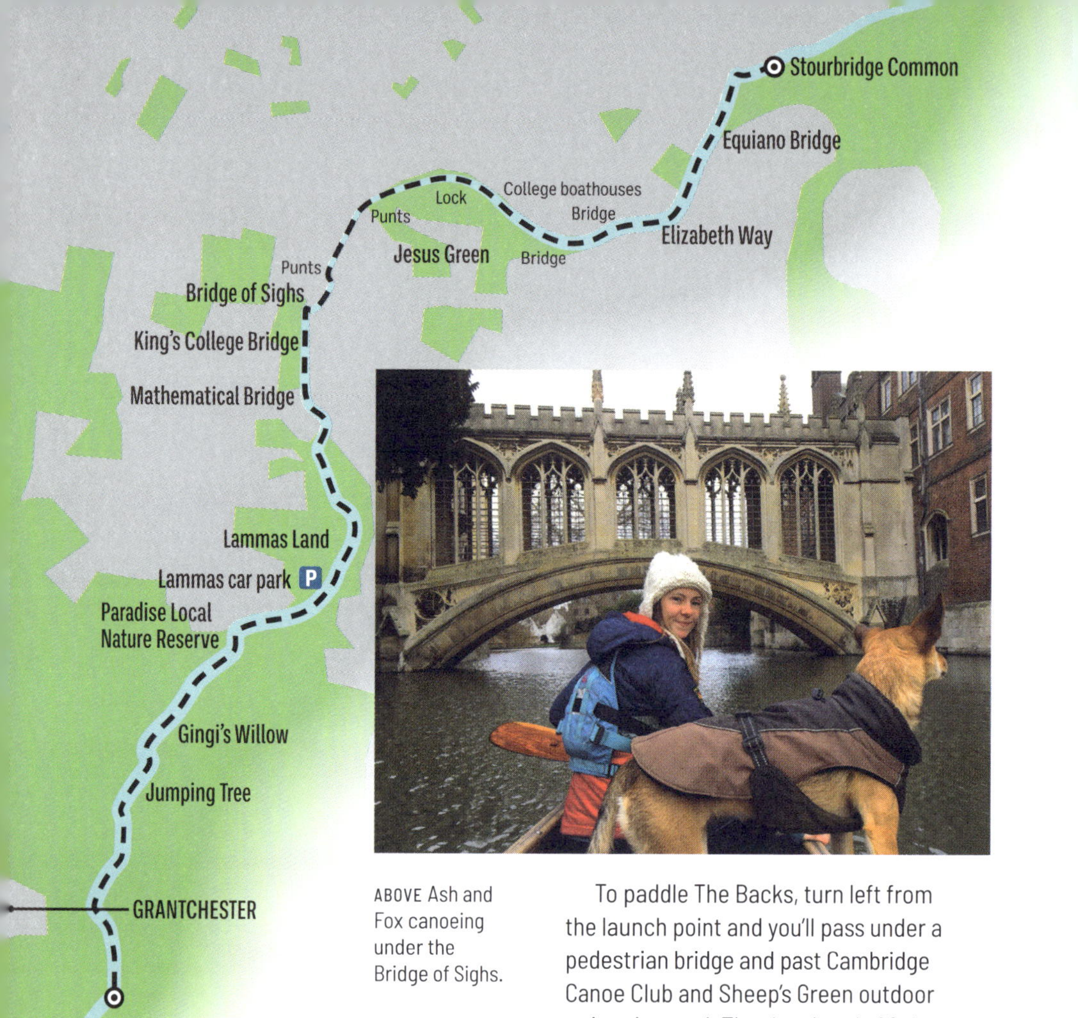

ABOVE Ash and Fox canoeing under the Bridge of Sighs.

ROUTE Facing the water and turning left offers the breath-taking opportunity to paddle through the historic Backs of Cambridge. Turn right and you'll paddle south towards Grantchester and the rural countryside surrounding the Orchard Tea Rooms. We say this, as we always have to think about it and make sure to head off in the right direction.

To paddle The Backs, turn left from the launch point and you'll pass under a pedestrian bridge and past Cambridge Canoe Club and Sheep's Green outdoor swimming pool. The river bends 90 degrees to the left and then straightens as you paddle under the Fen Causeway towards iconic colleges and stone buildings of yesteryear.

After more bridges, you'll pass under Crusoe Bridge before you need to undertake a short portage onto The Backs via the boat rollers on the left-hand bank before Scudamore's Punting Station. You're now several metres lower than the top river. The river bends around to the right in a

loop as if you're paddling around a roundabout. Left on the lower river takes you to the Old Mill and the Granta riverside pubs, which you can get to by road if you wish to end your day here later.

If you don't want to stop now, paddle under the first of many bridges (not sure of the collective name for bridges – perhaps a cam?). You'll reach Silver Street Bridge first before the more interesting wooden Mathematical Bridge. King's College Bridge is next, which – you guessed it – leads to King's College, a beautiful stone affair where you will most likely be photographed.

Photographs are often one of the main pastimes of any Cambridge paddling trip,

ABOVE Portaging onto The Backs at the boat rollers.

so next up are Clare Bridge, Garret Hostel Bridge and Trinity Bridge. In case it is not obvious, the left and right banks are college land, paddocks and private gardens for students, all part of the magic of studying in the city. Ahead of you is a dog leg in the river and the impressive St John's College.

Sweeping to the right and then straightening, you'll see the traditional stone works of Kitchen Bridge and then the iconic covered arch Bridge of Sighs, which dates to around 1831. The final bridge of this part of the Cam is Magdalene Bridge,

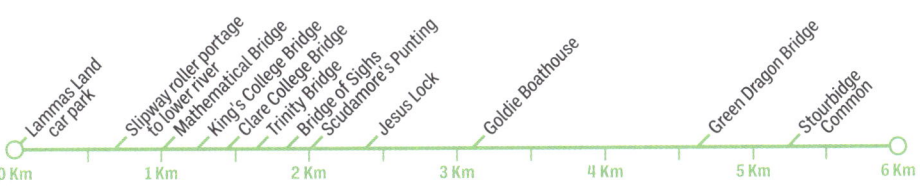

ABOVE Stewie on a doggy paddle, passing under historic bridges on The Backs.

located alongside Scudamore's Punting station and quay.

The river is usually less crowded from this point on as you paddle up to Jesus Lock, where you need to portage. There are toilets here and just past the lock is Jesus Green Lido on the right-hand side. You'll discover college and Cambridge boat houses including the Goldie Boathouse on the left bank as you continue under Victoria Street Bridge, so beware of rowers on this stretch of river (it is possible to exit here). The left bank behind the boat houses is primarily a residential area whereas the right bank is Jesus Common, more green meadows that are always bustling with energy and life.

Your paddle now passes under a cycle/pedestrian bridge and then Elizabeth Way, signalling more boat houses. This part of the river has a lived-in feel with moored canal boats festooned with colourful plants, bicycles and random homely attire.

The more futuristic Equiano Bridge, with its ornate curves and suspension arches, is next followed by Green Dragon Bridge as you reach Stourbridge Common. Chisholm Trail Bridge, with its parallel rail bridge, takes you on to Ditton Meadow and Fen Ditton. St Mary the Virgin's church tower should be visible. We've stopped several times on Ditton Meadows to picnic and relax and usually you have the place to yourselves. There's also a short inlet from the Cam on the bend.

This is our turn-around point on the north side of Cambridge, and you can now return and count the bridges heading in the other direction.

Alternatively, if you're wanting to head south from the outset to Grantchester and the Orchard Tea Rooms, turn right at put in. Paddling off from here you'll see Hodson's Folly on the opposite bank. Despite being a city centre, Cambridge is blessed with many green spaces and plenty of flora and fauna. The riverbank on the right is Paradise Local Nature Reserve, and the river threads through heavily wooded banks and tree plantations on the outskirts of the city.

If you inspect a map you'll see you are surrounded by parks and sports grounds known as Grantchester Meadows. Cambridge Rugby Club is only a few fields away and the Skaters' Meadow nature reserve is home to a wide selection of flowers and other wildlife. Cambridge University Canoe Club is tucked away in the trees just in front of Skaters' Meadow so you may see other boaters and paddlers relaxing in the waters.

At 950m the river has an unusual kink in its navigation before straightening and running south. In this next section you may find groups wild swimming, using the jumping tree, or picnicking at Gingi's Willow (all of which are listed as places of interest). You may also find families swimming and wading on sunny days in the small beaches and launching spots along this stretch.

Enjoy this slower pace of life and don't rush the paddle as you approach Grantchester. You'll see the spire of the Church of St Andrew and St Mary as you get closer, which is a good reference point for the tea rooms. Pull into the right bank just before a wooded area on and you then need to walk across the fields to the tea rooms.

Once replenished, it's time to leave the tea and cake behind and get back to the paddling. Heading further downstream for 430m you'll paddle under the Brasley Bridge as you pass Trumpington on the left bank. The river then widens and is joined by Bourn Brook and Byron's Pool, a favourite with visitors for its nature reserve and woodland walks. You will need to organise a shuttle or loop back to the start. Be warned exiting here will require a carry to the car.

EXTEND THE TRIP You can of course continue and extend your paddling time and distance by exploring the limits of the route covered in this book. Past Byron's Pool the river is

RIGHT Incredible architecture lines this route.

narrow and passes through more woodland, making this a path less travelled and more overgrown. One obvious landmark is the giant bridge of the M11 viaduct.

Continuing north and east on the Cam beyond Fen Ditton takes you under the A14 dual carriageway and to Baits Bite Lock, which you need to portage. From here you'll head north-east, passing close to Waterbeach with more locks and nature reserves part of your route. At Ely the Cam joins the River Great Ouse and heads towards the sea.

OUR RICH ADVENTURE Cambridge has been a go-to destination for us over the years, as it is fairly close to Bedford, our home, and Rich even lived on the outskirts of the city for a while, which fit in well with his love of cycling. We've paddled the Cam and The Backs on a great many occasions and often take international paddling friends along with us, such as professional SUP'er Cody

> **WHERE'S THE MAGIC?**
>
> Cambridge is, in our opinion, like no other city, as you get to paddle through the very heart of some of England's most historic architecture and culture. The ornate bridges, manicured lawns, fantastic food and general ambience make it an exciting place to be. It's infectious.

White. And, of course, there's the small matter of a perfect day here with Ash and asking her to marry me...

CALORIE CREDITS There are plenty of places in Cambridge city centre to satisfy almost any palette. Of course, we absolutely adore the simplicity and beauty of The Orchard Tea Garden, which has served

BELOW St John's Meadow and New Court illuminated by the winter sun.

generations of poets, prime ministers and those who have shaped our country (W: www.theorchardteagarden.co.uk).

WILDLIFE SAFARI Cambridge has lots of green spaces so you don't have to paddle far to see wildlife on the banks and meadows. Swans, moorhens, cormorants and other bird life call the city their home.

OTHER ATTRACTIONS You won't struggle for things to do in this city. For starters, there's The Fitzwilliam Museum, which holds world-class collections of artifacts from antiquity to the present day (W: http://fitzmuseum.cam.ac.uk). While in the city, take some time to step outside the hubbub and seek out a variety of book shops hidden down small back alleys.

If you're up for something a little more invigorating, visit Jesus Green Lido situated on Jesus Green (T: 01223 302579), which is open for public swimming year round and even has a sauna.

Beyond the city, the Imperial War Museum at Duxford definitely warrants a visit (W: www.iwm.org.uk/visits/iwm-duxford) while it's always worth a walk around house and gardens of Anglesey Abbey, run by the National Trust (W: www.nationaltrust.org.uk/visit/cambridgeshire/anglesey-abbey-gardens-and-lode-mill).

THE SHARED ECONOMY SUP Cambridge operates a hire service from Grantchester (W: https://supcambridge.com).

BELOW A guided punting tour passing King's College.

MIDLANDS

21 GRAND UNION CANAL

Paddle part of Britain's canal super highway – the Grand Union Canal, which runs from London to Birmingham. This major artery connects villages, towns and other waterways around middle England, and in the industrial past was one of the main supply routes for transporting building materials, goods and other supplies around the country. This is a straightforward paddle, though no less fascinating, and you can launch at one of several points, depending on the distance and time you want to spend traversing this historic part of the canal network.

The Lowdown

DIFFICULTY
A simple paddle but allow time to portage the locks, sample the riverside pubs.

DISTANCE Willen Lane, Milton Keynes to Stoke Bruerne A to B: 20km.
Circular route from either end of the A to B route, covering a distance to suit (1hr to half a day).

DIRECTIONS If you opt for the A to B route from Milton Keynes, park near Willen Lane at the Brick Kiln car park. It's a 25-minute shuttle and 20km by road back up the A5 from Stoke Bruerne.

HAZARDS

CRAFT
*craft choice dictated by conditions and experience

	LOCATION	GRID REFERENCE	POST CODE	WHAT3WORDS
START OR CIRCULAR	Brick Kiln car park, Milton Keynes	SP860416	MK14 5BB	transmits.imported.surround
	Galleon pub, Ouse Valley Park	SP806413	MK12 5PW	places.pills.porridge
FINISH OR CIRCULAR	Stoke Bruerne	SP743499	NN12 7SQ	forgives.punctuate.halt

21 • GRAND UNION CANAL

BACKGROUND The Grand Union canal was a workhorse of a trade route, connecting major cities and resources in Britain. It played an important part in the industrial revolution and was a template for canal infrastructure all over the world. The paddle starts in Milton Keynes, a new and pioneering city with green spaces, cycle ways and even concrete cows; it is one of the fastest growing conurbations in the UK. Once out of the city you travel through the rural farmlands of middle England.

A SLICE OF HISTORY Construction of the Grand Union Canal began in in 1894 and was completed in 1929. It covers some 220km between London to Birmingham and features 177 locks.

Blisworth Tunnel, between the villages of Stoke Bruerne and Blisworth, is the third-longest navigable canal tunnel (2,813m) on the UK canal network and was completed in 1807. Until the 1870s, travel through the tunnel was done by men lying on their backs and pushing the boats with their feet in a method known as 'legging'.

As Britain's newest city, Milton Keynes has grown from a 1960s government initiative to build new towns in the south of England to a major city and overflow town for commuters working in London. It's most famous for its roundabouts, concrete cows and shopping centre, but it is also a vibrant city with lots of green and blue spaces.

ABOVE Iron Trunk Aqueduct crossing the River Great Ouse.

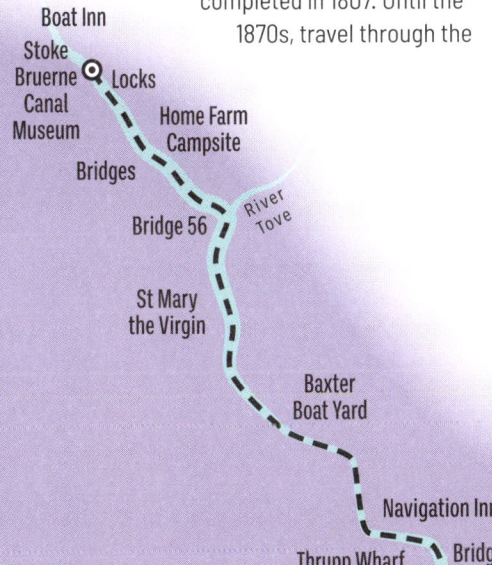

ROUTE Navigate your way around the new city of Milton Keynes using the American-style grid system with its horizontal and vertical streets to find Willen Lane and the Brick Kiln car park. From there you're straight onto the Grand Union Canal. Don't worry if the car park is full, you can soon find another space close by in the maze of residential streets.

Once on the water, relax and enjoy a leisurely paddle north (turn left). As you round the first bend you'll pass a small orchard, Willen Lane Orchards, and then a bridge over the canal. You're skirting around Great Linford Manor Park on the left bank and there's plenty of green space here, including sports pitches and a playground.

After 700m you'll reach another bridge over the water and the canal turns west with a left-hand bend, remaining tree-lined on the left bank with residential housing including a pub on the right. About 700m later there's another bridge and on the left bank is a wooden sculpture of three sheep, created by artist Luke Chapman (and you thought Milton Keynes was famous only for its concrete cows!).

The canal straightens for 600m or so and the left bank is home to the leafy and wooded Blackhorse Wood. The river bends right as you pass under a bridge and a few hundred metres later you'll reach a bridge and the Black Horse pub on the right bank, and a stone circle (Stonepit Field, looked after by The Parks Trust) on the left bank.

The canal heads west for a kilometre, weaving past more green and blue spaces with Stanton Low Park and various lakes including Bradwell, and passes close to the River Great Ouse. The canal heads generally southwards and south-west for a couple of kilometres, passing under Newport and

ABOVE Paddling under the Iron Trunk Aqueduct.

ABOVE Morning reflections on the Grand Union heading north.

Bradwell road bridges, before you reach the New Bradwell Aqueduct, which passes over V6 Grafton Street.

The canal turns another corner, heading back north as you pass under the railway bridges at Wolverton and by the secret garden, which sometimes runs events such as Easter egg hunts for kids and families. The next half a kilometre is various bridges crisscrossing the canal as it turns westwards and passes through more of an industrial area for about 1.5km. You'll then reach one of my favourite bits of the canal as you pass the Galleon canalside pub with the Ouse Valley Park car park opposite. This is another potential launch site for your trip to shorten the paddle.

Old Wolverton Castle and Holy Trinity Church are set back in the park, surrounded by open parkland and great walks. Then, 500m later you'll reach the Iron Trunk Aqueduct, which spans the River Great Ouse. We've walked, scrambled, and paddled over and under this remarkable piece of engineering. The canal straightens

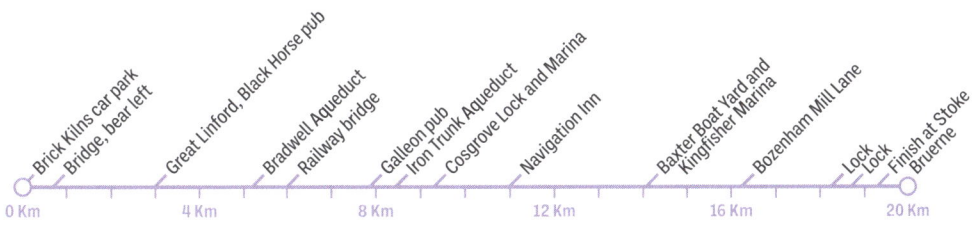

for about 500m as it passes Cosgrove Park, nestled among lakes and treelined avenues for touring and static caravans.

At Cosgrove you'll need to portage the lock, which is a short carry on the right side by the towpath. The canal winds northwards now for 1.7km, passing under a road bridge with another watering hole, the Navigation Inn, and a marina alongside. You could use this as a pick-up or start location if you want to shorten or change the route.

It really does feel like you're leaving towns and cities behind now to enjoy rolling countryside. The canal weaves generally north-west for another 3km, passing under a couple of small bridges and alongside farms and the odd building before arriving at Kingfisher Marina near Yardley Gobion. The canal runs more northwards now for a couple of kilometres, passing under a few more small bridges and skirting behind Grafton Regis, where you can see the church tower of St Mary the Virgin. You'll also pass under the road bridge at Bozenham Mill Lane.

Bridge 56 is just under a kilometre further on as the canal turns west slightly and follows the tiny River Tove alongside. About 1.5km on you'll reach another lock

BELOW Rob taking a break on the Aqueduct.

with a short portage to navigate. A few hundred metres on is a second lock with parking alongside. Both are easily portaged on the right side. A third lock is a few hundred metres on, under the A508 Northampton Road flyover.

It's groundhog day, so you still have two more locks to negotiate in the next few hundred metres. You should by now be a dab hand at this portaging gig, making light work of it. It's half a kilometre north until – you've guessed it – another lock, this time Lock 15. The Navigation Inn is on the right bank as you approach Stoke Bruerne, your destination. You'll need to navigate Top Lock no. 14 to access the basin and the museum. If you want to enjoy the last stretch of water above the lock you can paddle up to the Blisworth Tunnel, which is not accessible to paddle craft.

EXTEND THE TRIP Paddling north past Stoke Bruerne and the tunnel involves a long, tough portage of about 3km around the tunnel, so it might be worth using a shuttle or a trolley. If you do explore further north, you'll wind your way past many sleepy Northamptonshire villages and towns including Bugbrooke, Weedon Bec, Nether Heyford and Daventry.

Extending your route south offers the chance to paddle through the backwaters of Milton Keynes and on towards Leighton Buzzard as the canal threads past.

OUR RICH ADVENTURE We know the Grand Union Canal very well, having paddled its waters for decades. Rob Campbell and I used it for training for our 2016 Yukon race, paddling up and down the canal and using the portages around it as cross training.

We also undertook one of our Project 24 challenges paddling the river here, walking and paddling (canoe and kayaks on

ABOVE Rich and Rob heading over the Aqueduct in a racing canoe.

separate occasions) for 24 hours around the River Great Ouse from near its source in Buckingham. We paddled under the Grand Union Canal Aqueduct and pushed on to achieve 78km in 24 hours, which included some tough portages as the river is non-navigable (allegedly!).

We've also spent a lot of time playing and paddling in two of Milton Keynes' local waterways, Caldecotte in the south and Willen Lake in the north. We also ran the watersports at the Big Outdoor Show, where we had the pleasure of first meeting Sir Ranulph Fiennes.

One of Rich's big adventures was the New York Spare Seat Kayak Expedition, from Niagara Falls to the Statue of Liberty via the Hudson River and Erie Canal. The Americans studied Britain's canal systems and took them back to the United States to open up the interior.

CALORIE CREDITS Visit The Black Horse at Great Linford for great food and drink options (W: www.theblackhorsegreatlinford.co.uk). Or try the Galleon at Wolverton, which is a great pit stop (W: www.thegalleonwolverton.co.uk/index).

There are several pubs at Stoke Bruerne when you get there, including the wonderful Navigation (W: www.navigationstokebruerne.co.uk), and there's also a coffee shop in the town where you can grab a hot drink and snack.

WILDLIFE SAFARI There is an abundance of wildlife on this waterway including kingfishers, herons, swans, ducks, Canadian geese and wild ponies by the river.

> **WHERE'S THE MAGIC?**
>
> Canals are incredible feats of engineering, irrespective of the era in which they were built. And considering they were built over 200 years ago, and mostly dug by hand without machines, they are something we should all be proud of. Britain led the way when it came to canals, locks, aqueducts, sluices, balancing ponds and other ingenious solutions to travelling by water. You'll get to experience many of these engineered solutions as you paddle on this historic canal.

OTHER ATTRACTIONS There's outdoor crazy golf north of Milton Keynes at Mr. Mulligans, great fun for all the family or as a way to show off your skills (W: https://mrmulligan.com/milton-keynes-outdoor).

Planet Ice in Milton Keynes is home to the Milton Keynes Lightning ice hockey team, and provides a great evening of fast-paced sport and entertainment (W: https://planet-ice.co.uk).

Visit Stoke Bruerne Canal Museum, which is located at the end of your trip to learn more about the history of Britain's canals and waterway heritage (W: https://canalrivertrust.org.uk/places-to-visit/stoke-bruerne).

If you're planning a longer stay in the area, try Cosgrove Park Holiday Home and Touring Park (W: www.cosgrovepark.co.uk).

THE SHARED ECONOMY Visit the team at Willen Lake for a wide range of activities. There's an aquapark, pedalos and other watersports kit (W: www.willenlake.org.uk).

The Canoe The Ouse Company operates on the Grand Union Canal and a small section of the Great Ouse near Milton Keynes (W: www.canoetheouse.co.uk).

Or head across to Bedford and paddle the stunning River Great Ouse further downstream, as it passes through the market town and its Victorian Embankment with Canoe Trail (www.canoetrail.co.uk).

22 RIVER WYE: KERNE BRIDGE TO SYMONDS YAT

The River Wye is one of Britain's most popular paddling destinations, with classic meanders and the towering presence of Symonds Yat. It was historically frequented by canoeists and kayakers, but since the advent of the SUP revolution SUP'ers have also joined in the action and the Symonds Yat rapids were remodelled, making them more user-friendly, although they may still present a risk of a swim if you're not experienced. Just mind any shallows to avoid the rapid dismount.

The Lowdown

DIFFICULTY

Avoid Symonds Yat, a small Grade 2 rapids, by exiting the flow before the whitewater, the rest is Grade 1.

DISTANCE 15km

DIRECTIONS Park at the car park just below Kerne Bridge to access the beautiful River Wye from the layby beach area. The paddle down to the bottom of Symonds Yat rapids is just over 14km in distance going with the flow. The shuttle distance is about 6.5km but can take longer than the estimated 15 minutes due to narrow roads and tourist traffic; various small roads follow after the B4234, but they can be very congested during peak season.

HAZARDS

CRAFT

*exit before Symonds Yat rapids

	LOCATION	GRID REFERENCE	POST CODE	WHAT3WORDS
PARKING	Car park at Kerne Bridge	SO581188	HR9 5QT	aware.refreshed.upstairs
START	Kerne Bridge	SO582187	HR9 5QT	latches.hopeless.adventure
PORTAGE	Steps below Symonds Yat rapids	SO559155	HR9 6JL	kitten.district.deleting
FINISH	Car park above Symonds Yat rapids	SO560157	HR9 6JL	fights.endings.corrupted

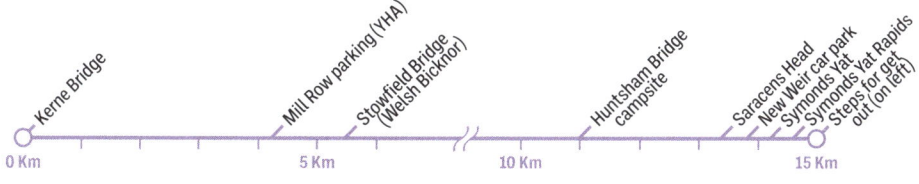

ABOVE Heading down the River Wye with Marc Nicolson.

BACKGROUND Symonds Yat escarpment is managed by Forestry England with trails and vantage points over the River Wye Valley. Over 2,500 years old, it was originally an Iron Age hill fort, and is a designated ancient monument. There is plenty of birdlife, with peregrine falcons, goshawks, owls and more. The valley floor hosts the bubbly River Wye with pubs and campsites along its route.

A SLICE OF HISTORY The Wye Valley was mined for iron ore as far back as 1590 and hand ferries and bridges were used to transport supplies across its switchback loops. Its high ground also made it the perfect location for an Iron Age fort and Roman forts, while standing in open countryside above the River Wye, Goodrich Castle is one of the finest and best preserved of all English medieval castles and now under the care of English Heritage.

ROUTE Launching at Kerne Bridge, there's parking and a layby space to unload kit and an easy launch point. Be warned: in summer Symonds Yat is a tourist trip, which means crowded parking and tight traffic on the narrow lanes. Head there outside of the main holiday times to enjoy this classic river for a route less paddled.

Once on the river the stresses of any parking and shuttling are soon forgotten as you lilly dip downstream from the bridge. After 1.6km the river begins a gentle bend to the right and depending on levels there may be a small riffle. The river straightens after the bend for a kilometre or so before again bending lazily to the right, passing Joy's Green village in the Forest of Dean.

The river straightens for another 750m as you cruise up towards the superbly named Welsh Bicknor on the north bank, which is home to the YHA Wye Valley hostel. You may not be surprised to find the river bending around again, such is the geology of the Wye. This time it bends around to the left and about 400m later you'll pass under Stowfield Bridge, known as the Black Bridge.

The river continues its meandering ways for another 2.7km until it enters the larger switchbacks approaching the Symonds Yat Escarpment. The river does a full loop back on itself to the right and heads north again for another 2km towards Huntsham Bridge, which has a small campsite if you're wanting to break the trip down over more than one day. The river loops around the top of the bend to the left after the bridge, before heading back down towards Symonds Yat.

The river then straightens again and the quiet backwaters are replaced with caravan and camping sites on the right bank, but it never loses its charm. You'll pass the tiny St Dubricius Church on the right bank. Paddle on, carried by the excitement of the cliffs, Yat rock, soaring birds of prey and climbers on the wall as you approach Symonds Yat. The last 2km of paddling are

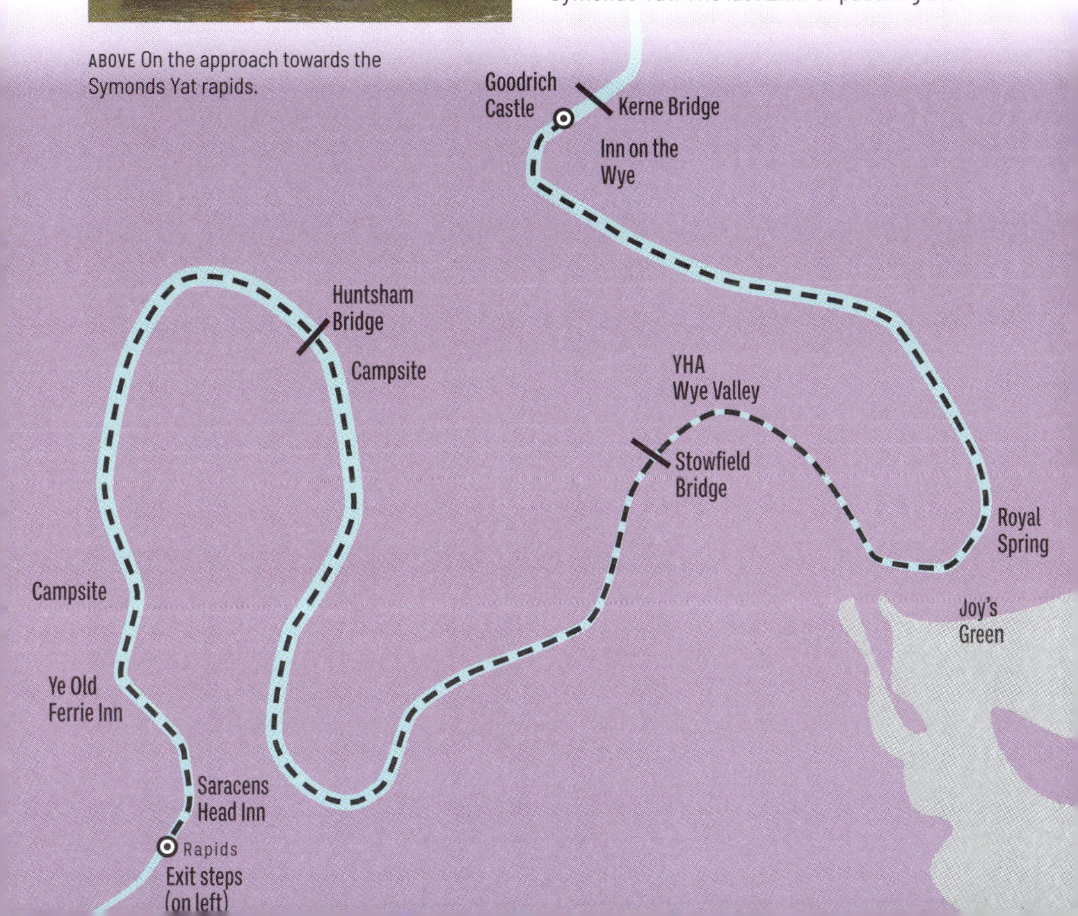

ABOVE On the approach towards the Symonds Yat rapids.

ABOVE The get out steps on river left at the bottom of the Symonds Yat rapids.

and start of the short section of rapids (Grade 2). You can either pull over and exit the river at this point or run the rapids to the bottom (canoe or kayak only). As always, make sure you've checked the flow levels and paddle within your ability. If you do shoot the rapids then you can opt to paddle straight down the middle of the downstream V-shape (tongue of water), holding the craft straight to keep things simpler.

Just below the island, about 150m below the start, are steps on the left-hand side to portage up to the track and return to the car park above.

delightful, with a bit of a sensory overload of activities and river life in full flow.

The main car park is on the left and is where Wyedean Canoe and Adventure Centre is based, followed by the Saracens Head Inn, captured in so many photographs of the waterfront here. As you round the bend just after the inn you'll see the island

EXTEND THE TRIP There's plenty more to paddle on the Wye, essentially continuing the flatter sections below Symonds Yat towards Monmouth. You'll crisscross the Wales–England border towards the A40 for 4km and then the river turns a sharp left following the road down to the town.

ABOVE Marc on the Symonds Yat in spate.

It's about another 4km to the town bridge. Over the years we have explored much of this stunning river, including competing in the 100-mile (161km) CHAR raft race over three days.

Paddling further upstream leads to more exciting whitewater, taking in features such as Hell Hole, and the beauty of Hay-on-Wye and Glasbury. You can go even further by heading up or downstream, but we think Kerne Bridge to Symonds Yat is the perfect family adventure.

OUR RICH ADVENTURE We've enjoyed the Wye River in all four seasons at different locations. I first paddled the Wye about 25 years ago, when we stayed there as a family on holiday. We took our plastic-fantastic kayaks and an inflatable dinghy we used on the local weir to 'run the rapids'. Unbeknown to me, the floor had holes in it and would quickly fill up the inner dinghy, making it more like a giant rubber ring! My dad took the helm and paddled off into the flow with my two young cousins as junior ratings. As the leak became visible, I could see he was not amused. His vex and anger made me laugh nervously, making him more furious by demanding I do something...!

My gran also expressed her annoyance at the jeopardy of her two young grandchildren. By now I was helpless to assist due to crying with laughter. The statute of limitation on holding a suitable grudge remained in place within the family for at least a decade...

Since these troubling times we have paddled and rafted the Wye many different times and from low flows in summer to full bore in spate. The wildlife, beautiful surroundings and of course the views never disappoint.

CALORIE CREDITS Visit the Paddle Café Firetruck at Kerne Bridge during normal season for snacks (W: www.thepaddlecafekernebridge.com).

The Hatter and Hound Café on the right bank and Ye Old Ferrie Inn (W: www.yeoldferrieinn.com) (which apparently is quite old, being opened in 1473), also on the right bank, are accessible from the water, while The Saracens Head Inn marks your finish point, and we've frequented this pub over many decades (W: www.saracensheadinn.co.uk).

BELOW Ash winding her way downstream.

ABOVE Blue sky days as we head down to Symonds Yat from Kerne Bridge.

WILDLIFE SAFARI Symonds Yat is home to a wide range of birds of prey, including the speedy peregrine falcon, hobby and osprey, which all use the towering escarpments to hunt.

> **WHERE'S THE MAGIC?**
>
> The natural geography of the River Wye between Symonds Yat east and west is extraordinary. Visit the viewing points early or later in the day to capture stunning misty shots at sunrise or sunset.

OTHER ATTRACTIONS King Arthur's Cave Nature Reserve is just downstream from Symonds Yat, making for another interesting place to visit (W: www.herefordshirewt.org/nature-reserves/king-arthurs-cave).

You'll also pass close to Offa's Dyke, the legendary defence ditch spanning Wales and built by King Offa (757–96) in the 8th century, which makes for a fantastic walk along the Offa's Dyke Path (W: www.nationaltrail.co.uk/en_GB/trails/offas-dyke-path).

The remains of Little Doward Iron Age Fort can be found up on the hill if you fancy a wander after the paddle, or take time out to visit Goodrich Castle, which is seriously impressive and appears impregnable (W: www.english-heritage.org.uk/visit/places/goodrich-castle/).

THE SHARED ECONOMY There are plenty of paddling companies lining the banks of the River Wye, so you can really take your pick of the different start locations, shuttles and services.

23 WARWICK CASTLE AND THE RIVER AVON

Perched on the banks of the River Avon, Warwick Castle towers over the river, making you feel a very small cog in a much bigger wheel. This short backwater of the Avon, however, feels intimate, with its weirs, small islands and boating life, belying the fact that further down the river is a world-famous international tourist attraction, the 16th-century birthplace of the world's most famous playwright.

The Lowdown

DIFFICULTY
An easy accessible and short paddle around Warwick's Avon.

DISTANCE 4.5km around the loop from the castle up the backwater weir and onto the River Leam spur can either take a couple of hours or be extended to longer with lunch.

DIRECTIONS You can launch at a number of places on the north bank. Park in residential streets or even at the Tesco Superstore and walk to the river, which is typically 150–200m depending on parking.

HAZARDS

CRAFT

	LOCATION	GRID REFERENCE	POST CODE	WHAT3WORDS
START	Near housing	SP308653	CV34 6QX	shield.proper.middle
FINISH	End of the line	SP284646	CV34 4SP	bits.grin.knots

BELOW An elevated view from the aqueduct over the Avon at Warwick.

BACKGROUND
A paddle down the River Avon, adjacent to the walls of the mighty Warwick Castle, makes you feel like you've time-travelled to an ancient way of life. The castle and associated bridge and ruins make this a classic selfie moment for all paddlers. Note, this is a popular destination and can be busy on hot days and during holidays.

A SLICE OF HISTORY
The medieval Warwick Castle was developed from a wooden fort first built by William the Conqueror in 1068. The original wooden motte and bailey castle was rebuilt in stone during the 12th century. During the Hundred Years' War (1337-1453), the facade opposite the town was refortified, resulting in one of the most recognisable examples of 14th-century military architecture in Britain.

ABOVE Rich and Arafat pose in front of Warwick Castle on the River Avon.

ROUTE
We launched on the River Leam close to the Princes Drive Weir and followed the river about a kilometre down to the confluence with the River Avon. Once on the Avon it really does feel like you are ready to explore. Turning right and heading upstream, the green spaces and small islands capture your imagination. There are a couple of bridges to pass under before you find the small islands. River left continues upwards and around a slight

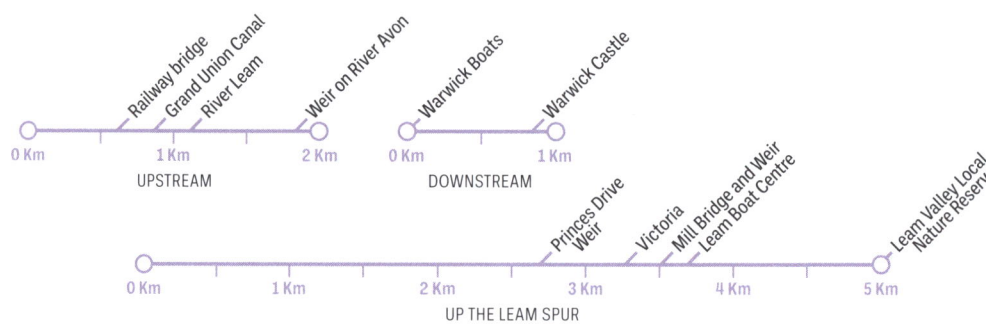

bend, and 750m upstream you reach a small-sloped weir.

You could portage this from the bank and continue upstream towards Guys Cliffe House, a historic Gothic manor on the banks of the Avon, but we chose to head for the main prize: Warwick Castle. Retracing the 700m back to the River Leam we headed downstream to pass under the Grand Union Canal aqueduct and past the Saltisford Canal Trust 210m away. There's a railway bridge 250m further on, adjacent to a Tesco Superstore, where you could also opt to park and portage a couple of hundred metres with canoe, kayak or SUP.

Just over 600m downstream, after a gentle S-bend, you'll paddle under National Cycle Route 41, which crosses next to the Kingfisher Pool (which you can't see from the river but is a large heart-shaped lake). The 2nd Warwick Sea Scouts have their scout hut and a launching space on the north bank. The riverbanks begin to feel more manicured as you get closer to the parks and green spaces of Warwick.

On the right bank located next to the road bridge you'll find Warwick Boats, hiring all manner of craft from kayaks to canoes and pedalos. You've covered 700m from the last bridge with the end in sight, Warwick Castle. Be aware, both the bridge and ruins before you reach the castle are crumbling and signs advise against getting too close to avoid falling debris.

Once you pass the last ruins you are at the castle and you can take pictures galore. Enjoy this historic location and take in the moment (we recommend stopping short of storming the castle!).

ABOVE Heading upstream under bridges, away from Warwick Castle.

EXTEND THE TRIP Paddle and explore parts of the River Leam. Heading upstream from the confluence with the Avon you reach the Princes Drive Weir after 920m and then a second weir after 2.3km, which is just before you reach the Leam Boat Centre on the right bank as you head upstream opposite a small island. Portage the weirs to continue upstream. There are various bridges as you continue, and you'll pass by Leamington Spa Sailing Club, which is on the lake next to the river. About 1.25km after the centre you'll pass through the Leam Valley Nature Reserve. Another 2km and the River Leam approaches a sharp left-hand bend, which is right next to canal and Cycle Route 41. You could switch onto the canal and paddle back to the aqueduct, making an adventurous loop and a longer day spent exploring.

OUR RICH ADVENTURE
We paddled this historic stretch on a cold winter's day and enjoyed the river to ourselves. We had various foster dogs press-ganged into our craft. All was going well until we lined up for the obligatory photos. Ash took the first round, like a pro, and little Stewie, one of our foster dogs, was anxious to get to her as soon as possible. He didn't realise that his ability to walk on water was short lived and he plunged into the river. Undeterred he demonstrated his best doggy-paddle skills, powering over to Ash. He then sat shivering, despite multiple coat layers and cuddles, for the next hour or so. I, of course, lost my front engine (my wife Ash) to the cuddling process...

CALORIE CREDITS
You're spoilt for choice in Warwick when it comes to restaurants, pubs and cafés. Or why not pack a picnic to enjoy your time on the river? Near the Leam Boat Centre, Temperance Bar has delicious food (W: www.temperance.bar/menu).

WILDLIFE SAFARI
Kingfishers, swans, ducks and, of course, a small dog swimming all made an appearance during our paddle. You might spot birds of prey at the castle, where they fly eagles, vultures, owls and even a condor during displays.

OTHER ATTRACTIONS
Tour Warwick Castle (W: www.warwick-castle.com) to find out more about our history, but be warned: some of the live actors can be a bit scary! Nearby Stratford-upon-Avon is a must for all Shakespeare fans (W: www.visitstratforduponavon.co.uk), while for those more mechanically minded there's the National Motorcycle Museum in Solihull, with its collection of over a 1,000 British-made bikes (W: www.nationalmotorcyclemuseum.co.uk).

THE SHARED ECONOMY
The highly experienced paddler team at the Leam Boat Centre offers canoe and kayak hire, British Canoeing courses, SUP courses and much more (W: leamboatcentre.com). Warwick Boats hire row boats, canoes and kayaks, as well as the highly desirable large swan and dragon pedalos (W: warwickboats.co.uk).

> **WHERE'S THE MAGIC?**
> Location, location, location. Paddle through history as you approach Warwick Castle. The more hidden parts of the Leam and upstream on the Avon are also an absolute delight to explore, away from the hustle and bustle of the city.

LEFT Portage required at the weir on the River Leam.

24 IRONBRIDGE GORGE AND THE RIVER SEVERN

Boost your fresh-air miles by paddling the iconic waters of the Ironbridge Gorge, the birthplace of the Industrial Revolution and now a UNESCO World Heritage Site. At its heart is the red Iron Bridge, with multiple old manufacturing plants and machinery, a true testament to the skill, vision and enterprise of this region's pioneering ironworkers. The Blists Hill museum, tunnels and surrounding history can take a day on its own.

The Lowdown

DIFFICULTY
A charming paddle with a short section of exciting rapids at Jackfield (not for SUPs), Grade 1 with the exception of Jackfield, Grade 2.

DISTANCE Iron Bridge to Woodbridge Inn: 4km. Iron Bridge to Severn Park, Bridgnorth: 15km.

DIRECTIONS You can launch at several places along the River Severn around Iron Bridge and the Gorge. Park at Dale End or Wharfage car park to access the riverbank. In recent years, one of the local activity providers has appeared to have become a little overprotective of the Wharfage launch spot, so head a little upstream.

It's a 14km shuttle from the finish at Bridgnorth, taking 25 minutes or so by road.

HAZARDS

CRAFT *

*kneel down or get out to avoid Jackfield

	LOCATION	GRID REFERENCE	POST CODE	WHAT3WORDS
PARKING	Wharfage	SJ665037	TF8 7DG	keyboard.gymnasium.goods
START	River Severn above Iron Bridge	SJ666036	TF8 7DG	skippers.uptown.havens
FINISH	Severn Park, Bridgnorth	SO721934	WV15 5AF	blemishes.rungs.verdict

BACKGROUND There's an obvious magnetic quality to Iron Bridge, which seems to draw paddlers back over multiple visits to witness this icon of form, function and engineering spanning the magnificent Ironbridge Gorge.

The River Severn itself has eroded the gorge-over time, with steep walls and high hills flanking its waters. Once past Iron Bridge itself, don't fear, as there's plenty of exciting and interesting paddling to come. There is a wide range of manufacturing museums and attractions including the Tar Tunnels, Tile Museum, Darby Houses, Iron Museum, Pipeworks and china museum.

A SLICE OF HISTORY Built by Abraham Darby III in 1779, the world's first cast-iron bridge is an iconic tribute to Britain's industrial past and features the Toll House on the far side. The Toll House was built to recover some of the £6,000 building costs and the original prices remain displayed on the toll boards.

Nearby Much Wenlock is home to the Wenlock Olympian Society, which was founded by William Penny Brookes in 1850 and is said to have inspired the modern Olympic Games, introduced in 1896.

ROUTE Launch on the beach close to the river and join the gentle flow downstream and around the bend where one of the top-drawer prizes of the day – Iron Bridge – soon comes into view. Each time we've visited we've grabbed photos from upstream and downstream selfie style, enjoying the varied light.

The left bank is high stone with some old rickety stairs and the shop fronts that grace the streets of this famous venue.

As you pass under the bridge, once out of the way of the general public, it becomes more enchanted, with higher banks and trees. You feel like the river is now your own to explore. About 900m downstream, as you pass old boulders and green mossy banks, you'll reach the Lloyds Head Free Bridge and quickly afterwards, about 350m on, is the top of Jackfield Rapids.

The short but brilliant Jackfield Rapids can trip up even the most experienced paddler if it is not given due respect. There's a simple line running from left of centre towards river right and the rapid itself is less than 150m long. There are some obvious places to break out on river left to slow your speed and practise some moves. At the bottom of the rapid is a large pool on river left and it is possible to line and pull craft back upstream to play further. It's a paddling mission to paddle

BELOW Rich, Foxy and Lara below Ironbridge for picture postcard perfect shots.

LEFT Ironbridge – one of the most famous bridges in the world.

back up, but you can make it up the bottom sections with the appropriate skills.

Around 700m downstream you'll reach the first of several public houses lining these banks, The Half Moon Inn, and 500m downstream of that is The Woodbridge Inn, just past the stunning spans of Coalport Bridge.

The river bends right just over a kilometre later and begins to wind gently back and forth, with dense woods above on the left bank. It then heads down towards the Apley Estate and park on the left bank and about 3km south passes under a smaller road bridge leading to the private estate and gothic mansion of Apley Hall, built around 1811. Around 2km past the bridge the river kicks around to the right before heading south on the run in to Bridgnorth.

About half a kilometre later you'll see the open park of Severn Park on the left bank, which is home to Bridgnorth Rugby Club and your end point for this electric paddle of rapids, wildlife and living history. (Our 100-mile paddle saw us get as far as Worcester on this route.) Further downstream there are hermit caves and chain ferries to excite your inner historian and earn even more fresh-air miles.

EXTEND THE TRIP You can launch further upstream at multiple locations, including a layby where the B4380 crosses the river

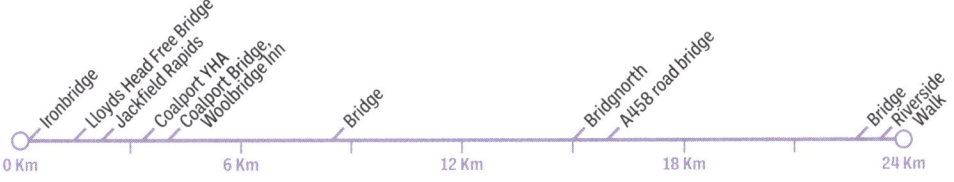

BELOW The inviting Woodbridge Inn offers a friendly stop for food and drink.

at Cressage, which will add about 11km of winding river switchbacks along the Severn River valley. Various old bridges cross the flow here, so there's lots to see.

You can extend the trip further to suit your aspirations and available time; there are lots of incredible towns along the way, including Stourport-on-Severn, Bewdley, and Hampton Loade. Note, further downstream some of the portages around weirs and locks are not for the fainthearted, but it's particularly user-friendly for kayaks and canoes as you get down towards Worcester.

OUR RICH ADVENTURE

We've paddled the River Severn and Ironbridge Gorge on countless occasions, usually in canoes but also on kayaks and SUPs. The Jackfield Rapids are a great place to play and are generally pretty user-friendly, with a series of pools to break out on the left side (depending on levels), or you can bosh straight through.

Ash and I have paddled down here with the dogs plenty of times. I trained here with TV adventurer and presenter Andy Torbet in a canoe for the DW Canoe Race and the Yukon River Quest. Injury prevented us from competing together, but not before a superfast training paddle on the Severn in flood.

One of the funniest times I've had on this section was while training with replacement partner and paddling ninja Rob Campbell for the Yukon. We planned to paddle 160km by canoe in 24 hours, starting in Welshpool. Despite working extremely hard, by the time we reached Ironbridge it was dark and the bridge was floodlit. No problem, however, a discussion ensued about running Jackfield Rapids in the dark. The unflappable Rob concluded centre of river full tilt and we should be fine! Less convinced, I moved back to the centre thwart behind

ABOVE Heading upstream from the car park put on location.

RIGHT Jackfield Rapids, an exhilarating rapid to hone your whitewater skills.

the front seat, which was fortunate, as we shipped serious waves and water as we paddled down the rapids in the pitch black. Much laughter and banter followed, as well as extreme fatigue by daylight.

Last time we were on this stretch of river the local fire service were practising rescue skills in Jackfield Rapids. No rescues necessary, though (they seemed genuinely disappointed).

CALORIE CREDITS There are various pubs and eateries along the route with differing ease of access from the riverbank.

Stop at the Woodbridge Inn for a brew and fab food (W: www.brunningandprice.co.uk/woodbridge), grab drinks at the YHA at Coalport (W: www.yha.org.uk/hostel/yha-ironbridge-coalport) or visit Ye Olde Robin Hood Inn in Ironbridge itself for great food or somewhere to stay before or after your trip (W: www.robinhoodironbridge.co.uk).

WILDLIFE SAFARI Kingfishers, deer, red kites frequent the valley. We even rescued a lamb stuck in the mud during one paddle!

WHERE'S THE MAGIC?

The entire Ironbridge Gorge never gets boring with its incredibly well-preserved living history, Iron Bridge itself and the fun times of Jackfield Rapids adding a little spice to your paddling day.

OTHER ATTRACTIONS Make the most of your trip by thoroughly exploring this UNESCO World Heritage Site, known as the 'Valley of Invention'. There's several museums, Blists Hill Victorian Town, the Tar Tunnel, furnaces and more (W: www.ironbridge.org.uk).

The ruins of the 12th-century Cistercian Buildwas Abbey, which include a church and ornately carved chapter house, are close to Ironbridge and run by English Heritage (W: www.english-heritage.org.uk/visit/places/buildwas-abbey).

Extend your stay by resting at the absolutely fantastic YHA Ironbridge Coalport, which is situated on the banks of the River Severn and next to a world-class bike shop (W: www.yha.org.uk/hostel/yha-ironbridge-coalport).

THE SHARED ECONOMY A wide range of local canoe, coracle and rafting suppliers provide paddling trips, hire and even a handy shuttle service. Ironbridge Canoe Hire (W: www.ironbridgecanoehire.co.uk) offers canoe hire on the Severn, while Shropshire Raft Tours provide a whitewater rafting option on the river (W: www.shropshirerafttours.co.uk).

25 RIVER TRENT AND THE STAFFORDSHIRE CANALS

A serene looping paddle on the River Trent, along some of Staffordshire's hidden waterways between Stone and Wolseley Bridge. The route provides a real adventure with the potential for portages around fallen trees on the narrow waters. The start near Stafford and Stone Canoe Club offers some gentle moving water with rocky features and channels. Downstream of Wolseley Bridge you can loop back to the start, portaging on the Canal at Brindley Bank Aqueduct.

The Lowdown

DIFFICULTY
A long and winding adventure paddle with riffles, historic bridges, camping and an aqueduct to loop back on the canal.

DISTANCE
Crown Meadows, Stone to Wolseley Bridge (long day paddle): 24km.
Aston Bridge to Salt Bridge (leisurely half day paddle): 8km.
Aston Bridge to Mill Lane Bridge, Great Haywood (shorter day paddle): 16.1km.
Paddle from Stone to the campsite at Great Haywood, onto Brindley Bank Aqueduct for a 19km overnight camp paddle (using the campsite twice).

DIRECTIONS
There are campsites at Great Haywood, allowing you to extend your paddle downstream, or paddle back on the canal to Stone, making a micro adventure of it. The straighter canal paddle from Wolseley Bridge back to Stone is about 19.6km and 15.6km from Great Haywood. The vehicle shuttle from Wolseley Bridge to Stone is 22km and takes about 20 minutes.

Access restrictions: check the slalom websites for competition events at the Stafford & Stone Canoe Club to avoid paddling the slalom course when in use.

HAZARDS
*at start near Stone slalom course and weir

CRAFT

25 • RIVER TRENT AND THE STAFFORDSHIRE CANALS

	LOCATION	GRID REFERENCE	POST CODE	WHAT3WORDS
PARKING	Crown Meadows car park, Stone	SJ901337	ST15 0GY	clapper.refilled.gratuity
START	Crown Meadows, water's edge	SJ900336	ST15 0TT	notched.shoelaces.potato
ALTERNATIVE LAUNCH SITE WITH CAR PARK	Stafford & Stone Canoe Club, Westbridge Park, Stafford Road	SJ902334	ST15 0GX	cleansed.studio.losing
ACCESS POINT (START OR FINISH)	Aston Bridge	SJ914319	ST15 0BJ	happily.craziest.voting
ACCESS POINT (START OR FINISH)	Salt Bridge	SJ958278	ST18 0BT	decimal.headlight.stacks
DANGER WEIR (PORTAGE)	Weir drop and rapids	SJ995240	ST18 0RG	imitate.clumped.crawling
ACCESS POINT (START OR FINISH)	Mill Lane Bridge, Great Haywood	SJ993230	ST18 0RJ	casino.bound.stung
CAMPSITE	Mill Lane	SJ995230	ST18 0SD	trickles.tuxedos.screen
ACCESS POINT (START OR FINISH)	Essex Bridge	SJ995225	ST18 0ST	riverbed.laying.nuggets
FINISH (3)	Wolseley Arms pub, Wolseley Bridge	SK020203	ST17 0XS	cello.prop.spent
PORTAGE ONTO CANAL TO LOOP BACK	Brindley Bank Aqueduct	SK039195	WS15 2HP	thank.stream.above

BACKGROUND The River Trent is the third longest river in the UK, bisecting the country from south of Biddulph moor across to the east coast, from rural slack water to a large and wide body of water tracking out towards the North Sea. The River Trent and Trent and Mersey Canal offer a brilliant river to canal camping loop for a paddling adventure. The river itself is slow moving with riffles, lovely bridges and lots to see in this area of pottery prowess. The Trent has some stunning scenery and walks around Shugborough, and a range of small tributaries to explore including the Sow plus miles of canals.

OPPOSITE Mr Lincoln from Goldington Academy on our Duke of Edinburgh trip being chaperoned by the locals.

A SLICE OF HISTORY The name 'Trent' possibly derives from a Romano-British word meaning 'strongly flooding'. The river last froze 130 years ago, in January and February 1895.

On the southern fringes of Stoke-on-Trent, the river passes through the landscaped parkland of Trentham Gardens. The estate, which was previously owned for over 400 years by the dukes of Sutherland, includes Italianate gardens designed by Charles Barry in the 1830s and the UK's first 'barefoot' walk, as well as a children's adventure play area and maze (W: https://trentham.co.uk/).

The Trent and Mersey Canal, engineered by James Brindley, was the country's first long-distance canal. It is full of interesting

164 MIDLANDS

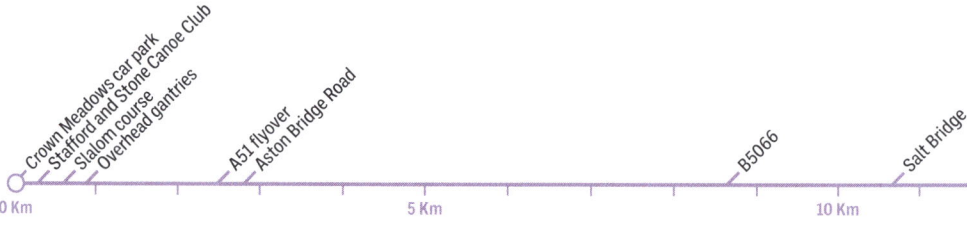

features, which reflect its diverse and storied history, including Harecastle Tunnel, the lengthy lock flight known as Heartbreak Hill, and the traditional canal town of Shardlow.

ROUTE Park at Crown Meadows car park and walk the short distance to the River Trent. Getting on at the bank here you would have no idea how monstrous and big the Trent becomes as you move eastwards – it's a tiny river at this point! After 270m you'll pass under the Stafford Road viaduct, where the Stafford & Stone Canoe Club is based, another possible launch site with a convenient adjacent car park.

The river now flows down a slalom course, so do check the website to avoid inadvertently entering a slalom race. The river is compressed slightly here, with the narrows of stone walls channelling the flow and producing well-defined eddies. About 100m after the bridges the river hangs a sharp right and then runs down for another 100m before bearing left. It remains tight, so avoid it in spate as it has overhanging trees and will be fast, presenting an increased risk to less experienced paddlers. The river continues its tight and ever-changing course with sharp bends around every corner. Running parallel to the general direction is the Trent and Mersey Canal, which offers a route back to the start if you want to create a paddling circuit.

Just before the A51 flyover, about 2.5km from the start, the Trent almost joins the canal and is a mere stone's throw away. Another 300m on is the Aston Road Bridge and then the spire of St Saviours and then St Michael Archangel. You could launch from Aston Bridge Road, on the National Cycle Route 5, if you prefer.

The Trent settles into a gentle, easy river with grasslands and meadows on each side and occasional trees along the way. The occasional looping bend and switchback reminds you that this river in flood is more powerful,

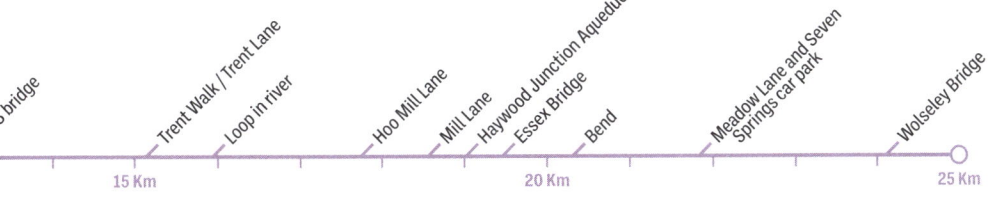

ABOVE The bridge at Great Haywood is one of many pretty bridges on this route.

eroding banks as it pushes through. You'll be forgiven for forgetting the time of day as you explore these charming upper reaches. There's little to break the day dreaming until you reach the B5066 bridge crossing at Sandon, which is about 6km of paddling and includes paddling close to the impressive Sandon Hall.

Salt Bridge is your next landmark, less than 2km on in the village of Salt, where the good news is The Holly Bush, apparently one of the oldest pubs in England, is only a short walk away from the bridge. The river returns closer to the canal and continues eastwards for several kilometres until Gayton Brook joins on the left bank and then you paddle under the A518 flyover leading to Weston, about 1.5km from Salt.

Another 2.8km onwards and you'll reach the Trent Walk to Trent Lane Bridge, which really can't seem to make its mind up about what it should be called. You're now passing by the village of Weston. After about 700m the river almost forms a circle and turns back on itself, almost kissing itself as it passes. Once the river straightens again you'll paddle past woodland plantations on river right. You'll reach Hoo Mill Lane about 1.8km on (a short walk up the road at the canal is the Bridge 76 Emporium, which has a café).

You're now close to Great Haywood and an obvious pitstop with the Canalside

ABOVE Ash, Toby and Jackson (plus Mr Lincoln) heading towards the campsite.

farm, shop and café just up Mill Lane. Be aware of the penultimate bridge, about 1km upstream of Great Haywood, with a rocky weir under the bridge which you need to portage around. You'll reach the Mill Lane bridge first after a kilometre, having passed Great Haywood Marina just over the canal. You can exit the river into a field before the road bridge and end your river trip at Mill Lane Bridge, or just keep paddling for more beautiful Staffordshire scenery. You could also initiate a return loop here on the canal. There's a canal side campsite here on Mill Lane, bookable via Pitchup or by calling 07396 799789. There is a second campsite nearby at White Lodge Camping (W: www.thewhitelodgesite.co.uk). Just past the road bridge is the Haywood Junction aqueduct on the Black Country Ring, and there are campsites here if you're making a longer journey. There is a multi award winning farm shop here to entice you to fill your bag with lots of indulgent snacks.

The next section of the river is more interesting, with lots happening in a short space of time. After 400m you'll reach the somewhat misplaced Essex Bridge, which marks the union of the Trent River with the River Sow, which joins on the right side having passed the impressive Shugborough Estate, run by the National Trust.

The river straightens for almost a kilometre as it passes Shugborough, and then hits a sharp left-hand bend. Another 1.5km on you'll reach the bridge on Meadow Lane near Little Haywood, having also paddled under the railway bridge. There's a car park on this road to the south if you do need to exit. You're not far now from a possible exit point at Wolseley Bridge with the Wolseley Arms by the river and roadside only 2.3km away. Exit river right under the bridge to the pub car park.

Enjoy the final few bends and loops and you're there. If you're really keen you can switch over to the canal and return back to Stone. There's a campsite at Carney Pools, which is about 2km from the river (so you will need transport) for getting a good night's rest before the return leg.

EXTEND THE TRIP

The Trent should by now have captured your heart, with its uncluttered and largely rural paddling off the beaten track. Continuing on from Wolseley offers more of the same paddling through rural Staffordshire and the Black Country. 2.4km downstream of the Wolseley Bridge is the Brindley Bank Aqueduct taking you onto the Trent and Mersey Canal.

Paddle back on the Trent and Mersey Canal, which is of course significantly straighter in course with fewer deviations winding in and out. It passes under various small road bridges and you'll need to portage the locks between Wolseley and Stone. The canal loops back past the canal side campsite so you can make it a 3 day and 2 night trip.

Downstream if you stay on the river it then passes Cannock Chase AONB and Rugeley, before turning north to the brewing town of Burton-on-Trent. The River Trent grows significantly as you paddle eastwards, making it a classic touring journey. Despite passing major roadways such as the M1, it remains largely off the beaten track as you then head for Nottingham and Holme Pierrepont, home to the National Watersports Centre.

If you're paddling the majority of the Trent, it's worth carrying on to Newark to see the castle and gardens on the river.

OUR RICH ADVENTURE We've been paddling on the Trent for as long as we can remember. I enjoyed many days out with my local paddling club, Viking Kayak Club, where I first started using Krakatoa Mouldings' (of Bedford) slalom kayaks and then old school 'plastic-fantastic' Dancers and Pirouette S kayaks to explore the river at different locations.

More recently, we've spent time at the National Whitewater Centre with the occasional trip to the whitewater course for rafting. We've also watched some of the world's best slalom kayakers compete here during major championship events.

RIGHT Heading down from the Stone slalom course onto a charming stretch of the River Trent.

Our last paddling trip on the Trent was from Stone to the lovely campsite at Canal Side Campsite, onto Wolseley Bridge and back on the canal for a Duke of Edinburgh Group for one of our schools customers. The river was in stunning colours with plenty of adventure around fallen trees, little rapids and lots of wildlife.

CALORIE CREDITS There's award-winning dining at Aston Marina, which has views over the waterways and domes and is a short walk from the river (W: www.astonmarina.co.uk). It's also a short walk from the river up the B5066 to the village of Standon and The Dog and Doublet Inn (W: www.doganddoubletsandon.co.uk), while The Holly Bush at Salt is listed as one of the oldest pubs in England and still retains a straw hat (thatched roof) today (W: https://thehollybushatsalt.co.uk).

Visit the Canalside café and farm shop, with a proper traditional butchers and even a pick-your-own-fruit section, located by the canal and river at Great Hayward Bridge. Better still, stock up with treats while setting up the shuttle and enjoy locally sourced food on the paddle (W: www.canalsidefarm.co.uk).

The Wolseley Arms is located at the get out for this trip by Wolseley Bridge, making for somewhere cosy and welcoming to wait if you're shuttling back at the end (T: 01889 883179).

WILDLIFE SAFARI The river is alive with eels and salmon, which both use the Trent as spawning grounds. The meadows and wetlands are also home to plenty of bird life.

BELOW Horse riders using the old railway bridge to cross over the River Trent.

ABOVE Foxy and Rich paddling down through Stafford and Stone slalom course.

OTHER ATTRACTIONS Stoke-on-Trent is the land of pottery, and Wedgwood is known the world over. Book a factory tour and, while you're there, check out the gift shop or sample their cocktail bar and Michelin 2-star dining (W: www.worldofwedgwood.com/).

As well as hosting weddings, Sandon Hall runs a literature festival and other events throughout the year (W: https://sandonhall.co.uk).

> **WHERE'S THE MAGIC?**
>
> The River Trent offers sublime paddling with quiet, stream-like characteristics looping vigorously yet silently back and forth while following the parallel Trent and Mersey Canal. Despite growing to a vast river downstream, it retains its distinct and tranquil nature, feeling remote yet never too far off the beaten track.

If you're looking for something a bit wilder, Trentham Monkey Forest is the only place in the UK where you can walk among 140 free-roaming Barbary macaques (W: https://monkey-forest.com/). Or visit The Wolseley Centre, run by Staffordshire Wildlife Trust, which offers educational walks, sensory gardens and a café (W: www.staffs-wildlife.org.uk/explore/our-visitor-centres/wolseley-centre).

If you're up for more adventures among the trees, Go Ape has aerial courses and Segways for hire (W: https://goape.co.uk/locations/cannock-chase). A little more sedate, the impressive Shugborough Estate has Europe's largest yew tree, extensive gardens and an arboretum to unravel with a tour, while the house is a Georgian mansion of global treasures (W: www.nationaltrust.org.uk/visit/shropshire-staffordshire/shugborough-estate). There's also a great fishery, camping and glamping site downstream of Shugborough at Carney Pools, less than 2km from the exit point at Wolseley (https://carneypools.co.uk/).

Further down the Trent in Nottingham, enjoy adrenaline-fuelled activities and family-friendly fun at Holme Pierrepont Country Park (W: www.nwscnotts.com/hpcp/activities). Or why not try their whitewater course, a great place to hone skills (W: www.nwscnotts.com/nwsc/water-sports/ww-course/)?

The National Forest Adventure Farm is the perfect setting for a family day out. It has plenty of creatures great and small, including miniature Shetland ponies, shire horses, reindeer and Boer goats, as well as indoor play areas, adventure activities and even a maize maze in summer (W: www.adventurefarm.co.uk/). Or for something a little different, why not visit the UK's largest network of caves – over 800 are hidden beneath Nottingham's streets (W: www.nationaljusticemuseum.org.uk/cityofcaves)?

Further downstream is the historic Newark Castle, which has defended the town for over 900 years. Explore the impressive 'Guardian of the Trent', where King John famously took his last breath... (W: https://visitnewark.co.uk/p/newark-castle).

THE SHARED ECONOMY If you see other paddlers on the Trent they may well be from Stafford & Stone Canoe Club, which is home to Olympic Gold medallist Jo Clarke as well as Olympians Lizzie Neave and Adam Burgess (W: www.staffordandstonecc.co.uk). Say hello!

Tittesworth Water is about 40 minutes north of Stone and offers canoeing, kayaking and SUP hire, as well as courses and qualifications (W: www.tittesworthwater.co.uk).

ABOVE A canalside campsite nestled between the canal and the River Trent.

26 CALDON CANAL: LEEK BRANCH

This fascinating journey through the heart of Staffordshire's picturesque Churnet Valley is filled with surprises, from an unusual 'canal flyover', where one navigation crosses another, to sightings of passing steam trains. Having long since moved on from its former industrial past, the canal is now a haven for outdoor enthusiasts and wildlife, with flora and fauna aplenty.

The Lowdown

DIFFICULTY
Some portaging around locks and back down from the top canal to the lower one.

DISTANCE Out and back of 9km including tunnels and the aqueduct.
This can be shortened if you find an access point by car for an A to B journey.

DIRECTIONS Park at The Hollybush Inn with an agreement to boost their coffers after your paddle. You won't regret it, as usually a bowl of chips and a hot drink (or something more substantial) make it a fair trade.

HAZARDS

CRAFT

	LOCATION	GRID REFERENCE	POST CODE	WHAT3WORDS
START/FINISH	The Hollybush pub	SJ955535	ST13 7JT	procured.riding.estuaries
OUT POINT	Hazlehurst Junction Bridge	SJ947537	ST9 9JE	trendy.tabs.calibrate
OUT POINT	Tunnel	SJ974543	ST13 7EA	exclaim.illogical.requests
OUT POINT	Barnfields Canal Aqueduct	SJ978551	ST13 5RJ	interviewer.momentous.bitter

BELOW Paddling the Caldon Canal with a Canoe Trail adventure group.

ABOVE A delightful paddle back in time on the canal.

BACKGROUND

We've been paddling Leek Canal, a short branch off the longer Caldon Canal (itself a branch of the much larger Trent and Mersey Canal), for donkey's years. It offers both shorter and longer canal paddles with all the trimmings: locks, tunnels and even an aqueduct. Even better, it starts and finishes at a local canalside pub in the beautiful Staffordshire Moorlands countryside. What more could you want?

A SLICE OF HISTORY

The Caldon Canal opened in 1779 and was built to carry limestone from the quarries at Cauldon Low, down to the Potteries and the industrial Midlands via three inclined tramways. A shorter branch was built 18 years later, connecting the Caldon with the Staffordshire market town of Leek. Mining subsidence meant the locks had to be rebuilt to ensure the water levels functioned properly.

Sadly, like many canals, Caldon fell into disrepair after the Second World War. It was eventually dredged and restored in the 1970s, before reopening for leisure purposes.

It's important to mention a literal slice of history here, as this county is famous for Staffordshire oatcakes and their sweet counterpart, pikelets. Written accounts of oatcake consumption date back to the 1600s, when officials noted that the local grain stock consisted of 'oats and not much else'.

ROUTE

Launch by The Hollybush, being careful to avoid other, often bigger craft. Head right and quite quickly you'll pass under a bridge, which is the aqueduct you'll be paddling over on your return. If you do want to take a short cut and miss some of the fun you can portage here and climb up the steps to the top canal (but we advise you to take the lower canal which we shall call the low road!).

You'll soon come to a gentle left-hand bend, with various canal boats moored up

on the left-hand side. We love seeing the adaptations those who live on the water have made to their floating homes, from overflowing planters to canoe and bike racks on top of boat roofs, to name a few.

A few hundred metres later you'll get to your first lock, which you can portage or travel through if you have a lock key. We generally share this paddle with young people on our residential courses, so traversing the lock is all part of the experience. A second lock at Hazlehurst Junction follows almost immediately, providing the height gain required to paddle back over the lower canal on the aqueduct. This is a good place for a snack break and there are footbridges to cross the canal here.

You are now on the high road and loop back, parallel to the lower canal in the direction you came from. You'll pass by moorings and then reach Hazlehurst Aqueduct, which is short but you can stop to peer over at your earlier paddling route.

Continuing on, you'll pass under small bridges and pass pretty houses as you get a view over the canal below and the Churnet Valley. There's an exit point if you need it where the canal passes under Denford Road Bridge. This section of the canal is extremely pretty with large trees and woodland flanking the waterway as you paddle past small local communities.

About 2km from the second road bridge you'll arrive at the tunnel, which is ~200m long and adds to the adventure. Typically, the call of a warming hot chocolate or food is enough to ensure you'll turn around near here, but there are options to extend your trip to the River Churnet, another kilometre along. We usually head back to the aqueduct and portage back down to the lower canal section using the steps. It's a little bit of effort, but saves returning via the locks.

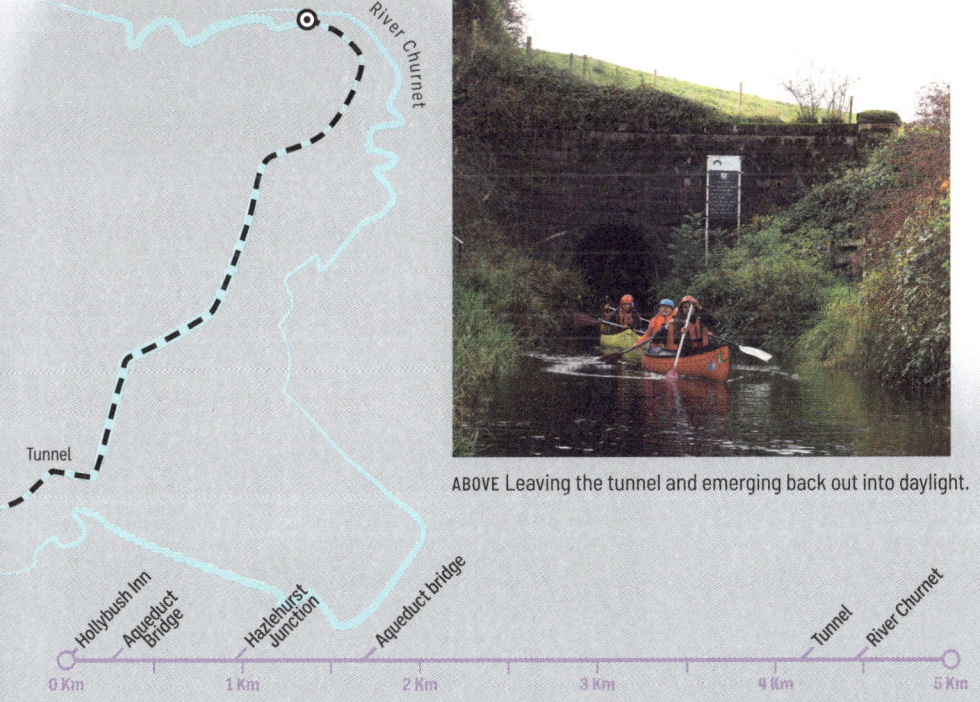

ABOVE Leaving the tunnel and emerging back out into daylight.

> **WHERE'S THE MAGIC?**
>
> Paddling through history is never more achievable than when exploring our ancient canal systems, through the murky depths of tunnels, lowering and raising locks and enjoying aqueducts, an ancient engineering masterpiece. Just as exciting is stopping off for Staffordshire oatcakes on the way to the paddle!

OUR RICH ADVENTURE We visited Leek Canal year after year when running residentials for young people from local youth charities.

CALORIE CREDITS The Hollybush Inn (W: https://hollybushleek.co.uk), a beautiful rural pub converted from an old flour mill, offers a great menu, which depending on the time of year you can enjoy outside in their canalside garden or inside with crackling fires. Of course, no trip to the Staffordshire Moorlands is complete without oatcakes – we recommend Leek Oatcakes in the nearby market town (W: https://jmaps.net/leek-oatcakes).

WILDLIFE SAFARI You'll usually have swans and ducks for company, and you might spot kites and buzzards over the meadows. You can visit the nearby Peak Wildlife Park to see more exotic species (see below).

OTHER ACTIVITIES The Roaches, which is managed by Staffordshire Wildlife Trust, is a prominent rocky ridge that rises steeply (505m) above nearby Tittesworth Reservoir, making it a great walking and/or climbing spot (W: www.staffs-wildlife.org.uk/nature-reserves/roaches). This is the gateway to the stunning Peak District National Park (W: www.peakdistrict.gov.uk), and attractions such as the Monsal Trail, the Wyedale Valley trail and iconic geological formations including Thor's Cave and Lud's Church.

Peak Wildlife Park offers a truly unique and immersive animal experience, where you get to come face to face with exotic and endangered animals from across three continents (W: www.peakwildlifepark.co.uk).

Book into one of the local Youth Hostel Association (YHA) sites, such as the 17th-century manor Ilam Hall near Dovedale or the Jacobean mansion Hartington Hall near Buxton, where it is claimed that Bonnie Prince Charlie once stayed (W: www.yha.org.uk/hostel/yha-hartington-hall).

THE SHARED ECONOMY Rapid Horizons, run by our good friend and former GB paddler Jon Best, offers tubing, rafting, canoeing and kayaking at nearby Matlock (W: www.rapidhorizons.com), while Canoe Trail runs several introductions to moving trips at Matlock each year. You can book on with our team (W: www.canoetrail.co.uk).

ABOVE The view from inside the Caldon Canal tunnel.

27 RIVER DERWENT AND MATLOCK BATH

The River Derwent is a fantastic introduction to moving water, with winding flows alongside tree-lined banks and the more challenging features of a town bridge and small fish weirs. At normal flows it's a great place to cut your teeth on whitewater, developing skills like breaking in and out, ferry gliding and reading the water. The gorge at Matlock Bath signifies a change of character, with more wave trains to play in, before ending at the Matlock slalom course.

The Lowdown

DIFFICULTY
Some small rapids and narrows at the town bridge, overhanging trees and a slalom course (which you can exit if preferred).

DISTANCE 6.8km paddle from Darley Bridge to Matlock Slalom Course.

DIRECTIONS Drive up to the put in at Darley Bridge and shuttle back or book taxis for the return leg from Matlock Bath, about 7km downstream. You drive over the bridge at Darley Dale DE4 2JZ spanning the river and unload on river right, your left after the bridge. By arrangement, you can also access at the Square & Compass pub, but you'll need to pay a launch fee.

HAZARDS
Flood risk – check water levels

CRAFT

	LOCATION	GRID REFERENCE	POST CODE	WHAT3WORDS
START	Darley Bridge	SK271620	DE4 2JZ	plants.stiletto.reassured
	Town bridge	SK297601	DE4 3LW	words.dating.pioneered
	Second railway bridge	SK297598	DE4 3RD	improvise.placed.reserving
FINISH (1)	Above slalom course, steps and exit	SK295589	DE4 3PT	estuaries.spell.always
FINISH (2)	Below slalom course, steps and exit	SK296586	DE4 3PT	hardback.guidebook.wallet

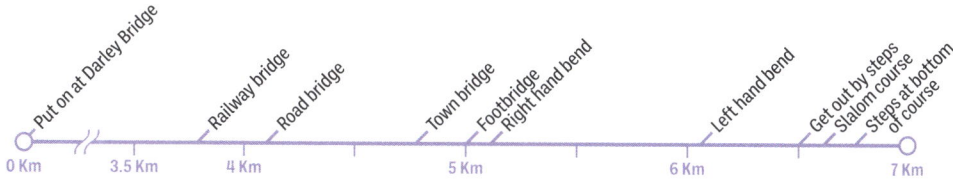

BACKGROUND Get busy in Britain's first national park with river valleys, enticing walks and steep walled gorges towering above you. This relatively short paddle introduces you to short rapids and moving water, while the Derwent has plenty of kingfishers and herons to awake your inner Attenborough. Check the river levels before paddling as the Derwent can rise to significant levels due to its narrow gorge and high water catchment.

ROUTE The start point near the Square & Compass pub has been a favourite of ours for over 20 years, but there's a new access ramp below Darley Bridge for the 11km paddle winding through river flat lands before the little fish weirs and drops of Matlock Gorge. You join the river below a small riffle rapid and then head downstream with a gentle but pressing flow. Trees and bushes line the bank sides and may represent a capsize risk, so hug the middle of the flow.

The river winds and loops and is of course faster on the outside of the bends. As it flattens out you'll see a barn and house on the right bank. You may also see the little steam train chugging along in the distance on the left bank. Further downstream on the left bank are some small beaches below a fairly steep bank area – perfect for a picnic. Depending on the river levels there's a small number of little sand bars and chutes that require you to set a course and paddle a good line. At lower levels there are a few rocks and islands, but at higher levels these are all underwater.

After a sharp left-hand bend you're now reaching the railway bridge near town. You'll need to follow the flow in an S-bend, from river right to left, avoiding the bridge pillar. You'll then pass under the road bridge tunnel and begin to see small weirs, which create a simple downstream flow or tongue

BELOW Paddling down the River Derwent.

BELOW Heading under the bridge at Matlock.

of water. Depending on the flow they can have small- to medium-size wave trains, making them a bouncy ride, but you can reduce this by slowing down or paddling out of the main flow.

Shortly after this comes the old stone town bridge, which requires you to set a course on the left arch. This can be tricky, with trees and debris catching on the arches, so make sure you have a good look for a clear passage. You can usually eddy out either river left above, or further upstream on river right. It is possible to portage the town bridge but it's a true mission hauling boats up the right-hand bank and carrying them over the bridge before relaunching from the river gardens on the left side.

The river now enters the gorge and the cliffs on the left-hand side are home to climbers pushing their vertical limits. You pass under another railway bridge after a right-hand 90-degree bend. You can opt to pass either side of the heavy stone pillar. It's now the homeward straight with a few more features of little weirs and small chutes. As you enter a long straight you'll see a small bridge pipeline in the distance and several slalom poles, which signify the last set of steps before the slalom course. This is a short section of Grade 2 with a small beach on the left-hand side and steps on the right. To exit above or below the slalom course you'll need to use the steps on river right. You can walk back up the rapids on river left and paddle back over to the top steps. It's a mission to get a canoe out here, so many opt to walk and or line their canoes back up the left-side beach and get out at the top steps.

ABOVE Nathaniel Barker paddling the S shape under the old railway bridge.

EXTEND THE TRIP You can paddle on below the slalom course, heading downstream towards Ambergate. About a kilometre downstream, after passing various footbridges serving the tourist industry, things begin to quieten down and you reach Matlock Bath Boats, where you may see hired rowing boats with motley crews. The river passes by Lovers' Walk here, a series of footpaths alongside the river and up over the cliffs (perfect for seeking love if the mood takes you). There's a weir just over half a kilometre on from the rapids, which you may need to portage, and several others on the route down to various get-out options, including the bridge at Whatstandwell. A canal runs adjacent the river so a return loop may be possible.

A SLICE OF HISTORY A popular tourist destination since the late 17th century when the spa waters were discovered, Matlock Bath's heyday was in the Victorian era, when getting outdoors and into nature became popular.

WHERE'S THE MAGIC?

The high cliffs and imposing nature of the gorge section make up the crown jewel of this stunning paddle. It really does offer so much, with lots of wildlife, the wider activities and opportunities of the Peak District National Park and a classic intro to whitewater.

OUR RICH ADVENTURE This paddle is like a second home to us, having completed British canoeing courses here, competed on the Matlock Slalom course (at the get out) and guided countless client trips. Canoe Trail has run intro and moving water trips on the Derwent for years, introducing customers to whitewater and journeys. We nearly always meet someone we know paddling here, running a course or out for a play. It's the perfect spot for learning about

RIGHT Arafat below the town bridge at Matlock.

BELOW Paddling under the second railway bridge, below the town bridge.

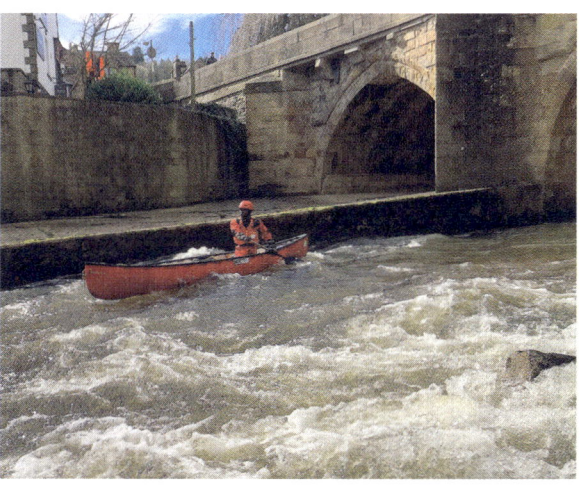

breaking in and out of flows and ferry gliding.

Over the years we have also run adventure camps and residential programmes in the Peak District for some of the young people, charities and schools we work with.

CALORIE CREDITS The Square & Compass at Darley Bridge offers a wide range of food and beverages and even has an adjacent campsite (W: www.robinsonsbrewery.com/pubs/square-compass-darley-dale/).

Matlock Bath itself is like a sunny beach day during holidays, with bikers and tourists flocking to one of the most popular destinations in the Peak District for fish and chips, ice cream and other essential food groups.

WILDLIFE SAFARI The Derwent is always teeming with kingfishers, mergansers and other bird life. We usually see kites and buzzards soaring above the meadows flanking the windy stretches of the river.

ABOVE Heading towards the slalom course.

OTHER ATTRACTIONS Woodland Ways, run by our good friend Jason Ingammells, runs bushcraft courses and activities across the UK. Their main base is just upstream of Matlock, in their ancient woodland (W: www.woodland-ways.co.uk).

Visiting the Peak District National Park (W: www.peakdistrict.gov.uk) is a real treat with so many interesting trails and stunning scenery. We recommend the Monsal Trail, Dovedale and Thorpe Cloud for walking, and the iconic geological formations of Thor's Cave and Lud's Church.

At Matlock Bath you'll find the Heights of Abraham cable car ride, with its 60-acre hilltop park including incredible vistas and cavern tours (W: www.heightsofabraham.com).

While in the mood, you may wish to tour the world-famous Blue John Cavern in Castleford (W: https://www.bluejohn-cavern.co.uk) or Speedwell Cavern, which features an underground boat ride (W: https://speedwellcavern.co.uk).

Book into one of the local Youth Hostel Association (YHA) sites, such as the 17th-century manor Ilam Hall near Dovedale or the Jacobean mansion Hartington Hall near Buxton, where it is claimed that Bonnie Prince Charlie once stayed (W: www.yha.org.uk/hostel/yha-hartington-hall).

THE SHARED ECONOMY Rapid Horizons, run by our good friend and former GB paddler Jon Best, offers tubing, rafting, canoeing and kayaking at nearby Matlock (W: www.rapidhorizons.com), while Canoe Trail runs several introductions to moving trips at Matlock each year. You can book on with our team (W: www.canoetrail.co.uk).

NORTH OF ENGLAND

28 RIVER RIBBLE

Welcome to the red-rosed Ribble Valley of Lancashire. The Ribble Valley is a gem with gentle riffle rapids and bedrock from Clitheroe downstream building in volume as the Calder and Hodder join the flow. Further down the rapids grow in size with the 'Wheel' being the feature rapid of the river. Enjoy this northwest gem with stunning scenery as well as great fun rapids.

The Lowdown

DIFFICULTY
A lively whitewater paddle with easy rapids and a few more technical but still simple features.

DISTANCE Edisford Bridge to Ribchester Bridge: 12.7km.

DIRECTIONS The shuttle back to Edisford Bridge takes around 15 minutes on the backroads.
You can paddle on to Ribchester for another couple of kilometres or go big and head to Preston, which is another 22km of delightful north-western countryside.

HAZARDS
Check water levels for good coverage of rocks at start of paddle. Greater than 0.5m on the level is best and over 1m – 1.5m makes a more exciting whitewater experience.

CRAFT

	LOCATION	GRID REFERENCE	POST CODE	WHAT3WORDS
START	By Edisford Bridge	SD726414	BB7 3LA	arriving.aspect.crackled
WEIR	Weir (portage)	SD721391	BB7 3LL	stirs.rosier.ticked
S BEND RAPID	Rapid by footbridge, Grade 2	SD685365	BB6 8AN	newsprint.slides.soak
RAPID	The Wheel rapid, Grade 2	SD676358	BB6 8AJ	slams.wordplay.oldest
MAIN FINISH RIBCHESTER	River exit by layby, Ribchester Bridge	SD662356	PR3 3ZQ	shuffle.muffin.owned
FINISH (2) NEAR SPORTS GROUND	Riverside, Broadgate, at Preston	SD532282	PR1 8ET	punchy.before.hardly

BACKGROUND The River Ribble is a classic touring river. It has a bit of excitement with simple slabs and smaller rapids as well as some bigger features, building to a crescendo with the pièce de résistance, the Wheel rapid. The river weaves through Lancashire's rural lands with absolutely stunning riverbanks and lovely rapids. It is boosted by several tributaries including the Hodder and Calder. The river is blessed with great wildlife, beautiful old bridges and the occasional watering hole.

ABOVE Lining the canoe over the weir on the River Ribble near the start of the route.

A SLICE OF HISTORY The Red Rose of Lancaster (blazoned: *a rose gules*) was the heraldic badge adopted by the royal House of Lancaster in the 14th century. In modern times it symbolises the county of Lancashire. The War of the Roses were fought between two rival groups of the House of Plantagenet, from Lancaster and York, between 1455 and 1487.

Clitheroe Castle has sat on top of its limestone mound and dominated the local skyline and river valley for over 800 years. The Castle and grounds are now open daily and free to visit.

Dominating the landscape to the south of Ribble Valley is the mysterious Pendle Hill, an area steeped in the history of witchcraft, where 10 people were accused of witchcraft and executed in 1612. Visit the Roman bath ruins at Ribchester, which means 'fort beside the Ribble'. The Romans knew it as Brematennacum where the bath house was built around 100 AD.

ROUTE The launch site at Edisford is as picturesque as they come with a beautiful park, toilets and walks as well as a miniature railway. We had to remind ourselves of the task in hand as opposed to sight-seeing! Once on the river, the water

ABOVE Ash with Toby and Foxy in the canoe heading under one of the Ribble bridges.

sparkles with light shows as it dances over little drops and rock ledges. We were in our happy place.

Once you push off it's an ongoing challenge of finding the right lines and scouting rapids through a read-and-run technique. Read the river features and follow the main flow to avoid unnecessary rock collisions and scrapes. The river bends around to the left after the first hundred metres or so and immediately you'll see little threads of rock and slabs. It then straightens out for about 400m as you pass the caravan park on the left bank, and then kinks right, covering about 900m before reversing its direction again, turning back to the left and almost back on yourself and then on to a course south.

More bending and winding and 2.75km from the start, you'll paddle under a small bridge. Around 250m from this you'll reach a steep 1m drop/step weir. We lined our canoe down the left side of the weir face and walked around with the dogs. It looked like it would be simple to kayak over the edge for fun, but obviously you'd

LEFT Foxy stays on the bank whilst Rich follows Ash down a shallow riffle rapid.

joins from river left. The Ribble then swings a sharp 90-degree bend to the right.

Like an old friend, the river retains the same qualities and characteristics as it twists further down the valley, with pronounced bends left and right, and after 2.3km it passes under a small pipeline gantry. You've skirted around Brockhill to the south of the river course. About a kilometre downstream, it bends around to the right with farm buildings and houses on both the left and right bank. As you round the bend you'll see a footbridge and the river drops a little more with a Grade 2 short rapid (this is south of Hurst Green).

We had a bit of an adventure at this point with our three dogs craning to see people and refusing to sit as we bobbed down the rapid, an S-shape from the centre of the river over to the right side. There are some rocks here and we managed to glance a couple while fussing over our four-legged charges acting like excited pinball wizards! If you do take a swim here then feet up and float down to the pool at the bottom to pick up the pieces, and hit solid laughter mode. The river relaxes again and eases off anything more than a riffle rapid for the next 1.2km, at which point you're in the run in to the main event of this paddle: the Wheel.

The Wheel rapid is where the Ribble drops in elevation, picks up speed and squeezes through a narrower gap with some

need to check levels and inspect to ensure it doesn't have a stopper, which would be dangerous.

After more bends and 800m you'll reach Mitton Bridge with its stone arches, which is conveniently located next to a riverside pub, the Aspinall Arms. On the right bank you can see All Hallows Church as you approach Mitton. Below the bridge the river shows small, lateral drops and rock features, which would hinder progress in low water. The river bands around to the left and passes by Mitton Hall.

The river then remains simple, with little riffles and small drops as it rounds several bends, and about 700m downstream it marginally picks up pace with some bigger rock ledges. About 200m later you'll reach the River Hodder, which joins from the right side. The fields are now littered with spinneys and woodlands as you paddle the next stretch. Like buses, one river comes along and then another as the River Calder

larger rock formations protruding from the left bank constricting the flow. There's a matching rock formation on the right and this can cause interesting flow patterns as the water backs up. In higher water levels you may well experience a wave and a wet ride. Approaching the rapid the main flow is on river right, offering an easier channel over several slabs before the squeeze, which is right of the middle river. It's about 150m from start to finish.

After the squeeze there's a big pool, so again you can paddle through the gap if your experience and mood align. If not, a portage or lining down the right bank may be an option. The pool below has a beach on river left to empty open canoes or kayaks.

After another left-hand bend the river straightens and slows as you see the Ribchester Bridge spanning the river. We pulled in at river right and hauled our canoe up the steep bank before using a taxi for the shuttle back to our van.

EXTEND THE TRIP You can extend your route slightly by starting upstream in a number of locations, from Sawley Bridge or from the bridge on West Bradford Road, but be aware that there's a big weir (Waddow Weir) between the West Bradford road ridge and Edisford Bridge.

Alternatively, instead of exiting the river at Ribchester Bridge, continue on the Ribble for another 22km down to Preston. The river retains the same features of small rock slabs, gravel beds and riffle rapids as it winds onwards towards the city. In general it is slower without the more challenging rapids of the Wheel and footbridge (near Hurst Green), and there are some larger gravel bars and farms along its banks. Note, there aren't many easy exit points between Ribchester and Preston, so go for broke and paddle to Preston.

BELOW Paddling under one of the bridges with small riffle rapids.

OUR RICH ADVENTURE

We paddled the Ribble between lockdowns and stayed the night in a car park adjacent to the Covid test centre, which was a surreal experience, like something out of a post-apocalyptic film. The paddling high life! The river was stunning, with small shelf drops and chutes offering excellent paddling and a true sense of adventure. In a few particularly shallow places we did wade the canoe, being careful with our feet. The main rapid, the Wheel, is a large constriction of the river through a gap in the rocks causing waves, eddies and boils in higher waters.

At the footbridge over the river there's an S-bend rapid, which proved quite a challenge with three dogs in the canoe. Everyone was shuffling for a view and excited to see people on the bridge. With some dog and edge control, we made it safely to town. We both loved the Wheel although we have vowed to return in higher water to experience the white-knuckle rapid version.

CALORIE CREDITS

Edisford Bridge Country Pub at the put in offers good food (T: 01200 422637). We also explored the pubs in Clitheroe the night before our paddling trip. Try the riverside Aspinall Arms, located in the Ribble Valley at Mitton Bridge, which offers good food and drink (W: www.brunningandprice.co.uk/aspinallarms).

Getting out at Ribchester, there are several good watering holes, spoiling you for choice, including the café at Stydd Gardens, The Glasshouse (W: www.glasshousestydd.com), The Ribchester Arms (W: https://ribchesterarms.uk) and the Potters Barn Tea Room, which has a café and pottery painting (W: https://potters-barn.com).

Edisford Bridge Farm Caravan and Camping Site is set in beautiful scenery and offers spacious pitches (W: www.edisfordbridgecaravanandcamping.co.uk/index.php). There's also an indoor swimming pool just 500m away.

ABOVE You will need to negotiate several small rapids like this on the River Ribble.

WILDLIFE SAFARI Dippers, kingfishers and herons all frequent the Ribble Valley. We saw the first two, but had to be content with reported sightings of the third species. The Wild Boar Park, while not on the river, is home to a massive and eclectic collection of animals (W: www.wildboarpark.co.uk).

> **WHERE'S THE MAGIC?**
>
> The Ribble is one of our favourite rivers to paddle, with cascading gentle rapids tumbling over shallow rock ledges and gravel bars that build to a more exciting climax with the Wheel. Along the river route you'll feel privileged to enjoy such unspoilt water; our paddle was almost entirely without people, allowing us to share the experience together. The final few rapids really add the 'cherry on top' to a gripping day on the water.

OTHER ATTRACTIONS For more wildlife, why not visit the Brockholes nature reserve, run by The Wildlife Trust for Lancashire, Manchester and North Merseyside (W: www.brockholes.org), or the Turbary Woods Owl and Bird of Prey Sanctuary in Preston offers a fun and informative day out (T: 01772 323323). Bowland Wild Boar Park has tractor rides, a café and a menagerie of animals making it a five-star attraction to visit with the family. There's also a lodge, camping pitches and glamping pods for hire (W: www.wildboarpark.co.uk).

If you're interested in history, check out the Roman Museum at Ribchester to discover more about this huge empire that transformed Britain (W: https://ribchestermuseum.org).

BELOW Navigating under the bridges and through rapids is worth it to see the stunning River Ribble from the water.

29 RIVER OUSE, YORK AND THE RIVER URE

Unlock your inner Viking and reward yourself at a floating ice cream boat on this stunning city paddle amid the historic waterfronts and bridges of York. Extend the trip by starting upstream on the Ure at Aldwark, or paddling down to Naburn Lock. This is an easy paddle, but be aware of the other craft sharing these waters.

The Lowdown

DIFFICULTY
A gentle river meander with easy paddling.

DISTANCE Wooden toll bridge, Aldwark to Landing Lane, A to B: c. 24km.
Landing Lane to A64 viaduct, loop: 13km.
Landing Lane to Naburn Lock, A to B: 12.2km.

DIRECTIONS Park at the small layby area near the RSPCA centre on the outskirts of York. You can launch on the riverbank there with a short scramble down to the water's edge and return to the same location, so no need for shuttling. If you chose to extend your route to the old wooden toll bridge at Aldwark on the River Ure, then it's a 20km shuttle, which will take about 30 minutes.

HAZARDS

CRAFT

	LOCATION	GRID REFERENCE	POST CODE	WHAT3WORDS
PARKING	Landing Lane	SE582524	YO26 4RH	sticky.bottom.soil
START (1)	River bank	SE584525	YO26 4RH	desire.became.tiger
START (2)	Wooden toll bridge at Aldwark, River Ure	SE467621	YO26 9SL	topics.moss.really
POSSIBLE TURNING POINT	Blue Bridge (canal entrance)	SE605510	YO10 4NL	calms.scary.shout
	Naburn Lock	SE594444	YO19 6HN	pipes.regaining.cubes

BELOW Ouse Bridge on the route into York city centre.

BACKGROUND The River Ouse (and its tributary, the Ure) is a fantastic touring river, with sandy beaches and treelined banks leading to the ancient city of York, or Jorvik, as the Vikings knew it. The city is steeped in history and seeing it from the water gives you a whole new perspective on this beautiful place. Make sure you allow time to explore the old canal locks and bridges around the city. There are so many backwaters and interesting slipways, riverside cafés and restaurants, and even floating ice cream parlours!

ABOVE The fine detail on the beautiful Ouse Bridge.

A SLICE OF HISTORY York has enjoyed many names over time. The Romans knew it as Eboracum whereas the Saxons called it Eoforwick. After the Vikings, led by Ivar the Boneless, conquered the city in AD 866, Ivar and King Halfden renamed the city Jorvik.

The Foss Tributary that rises in Foss Crooks Woods travelling through the Vale of York is likely to have been named after the Roman word 'fossa' meaning ditch. At 31km that is some ditch by modern standards.

York has been declared one of the most haunted cities in Europe with over 500 sightings and hauntings reported according

ABOVE Old city defences overlooking York city centre.

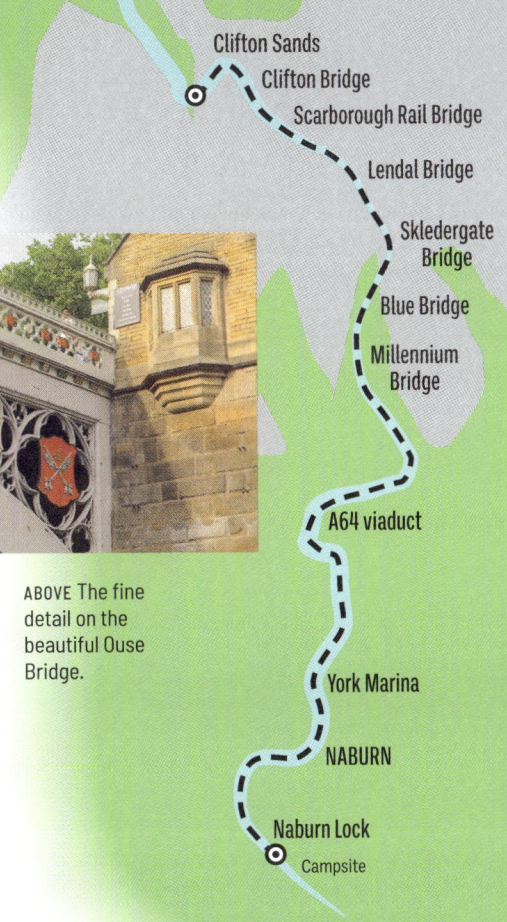

to the International Ghost Research Foundation. It is reported that one of those ghosts may be Guy Fawkes, famous for the gunpowder plot where he tried to blow up James I and Parliament. He was born in York in 1605.

ROUTE Launching from the small beach area outside the city, it's a short scramble down to the water's edge. Head downstream towards York, rounding the first bend, with sandy beaches (Clifton Sands) where you're likely to see dog walkers throwing sticks for their hounds. You've already covered 650m by the time you reach Clifton Bridge.

The banks are meadow-lined green spaces and the left bank is home to St Peter's School (you'll pass their boat house).

About a kilometre from Clifton Bridge you'll reach Scarborough Rail Bridge. The left land bank is home to Dame Judi Dench Walk, with York Observatory and Museum set back from the waterfront in the park. Around 400m later is Lendal Bridge, with The Perky Peacock café and bar on the south bank and the Full Moo Ice Cream Boat on the opposite bank. What a choice! Within a few paddle strokes you can enjoy both.

By now you should be getting into the tourist vibe and enjoying the sightseeing from your craft. About 400m on is the Ouse Bridge and the river opens up with converted warehouses on one bank and cafés and pubs on the north bank. We moored up at King's Staith Landing (City Cruises), where there's a slipway and variety of refreshments at the Esplanade.

Tower Gardens occupies the next section of the bank, just before Skeldergate Bridge, offering an oasis of green foliage. Skeldergate is 350m downstream from the Ouse Bridge. A further 250m on and you'll see the river widen, as the River Foss enters the Ouse. Spin around off the main flow and back on yourself and you can explore the Foss Basin, with its enormous bridge gates.

About 800m downstream you'll reach the Millennium Bridge. Look around, as the second roving ice cream parlour, Two Hoots Ice Cream Boat, is usually moored here. About 1.5km later and the river bends sharp right, and 500m after the bend you'll paddle under the A64 dual carriageway. This is a possible place to turn around, however, if you wish to paddle for longer, or do an A to B route, you can continue on. Returning

back to the start is an easy paddle, as the river is generally slow moving.

EXTEND THE TRIP Starting upstream at Aldwark Toll Bridge (W: https://www.aldwarkbridge.com), a privately owned toll bridge on the River Ure, which feeds into the Ouse, provides a fantastic blend of rural countryside and iconic English touring rivers combined with York's history and majesty. This section of paddle includes passing Linton-on-Ouse, Linton Lock with its whitewater feature, and the Linton Lock Inn and adds about 18km to your day. You can of course reduce the city element if you arrange a shuttle.

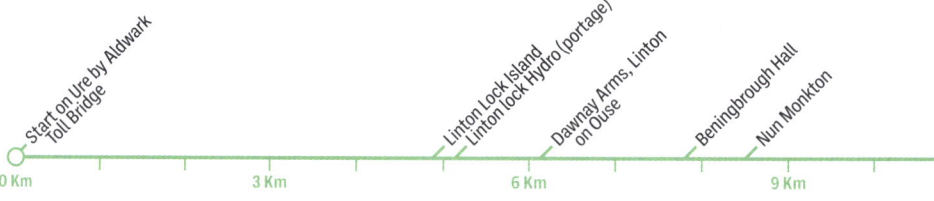

ABOVE The hubbub of York city centre.

Alternatively if you want to create the perfect A to B paddle through the city onwards to Naburn Lock, just keep paddling once you reach the A64 viaduct. The river loops and bends southwards past Bishopthorpe Palace, Bosun's Restaurant and onwards to the large York Marina, about 3km downstream. The river enters a large, meandering S-bend heading right at Naburn and swinging around to Acaster before the final straight down to the lock.

You can of course keep paddling beyond the lock towards Selby and on to Goole if you're seeking more adventure.

OUR RICH ADVENTURE

As a youngster, Rich and his family lived in Yorkshire while his dad, Alan, was working as an engineer, and there were plenty of visits to explore the North York Moors, the National Railway Museum and, of course, boat cruises on the Ouse. It was therefore such a delight, after a lifetime of paddling, to finally paddle this iconic stretch of water.

Our paddling trip on the Ouse involved playing on the Ure, throwing sticks for the dogs from the sandy banks, and paddling into the city to explore and enjoy an ice cream from a floating parlour. We also spotted various wild swimmers enjoying a secluded dip.

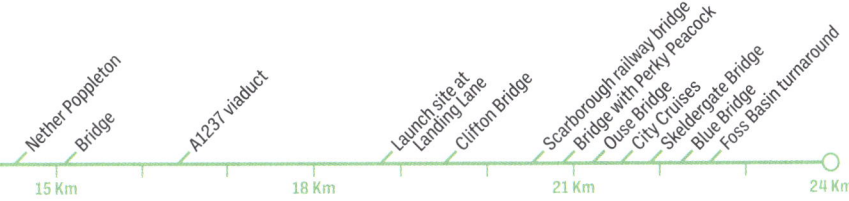

CALORIE CREDITS Grab a brew at The Perky Peacock, set in the 14th-century Barker Tower at Lendal Bridge (W: https://perkypeacock.co.uk).

Grab a 99 from The Full Moo Ice Cream Boat at Lendal Bridge (T: 07392 832893). Find Two Hoots Ice Cream Boat (T: 07835 044421) further down at the Millennium Bridge.

There's a wide range of restaurants, cafés and pubs on the Esplanade, just downstream of the Ouse Bridge. The iconic Bosun's Restaurant, located on the south bank, has panoramic river views (W: https://bosunsrestaurant.co.uk).

If you paddle as far as Naburn Lock you can enjoy tea and cake at the fabulous Tea by the Lock (W: www.teabythelock.co.uk).

Finally, reportedly there are 365 pubs in York, one for every day of the year – so enjoy!

WILDLIFE SAFARI We spotted cormorants, swans, geese and moorhens and plenty of kingfishers flitting along the riverbanks. Upstream, we saw plenty of coots and moorhens on the quieter stretches.

OTHER ATTRACTIONS The Jorvik Centre is a York institution, with its interpretive

> **WHERE'S THE MAGIC?**
>
> The River Ure leading into the River Ouse is one of our favourite touring rivers – wide-ranging countryside before hitting the historic cityscape that is York. There's so much to see and do here, it's well worth exploring for a few days.

exhibition capturing archaeological digs and animated characters showcasing Viking life (W: www.jorvikvikingcentre.co.uk).

Visit the National Railway Museum with exhibits including the *Flying Scotsman*, a bullet train, steam engines galore and the *Mallard*, the world's fastest steam locomotive (W: www.railwaymuseum.org.uk).

As outdoor folk, the Coast to Coast walk may entice you. It's an incredible national trail from St Bees in Cumbria to Robin's Hood Bay in North Yorkshire. Alfred Wainwright's famous walk takes in the North York Moors, the largest area of upland heather moors in the country, and the Yorkshire Dales (W: www.coasttocoast.uk).

Camp, glamp or caravan at the Mill Bridge Farm campsite just 6km outside of York and close to the river. Call 01904 656255.

Linton Weir is also a popular spot for playboaters. There is a new whitewater facility at the lock, which combines hydropower, fish passage and a short whitewater course all in one place.

THE SHARED ECONOMY Hire a canoe or kayak from The Boatyard, downstream from York (W: https://the-boatyard.co.uk/boat-hire).

ABOVE Old warehouses line the river in the city centre, though many have been converted into chic residences or businesses.

30 RIVER TEES: COTHERSTONE TO BARNARD CASTLE

This whitewater paddle has lots of solid Grade 2 technical features along the River Tees and traversing some of northern England's finest river valleys. The short river section has some lovely slab rapids and ends just downstream of the high imposing town bridge of Barnard Castle. There is a great small set of rapids, perfect for training, just below the get out, where you can practice skills. End your day by heading into Barnard Castle to enjoy its hilltop ambience.

The Lowdown

DIFFICULTY

A bubbly whitewater section with great rapids (Grade 2 river).

DISTANCE 6.2km, A to B.

DIRECTIONS Park in Cotherstone village, having unloaded near the football field (but don't park there). Carry down along the narrow track to access the river on the bend near the confluence with the River Balder. The shuttle by road is 6.5km and takes 8 to 10 minutes. There's a narrow layby adjacent to the wall at the get out by the Sills. Be sympathetic to other paddlers and leave room where possible. Access restrictions: ensure the river gauge is reading above 0.55 on the River App.

HAZARDS

CRAFT

	LOCATION	GRID REFERENCE	POST CODE	WHAT3WORDS
PARKING	Layby, Cotherstone	NZ047159	DL12 9BE	trend.teaspoons.shame
START	On bend near River Balder confluence	NZ013200	DL12 9NW	purest.untruth.indulges
RAPID	Reef rapid – paddle hard right	NZ039178	DL12 9BP	puddles.crumples.upholds
PORTAGE POINT	Portage the big weir	NZ046166	DL12 9AZ	evenings.monopoly.taller
FINISH	Steps by the wall	NZ047162	DL12 9BE	scrapped.glassware.twists

BACKGROUND The River Tees in the far-flung northern flanks of our land is one of the finest whitewater rivers in the country, with tight gorges, drops and weirs, and serious rapids with crux points where the river channels into narrow features that test the paddler. The route we have selected is a delightful whitewater section with great rapids to develop moving water skills such as breaking in and out, ferry gliding and reading the water.

A SLICE OF HISTORY

Set on a high rock above the River Tees, Barnard Castle takes its name from its 12th-century founder, Bernard de Balliol. It was later developed by the Beauchamp family and then passed into the hands of Richard III. With fantastic views over the Tees Gorge, this fortress sits on the fringe of an attractive working market town, also known as 'Barney', so there's plenty to do for families on a day out.

Stanwick Iron Age Fort is 15km from Barnard Casle and was an iron age fort utilising the natural bedrock as part of it defences. The ramparts and fort, over 6.5km of defences covering 766 acres, were important to the Brigantes, one of the most significant pre Roman tribes in Northern Britain.

Kirkcarrion is a Bronze Age round barrow burial site with a copse on top

ABOVE Ken Hughes side surfing a wave on the Tees Rapids (photo: Ken Hughes).

of a earth and stone mound. The site is surrounded by myth and mystery with it believed to be the grave of the Brigante Chieftain Caryn. Caryn's ashes were supposed to be buried there on the remote hilltop to pay respect with a stone cairn and the Welsh-Celtic words *Carreg Caryn*, meaning 'Caryn's burial heap', hence the site's present name.

The mystery continues with Peg Powler, a water sprite or perhaps a mermaid who is said to reside deep in the waters of the River Tees. Known for her long green, water-drenched hair, you might get an inkling of Peg's presence in the river if the surface suddenly takes on a frothy appearance. You have been warned.

Map labels:
- River Balder
- Gravel bar island
- River Tees
- Red Lion PH
- COTHERSTONE
- Gravel bar island
- Rapids
- Riffles
- Riffles
- Rapids
- Silver Bridge
- Weir (portage)
- Red Well Inn
- BARNARD CASTLE
- Country Bridge
- Steps on left
- Rapids

ABOVE Kayakers playing on the River Tees (photo: Ken Hughes).

The abbey of St Mary and St John the Baptist was founded at Egglestone between 1195 and 1198 for Premonstratensian canons. Remains include much of the 13th-century church and a range of living quarters, with traces of their ingenious toilet drainage system. It's free to visit and you pay a few pounds for parking.

Built between 1171 and 1187, Bowes Castle changed hands plenty of times in its history including being besieged by King William of Scotland (1165–1214). The impressive ruins of Henry II's 12th-century keep are on the site of a Roman fort and guard the approach to the strategic Stainmore Pass over the Pennines, not too far away from the river.

ROUTE This a solid route running from Cotherstone down to the historic and beautiful Barnard Castle and incorporating classic Grade 2 rapids. Once you launch near the meeting with the River Balder on the bend, turn downstream and head towards the castle. The levels need to read 0.55 and above on the river gauge to avoid scraping your craft all the way down. At lower levels you'll see gravel bars and beach areas.

As you round the bend to the right the water drops away into the first small rapid with riffles and smaller rocks to focus the mind. The river then straightens with more bouncy waves, which are all straightforward.

Around 800m on, the river bends slowly right with more rapids, waves and the occasional rock breaking the surface to contend with. Lance Beck joins on river right. The banks are lush and heavily tree-lined here, providing shade and shelter from the elements.

LEFT Big air on the River Tees (photo: Ken Hughes).

Another straight section follows, and 850m on the river completes a tighter S-bend, starting to the left. This river does require you to set angles to avoid hazards and avoid faster water pushing you into obstacles. As you round the bend there's an island ahead of you with the line down the right side of the island where the flow produces a chunky rapid with some rocks. You are passing West Holme House and then East Holme House on the map.

The river runs true and straight again here, with flow and small waves for about 500m. It's joined by Grise Beck on the right bank. Another S-bend follows, starting with a left-hand turn with a shingle rapid. The easy route is river left, with plenty of eddies to enjoy on river right to hone skills. Once round the bend the rapids continue at pace with 500m of simple but fun rapids and plenty of eddies to hit. The river bends hard right near Towler Hill with a few twists and turns coming up.

Once around the bend, Reef Rapid is coming up, where the rock bed forms a reef across the river. This is usually best run on hard river right. In some higher levels the centre channel can be run. There's a long, flat section after this for any rescues that might need completing.

The river now bends left now to straighten up for the last couple of kilometres into Barnard Castle. On the bend is the Viaduct Stanchion Rapid, where there is a clear channel and exit flow on river right with some waves and a potential wet ride.

The river still offers some riffle rapids on the final approach to Barnard Castle as you pass a tree-covered woodland on river right. You'll see a metal footbridge followed by a big weir. The safest option is to exit

BELOW Paddling one of the slower stretches of the River Tees (photo: Ken Hughes).

RIGHT Ash running the section above Barnard Castle (photo: Ken Hughes).

the river on the right side just after the footbridge at the small tributary and portage around the weir. Experienced paddlers can paddle the side of the weir if safe, but avoid the centre, which has a big stopper.

Once around the weir, the rapids continue down to the iconic Barnard Castle bridge. There are plenty of rocks in this section, so stay sharp as you finish the trip to avoid broaching (be careful of the bridge pillar, which presents a broach risk). Don't forget to grab some photos as you pass under the bridge. Exit on the right-hand side below the stone wall. There's a set of steps and a layby by the Sills roadway.

EXTEND THE TRIP There's a great small section for improving skills from the egress point down the short rapid below to above the green bridge located at the bottom of the rapid. This short section of whitewater is great for working on traditional skills. You can use the bank to line and track back up or there's a path on the right bank with a track back to a five-bar gate. Don't be enticed to paddle on from here without a solid plan, as there's some serious whitewater for more advanced paddling below this point.

EXTEND THE TRIP The Tees continues for many kilometres in either direction from the route described here. Sections upstream and downstream include technical river features such as big weirs, gorges and rapids that need to be respected. Typically, they are used for more advanced courses and coaching for experienced paddlers. We would recommend hiring a whitewater coach or guide to paddle them for the first time or join your local club to access coaches and leaders who can help you develop the necessary skills.

OUR RICH ADVENTURE Many of our Canoe Trail team have paddled and trained on the River Tees with Ken Hughes over the past decade or so, enjoying expert coaching from the canoe master. We've been able to explore these waters at the same time as raising our game with traditional skills such as lining and tracking, poling and lots of work on reading the water.

CALORIE CREDITS Stop off at Cross Lanes Organic Farm Shop & Café to stock up on wholesome snacks and lunch for your river journey (W: https://crosslanesorganics.co.uk).

Dating back to the 1750s and located on a stunning stretch of the River Tees in an AONB, The Fox & Hounds sits proudly on the west green in the picturesque village of Cotherstone and has a friendly and cosy atmosphere (W: www.cotherstonefox.co.uk).

WILDLIFE SAFARI The Teesdale Valley has plenty of wildlife and is a designated AONB. There's a chance to see dippers, otters and kingfishers enjoying life in the river valleys and gorges.

OTHER ATTRACTIONS Star gaze under the dark skies of the Tees Valley at Grassholme Observatory (W: www.grassholmeobservatory.com). Or why not pack a bike for your visit to Teesdale and enjoy the fantastic tree-filled trails of the Descend Bike Park near Bishop Auckland (W: www.descendbikepark.com)?

For history buffs there's Egglestone Abbey, the charming ruins of a small monastery set on the bend of the River Tees just upstream of the infamous Abbey Rapids, where the river cascades through a narrow gorge (W: www.english-heritage.org.uk/visit/places/egglestone-abbey).

While in the mood, make time to visit the magnificent 14th-century Raby Castle and deer park, which has spectacular gardens, lakes and a yurt café set in more than 22,000ha of beautiful countryside.

> **WHERE'S THE MAGIC?**
>
> The River Tees is enticing, like a great film or book you want to revisit time and time again. Rapids and features punctuate this river journey, ensuring there's excitement and inspiration around every corner.

A short drive takes you to High Force waterfall, where the Tees drops 21m across the Whin Sill. High Force is situated within the beautiful Upper Teesdale countryside in the North Pennines AONB.

THE SHARED ECONOMY Canoeing ninja Ken Hughes is local to the Tees and is one of the best coaches in the country on moving water and also sits on the British Canoeing technical panel. He offers courses to support and inspire his customers to challenge themselves to progress in the higher grade waters.

BELOW Sunset over Egglestone Abbey above the River Tees.

31 WINDERMERE: THE LAKELAND JEWEL

This lakeland jewel, a glacial ribbon lake with 18 islands along its length, is a tourism mecca and a hive of activity. You'll be joined by hire boats, steamers and other craft as you paddle these deep waters. The lake is massive and has multiple personalities, from the more remote Low and High Wray, Harrowslack and Wray Castle on the Western shore to the more lively Bowness on Windermere and Ambleside. Several days of exploring at a leisurely pace on land and water will make this an exciting and unforgettable break.

The Lowdown

DIFFICULTY
A charming paddle with circular route or A to B options on this open water lake.

DISTANCE Central islands including Belle Isle (2hr): 3.5km.
Ambleside and back to start, loop (full day): 16.5km.
Harrowslack to Ambleside, A to B (half day): 8.5km.
Harrowslack to Newby Bridge/Fell Foot, A to B (half day): 9.7km.

DIRECTIONS The only car ferry takes around ten minutes to cross the centre of Windermere. It runs from Ferry Nab, just south of Bowness, to Ferry House at Far Sawrey, and operates all year round.

Driving around or taking the ferry across to Far Sawrey gets you off the beaten track and away from the hubbub quickly. Launching from the Harrowslack National Trust car park offers a lovely paddle to the islands, or further if you fancy it.

HAZARDS

CRAFT

	LOCATION	GRID REFERENCE	POST CODE	WHAT3WORDS
PARKING	Harrowslack National Trust car park	SD388960	LA22 0LP	redouble.market.fleet
START	Water's edge, Windermere	SD389960	LA22 0LR	fearfully.jigsaw.headings
FINISH IF A TO B ROUTE NORTH	Ambleside Beach waterhead	NY376032	LA22 0EP	nickname.entitles.spouting
FINISH IF A TO B ROUTE SOUTH	National Trust, or onwards to Newby Bridge	SD379868	LA12 8NN	stun.marathons.cloud

BACKGROUND Windermere is the largest natural lake in England at over 18km long and 66.7m at its deepest point, and offers a variety of paddling. The islands located in the mid-section close to Bowness-on-Windermere are great for family paddling and exploring seemingly untouched lands.

A SLICE OF HISTORY With settlements dating back to more than 5,000 years ago, the region quickly became a source for stone axes and the site of many stone circles.

On the shores of Windermere, the well-marked remains of Ambleside Roman Fort date from the 2nd century. It was probably built under Hadrian's rule to guard the Roman road from Brougham to Ravenglass and to act as a supply base. Run by English Heritage, the fort is located at the top end of the lake.

A book entitled *Guide to the Lakes* was published in 1810, which changed the future of tourism in the Lake District forever. William Wordsworth's guide mapped not only points of significance, but also how the individual should view certain locations to feel a sense of the sublime.

In July 2017 the Lake District was awarded UNESCO World Heritage Status, which recognises the areas for its abundance of remarkable natural beauty.

ROUTE Carry your craft 100m to the water's edge from the National Trust car park at Harrowslack. Immediately you'll see the islands parked in the waters opposite Bowness-on-Windermere. There are lots of smaller islands, the largest of which is Belle Isle.

In terms of the route, it seems a little prescriptive to say paddle clockwise this way, or vice versa. Even in breezy conditions you can skip across to the islands using the lee as shelter. Given the

ABOVE Kayaking around the islands on Windermere.

length of the lake, in windier conditions it can produce waves and bigger swell, so check the forecast. It's about 200m across to Belle Isle as the crow (or swan) might fly, but you can reduce this by hugging the shore if needs be.

Around 550m to the north-west of Belle Isle are two smaller islands that you can paddle between, working your way north to round the top of the two furthest islands of the cluster, which are another 650m on. We practised rescues on this course and also grabbed a bite to eat on the foreshore of the islands, which was a calming place to spend some time. The total distance to circumnavigate these islands is 3.5km.

Alternatively, bay hugging and hopping north offers a different kind of trip, allowing you to paddle a much bigger circuit up to Ambleside, passing plenty of landmarks and places of interest before turning south back to Bowness and crossing back to the start. Typically, it is safer and more interesting to hug the bays and shoreline to complete the circuit rather than plough down the centre.

Head north past the islands and aim for the High Wray bay, which is 5km ahead on the shore with Wray Castle a further 500m on and the Low Wray Campsite another 500m. From there, depending on your meandering route, you're just over 2km from Ambleside on the far north banks. Depending on conditions, bay hopping across the bigger indents on the map on the east side will speed up your journey.

After about 1.3km you'll pass Low Wood Bay Resort & Spa. Paddle onwards to Brockhole Pier, a new transit landmark 1km south. Cut across White Cross bay, enjoying the cruising aspect of life on the water. The next few kilometres take you down towards Bowness and the bigger Belle Isle, but you'll pass several small islets on the right-hand side before the big island after 14.5km or so of your trip. You'll now see the familiar territory of Belle Isle, where you can paddle

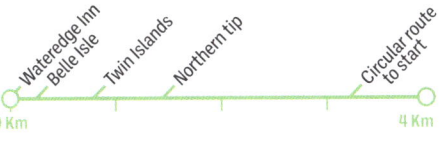

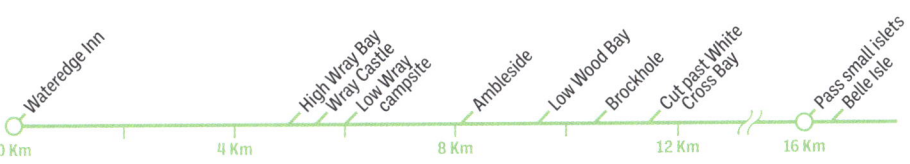

ABOVE Windermere gets into your bones. Expect to laugh out loud.

down either side, the eastern side being the shortest route back to the launch site at Harrowslack.

EXTEND THE TRIP

Once into the groove of Lakeland paddling, consider a trip to the far south of the lake to Newby Bridge, which is a slightly longer distance to the paddle covered above.

Departing your familiar and friendly foreshore near Harrowslack, head south past the ferry route and in essence just keep paddling. Again, hug the shores for more wildlife and interesting sights as you paddle past some great locations with unusual names, such as Green Naze Wyke, Lazy Bay (surely a place to stop and rest) and Karen Island!

Around 9.5km the mere (Saxon word for 'lake') narrows into the pretty River Leven, where life appears more busy as visitors descend on Fell Foot (National Trust). About 500m down the narrows is a car park. The river starts in a gentle fashion, changing course, heading right, and then bending south for about 1km down to the Swan Hotel and Newby Bridge. But heading past the bridge there's serious Grade 2 whitewater, with weirs and drops and then a solid Grade 3. This is technical and advanced paddling, so best avoided unless you're an experienced whitewater paddler.

OUR RICH ADVENTURE

We have paddled and explored Windermere on many occasions and have even used it as a detour for fish and chips on the water travelling back from our adventures in the north.

Rich also completed his British Canoeing

ABOVE Fun times SUP'ing on Windermere.

(now Paddle UK) touring leader provider assessment on Windermere in solid Force 4 conditions, spending lots of time upside down while demonstrating his rescues. Our adventures have also included exploring the islands on the western shore from Harrowslack and zigzagging across the lake. Ash and Rich love the film version of *Swallows and Amazons*, which was inspired by Windermere and Coniston, and always imagine ourselves as paddling pirates while adventuring here.

CALORIE CREDITS Set in the blissful countryside of the southern Lake District, the Masons Arms is a Lakeland institution, with accommodation and a locally sourced menu (W: https://masonsarmsstrawberry bank.co.uk). Or choose from light snacks to restaurant dining at The Boathouse at Bowness-on-Windermere (W: https://theboathouse-windermere.co.uk). There's also a coffee stand with light snacks at Far Sawrey ferry landing.

The Boardwalk Bar & Grill offers a broad menu to be enjoyed in their relaxed and friendly environment with views over the lake. Dogs are always welcome on the outdoor terrace and indoors on the ground floor (W: https://boardwalkbowness.com).

The Swan Hotel is nestled at the foot of Windermere by Newby Bridge just where the River Leven departs for whitewater adventures. There's gardens and great views as well as plenty of food and drink options (W: www.swanhotel.com).

WILDLIFE SAFARI Windermere wildlife is abundant and vibrant, with red squirrels, red deer and plenty of bird life on the water. The lake is home to cormorants, Canadian and greylag geese, coots, grebes and goldeneye. There are nesting ospreys around Cumbria too – visit the Cumbria Wildlife Trust to check webcams and get updates (W: www.cumbriawildlifetrust.org.uk/).

OTHER ATTRACTIONS The viewing platform at Claife Viewing Station was built in 1790 for the first tourists to the Lake District, with platform views framed by coloured glass. The café on site serves tea, cake and scrumptious delicacies (W: www.nationaltrust.org.uk/visit/lake-district/claife-viewing-station-and-windermere-west-shore).

Take a stroll to Stock Ghyll Waterforce,

> **WHERE'S THE MAGIC?**
>
> Windermere is the mighty jewel in the crown of the Lake District National Park. It is narrow and rambling in layout, offering a feeling of exclusivity and remote paddling despite obvious other users. The central islands allow for many an exciting island-hopping adventure.

a scenic 21m-tall waterfall in a wooded area with a great viewpoint and fascinating industrial heritage (W: www.visitcumbria.com/amb/stock-ghyll-force/).

If you're looking to stay a while in the Lakes, the homely YHA Ambleside offers self-catering or meals at their restaurant (W: www.yha.org.uk/hostel/yha-ambleside). Or you could book into Low Wray Campsite in Ambleside, which is set on the banks of Windermere. This stunning site offers a wide-range of camping options including traditional pitches with waterfront, lake, meadow or woodland views, or camping pods, safari tents, space for campervans and even two suspended tree tents (W: www.nationaltrust.org.uk/holidays/lake-district/low-wray-campsite).

Get inspired by reading Arthur Ransome's *Swallows and Amazons*, which drew inspiration from around the Lake District. At Windermere Jetty

LEFT Sunset over Windermere after a great day paddling.

ABOVE Paddling with a multi-craft group on Windermere.

Museum (W: https://lakelandarts.org.uk/windermere-jetty-museum/) you'll find the two 1950s wooden sailing boats used in the 2016 film adaptation, chosen because they're small enough for a child to sail, but can also hold a camera crew and their equipment!

This area is known for its literary legacy, and down the road you'll find The Magical World of Beatrix Potter, which has themed tea parties, trails and storytelling (W: www.hop-skip-jump.com).

THE SHARED ECONOMY

The Windermere Outdoor Adventure Centre offers canoeing, kayaking, windsurfing and sailing with courses, multi-activity days and guided tours (W: www.better.org.uk/leisure-centre/south-lakeland/windermere-outdoor-adventure-centre).

The Hodge Howe Watersports Centre at Windemere School is a Royal Yachting Association (RYA) Training Centre and RYA British Youth Sailing Recognised Club. It offers expert instruction to children in all manner of exciting activities (W: www.windermereschool.co.uk/beyond-the-classroom/water-sport-centre).

Visit the team at Stoked Watersports at Fell Foot to get active and on the water (W: www.stokedwatersports.co.uk/locations/fell-foot-park-windermere-sup-and-kayak-hire)., or check in with LakeSUP at YMCA Lakeside at Newby Bridge for SUP hire and tuition (W: https://lakes-sup.co.uk). Finally, Windermere Canoe Kayak is a large shop and hire fleet covering all your paddle sports needs, situated at Bowness-on-Windermere (W: www.windermerecanoekayak.com).

32 LAKE DISTRICT: ULLSWATER

Plot a course for one of William Wordsworth's favourites, one of Britain's most iconic lakes, offering towering peaks, a waterfall, and a relaxed paddling location amid the beautiful Ullswater Valley. There's so much to do in the region, you can lose yourself for days – or longer, depending on how the mood takes you.

The Lowdown

DIFFICULTY
You can opt for short or longer paddles and explore this water at your leisure.

DISTANCE Enjoy a 7km circular paddle around the Western End of the lake going around the islands to Glenridding or a 12km paddle to Pooley Bridge making it a memorable A to B trip. The shuttle is 13km from Pooley Bridge to Glenridding taking about 20 minutes.

DIRECTIONS Our recommended launch site, the Glencoyne car park run by the National Trust, is a bit more off-grid, but you can also launch from Pooley Bridge at the head of Ullswater or at Glenridding near Ullswater 'Steamers' to get on the water quickly.

HAZARDS

CRAFT

	LOCATION	GRID REFERENCE	POST CODE	WHAT3WORDS
START	Beach near Glencoyne car park (south bound), A592	NY387188	CA11 0JS	headless.tumblers.tracking
FINISH (1)	Ullswater Steamers, Glenridding	NY389169	CA11 0PB	shows.saunas.multiples
FINISH (2)	Granny Dowbekins Tearooms, Pooley Bridge	NY469244	CA10 2NP	decking.treble.president

BELOW SUP'ing across to Norfolk Point towards Glenridding.

LEFT Rich and Foxy departing from Glencoyne car park and beach.

BACKGROUND At 14.5km long, about 1.2km wide and 60m deep, Ullswater is the second-largest lake in the Lake District and widely considered to be one of its most beautiful, with its distinctive bend two-thirds of the way down and views to Helvellyn. Glenridding on the southern end of the lake offers plenty of outdoors shops and great walking, while Ullswater Steamers has been providing cruises on the lake in its heritage 'steamers' for more than 160 years.

A SLICE OF HISTORY Ullswater was formed after the last Ice Age when a glacier scooped out the valley floor, which was then filled with meltwater when the glacier retreated.

The lake is said to be the most beautiful in Lakeland, inspiring perhaps its most famous visitor, English poet William Wordsworth, to write of it, 'It's the happiest combination of beauty and grandeur which any of the lakes affords'. Such was his admiration for the area, Wordsworth produced his own Lake District guide book – anonymously at first, but it was eventually published in 1822 and proved to be so popular it reached its fifth edition.

Ullswater is also famous for its fleet of heritage 'steamers', which have been cruising these waters for more than 160 years, come rain or shine. Built in 1877, the MY *Lady of the Lake* is believed to be the oldest passenger ferry in the world.

ROUTE Launching from the beach near the Glencoyne car park, used by a lovely little community of like-minded paddle folk, you can opt to head in either direction or plan a shorter loop to take in the small islands close by, including Norfolk, Cherry Holm and Wall Holm. There are a couple more smaller islands close to the far shore at Glenridding, allowing the chance for a simple bimble at the western end of the lake. Note, the route down to Pooley Bridge is a much longer

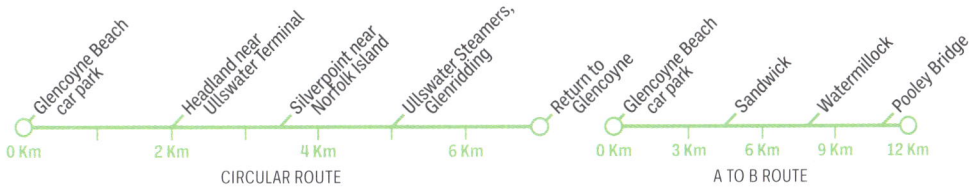

CIRCULAR ROUTE — A TO B ROUTE

paddle and certainly one for the more committed.

If you head south on the lake, your first main target is Norfolk Island, which is about 600m away, with Silver Bay and Silver Point sitting behind it. Heading in the general direction of Glenridding, there are various small islets close to the east shore. First comes Lingy Holm and then Wall Holm as you paddle past Blowick Bay. The last time we paddled here we raced one of the lake 'steamers' as it cruised past us back to base.

Roughly 2km down the lake you'll arrive at Cherry Holm, the last island, and be level with Glenridding Beck and the 'steamer' ferry landing. At this end of the lake there are small bays around the edges and at St Patrick's Boat Landing a little café serving cake, ice cream and hot drinks. The end of the lake is now less than 3km from your start point. Goldrill Beck enters the lake roughly in the middle at the southern end. The large hill to the south is Place Fell and if you fancy a surf 'n' turf experience, it's 657m to the summit.

Returning to Glencoyne offers a lovely paddle with plenty to explore and enjoy – perfect for a family trip and messing about on the water.

EXTEND THE TRIP If you'd like to spend longer on the water you can head north-east along the lake towards Pooley Bridge about 10km away, and if prevailing winds are assisting this makes for a lovely canoe sailing trip. The protruding headland where Aira Beck joins the lake is about 2km away and beyond this the lake has a noticeable dog leg at 5km, close to the Outward Bound Trust centre at Gowbarrow Bay.

WHERE'S THE MAGIC?

The magic is in the hills that surround these waters; they truly lift the spirits as you paddle this gorgeous lake.

OUR RICH ADVENTURE We've paddled every nook and cranny of this lake, and even climbed the hills to enjoy the views of the water from a different angle. We've camped on these shores, including a stay just as we came out of lockdown, and I also completed some of my touring leader provider course here. The lake is often a hive of activity with wild swimmers, hikers, paddlers and dog walkers all sharing this lovely space.

CALORIE CREDITS Fantastic tea rooms and cafés are dotted around the lake. Granny Dowbekins Tearooms and Gardens at Pooley Bridge has fab home-cooked and locally sourced food (W: https://grannydowbekins.co.uk), while the family-run Sun Inn and hotel serves award-winning ales and great food (W: https://suninnpooleybridge.co.uk).

Aira Force Tea Rooms are midway down the

ABOVE Kayakers out on Ullswater.

ABOVE Ash and William spending quality SUP time on Ullswater.

lake in the National Trust-run Aira Force and Gowbarrow Park (www.nationaltrust.org.uk/visit/lake-district/aira-force-and-gowbarrow-park), or check out Fellbites Café in Glenridding (W: www.fellbitescafe.co.uk).

Grasmere is 40 minutes' drive away, but it's worth the detour for its world-famous gingerbread (W: www.grasmereginger bread.co.uk).

For those not in the know, we'd highly recommend using the Tebay services just north of Junction 28, where you can get a delicious home-cooked meal or stock up on farm shop goodies for your paddling adventures (W: www.tebayservices.com).

WILDLIFE SAFARI

The Lake District is a stronghold for the elusive red squirrel, which remains one of the key wildlife draws to this area. You may also be lucky enough to see ospreys fishing in the lake or peregrines hunting over the hills and rocky crags.

OTHER ACTIVITIES

Walk the mighty Helvellyn (950m) or even take a wander up the hills overlooking the lake. If you'd rather stay at lower levels, you can cruise the lake with the world-famous Ullswater Steamers (W: www.ullswater-steamers.co.uk).

You can also hire SUPs and have a go with wake boarding at Wake & Surf (W: www.wakeandsurf.co.uk), or Alfresco Adventures offer a wide range of activities including gorge walking, SUPs, caving and rock climbing (W: www.alfrescoadventures.co.uk).

THE SHARED ECONOMY

Set sail, paddle a canoe or book team-building activities with the Glenridding Sailing Centre near the jetty (W: www.glenriddingsailingcentre.co.uk), while Ullswater Paddleboarding SUP hire and coaching is on the northern shore of the lake offering hire and lessons (W: www.ullswaterpaddleboarding.co.uk).

33 DERWENT WATER AND RIVER

The Lake District is a wondrous place, known for its rolling hills, waters and meres (as opposed to 'lakes') and lots of activities to get you excited for the great outdoors. This charming day-trip paddle will see you exploring two stunning areas of open water, one the only official 'lake' in the Lake District National Park, joined by a small and narrow river, making this feel like a real adventure.

The Lowdown

DIFFICULTY

DISTANCE Derwent Water to Bassenthwaite Lake: 11km (+6-7km to explore the lake).

DIRECTIONS Park at the National Trust Kettlewell car park on the south-west corner of Derwent Water, just off the B5289. There's another car park further up near Ashness Pier. Access restrictions: you need to purchase a permit to paddle on Bassenthwaite Lake, which you can get online from the National Park website at £7 per day. https://www.lakedistrict.gov.uk/visiting/things-to-do/water/bassenthwaite-permits

HAZARDS

CRAFT

*kneel down as necessary

BACKGROUND Derwent Water is the third-largest lake in the Lake District National Park, covering 5 square kilometres and containing two islands. The River Derwent sneaks east from here into Bassenthwaite Lake, the only official lake by name in the Lake District (the other fifteen are known as waters or meres). At the western end of Derwent is the outdoor centre and shallows decorated with reeds and lots of bird life. The lake has plenty of small beaches and access points via National Trust car parks, so it's worth getting membership for the free parking.

The eastern end is more developed, with a marina and other facilities offering plenty for tourists to enjoy. The entrance to the narrow river is hidden close by the marina and you feel like you're exploring a bayou, which wouldn't look out of place in the American Deep South. It winds delicately through the scrub land, a small weir and stony beaches, and under several small bridges, including a Victorian-looking suspension bridge.

33 • DERWENT WATER AND RIVER

	LOCATION	GRID REFERENCE	POST CODE	WHAT3WORDS
PARKING AND LAUNCH SITE	Kettlewell car park	NY266195	CA12 5UU	ghost.cashier.relieves
PARKING FOR SHUTTLE	Woodend Brow car park	NY218276	CA12 5SJ	amends.overtime.housework
START	Derwent River	NY255232	CA12 5NS	layover.slippery.committed
	Footbridge	NY253237	CA12 5RE	tame.downcast.sculpting
	Small weir	NY251238	CA12 5RA	serves.chat.gracing
	Start of Bassenthwaite Lake	NY230274	CA12 4QD	amazed.inserting.imitate
FINISH	Car park, Old Coach Road	NY218276	CA12 5SQ	brand.printout.machine

ROUTE Derwent Water is shallow near the launching point and depending on your paddling plan you can explore the outer reaches of the lake or make a beeline for the islands, or mix the two. The two main islands – St Herbert's and Rampsholme – are easily visible from the shore about 1.8km respectively from the beach. The Scarf Stones islet is nestled between.

Further up Derwent Water you'll also see Lord's Island on the right protecting Strand Shag Bay. It reminded me of our orca experience off another Lord's Island when we sea kayaked off Alaska. Paddling

ABOVE Ash paddling the small weir drop on the River Derwent.

past Friar's Crag on the eastern shore, you have Derwent Isle directly ahead of you to the north.

All the islands have stony beaches and are clad in trees, making them look like something straight out of *Swallows and Amazons*, although the classic children's novel was actually inspired by a cross between Windermere and Coniston. Keswick, up on the hill, and Crow Park sit behind and to the right of Derwent Isle and now if you want to paddle on the Derwent River, you need to head to the north-west (top corner) towards Derwent Water Marina and Portinscale village.

Depending on the time of year and whether there are rushes or not, access to the river is obvious or a little more hidden. It sits alongside the Keswick Camping and Caravanning Club site and is a narrow, treelined corridor to Bassenthwaite. The river bends slightly to the right as you pass the campsite and then meets up with the River Greta.

The river then completes a massive S-bend from left and back to right again, with lovely little gravel beaches and a gentle flow carrying you onwards. You'll pass under a pedestrian suspension bridge with a much larger and longer gravel beach on the right. We stopped here for snacks and a picnic with the dogs to play in the sun. There's plenty of room for skimming and stone-balancing challenges to occupy family and friends.

The river straightens out for 150m and then drops over a small measuring weir for river level monitoring height. This weir is easily shootable in a canoe or a kayak, but if you'd rather not, you could scramble up the bank and walk around. After the weir the river kinks around to the right, passing under the bridge for High Hill Road and then a second one for the Old Coach Road.

You can relax and enjoy the very slow-flowing river for the next 4.75km to the lake, looking out for wildlife such as otters and kingfishers. This definitely felt like a good place for some outdoor alone time, as we didn't see another person for the majority of the day. If it feels deeply spiritual and as old as the hills, then it probably is and that's a good thing.

BELOW SUP safari on Derwent Water with Ash heading for the islands.

The river runs slowly, unhurried by time, but still has plenty of bends, pools and small islands to occupy your attention. There are a couple of farm tracks past the river buildings, reminding you that you need a permit to paddle in Bassenthwaite Lake. The river shallows as you reach the southern shores of the lake (this one is actually a lake!) and you can explore its 6.4km length. We exited via the small car park on the Old Coach Road. It was definitely a tricky portage to carry across

LEFT A family lunch stop on the River Derwent by the footbridge and beach area.

the A66, but we were there out of season, meaning limited traffic. The other exit point on the lake is almost opposite St Bega's Church on the eastern shore where there is another car park.

Note, on the foreshore between Calf Close Bay and Broomhill Point is a remarkable stone carving called the Hundred Year Stone, made from glacial stone carved by Peter Randall Page. It was commissioned by the National Trust to mark the organisation's centenary.

EXTEND THE TRIP

The River Derwent leaves Bassenthwaite to the north opposite the Herdcroft Caravan Park. It continues up to Cockermouth before meeting the sea there. It also passes the Lakes Distillery, which is worth a visit.

Spend more time enjoying the tranquillity of Derwent Water heading. There's an activity centre and plenty of bays to explore with small islets and islands. Or you could check out the other Lake District paddles provided in this book (see Route 31, page 199 and Route 32, page 206).

A SLICE OF HISTORY

The geological origins of Keswick and the North Lakes lie in the Ice Age, when glacier erosion shaped the landscape of mountains, valleys and lakes. The first evidence of settlement dates back to the Stone Age, when Neolithic man used stone axes to make clearings in the forested hills and valleys to grow crops and keep livestock. Three axes have been found inside Castlerigg Stone Circle, which dates back some four thousand years to around the time of these early farming communities.

Castlerigg is an English Heritage managed stone circle perched above Derwent. It is magnificently set on a hill with panoramic views and the mountains of Helvellyn and High Seat as a backdrop. It is also believed to be among the earliest British circles, dating to 3000 BC, during the Neolithic period.

The George Hotel is Keswick's oldest coaching inn, dating back to the 16th-century.

Mirehouse has been added to over the centuries, while Wordsworth and other famous poets were regular guests here. The Spedding family still live in the house, which they inherited in 1802.

Force Crag Mine, located near Braithwaite, is a long-serving mine and Threlkeld Quarry provided a century of employment for the local workforce. The first records for quarrying at Honister Slate Mines date back as far as 1643 and they employed over 100 men until its final closure in 1986.

OUR RICH ADVENTURE After the confinement of the Covid-19 lockdowns, we were able to get out in our van for several nights in the Lake District. We watched the open water swimming and paddling communities come and go like a never-ending time-lapse of fun in the outdoors, and we too enjoyed a sunset paddle on SUPs and kayaks.

The following day, with dogs on board, we had one of our most memorable paddles following the Derwent River to the more

ABOVE Sunset silhouettes on Derwent make for the happiest memories.

secluded Bassenthwaite Water. We stopped close to the suspension bridge, lunching on the little beach with the dogs playing tag in the bubbling waters. It was literally timeless, as we enjoyed the pebble beach, making cairns and snacking in the hot sun. We didn't see another soul. When it felt like time to move on we paddled on to Bassenthwaite and across to our exit point. A perfect paddling day.

CALORIE CREDITS The Pheasant Inn at Keswick is an olde-worlde pub offering pub meals and good beer (W: https://thepheasantinnkeswick.co.uk), or visit Lake Road Brunch Keswick for a light menu (W: www.lakeroadbrunch.co.uk).

The Grange Café is south of Derwent Water at Borrowdale (T: 01768 777077), while the Chalet Tearooms Portinscale are on the opposite side of the lake from Keswick, with a wood burner, making it a cosy treat (W: https://thechaletportinscale.co.uk).

WILDLIFE SAFARI This region is teeming with bird life, including kingfishers and ospreys nesting on Bassenthwaite.

> **WHERE'S THE MAGIC?**
>
> Being able to paddle the small, secluded river from Derwent Water through to Bassenthwaite makes this paddle feel like a proper and worthy adventure.

OTHER ATTRACTIONS The Lake District has a wealth of ancient stone circles, including one its most famous and one of the UK's most ancient, Castlerigg. At 30m in diameter and with 42 stones, it's a dramatic

BELOW Glorious red and gold hues to finish a magical day on the water.

ABOVE Kayakers landing at National Trust Kettlewell Car Park.

sight and free to visit (W: www.english-heritage.org.uk).

For a shot of the arts in a stunning location, check out the Theatre by the Lake in Keswick. It's jam-packed with all manner of exhilarating shows to get your feet tapping and bring a smile (W: www.theatrebythelake.com).

The Keswick Mountain Festival has been a feature on the outdoor calendar for years. While it has taken on more of a trail running theme, it should inspire all outdoor-loving adventurous types (W: www.keswickmountainfestival.co.uk).

For something a little different, try the cerebral challenging puzzles of the Puzzling Place, a strange mix of optical illusions (W: www.puzzlingplace.co.uk). Or head to the world-famous Derwent Pencil Museum (W: www.derwentart.com/en-gb/c/about/company/derwent-pencil-museum).

Check out the Honister Slate Mine, England's last working slate mine, which is the scene of much adventure, from mine tours to Via Ferrata, the Infinity Bridge and Adrenaline Pass (W: https://honister.com). Or why not try Kong Adventure, which has both indoor and outdoor climbing, children's play areas and an indoor caving feature (W: www.kongadventure.com)?

Extend your stay in the National Park by booking into a YHA in Keswick, giving you more time to wander (W: www.yha.org.uk/places-to-stay/keswick).

THE SHARED ECONOMY Keswick Canoe and Bushcraft is based on Derwent Water, literally at the water's edge (W: www.keswickcanoeandbushcraft.co.uk), or check out Keswick Adventures (W: https://keswickadventures.co.uk) for a range of watersports including ghyll scrambling, SUP, kayak and canoe activities.

The Calvert Trust provides watersports and adventure activities for participants with disabilities at Calvert Lakes (W: https://calvertlakes.org.uk).

34 LINDISFARNE – THE HOLY ISLAND

One of Britain's best-kept secrets, Holy Island is a deeply spiritual bolthole perched in the North Sea just off the magnificent Northumberland coastline. A circumnavigation of this tiny island, equal parts enchanting and rugged, takes in rare wildlife, lighthouses and the historic Lindisfarne Priory. The small island also has a castle and lime kilns and is listed as a national nature reserve.

The Lowdown

DIFFICULTY

Can be choppy, with big waves on the sand bar at the island's northern tip.

DISTANCE Circumnavigation of Holy Island: ~15km.
Paddling around the Lindisfarne Nature Reserve and Holy Island: 17.6km.
South to Bamburgh Castle: +8.5km.

DIRECTIONS Launch near the causeway on to the water – you'll need to park elsewhere and walk back. Be aware that it's a long carry (~300m) from the car park to the water's edge at Bamburgh Beach.

Use these tide tables to determine high and low tide before your paddle (W: www.tidetimes.co.uk/holy-island-tide-times).

HAZARDS

CRAFT

*craft choice dictated by conditions and experience

	LOCATION	GRID REFERENCE	POST CODE	WHAT3WORDS
START/FINISH	Causeway to Holy Island (drop-off)	NU079427	TD15 2PL	graphics.link.outermost
PARKING/POSSIBLE EXIT ON A TO B ROUTE	Bamburgh Castle car park	NU184349	NE69 7DF	awoken.crate.slopes

BELOW Holy Island standing proud on the horizon.

BACKGROUND Holy Island saw the spread of Christianity with the pilgrimage of St Cuthbert (see St Cuthbert's Way) to this eastern spiritual destination. Lindisfarne has plenty of history and monuments to visit, food and drink including Lindisfarne Mead. Part of its mystery is the remote nature of island accessible by its causeway. The northern beaches and dunes provide a more rugged backdrop and place to paddle or walk.

A SLICE OF HISTORY Holy Island has a recorded history dating to the 6th century AD. It was an important centre of Celtic Christianity under saints Aidan, Cuthbert, Eadfrith and Eadberht of Lindisfarne. After the Viking invasions and the Norman conquest of England, a priory was re-established. A small castle was built on the island in 1550.

Crowning 3.5ha of the Great Whin Sill, Bamburgh Castle has stood guard over the Northumberland coast for thousands of years. It was home to the Anglo-Saxon kings of Northumbria and a succession of monarchs from Henry VI to James I. Visionary inventor, industrialist and philanthropist William George Armstrong bought the castle in 1894, and today it is run by the National Trust.

ROUTE Launching near the causeway gives you a useful datum point for navigation, as well as the island in front of you. If conditions are lumpy on the North Sea, the eastern side of the island, then you can stay in the shelter of the islands and explore the inner sound and along the width of the island, which is less exposed.

Paddling anticlockwise gets you up close and alongside the castle on the southern side of Holy Island. You'll also see the Old Law Beacons on Guile Point (see below) and the Lindisfarne NNR. It's ~1.7km across to the island following the causeway, which is two car lanes wide, which will no doubt cause much amusement during tourism season as you paddle past. Failure to time the tides can leave walkers and motorists stranded or in deep water!

RIGHT Circumnavigating Lindisfarne on the spring tides to complete the loop before the causeway is dry.

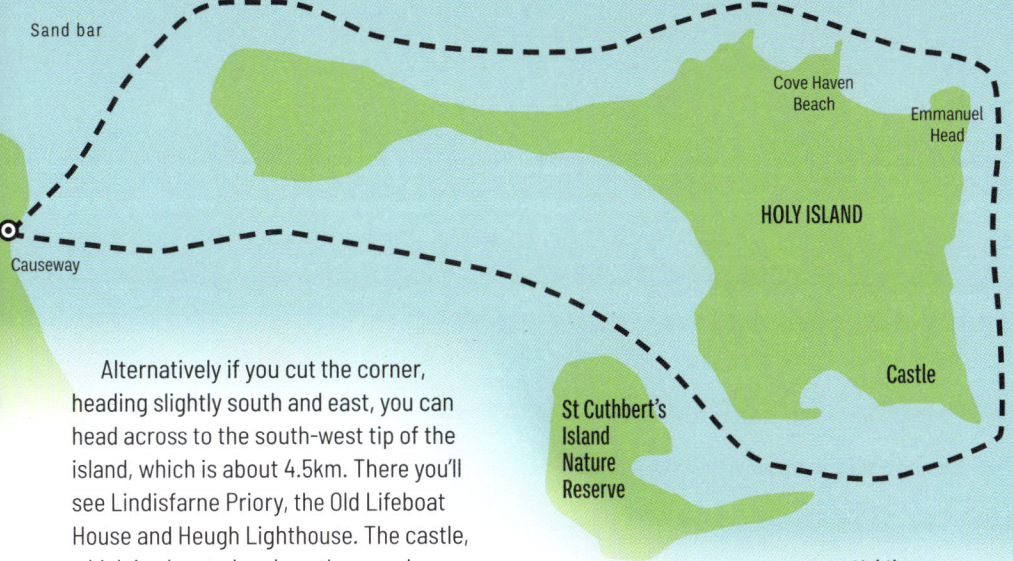

Alternatively if you cut the corner, heading slightly south and east, you can head across to the south-west tip of the island, which is about 4.5km. There you'll see Lindisfarne Priory, the Old Lifeboat House and Heugh Lighthouse. The castle, which is elevated and another good landmark, is further round the island. Just off the south-west tip is St Cuthbert's Island (also known as Hobthrush Island), which you can walk to at low tide or paddle when water allows.

It is another half kilometre to the lighthouse and a few hundred metres later is the gorgeous Holy Island beach, where you can stop for a paddle and explore. Lindisfarne Castle is 600m onwards from here and definitely worth a visit.

Just past the castle and below it in elevation are the lime kilns, which make for a great photo and were our home for a night a few years ago. The south-east tip of the island is now about 250m away and then there's the opportunity to turn north and paddle up the side of the island. Please do check tides and conditions and consider if it is achievable on the day of your visit for you and your group. If not, there's still plenty to explore in the calmer waters in the island's channels.

Once you turn north you'll follow the eastern side of the island for 2.3km, hugging the rocky shores until you reach Emmanuel Head with a marker on the headland. Once you round the head you'll begin to head west and there are two bays with beaches offering shelter and a place for a picnic. The first bay is about a kilometre across on this north shore with a beach set back, and then it is another 400m to cross the second bay. The North Shore is a long, sandy beach, running from this point on for about 3km. You'll need enough tide height to allow you to paddle back around this section.

Once you reach the north-west tip, turn back around and look for the channel to take you back behind the island. If you

get the tides wrong then be prepared for a long walk and carry. We had lots of fun surfing the waves around this northern tip, but it does land you in shallows and there's a beach to pick up any pieces if you do capsize. From here it is about 2.5km back to the causeway and celebrations of rounding this special island.

EXTEND THE TRIP Paddling to Bamburgh Castle along the Bamburgh coastline will add another 8.5km to your trip. Check tides, winds and forecasts so you don't bite off more than you can chew.

Leaving the bay and island south of Holy island, it's about 2km until you reach the wider sands of Ross Beach. Around 3km down this vast expanse of beach you'll reach the inlet of Budle Water, where you'll see Newtown Gun Emplacement. The coastline kicks out here and 2km south you'll reach Bamburgh Lighthouse, which guards Harkness Rocks. It's then a final kilometre down to Bamburgh Castle, where you can capture some fantastic pics of the day you captured the castle – allegedly!

If you want to visit the Farne Islands (landing is not permitted) it's 3km each way from Bamburgh Beach out to the Inner Farne Islands. The surf here can be meaty on windy days and where tide and wind collide. As always, get the forecast and ask a local before venturing out.

OUR RICH ADVENTURE We've paddled different parts of Northumberland for over two decades and Holy Island is one of our all-time favourite paddles, with its incredible history and wildlife.

One challenge is to circumnavigate the island on the spring tides, passing over the causeway before it is impassable. We started in the dark, paddling anticlockwise at night, which was fantastic.

On other occasion, Ollie Jay (of Active 4 Seasons) and I decided to canoe the 17km around the island. It was quite an adventure. We camped in the lime kilns

ABOVE Launching from the shore in canoes to paddle around the island.

below the castle and I was awoken by a dog walker proclaiming they'd found a tramp! We reassured them we were just paddlers out wild camping. On the paddle north we had dolphins riding shotgun, which was a real privilege. When we got to the northern peninsula there were sizable waves with a sand bar. Surfing in on big waves, we ended up capsizing and swimming, which Ollie has never let me forget!

CALORIE CREDITS Visit Pilgrims Coffee for great coffee and cake on Holy Island itself (W: www.pilgrimscoffee.com). There are also several pubs, including the Ship Inn (W: www.theshipinn-holyisland.co.uk) and the dog-friendly Crown and Anchor (W: www.holyislandcrown.co.uk).

The Barn at Beal just off the A1 towards Lindisfarne is home-from-home, with its welcoming campsite, bothy bar, restaurant and café. We've stayed here a few times, usually detouring to check in (W: http://barnatbeal.com).

The Hut at Bamburgh (find them on Instagram) offers great food, as do the Clock Tower Tea Rooms at Bamburgh Castle (T: 01668 214487).

WILDLIFE SAFARI Keep your eyes peeled for dolphins and seals when paddling around the Lindisfarne bays. There are also guillemots and puffins locally. We usually see cormorants drying their wings on the shore.

WHERE'S THE MAGIC?

The Northumberland coastline, Holy Island, Lindisfarne and the rugged North Sea swells make this paddle a true adventure, with ancient backdrops as well as rare wildlife to warm your heart.

OTHER ATTRACTIONS There's plenty to entice lovers of history along this coastline. St Cuthbert's Cave, also known as Cuddy's Cave, near Belford is said to be the final resting place of the ancient monk and patron saint of Northumbria. Bamburgh Castle and the beaches south of Berwick radiate the wild beauty of the Northumberland coast (W: www.bamburghcastle.com/), while Holy Island and Lindisfarne are magical spiritual enclaves (W: www.lindisfarne.org.uk).

BELOW Wild camping near the castle.

Or why not visit the Old Law Beacons on Guile Point, two obelisk navigation beacons that when lined up formerly directed boats into Holy Island harbour (W: https://fabulousnorth.com/old-law-beacons-on-guile-point/)?

If you're up for a hike, you can enjoy visualising the seascape as artist LS Lowry saw it on the Berwick Lowry Trail (W: https://berwickpreservationtrust.co.uk/lowry-trail). Stay at nearby Pot-A-Doodle-Do, which has playgrounds, pedal cars and a range of top-notch glamping activities (W: https://potadoodledo.com).

THE SHARED ECONOMY Check out Canoe Trail's Sea Kayak the Northumberland Coast expedition to experience world-class sea kayaking to the Farne Islands, Berwick and Holy Island (W: www.canoetrail.co.uk/canoe-camp/expeditions/kayak-northumberland-coast). Alternatively, you can sea kayak to the Farne Islands or explore the River Tweed with our expedition buddy Olly Jay and Active 4 Seasons (W: http://active4seasons.co.uk).

ABOVE Ollie Jay of Active 4 Seasons canoeing around the island by the castle.

BELOW The coast around Bambergh Castle.

SCOTLAND

35 RIVER TWEED: KELSO TO BERWICK

This route along the Scottish-English border takes in the River Tweed, famed for leaping salmon, ospreys and otters. The river offers classic whitewater touring with interesting fish weirs and meandering flows. Outside the paddle, Berwick-upon-Tweed is one of Britain's finest walled towns, with viaducts, stone bridges and the Lowry Trail, which celebrates LS Lowry's seaside paintings.

The Lowdown

DIFFICULTY

Weirs, eddies and some whitewater requiring good boat control; the bottom section is tidal Grade 2 waters.

DISTANCE Kelso to Coldstream: 19km. Coldstream to Berwick: 27km.

DIRECTIONS You'll need to arrange a shuttle, as the river flows fast towards Berwick (shuttle from Berwick to Kelso is ~45km). Check tides to avoid an unnecessary battle in the tidal bottom section. You can break the trip into shorter sections to reduce the daily distance.

HAZARDS

CRAFT

	LOCATION	GRID REFERENCE	POST CODE	WHAT3WORDS
START	Kelso, above bridge at Junction Pool viewpoint	NT724338	TD5 8LT	recliner.arrives. radiated
STEPPED WEIR WITH BIGGER DROP	Left-hand side of river	NT760369	TD5 7QA	fists.biked. spooned
COLDSTREAM	Small layby and steps	NT806393	TD12 4LN	zaps.mended. corrupted
NORHAM	End of Pedwell Way	NT898476	TD15 2LD	yelled.blank. reviewed
FINISH	Tweedmouth Slipway near lifeboat station	NU000519	TD15 2AY	props.cubs.resort

ABOVE Bridges at Tweedmouth.

BACKGROUND The River Tweed is a one of our favourite rivers of all time, offering a continuous conveyor belt of moving water, small weirs and whitewater features with inspiring landscapes and wildlife along the way. Any trip along this route should be combined with exploring one of Britain's best-kept secrets: Northumberland.

A SLICE OF HISTORY Explore the lively border town Kelso, which boasts plenty of outdoor activities, fishing on the River Tweed, folk music traditions and, of course, Kelso Abbey, which dates to the 1100s. King David first invited Benedictine monks from France to found the abbey in around 1128 after relocating from Selkirk to be near Roxborough Castle.

Wark on Tweed Castle, sometimes referred to as Carham Castle, is a ruined motte and bailey castle built around 1136. It was reputed to be significant in history as the founding place of the Order of the Garter and was destroyed and rebuilt during various battles over the centuries.

Coldstream gave its name to the regiment that marched from here to London in 1660, an action that resulted in the restoration of Charles II. The Coldstream Museum highlights the history of the regiment and is located in the original barracks.

Twizel Viaduct, known as St Cuthbert's, was built between 1846 and 1849 by the Newcastle & Berwick Railway, to carry the Tweedmouth to Kelso railway branch line over the River Till at Twizell.

For 450 years Norham Castle, first built in the 12th century, was one of the great English strongholds along the River Tweed, a barrier against the Scots. The Scots besieged it nine times, capturing it on four occasions.

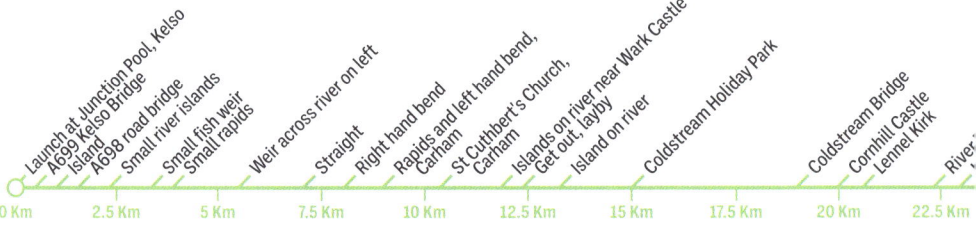

35 • RIVER TWEED: KELSO TO BERWICK

ROUTE Launching on the small beach at Kelso, the A699 road bridge immediately captures your attention about 330m downstream. Depending on levels it can be shallow here and hence quite fast, so set your line through the bridge arches early. Like so many of the bridges crossing the Tweed, this one is large and imposing. The river bends left and there are some small islands on the right-hand arch. About a kilometre downstream you pass under a second bridge with the river having continued left and now straightening as you pass through Kelso.

The river threads through a weaving cluster of islands, both large and small, about a kilometre downstream, where the centre line is obvious as the main flow. These are simple Grade 1 riffles and small rapids. About 600m on from the island you encounter your first fish weir pool, a rock weir (or cauld) extending across most of the river with an obvious exit flow through a gap in the weir. These are excellent for enjoying small wave trains and fast small channels where the water accelerates through the gap. More experienced paddlers may want to practise tight turns, ferry gliding and breaking in and out on these features. The main channel is on the left hand side of the weir, making it a simple task to enjoy. About 600m downstream the river bends left and there is a small riffle rapid with the main channel in the middle of the river as you pass Sprouston on the right bank.

The river twists and turns for another 1.7km or so before you reach another weir and pool across the river, with channels in the river centre. Small islets and islands extend into the flow on river right. The river left channel is the course (to the left of the main island), where there is a 1.5m-high stepped weir with much bigger waves and the line down the centre, followed by a second, less committing weir. Usually you need to empty canoes at this point as it can

RIGHT The viaduct at Berwick.

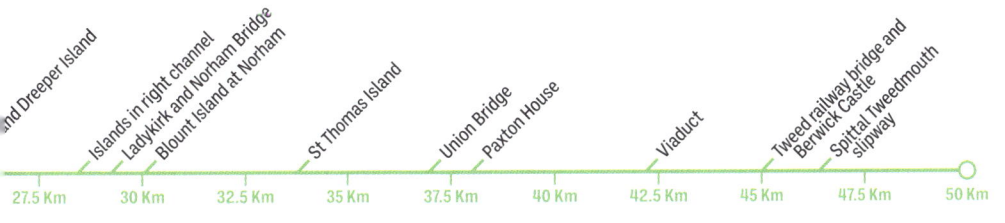

be a wet ride. You can portage if you don't fancy it. The water remains frothy and can be a little turbulent for a couple of hundred metres downstream. The river straightens for about 1.5km and then bends around to the right with a small rapid and riffle, where you can paddle down the middle or centre line.

The Tweed straightens for 1.5km and then bends almost back on itself for another 1.5km before entering a straightforward bubbly rapid and riffle, which is about 200m long. It then kicks a sharp left as the Carham Burn pours in, and then 150m downstream is an island with the flow pushing river left. After ~1.25km you pass Carham Church on the right bank and then the river relaxes with about 2km of simple riffles before you arrive at the first of two islands. The second island is larger but across from a farm and is 800m on downstream and just upstream of Wark Castle, a ruined motte and bailey castle.

It would be possible to camp here but do remember to leave no trace and be gone early, as this is a prime fishing river and we don't want to spoil things for future paddlers. Just upstream of the islands is the get out to a layby used by the fishing folk, so please be mindful and share the space.

Coldstream Holiday Park is about 2km from the islands and although a steep climb up, you could exit and stash kit or shuttle back from the get out. From the islands it's about 6km of classic winding riverbanks with a few small islets to the approach to Coldstream Bridge, which is always a welcome sight. Put simply, we love this stone bridge: a beautiful seven-span feat of engineering, built by John Smeaton (who features on several routes in this book) and opened in 1767. On the hill there's a very tall monument to Charles Marjoribanks, a Scottish Liberal MP who helped reform the voting system.

Head through one of the right-hand arches and be aware the river does a dog leg around further right, behind the bridge pillar. You can also opt in sensible water levels to portage over the breakwater on the left side. Once through the bridge steer right and then straighten through a 3m-wide gap in the breakwater and off downstream through some riffles where it is shallow. You can break out river left into a big eddy and practise skills in this fast-moving chute.

About 800m downstream you pass the ruins of Cornhill Castle, a medieval tower house and *barmkin* (Scots for 'defensive enclosure') from around 1385, with ditches set on a naturally defended promontory, the banks of the Tweed. Another historic reference point, the 12th-century church and graveyard of Lennel Kirk is passed on the left bank about 700m on.

ABOVE Passing under Coldstream Bridge.

ABOVE Canoeing the River Tweed.

About 3.5km downstream of magnificent paddling through the Scottish and English borders, depending on which side of the river you favour (wars have been fought over this) you reach the confluence with the River Till tributary. There is a flood defence here, so you need to stay river left. If you tuck behind the small, overgrown island you'll find the river mouth and can paddle up easily to the Twizel Viaduct. Last time we were here a large stag swam the river.

Around 400m downstream you reach a set of large gravel-bed islands, where the river splits through different shallow channels. You can paddle far left or far right when the levels are good. Look for the main flow if levels are lower. Then, 1.2km downstream, the river splits around Dreeper Island, with the main flow on the main obvious channels left and a long fish weir across the river. Identify the small tongues of water and exit flows on the weir and paddle on.

The Tweed straightens for another 2.5km and then bends around to the left. Around 750m after the bend look for a channel on the right on Canny Island. The backwater is reminiscent of Canadian sloughs so look out for wildlife. This is a better route to avoid the prime fishing spot if you don't turn. After 200m turn left and paddle the 500m before you arrive at the Ladykirk and Norham Bridge, which is another stunner.

After the bridge the river bends right and 1.2km later you pass Blount Island, with the main flow on river right. You are passing Norham where you can arrange to stop and meet vehicles. Stick with it and you get to enjoy Tweedmouth, more iconic bridges and the incredible walled town of Berwick-upon-Tweed. The river remains true to form, with more exaggerated twists and turns as you get closer to your destination, our coastline.

The river twists for another 3km until you reach St Thomas's Island, upstream of Horncliffe. When the river is flowing well here you get a mini-whirlpool. You can take the middle or right channel as the river bends more aggressively around to the left for over a kilometre. Two more kilometres of slower paddling without any riffles and

you reach the wrought-iron Union Chain Bridge, which opened in 1820.

As you head around the next big bend you pass the impressive Paxton House a kilometre on. Then head east for about 4km, passing a small island and Whiteadder Water, a river that joins just before you pass under the A1 road bridge. Beware: this section is tidal, so make sure you have timed your trip to avoid the pain of paddling against a flood or incoming tide.

The river expands now, widening as it takes on the characteristics of an estuary, and around the corner is the stunning multi-arched railway viaduct and Berwick Castle. You have 1.4km to cover to reach the end of your trip but it flies by with picture opportunities and the impregnable walls of Berwick town. On your left side is the town, stacked up the hill, while to the right is more of the fishing port. You pass under the twin road bridges serving the town's winding road system. Enjoy the final strokes of one of our all-time favourite paddles by paddling towards Spittal beaches, but do be aware that the North Sea waves can come at a real pace.

EXTEND THE TRIP You can start your paddling trip further upstream at Peebles and make it feel like a true paddling expedition. This section has further weirs and a significant technical rapid at Makerstoun, which includes the 'Goat Hole', a Grade 2/3 section.

Pay a visit to the much smaller tributary of the River Tweed by exploring the River Till and visiting the absolutely lovely Lavender Tearooms at Etal (see below).

OUR RICH ADVENTURE We've been making paddling trips to the Till, the Tweed and the Farne Islands of Northumberland for over two decades. We've sea kayaked and surfed in monstrous waves off Berwick Pier, paddled Makerstoun Rapids (above Kelso) in different levels and played under Coldstream Bridge. Our great friend and expedition buddy Ollie Jay, who runs Active 4 Seasons, lives locally, making it a go-to destination for us. Customers trips have always involved great food, worthy whitewater sections and fond memories of this hidden gem.

CALORIE CREDITS Kelso has several lovely cafés and eateries to help you recharge your

OPPOSITE Rocky outcrops and reflections where one year we watched an osprey catch a fish.

ABOVE Running one of the fish weirs below the River Till.

batteries. If you're visiting the wider area, we recommend the Lavender Tearooms at Etal (W: www.lavendertearooms.org.uk).

WILDLIFE SAFARI Every Tweed trip has provided something special, from red deer swimming the river to otters playing on the banks, ospreys catching fish and plenty of kingfishers displaying their electric-blue plumage. On one of our paddles we were accompanied by a young seal pup, who had followed the tide inland for a day trip.

> **WHERE'S THE MAGIC?**
>
> The River Tweed offers so much in terms of landscape, historic towns, places of interest and wildlife.

OTHER ATTRACTIONS St Cuthbert's Cave, also known as Cuddy's Cave, is near Belford and can be incorporated into a longer walk around the area.

Bamburgh Castle and the beaches south of Berwick capture the wild beauty of the Northumberland coast. Pay a visit to Holy Island and Lindisfarne for a paddle (see Route 34, page 217) or to take in the atmosphere of this spiritual enclave (W: www.lindisfarne.org.uk).

If you're up for a hike, you can enjoy visualising the seascape as artist LS Lowry saw it on the Berwick Lowry Trail (W: https://berwickpreservationtrust.co.uk/lowry-trail). Stay at nearby Pot-A-Doodle-Do, which has playgrounds, pedal cars and a range of top-notch glamping activities (W: https://potadoodledo.com), or the Coldstream Holiday Park allows camping and offers caravan and glamping options. From your elevated position on the banks you can walk down to the river, making it perfect for shuttling to here (W: www.coldstreamholidaypark.com).

THE SHARED ECONOMY Canoe and camp the River Tweed with Canoe Trail (W: www.canoetrail.co.uk/canoe-camp/expeditions/camp-the-tweed). Sea kayak to the Farne Islands or explore the River Tweed with our expedition buddy Ollie Jay and Active 4 Seasons (W: http://active4seasons.co.uk).

ABOVE Beginning a River Tweed expedition at Kelso.

36 FORTH & CLYDE CANAL: THE KELPIES TO THE FALKIRK WHEEL

With two iconic attractions at the centre of this paddle, including mythical beasts and marvellous mechanical motions, this is one of the most distinctive paddling experiences in this book. Combine this with picture-perfect Scottish backdrops, incredible views and a modern take on this ancient mode of travel, the ambience and energy of this fairly easy route is infectious.

The Lowdown

DIFFICULTY
Easy paddling but lots of portaging.

DISTANCE The Kelpies, Helix Park to the Falkirk Wheel (half-day paddle) – 7.5km. You can shorten it by only paddling some sections and avoiding the portages.

DIRECTIONS There are good public transport links along this route and excellent parking at both tourist locations. It is more relaxing to opt for an A to B route to avoid retracing your steps.

Be aware that paddling between destinations involves portaging plenty of locks, so a trolley and straps may prove useful.

Note: passage through the Falkirk Wheel is restricted and should be booked at least 24 hours in advance by calling 01324 676912.

HAZARDS

CRAFT
*kneel down as necessary

	LOCATION	GRID REFERENCE	POST CODE	WHAT3WORDS
START	The Kelpies at Helix Park	NS906820	FK2 7ZT	itself.sparks.loyal
FINISH	The Falkirk Wheel	NS852801	FK1 4LS	squish.earliest.quoted
	Falkirk Tunnel	NS881789	FK1 5LE	spines.picturing.dignitary

Kelpies, Helix Park — Right turn bend — Lock to portage — Lock by Main Street bridge — Lock portage — Lock portages — Bottom of lock flight — Top of lock flight — Falkirk Wheel — Roughcastle Tunnel — End of Roughcastle Tunnel — Left hand bend to lock — Falkirk Tunnel — End of Falkirk Tunnel – turnaround point — Grange Community Centre jetty

0 Km — 5 Km — 10 Km — 15 Km

BACKGROUND You'll pass two iconic tourist attractions on this route, the first at Helix Park, 350ha of green space between Falkirk and Grangemouth. Designed by artist Andy Scott, *The Kelpies* are two giant steel horse's heads, 30m high and weighing 300 tonnes each. Together they are the world's largest equine sculpture, depicting the shape-shifting beasts that, according to local legend, exist beneath the water.

Towards the end of this route, you'll get to see the monumental Falkirk Wheel, which lifts up the water and craft from the Forth and Clyde Canal to the ongoing navigation of the Union Canal. The Falkirk Wheel sits below the Roman Antonine Wall and garrison, a lesser-known version of Hadrian's Wall (to the south) and a UNESCO World Heritage Site.

A SLICE OF HISTORY Britain's canals are a living testament to the prowess of our engineering skills and the industrial age. The idea of a canal crossing central Scotland became more than a dream in 1763 when John Smeaton surveyed the route (Smeaton was also responsible for projects from Scotland to Cornwall, including the Coldstream Bridge and Cardington Sluice, both of which are referenced in this book). By 1790, after various funding setbacks and lots of hard yards digging and building, the Forth and Clyde Canal was finally opened to enormous fanfare.

The Union Canal connects Scotland's capital, Edinburgh, to the trade and coal from the west. It was built later, in 1822, after four years of construction. Head up to the hill above the Falkirk Wheel to explore the sprawling ruins of the impressive Antonine Wall (known to the Romans as Vallum Antonini) and Roman Garrison, dating back to AD 142. Spend time visiting the different sections and reading about the lives of those defending the northern flank. The wall was abandoned less than a

ABOVE Rich and the majestic Kelpies at Helix Park.

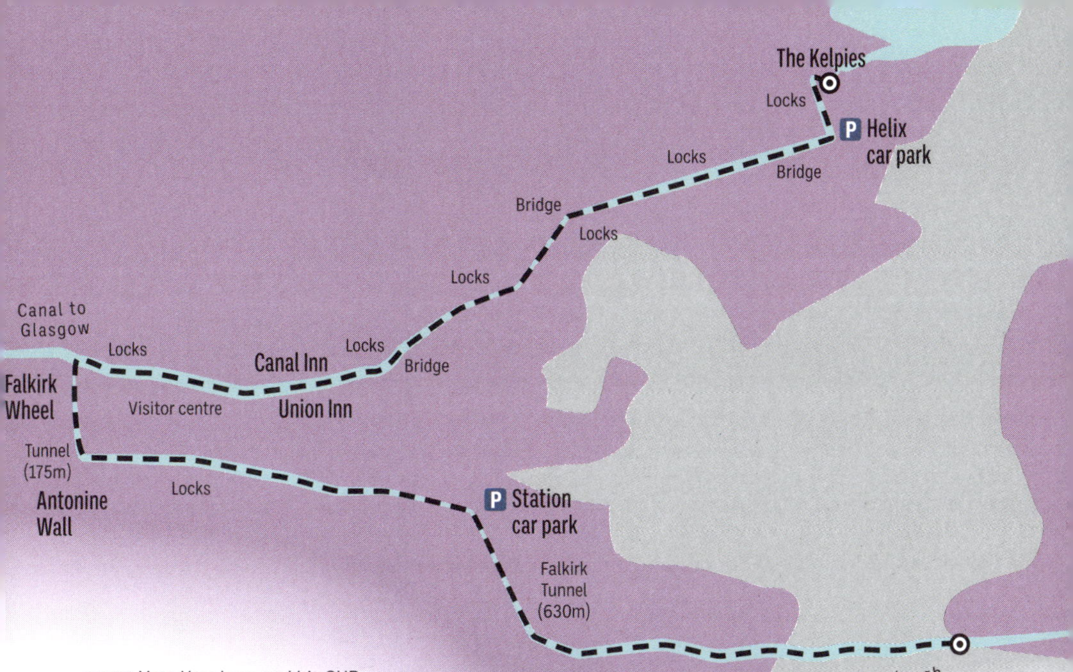

BELOW Matt Harpham and his SUP mates at the top of the Falkirk Wheel.

decade later, when efforts switched to the better known Hadrian's Wall.

The 650m-long Falkirk Tunnel has an eerie history. It attracted two men from Ireland in 1828, William Burke and William Hare, who killed 16 people during their time in Scotland and sold their bodies to Dr Robert Knox at the University of Edinburgh for medical experiments, transporting them in secret via the canal tunnel.

Things have quietened down since then, with no recent reports of macabre activity...

ROUTE Launching at either end of the trip offers shorter paddles without the need to portage the large number of locks in between *The Kelpies* and the Falkirk Wheel. That said, if you want to earn your spurs on the longer 7km paddle then go for gold.

From *The Kelpies*, the basin in front of the giant horses provides the majestic action shot. The canal loops back behind the horses and heads towards Falkirk, in the direction of The Helix car parks. You will see other canal users – mainly barges and boats – lining your route. About 430m from *The Kelpies* you'll reach the first lock adjacent to the car park, where you need to dismount. There's a sharp right-hand bend after 50m and the canal runs straight now for almost 2km, with locks approximately 1km apart. As

ABOVE Enjoying the view from the top of the Falkirk Wheel.

the canal passes under the second bridge at Grahams Road, it bends slightly left and then runs straight for another 500m before – you guessed it – another lock. It bends right slightly and after another 500m is the next lock. The locks come in quick succession, with three in less than a kilometre as you pass under the road bridge adjacent to the Premier Inn. In case you think that's it there is a flight of locks of six locks in about 700m uphill. Keep an eye out for the silhouetted figures on the bank and the lovely Canal Inn on the right-hand side, chip shop if you need it and then the Union Inn on the left at the top of the lock flight.

The canal gently zigs and zags with the canal path in tow, a running route we know well. There are unspoilt woods on the left bank and plenty of canal boats with hire fleets and restoration projects parked close by. About 1.6km after the top lock, the impressive Falkirk Wheel looms into sight.

Continuing onwards past the Wheel you'll travel westwards towards Glasgow.

At the Wheel you'll pass from the main canal into the Wheel basin and then once authorised (in advance, at least 24 hours) you can paddle into the lift wheel. The sluice doors are then shut and the lift begins its slow journey above the pool to the top waterway, where you can explore the waterways above Falkirk near the Antonine Wall. The Roughcastle Tunnel at the top is 180m long and has a traffic light system in place, which replaced the locks that once stood there. Once through the other side you can paddle towards Edinburgh, over 40km away, on the Union Canal.

If you choose to portage the Wheel it's a 650m carry or trolley from bottom to top avoiding the basin, Wheel and Roughcastle Tunnel. The tunnel is well lit, with pretty colours setting the mood. The view from the top of the lift across Falkirk and the hills beyond is truly breathtaking, so it's worth the effort, either by hand or on the Wheel.

Around 150m after the tunnel you'll arrive at the first lock and almost 500m later you'll pass under a footbridge for the bike trail. The canal becomes more picturesque here, with treelined banks and wooded areas, and 700m later it passes under the road bridge where there's another lock to portage. Wider passing gaps, more woodland and old cottages line the route here.

After 1.7km you'll arrive at the tunnel entrance to the 650m-long Falkirk Tunnel, with its interesting and dark history. You'll need lighting to continue, to ensure you're seen by oncoming traffic. A walkway towpath follows the canal along its hidden route.

The canal then winds on through industrial centres to woodland-lined banks and 9.5km later reaches the Avon Aqueduct, which passes over the river of the same name. Another 4km on and you'll reach the Linlithgow Canal Centre and finally, 26km later, after many bridges and locks, you'll reach the outskirts of Edinburgh.

EXTEND THE TRIP You can literally extend your route in any direction, with a long paddle towards Edinburgh on the Union Canal (26km) or a multiday trip to Glasgow (80km).

You can also extend your trip significantly by paddling the Glasgow to Edinburgh Canoe Trail, 80km of tunnels, aqueducts and portages taking you across Scotland's Central Belt. Paddlers attempting this trip should register with Scottish Canals at the Lowlands Canal and Waterways office (T: 01413 326936) for updates and support. West to east is best, following prevailing winds, but do ensure you get an up-to-date forecast when you register.

You can also access the River Caron from *The Kelpies* via two locks and an

ABOVE Heading into the Falkirk Tunnel.

LEFT Emerging from the Falkirk Tunnel.

800m paddle. From there it's just over 2km before you are on the Firth of Forth. We've paddled under the Forth Rail Bridge on several trips, exiting at Queensferry, but be warned: the tides can be meaty here. You'll also need to arrange a shuttle back or use one of the local companies providing shuttling services on the trail (W: www.scottishcanals.co.uk/activities/paddling/paddling-activity-providers).

WHERE'S THE MAGIC?

Getting to see and interact with world-class sculptures and feats of engineering makes this paddle one of the most unique in the book.

OUR RICH ADVENTURE We've paddled different stretches of the canals around Falkirk many times, as Rich's brother, Matt, lives a stone's throw away from the canal, near Loch 16. *The Kelpies* and the Falkirk Wheel are, of course, tourism hotspots, so you can be sure of becoming a social media sensation as you paddle by. These busier spots are balanced by the quieter stretches of this iconic canal, where you can enjoy much peace and quiet.

CALORIE CREDITS Great cafés and coffee shops can be found either end of this paddle. Grab a brew and a slice of cake before you set off at Helix Park (W: www.thehelix.co.uk/) to ensure you're fully fuelled, or take advantage of Scottish hospitality at the Canal Inn, close to Lock 16 (T: 01324 610637).

WILDLIFE SAFARI Many parts of this canal system truly feel remote and are teeming with wildlife. Swans, mergansers and a host of other birdlife are common on this route. While out jogging the canal section we have also seen deer in the wooded areas.

ABOVE Paddling through the Falkirk Tunnel is a surreal experience.

OTHER ATTRACTIONS

While *The Kelpies* is its crown jewel, Helix Park (W: www.thehelix.co.uk) has so much to recommend it. From an adventure zone playpark and splash play area to cycle paths aplenty, you'll be spoilt for choice.

The Falkirk Wheel (W: www.scottishcanals.co.uk/falkirk-wheel) is another fantastic attraction for a number of reasons. There are stunning walking trails, both high and low, and you can also follow the canal pathways by bike, paddle or on foot. Besides the fantastic visitor centre, you can hire bikes or bigger craft to explore the waterways, go on a Segway Safari or play a round of mini golf. There's also a splash park, adventure zone and bumper boats (like dodgems on the water!)

Visit the Edinburgh Indoor Climbing Arena on the outskirts of the city to enjoy incredible climbing routes and aerial courses in this old quarry site (W: www.edinburghleisure.co.uk/venues/edinburgh-international-climbing-arena), or for more outdoors run head to Arthur's Seat by Holyrood Park and the 251m summit for unapparelled views of Scotland's capital city.

If you're up for even more Scottish history, Stirling Castle (W: www.stirlingcastle.scot) and the National Wallace Monument (W: www.nationalwallacemonument.com) are less than an hour's drive from here.

THE SHARED ECONOMY

You can hire canoes and SUPs at the Falkirk Wheel to explore the canal areas. Or visit Pinkston Watersports, which runs a whitewater course near Glasgow as well as open water swimming and tubing (W: https://pinkston.co.uk).

BELOW Sunset over the Falkirk Wheel.

37 LOCH LOMOND

Known the world over for its majesty and stunning scenery, Loch Lomond is a must-see on any trip to central Scotland. The largest lake in the UK by surface area, it lies in the Loch Lomond & The Trossachs National Park and offers breathtaking landscapes, some of the UK's rarest wildlife and outdoor activities galore. Pack your bags and head out for a circular day paddle or plan a multiday trip and really lose yourself in this beautiful location. Ben Lomond at 974m is the most southerly of the Munros and is on the eastern shore.

The Lowdown

DIFFICULTY

A chance to explore one of Britain's most famous lochs from short bumbling paddles to overnight adventures.

DISTANCE A circular route and short paddle exploring the closest islands: 10km.
Another out and back journey which is a longer route around the main islands: 20km.
An A to B route from Luss to Ardlui Beach (heading north): 25km with a 25km and 30 min shuttle.
A southerly A to B route from Luss to Balloch Beach (heading south) which is 12km and requires a 14km road shuttle which takes about 15 minutes.
Better still plan your own route to explore and take in the sights.

DIRECTIONS Park at the car park near the Old Toll House at Luss, carry down to the beach and the water's edge.

HAZARDS

CRAFT

	LOCATION	GRID REFERENCE	POST CODE	WHAT3WORDS
PARKING AT THE OLD TOLL HOUSE	Inveruglas	NN322098	G83 7DP	cement.conclude.images
START/FINISH	Luss Beach, near car park	NS360931	G83 8PG	noted.operating.upsetting
POSSIBLE START OR FINISH	Ardlui Beach (heading north)	NN317156	G83 7ED	drop.studio.inclines
POSSIBLE START OR FINISH	Balloch Beach (heading south)	NS385824	G83 8QL	mailboxes.imprints.hushed

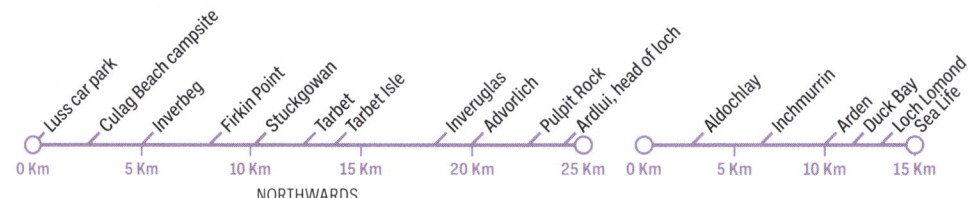

BACKGROUND
Flanked by Munro mountains (including Ben Lomond), ridges and buttresses, island hideaways and vistas beyond compare, Loch Lomond is an outdoor enthusiast's dream. At 39km long and 5km wide at the largest span, and with the West Highland Way national trail (154km) running along its eastern side, this is a true natural adventure playground.

The loch has various amenities, but once you paddle out it feels remote and serene, thanks to byelaws that were introduced to protect this precious area from overuse.

A SLICE OF HISTORY
Loch Lomond dates back to the neolithic era so you are paddling ancient waters. Like Loch Tay there is evidence of Cranogs, artificial manmade islands, one of which was called the Kitchen. Later the Romans built a fort with views of the loch from Drumquhassle. Vikings followed, hauling long boats over land to reach the narrows at Tarbet. It has subsequently been a destination for travellers and featured in the tour of the Wester Isles in 1773 by Dr Samuel Johnson and James Boswell. Loch Lomond was voted the 6th greatest wonder of the British Isles inn a 2005 *Radio Times* poll.

ABOVE Open canoe ninja John on Loch Lomond.

ROUTE
Park at Luss Beach and take to the water after a short carry to the beach. There's a little café nearby for last-minute sustenance.

Once you hit the waters on the small beach area you'll see the mighty Ben Lomond above you. To the right is a cluster of islands, perfect for a picnic or overnight camp (leave no trace). There are rare fallow deer white stags and horses on the islands, a ruined house and even wallabies on Inchconnachan.

This part of Loch Lomond feels more remote and far away from the crowds. It's ~1.5km across to the first landing points on the closest islands and a 10km paddle to circumnavigate all the islands in the closest group, which includes Inchconnachan, Bucinch, Inchcruin, Inchmoan and Inchtavannach. You can opt for double or quits for the 20km paddle by including the northern and southern islands of Inchlonaig and Inchmurrin. The loch is about 3.5km to 5km across at the middle, depending on which headland you aim for.

One of Loch Lomond's best-kept secrets is the well-hidden Inchgalbraith Castle, the ancestral home of Clan Galbraith, located on the islet of the same name south of Inchmoan. Further on, Inchmurrin is the largest and most southerly of the islands on the loch and has been owned by the appropriately named Scottish family for three generations. During the tourist season there's a restaurant and accommodation available.

There are some lovely small beaches on the main islands, perfect for a picnic as you thread through small narrows and little backwaters. Out of season there is limited traffic, giving you the sense of being Lord or Lady of the Loch for a day. Spotting the resident wildlife from the water is a fun pastime to occupy children when paddling as a family group.

EXTEND THE TRIP At ~11.5km due south of the launch point at Luss, Balloch is the most southerly point of the loch and has a beach and a variety of places to eat good food. Nearby caravan parks offer comfortable accommodation, and you can visit Balloch Castle and Country Park.

Heading north towards Tarbet, Inveruglas and Ardlui offers a beautiful paddle flanked by higher mountains and an incredible, wide vista that reveals itself as you progress. We recommend hugging the shore to avoid getting into any difficulties in inclement weather. Around 5km north of your launch you'll arrive at Inverbeg, with a caravan park and inn on the loch that is also accessible from the A82, making shuttling possible.

At Tarbet, 12km from your launch point, there's a lochside hotel and the narrow, winding A82, so you could run shuttle up to the beaches there. There's also a mainline station there, so you could travel from far and wide with an inflatable SUP in a rucksack or wheelie case.

RIGHT The Best of Scotland crew with Foxy, heading over to islands on Loch Lomond for wild camping.

Inveruglas is a committing paddle 17km north of Luss, but you can punctuate it with rest stops on the western shore. You'll pass by the small islet of Inveruglas as you continue on the final section of the loch past Ardvorlich and on to the most northerly point of Ardlui and the River Falloch, which is 25km from your start point. There are various bays and small outcrops at this northern end to explore.

If you're planning to wild camp, the eastern side of the loch is more remote and away from any road noise. As always, leave no trace and collect other people's debris to keep our parks and green spaces looking pristine. You need to be prepared in midge season: bring serious bug nets and insect repellent to avoid being sacrificed to the god of no-see-ums! (It's worth noting that some insect repellents are harmful to paddling kit.) Also, beware that there's a camping permit system for some areas of the loch and National Park, which runs between 1 March and the end of September (the byelaws don't affect designated campsites).

WHERE'S THE MAGIC?

There's magic at every turn, from plotting a route around the many pretty islands, to capturing reflections of Ben Lomond and the giant vistas in the water, or just simply exploring all the fascinating nooks and crannies of this iconic loch. This is the place of legends and songs (we've heard the rousing anthem 'Bonnie Banks o' Loch Lomond' sung at Murrayfield, home of Scottish Rugby, on many an occasion).

OUR RICH ADVENTURE We've adventured in, on and around Loch Lomond for many years, including driving the A82 road to Glencoe and walking the incredible West Highland Way from Milngavie to Fort William. Despite the incredible views and even spotting otters on that trip, we incurred the wrath of the midges whilst camping close to the loch. On our last visit with Canoe Trail customers we wild camped on one of the islands, where we enjoyed wild swimming, campfire food and more exploring.

CALORIE CREDITS Visit the local hostelries in Luss, including The Loch Lomond Arms (W: www.lochlomondarmshotel.com) to grab a pint of 70-Schilling beer, a hot beverage or even a can of Irn Bru, made from girders, as the advert said! There's also the Village Rest (W: www.the-village-rest.co.uk), Colquhouns restaurant (W: www.colquhounslochlomond.co.uk) and Sassenach Café, which is a lovely coffee shop (T: 07368 464717). If you're camping out, make sure you grab snacks and rations so you can enjoy the wilder spaces.

During the tourist season, a restaurant and hotel are available on the island of Inchmurrin and you could even book a wedding here (W: www.inchmurrin-lochlomond.com/restaurant).

BELOW Misty days on Loch Lomond in search of a good wild campsite.

ABOVE Heading past Luss by canoe.

WILDLIFE SAFARI Incredibly, there is a rare white stag on one of the islands, horses, and masses of bird life. There are also between seven and ten wallabies living on Inchconnachan island, dubbed Wallaby Island, which is an SSSI and, as such, is protected.

OTHER ATTRACTIONS Take a stroll up Ben Lomond and enjoy a view to to make a great postcard. Once you've breathed in the rarefied air, add the West Highland Way, which is over 40 years old, to your bucket list (W: www.westhighlandway.org).

Paddle some of the nearby locations included in this book, including the River Teith (Route 38, page 244) and River Tay (Route 39, page 250).

On land, check out The Helix, home of *The Kelpies*, the world's largest equine sculptures, and the Falkirk Wheel, then paddle on the canal there (W: www.thehelix.co.uk).

Top up your connection to our natural world by visiting Loch Lomond Sea Life (W: www.visitsealife.com/loch-lomond) or Loch Lomond Bird of Prey Centre (W: https://llbopc.co.uk).

If you want a bit more action, then book a TreeZone Aerial Adventure course through In Your Element (W: https://iye.scot/treezone-loch-lomond) or a canoe or kayak with Loch Lomond Leisure (W: https://lochlomond-scotland.com/).

THE SHARED ECONOMY The top end of the lock offers plenty of watersports action via Loch Lomond Wakeboarding (W: www.lochlomondwakeboard.com/watersports).

Canoe Trail's Best of Scotland trips include a wonderful paddle and camp on Loch Lomond (W: www.canoetrail.co.uk/canoe-camp/expeditions/best-of-scotland-canoe-expedition).

38 RIVER TEITH (EAS GOBHAIN)

This is a lively whitewater paddle with easy rapids and a few more technical yet still simple features. The River Teith is located near Stirling in Perthshire. The river trip A to B starts in the gentle flows of the mill pond at Callandar before taking you on a whitewater conveyor that gathers in pace. If you extend the trip down to Deanston then avoid the weir, though. The Teith is one of those river trips you always look back on and plan the next time you can return to try to tame it.

The Lowdown

DIFFICULTY
A fantastic beginners' whitewater river with bouncy Grade 2 rapids, the portage out is demanding.

DISTANCE Callander to A84 get-out (with time to play on features): 7.5km.
Callander to Deanston village: 13km.
Callander to Old Stirling Bridge: 26.5km.

DIRECTIONS The shuttle back from the A84 get-out is 6.5km and takes about 10 minutes. From Deanston village it's 13km (~15 minutes), and if you're coming back from Old Stirling Bridge, it's 25km (~30 minutes).

HAZARDS

CRAFT

BACKGROUND The River Teith (113km long) is a classic beginner's whitewater river, offering continuous small rapids from the picturesque start in Callander, though it is more narrow and intimate than some of the bigger rivers we've included in the book, such as the Spey and the Tay. The Teith name may come from the Gaelic *Uisge Theamhich*, which translates into English as "quiet and pleasant water" or more likely *uth/tith* meaning "to trot" so conveying the meaning "(the river which) flows smoothly and steadily". The River Teith is know for its fishing ands also a beautiful arched bridge ½ mile (800 metres) southwest of Doune.

A SLICE OF HISTORY There is so much to entrance any lover of history in and around Stirling that you could spend days exploring.

Doune Castle is a medieval stronghold close to the village of Doune near Stirling, made famous with appearances on the TV drama series *Outlander* and the film *Monty*

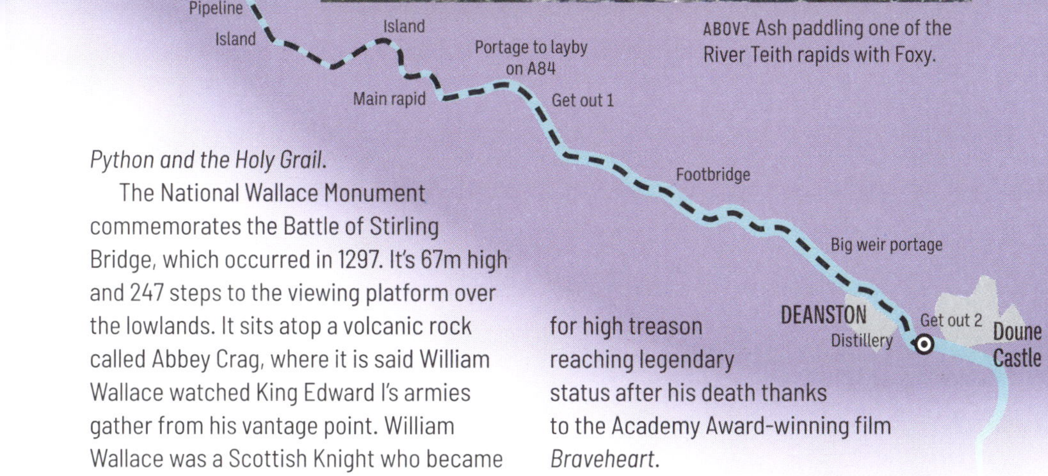

STUDLAND
P Meadows car park
Footbridge
Fish weir
Pipeline
Island
Island
Portage to layby on A84
Main rapid
Get out 1
Footbridge
Big weir portage
DEANSTON
Distillery
Get out 2
Doune Castle

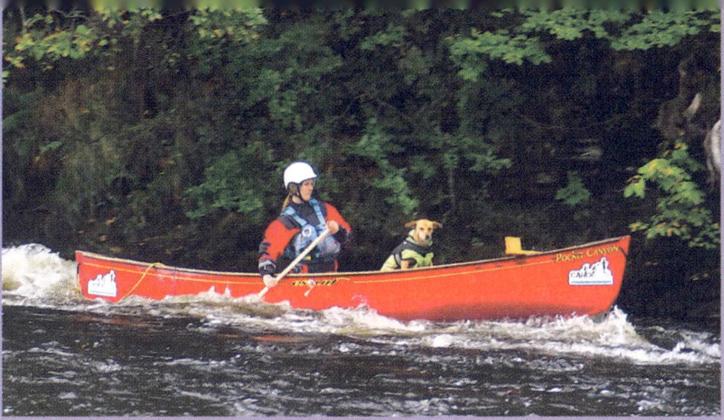

ABOVE Ash paddling one of the River Teith rapids with Foxy.

Python and the Holy Grail.

The National Wallace Monument commemorates the Battle of Stirling Bridge, which occurred in 1297. It's 67m high and 247 steps to the viewing platform over the lowlands. It sits atop a volcanic rock called Abbey Crag, where it is said William Wallace watched King Edward I's armies gather from his vantage point. William Wallace was a Scottish Knight who became one of the main leaders in the First War of Scottish Independence from 1296 to 1328. He became Guardian of Scotland and fought at the defeat of Battle of Falkirk Bridge in 1298. He was captured in 1303 and executed for high treason reaching legendary status after his death thanks to the Academy Award-winning film *Braveheart*.

Before the union with England, Stirling Castle, with its impressive architecture and ambience, was also one of the most used of the many Scottish royal residences – very much a palace as well as a fortress, with

	LOCATION	GRID REFERENCE	POST CODE	WHAT3WORDS
PARKING/START	Meadows car park, Callander	NN625079	FK17 8BB	cook.these.processes
RAPIDS	Torrie rapid, Grade 2	NN662043	FK16 6HJ	inherit.chop.cyber
FINISH (1)	A84 get-out, river height gauge	NN670044	FK17 8LL	pats.zest.protects
PARKING FOR FINISH (1)	Layby on A84	NN668045	FK17 8LL	barefoot.chickens.activates
	Deanston Weir, Grade 3 with dangerous stopper	NN702026	FK17 8LL	increases.browser.lunge
FINISH (2)	Deanston village	NN714017	FK16 6AH	engraving.wiser.busy
FINISH (3)	Stirling Old Bridge	NS796945	FK8 1AQ	evoke.website.readily

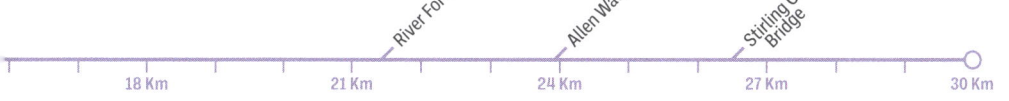

records suggesting early Stewart Kings, Robert II and Robert III, building parts in the 1300s.

ROUTE Launching at Callander is like taking to a duck pond and often you are literally surrounded by bird life. It's a great launch site, as you simply unload and step from the car park to the water. It is, however, a marked contrast to the egress from the river, which requires a bit more effort and energy. Once on the water, you can warm up by the car park or explore upstream towards the confluence with the River Leny (Garbh Uisge). Once you are good to go, paddle downstream to the stone bridge (A81 road bridge) and float onwards. The river is slow-moving at this point and the bend and pool inlet before the bridge on river right offer a good opportunity to work on crossing flows and breaking in and out.

About 200m downstream you'll pass under a footbridge and follow the river for a series of gentle bends, passing the Roman Camp Hotel, built in 1625 as a hunting lodge for the dukes of Perth. Riffles and small rapids, which add to the fun, start to appear about 500m after the foot bridge and another 500m on you'll reach the first fish weir-type rapid, with boulders and rocks forming a simple weir with obvious downstream 'V's (tongues of water) to follow. The river then exaggerates its winding motion with a sharper left-hand bend followed by a sharper right-hander.

On the map you are passing the cemetery and Callander Woods Holiday Park, which is 2km from the start of your paddle. Depending on how much playing and coaching we've been doing, we often use these spots as a good place for a tea break, as in normal water there are stony beaches on the shore.

BELOW Negotiating our way down the River Teith with our Best of Scotland group.

RIGHT Tackling the Torrie Rapids.

As you leave Callander behind, the pattern of small, simple, riffle-y rapids continues on amid the treelined banks. You'll pass an angling lake on the right ride (visible on the map) and continue southwards until you pass under a small bridge (carrying a pipeline for the quarry). The River Teith sweeps a long left-hand bend and begins to head eastwards, where shortly after it meets Keltie Water (Allt a Choire Bhric). Just at the top of the bend there's a small island with several islets and boulders (we did have a client take a swim here, as an angler was hidden on the left bank). The right channel is the main flow.

The Teith now becomes a little bit more urgent in its course and the bends tighten for 1.5km, with S-bends snaking right, left, right, left as if following a marching beat. There's a small gravel bar island after the first right-hand bend, which can be a good stop for a snack and breather. We've also used it for practising poling and rescues on different trips.

The final left-hand bend of the four is sharp and the start of the short, but fun, Torrie Rapid. There's generally a slab and ledge visible on river right with the chute and fun wave on the left-hand side. As you paddle onto the wave train, set your angle towards the right to avoid the slabs and rocks on the left side. You can break out on river right for pictures and play.

The end of our recommended shorter paddle is about 900m on, where the A84 almost kisses the river. Pull out before the bend on river left (look for a river height gauge) or land and find the track. It leads up to the road where you'll have a few hundred metres' carry to the layby. Team work and encouragement is the key to a sharp operation.

EXTEND THE TRIP Paddle on for more bubbly whitewater, continuing your route down to Deanston or beyond. Our first couple of trips on the Teith we explored further downstream, enjoying more rapids and whitewater. A couple of kilometres past the get-out for the recommended route is a bridge over the river, Lanrick Bridge linking footpaths and leading to Lanrick Macgregor Monument. The rapids remain fun, with nothing much to worry about. However, another 1.6km after the bridge is Deanston Weir, which is a beast and looks imposing. There's an option to portage on river left using a track in the treeline. We've tended to line our canoes down the fish ladder on the right (which is obviously much easier if your canoes are set up with bow and

stern lines). The main walkway for lining is solid so you won't have to perform any complicated acrobatics, but avoid sluices and the main weir. In low levels you can lift craft over the weir face.

After the weir you can re-join the flow and paddle down to a number of possible get-outs, including one we favour at the bottom of Deanston Village just after the sewage works, where you can access the track. Good news: Deanston Distillery is also located there.

You can then paddle on eastwards past Doune and Blair Drummond. The River Forth joins about 9km downstream and then Allen Water 2.5km after the M9 and on to Stirling. Check out access points to plan your escape, but by Old Stirling Bridge is a solid option. We used to visit and paddle here regularly when my brother lived in Stirling.

ABOVE Alex Bonney boofing off the rock bed on the River Teith.

OUR RICH ADVENTURE

We have paddled the River Teith on lots of occasions and it always delivers a classic Grade ½ whitewater trip with short sections of fun rapids.

We first paddled it during winter, while we were exploring new rivers to add to Canoe Trail's Best of Scotland expedition. Starting at Callander, two of our team got in and faced in opposite directions, which we fondly dubbed the 'love boat'!

Our last trip there was with a client group who simply loved the technical sections of this fantastic whitewater river. The egress on to the A82 road is a bit of a team effort, which always brings big smiles and lots of huffing and puffing in equal measure.

CALORIE CREDITS

The Dunkeld Fish Bar offers fantastic fish and chips, the classic deep-fried Mars Bar and even deep-fried Brussels sprouts at certain times of the year (T: 01350 727486). My brother always manages to find a good detour so we can walk near The Hermitage national forest and refuel here.

Before your paddle, stock up on locally sourced food and drink at Deli Ecosse, based in the old church hall (W: https://deliecosse.co.uk).

Extend your stay at Callander Hostel, which also offers glamping pods as well as hostel accommodation (W: https://cyp.org.uk/holidays).

WILDLIFE SAFARI The river is narrow and bubbly making it perfect for salmon and trout as well as the more mysterious lamprey, a throwback to more ancient times. We've often seen dippers and kingfishers on the Teith, too.

> **WHERE'S THE MAGIC?**
>
> The River Teith is a fantastic beginner's river for tackling a short or longer stretch of whitewater and simple rapids. The Torrie Rapid is always a favourite with our team and clients, offering some great waves to bounce through and over.

OTHER ATTRACTIONS Get out on the hills and trails near Callander to see the Bracklinn Falls, which tumble down through a gorge. You can park close by and complete the circular wooded walk including the bridge to see the falls, which were visited by Queen Victoria (W: www.lochlomond-trossachs.org/things-to-do/walking/short-moderate-walks/bracklinn-falls-circuit).

Loch Lomond is not far from here (see Route 37, page 238), with half-day to overnight paddling as well as plenty of stunning Munros (a mountain in Scotland more than 3,000 feet (914m) high). Matt, Ash and I have walked plenty of these mountains over the years.

THE SHARED ECONOMY Canoe Trail's annual Best of Scotland paddling trip includes the River Teith as a great training ground for whitewater paddling (W: www.canoetrail.co.uk).

BELOW Roger Palin dropping over the slab rock to the side of the Torrie Rapids.

39 LOCH TAY AND RIVER TAY

Loch Tay and the River Tay system offers so much to paddlers looking for adventure, including continuous stretches of Grade 2 whitewater, remote paddling and beautiful towns. At 24km long, the Tay can be paddled in one-day stages or as a committed multiday trip. There are fantastic campsites and wild camping along this route, and you can portage rapids that are above your level to avoid any unnecessary swims.

The Lowdown

DIFFICULTY
Decent loch paddle before river section with Grade 2 rapids.

DISTANCE Killin to Kenmore Bridge (loch): 24.75km.
Kenmore to Aberfeldy (River Tay): 13km.
The shuttle from Aberfeldy to Killin is 36km and takes 45 minutes.

DIRECTIONS Loch Tay and the River Tay can be tackled as a short 2-4-hour paddle or increased to a full day or multiday paddle with wild camping to allow you space and time to breathe in this spiritual wonderland. Park in Killin at the village hall car park (FK21 8UT) to access the loch and arrange to shuttle back from Aberfeldy, allowing two full days from loch to river. The A827 follows the loch and river.

You can extend the trip to Perth, allowing 5-6 days depending on your aspirations and paddling experience. Be warned: the Tay has some technical rapids, particularly below Aberfeldy.

HAZARDS

CRAFT
*loch only

BACKGROUND Loch Tay and the River Tay offer world class river and lake paddling set in the stunning Highlands starting in the west and running east. The River Tay itself is the longest river in Scotland and is 193km long. It originates on Ben Lui near Oban and flows into Loch Tay at Killin, a sleepy but delightful town. It's home to beavers, otters and salmon with the largest salmon weighing 29kg being caught there is 1922. The River Tay is fed by big tributaries including the Earn, Tummel and Lyon. It feeds the North Sea at Dundee, passing the fantastic Discovery Point, home to RSS *Discovery*, a ship shared by Scott and Shackleton on the same polar voyage.

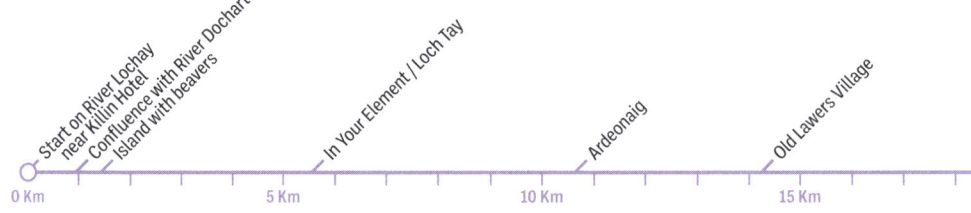

RIGHT Gemma and Calum on Loch Tay as part of their Best of Scotland expedition.

A SLICE OF HISTORY

Crannogs are artificial Iron Age Islands built by dropping rocks into the loch to build a platform or islet before building a timber house on stilts on top of the artificial island. You can see a fantastic Crannog site (currently being rebuilt due to fire) at the southern end of Loch Tay, where you'll find a fantastic museum, the Scottish Crannog Centre.

Old Lawers Village is located on the banks of Loch Tay. The Scottish king, Malcolm IV, granted the McMillan barony in 1160. It has been a vibrant fishing village, also milling flax, and even had a pier for steamships, but it was last inhabited in 1926.

The Lady of Lawers was famous for her many prophecies, originally stated in Scots Gaelic, which included 'fire-coaches yet to be seen crossing the Drumochter Pass', almost 200 years before the introduction of steam trains along the Highland Railway.

Around most corners in this region there is a historic bridge, stone circle or castle. A search of the local surroundings will reveal plenty to unlock your inner archaeologist.

	LOCATION	GRID REFERENCE	POST CODE	WHAT3WORDS
START/FINISH	Killin	NN572332	FK21 8TJ	together.intrigued.animated
START OF RIVER TAY AT KENMORE	Kenmore Bridge	NN771455	PH15 2EP	just.backfired.plump
POSSIBLE PORTAGE AROUND RAPID	Chinese Bridge	NN782467	PH15 2NT	hurtles.bulletins.eaten
FINISH	Exit river at slalom course, Beyond Adventure, Aberfeldy	NN865497	PH15 2EB	dunk.scrum.composes

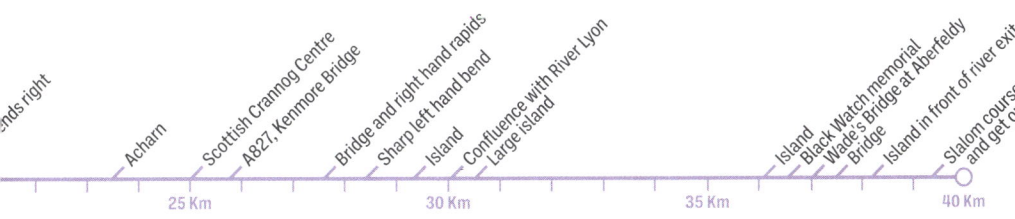

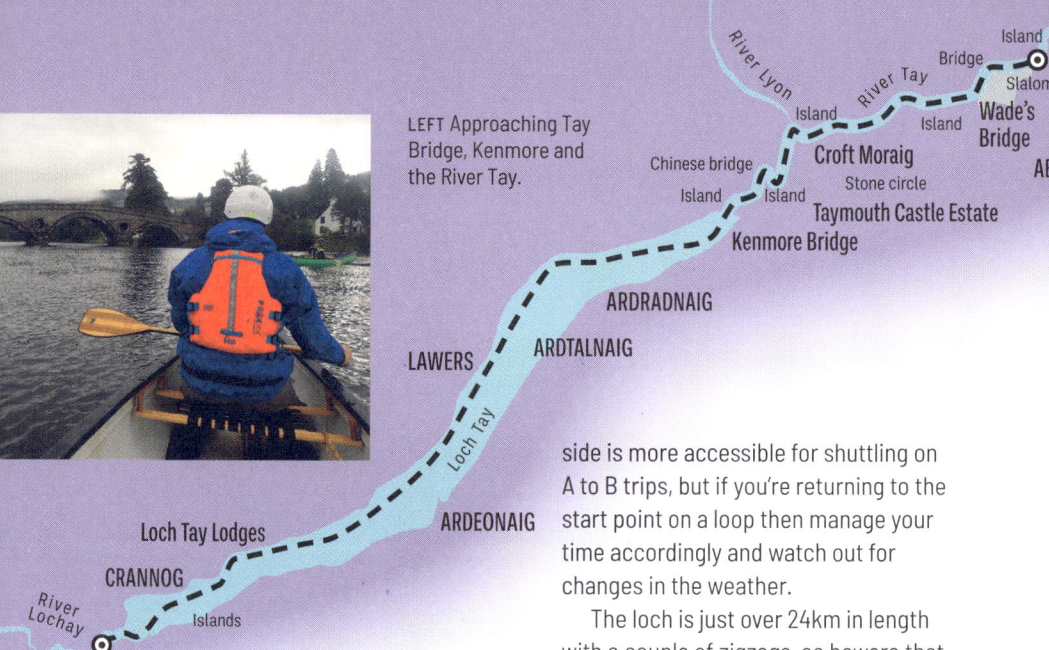

LEFT Approaching Tay Bridge, Kenmore and the River Tay.

ROUTE You can launch at Killin to access the loch on a short section, or further down at Loch Tay Lodges, where you'll have to pay a lunch or hire fee. From Killin, you can practise whitewater skills heading upstream on the Grade 1 River Lochay about 1km, which can be travelled with a mixture of lining, paddling and polling. Under the bridge there's a lovely chute and tiny stretch of rapids, which is great for breaking in and ferry gliding practice.

Leaving Killin, you'll pass under the old wooden railway bridge after 250m heading out towards the loch. Another 500m later and the River Dochart joins the River Tay, although all of the flow is slow moving at this point. There is a series of small islands here, home to a local beaver population and also to us, on some wild camping paddling trips with clients. About 2km from the launch point you'll reach the serene waters of Loch Tay and have options to hug the northern or southern shores depending on the weather. As a general rule, the north side is more accessible for shuttling on A to B trips, but if you're returning to the start point on a loop then manage your time accordingly and watch out for changes in the weather.

The loch is just over 24km in length with a couple of zigzags, so beware that you can't see your destination until the last third of your paddle. Following the left bank, you'll pass by plenty of small bays and about 3.5km down the loch is Loch Tay Highlands Lodges & Glamping Park (a possible launch or hire site). On the right bank you'll have already passed Firbush, the University of Edinburgh's outdoor centre. Access to and from the water is now limited and it would be a mission with kit until you reach Old Lawers Village, another 8km past the lodges. This is worth a visit and on the southern shore is the Tomnadashan Mine if you fancy the exercise and a detour. There's road access nearby on the north shore, as a small lane runs close to the water's edge from the A827 opposite Ardradnaig on the opposite shore, while the main road is also much closer at this point.

Paddling at a reasonable pace, Loch Tay itself gives a good day's worth of exploring and enjoying this pristine location. There are plenty of beaches for lunch or wild camping. After 17km, the final dog leg of the waters reveals the loch end, a welcome sight. At the southern end is a museum, the Scottish Crannog Centre.

There's camping all the way around Loch Tay, either on the few small islands at either end or on secluded beaches and bays. Be sure to follow the wild camping code and leave no trace. We've camped on the beach near here at the mouth of the Acharn Burn confluence, which offered a sheltered site when heavy rain was forecast. Walking up the hill from here will bring you to the mighty Falls of Acharn.

There's a sense of excitement and anticipation as you paddle across the loch, past Kenmore Beach and under the beautiful stone bridge on to the River Tay. The first couple of kilometres are gentle, sweeping bends left and right before you arrive at the Chinese Bridge after 1.8km from the river mouth. Hidden from view is Taymouth Castle Estate.

Chinese Bridge is the first real test of paddling skills and leadership on bigger water. You can inspect the rapid and walk below to some gravel bars and small islands before attempting it. The river bends to the right, so you can see the wave train below. If needs be it can be portaged.

The main rapid is a wave train and small drop under the bridge before the ongoing waves and a few holes, lasting about 150m in total. Be aware that the bridge

ABOVE A dramatic flyby over Loch Tay ensures this particular trip was far from boring.

stanchions can hold trees and snag hazards. The last time we paddled this section two of our young instructors got well acquainted with this rapid, gaining the 'fish award' for swimming.

Once past this rapid the riffles continue and 600m later the river does a sharp left, so set your angle towards the inside of the bend to avoid overhanging trees on the outside of the bend. Around 400m on there's a small island to the left and then another back channel on the right with a larger forested area behind. Another 500m after the first island the main flow forks right and there are gravel beaches and more back channels, which are usually overgrown.

You'll now pass by Balloch Park Lodges on the left bank before a long, sweeping right-hand bend, which signals the arrival of the River Lyon on your left side, which is 800m after the last islands. The river snakes around a much larger island and then begins to straighten out a little. About 1.3km after the River Lyon you'll pass a farm on the left bank and some more islands on the river. After another slow right-hand bend and about 2.75km from the farm you'll see another, longer island on the right bank, with gravel shores and the twin trees of Lord and Lady Breadalbane close by on the road.

The slower, smaller rapids towards Aberfeldy are perfect for practising breaking in and out and making eddies. After just over a kilometre you'll arrive at the outskirts of Aberfeldy and the final bends of your journey. There's a small island on river left and then you'll paddle under the stone bridge at Aberfeldy, which usually has some nice eddies and places to play. There's a second footbridge downstream of this. Roughly 2km past this is a small island ribbon, where you can sneak in at the top or paddle to the bottom and turn in

BELOW Investigating the Crannogs on Loch Tay with Calum, Alex and Damien.

> **WHERE'S THE MAGIC?**
>
> Reflections to capture the wildest imaginations, RAF flybys, beaver lodges and some classic whitewater excitement make this one of our favourite paddling locations in Britain. The whitewater sections of the river draw paddlers from around the world.

by the slalom gates. You've made it! Exit up the bank to the pathway, which leads up to Beyond Adventure and their car park.

EXTEND THE TRIP You can start higher up on the short section of the River Lochay near the power station and paddle back down to Killin, which is a 4km paddle with Grade 1 rapids and a slightly bigger, but short, rapid just under the A827 road bridge.

Or you can paddle onwards towards Grandtully, location of one of the Scottish Canoe Association's (SCA) slalom training sites, which is about 6km downstream. With names such as Boat Breaker, the main rapid here is more advanced water but can be portaged with care. There's an SCA campsite here, too. You could join a trip or hire a guide to help with this section. Beyond Grandtully you could head down towards Perth, which is typically a 4–5 day river descent trip in total.

OUR RICH ADVENTURE Paddling Loch Tay and the River Tay is a relatively recent experience for me. I first paddled Grandtully as part of my advanced canoe leader training and enjoyed challenging rapids. I was brought down to earth with a bump, though, as two very experienced whitewater SUP'ers paddled the same course. Very inspiring to see these full-faced, helmet-clad ninjas paddle past me.

A few years later, Canoe Trail ran a Best of Scotland trip and we based ourselves at the Loch Tay Lodges near Killin, enjoying fantastic canoeing, gorge walking and exploring the crannogs by canoe. We were treated to the most incredible day of mirror-like reflections on the loch with clear blue skies dotted with clouds, making it near perfection. An RAF flyby made the day complete.

One of our other trips turned out to be a canoe expedition of epic proportions, as we paddled the River Tay from Killin to Perth, 105km downstream, in huge flood conditions. We were chased by massive slugs of powerful water charged by continuous and heavy rainfall the entire day. We asked our clients two key questions: are you happy paddling it, and are you happy swimming it? We portaged several section to keep them out of harm's way.

CALORIE CREDITS Killin has a great vibe with the Falls of Dochart crashing down through the village just past the pub of the same name, the fantastic outdoor shop run by the eccentric Dutchman Robert and various other places to eat and relax.

Check out the Falls of Dochart Inn by the

bridge (W: www.fallsofdochartinn.co.uk/food-and-drink) or the Shutters Restaurant on the high street (T: 01567 820314). For paddling trips, stock up at the Co-op supermarket.

WILDLIFE SAFARI Beavers are one of the highlights of this very special place, along with ospreys, kingfishers and of course red deer.

OTHER ATTRACTIONS While in the area, walk the Falls of Dochart and dream of paddling this explosion of whitewater with huge waves, drops and very technical lines. There's also a stone circle above Killin and plenty of others along the Tay Valley, as well as the Clan MacNab burial ground.

If you're up for even more Scottish history, Stirling Castle (W: www.stirlingcastle.scot) and the National Wallace Monument

ABOVE Gemma and Calum take Foxy for a trip across Loch Tay.

BELOW Exploring the wide expanse of Loch Tay.

(W: www.nationalwallacemonument.com) are less than an hour's drive from here. There's also a great graveyard walk near the castle and a fantastic YHA on the rocky buttress of Stirling.

Visit the Scottish Crannog Centre to learn more about life on the loch over 2,500 years ago (https://crannog.co.uk).

THE SHARED ECONOMY If you book into Loch Tay Lodges you can hire canoes and kayaks. They also offer gorge walking and other activities (W: https://lochtay-vacations.co.uk/local-activities).

At Grandtully Slalom Course you can try your hand at whitewater rafting and splash rafting, set up by the amazing Peter Syme (W: https://rafting.co.uk).

Beyond Adventure is based by the slalom course in Aberfeldy just after the bridge and offers a huge range of outdoor activities, including kayaking, stand up paddle boarding, canoeing, canyoning and even adventure photography courses (W: www.beyondadventure.co.uk).

ABOVE Calum canoeing on Loch Tay.
BELOW Roger sailing on Loch Tay.

Canoe Trail runs an annual Best of Scotland trip and a Tay Descent that includes part or all of the Tay system from Loch Tay and Killin down to Perth (W: www.canoetrail.co.uk/canoe-camp/expeditions/best-of-scotland-canoe-expedition).

40 LOCH INSH AND THE RIVER SPEY

This beautiful and accessible paddle allows for small loch exploration amongst world-class wildlife, as the main island in these waters is home to nesting ospreys as well as other fascinating bird life. The River Spey is upstream towards Kinghussie or downstream under the road bridge towards Aviemore. Loch Insh watersports centre is located on the south east shore.

The Lowdown

DIFFICULTY
A short and easy paddle around the small loch with the Spey River at each end.

DISTANCE The loch is just 1km wide and 1.8km long, and is easy to navigate. Plan a route around the Loch with some time exploring the Spey upstream or downstream which add 7.6km to your tally.

DIRECTIONS Park at the layby and carry your craft down 100m to the loch edge. If you're paddling out and back from the same location, you can extend the trip by heading upstream and or downstream for small sections for fun and variety.

HAZARDS
* if you extend route

CRAFT

	LOCATION	GRID REFERENCE	POST CODE	WHAT3WORDS
START	Layby on B9152	NH821043	PH21 1LX	pegged.rolled.dumplings
FINISH	Beach at Loch Insh	NH822043	PH21 1LX	laminated.shaky.shower
POSSIBLE EXTENDED FINISH	Old Bridge Inn, Aviemore	NH895117	PH22 1PU	denoting.beans.routines

BELOW Loch Insh is a small loch ideal for new paddlers.

BACKGROUND Loch Insh is a charming small loch tucked away just upstream of Aviemore and known for stunning wildlife, in particular its nesting ospreys. The River Spey flows gently through the loch near the start of its journey to the sea.

A SLICE OF HISTORY Ruthven Barracks (Ruthven is derived from the Scottish Gaelic *Ruadhainn*, meaning 'Red Place'), near Kingussie, is where the Highland army gathered in 1746 after the Battle of Culloden only to be told to disband, bringing an end to the final Jacobite rising.

Further along the A9 is the historic Dalwhinnie, built in 1898 and now one of a multitude of the world's finest whisky distillers.

ABOVE Rich coaching on Loch Insh.

RIGHT You may be more likely to spot some of the copious wildlife around Loch Insh when away from a big group.

ROUTE Park at the car park layby adjacent to the old railway line to unload kit. Pass under the tunnel and enter the field a few hundred metres from the lapping water of the loch edge. You'll typically see a couple of ghillies' fishing boats lying in wait for busier days on the foreshore. Once onto the water you can explore this small but perfectly formed loch, including heading up or downstream on sections of the River Spey.

If you head anticlockwise on the loch to the furthest top corner from your launching

40 • LOCH INSH AND THE RIVER SPEY

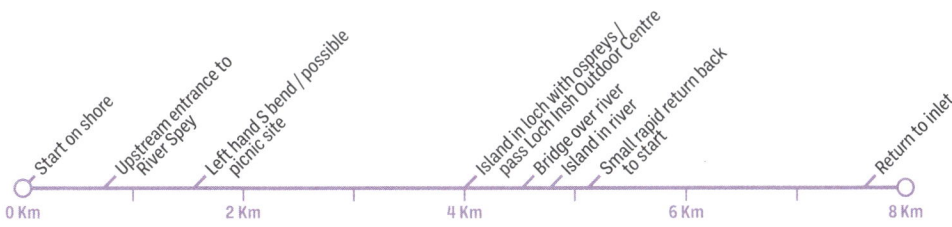

point you'll find the River Spey entering Loch Insh, heading down from Newtonmore and Kingussie. It's ~600m across the loch to the upstream start of the river. Hugging the bank makes progress up the flow easier, but it's usually pretty straightforward. The Spey winds gently right and then left for the first 500m or so, with old trees adorning the low banks. It then enters a double S-bend round to the right and then left for another 500m (we often use the beach and bank at the end of this bend as a picnic stop). Continue upstream in this slow-moving flow of the Insh Marshes as far as takes your fancy. It's straighter now for over a kilometre before bigger bends kick in.

Heading back onto Loch Insh, you can explore the far shore – literally called Farr. About 1.25km down the far shore you'll reach the stunning Loch Insh Outdoor Centre, a family-run activity centre delivering a passion for the outdoors and learning. They offer instructor training, archery, sailing, fishing, SUP'ing, kayaking, canoeing and more besides.

Hugging the far shore it is 600m to the shallows of the osprey nesting island. You can of course paddle around the island and, depending on your plans, return to your starting point, content with a lovely outing on the water. It's about 2km back hugging the shore closest to the start beach. Or head downstream a little further and explore the first sections of whitewater that beckon.

Around 200m down from the end of the island you'll reach the picturesque Alvie & Insh Church and then the old bridge a couple of hundred metres on. The river splits around the small island and you can paddle either side. This section of the river is prone to fallen trees and overhanging branches, so not SUP territory. About 200m past the island the river kicks left on a small rapid and we usually make this our turnaround

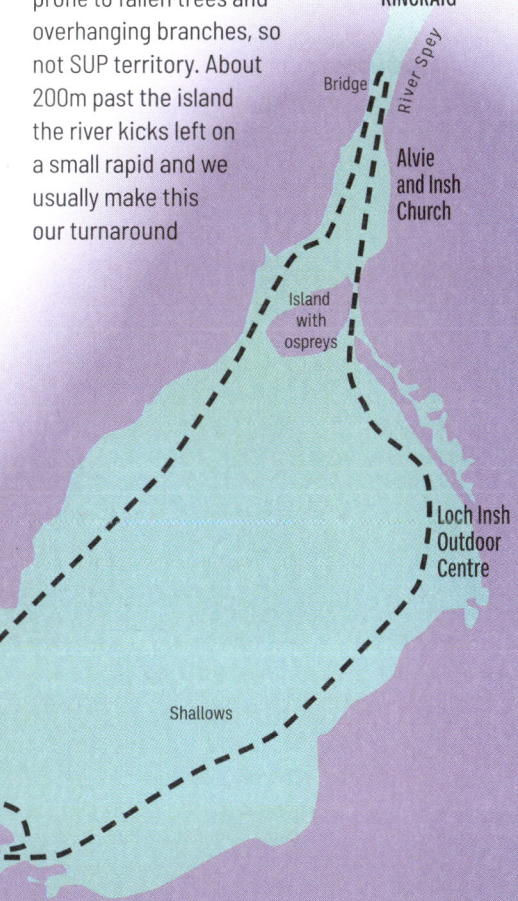

point with beginner groups if we're not paddling down to Aviemore. You can work on skills in the small rapid and then walk or line your craft back up above the small shingle bar (conditions permitting). Once you've played and enjoyed this section it's time to walk, drag or paddle back to the osprey island, finishing up by the layby.

EXTEND THE TRIP   You can get on the river at Kingussie and paddle down to Loch Insh (about 8km to the loch's smooth, open water). Or leave the comfort of Loch Insh and paddle 10km down to the Old Bridge Inn at Aviemore, which adds some small sections of Grade 1 rapids to your journey. Do watch out for trees blocking some channels and pick your route carefully.

OUR RICH ADVENTURE   Loch Insh has been a favourite place to share with our clients for over a decade. Our great friends Davey and Cherryl used to run the Crubenmore hunting lodge, so we lived like paddling royalty for a couple of weeks a year! It's also a great place to get clients paddling with some gentle moving water skills at the inlet and outlet of the loch, which helps build skills and paddling experience at the start of a week together. We'd always head upstream first to practise some simple ferry gliding and even poling.

CALORIE CREDITS   Pack a picnic and enjoy snacks on the loch, allowing time to enjoy this beautiful space. Or why not visit the Old Post Office Café Gallery with tea, cake and local art (W: www.kincraigartcafe.com) or the Boathouse Restaurant at Loch Insh Outdoor Centre (W: https://lochinsh.com/about-us/boathouse-restaurant/)? Definitely allow time in your travel plans to sample the numerous cafés and the Old Bridge Inn at Aviemore (W: www.oldbridgeinn.co.uk).

BELOW Loch Insh can be suitable for solo paddlers with enough experience.

ABOVE Loch Insh is a stunning place to stop and reflect.

WILDLIFE SAFARI Ospreys are famous for nesting on the island, close to Alvie & Insh Church at the head of the loch. Otters and kingfishers are waiting to escort you around the loch or down this beautiful river.

WHERE'S THE MAGIC?

Loch Insh has a deeply spiritual quality and you often have the place to yourselves. There's also plenty of opportunity for lining and tracking, poling and good old-fashioned exploring on the River Spey.

OTHER ATTRACTIONS If you're craving more wildlife, visit the Royal Zoological Society of Scotland's Highland Wildlife Park, almost opposite Loch Insh (W: www.highlandwildlifepark.org.uk), or walk the Wild Cat Trail to see 132 painted model wildcats on the (W: https://wildcatcentre.org).

If you're still feeling adventurous, swap your paddles for pedals and head out on over 30km of bike trails set in Scottish woodland at Laggan Wolftrax Mountain Biking Trail Centre (W: www.lagganforest.com/mountain-biking). Or why not try the TreeZone, situated right in the heart of the Rothiemurchus estate in the Cairngorms National Park (W: https://iye.scot/treezone-aviemore)? Come back in winter to enjoy Aviemore's ski ranges, minus the canoe or kayak!

THE SHARED ECONOMY Check out Canoe Trail's Best of Scotland expedition for a week of paddling in the Scottish Highlands (W: www.canoetrail.co.uk).

You can hire equipment from Loch Insh Outdoor Centre or learn from the experts. There's a jungle float water park, kayaking, paddleboarding, canoeing, sailing, windsurfing, rowing boats, fishing, pedalos and self-led river trips in canoes or kayaks (W: https://lochinsh.com).

41 RIVER SPEY: AVIEMORE TO BOAT OF GARTEN

The River Spey is a magnet for paddlers looking to tackle a little more flow, and get off-grid and into the wilds of the Scottish Highlands. The section from Aviemore to Boat of Garten is a favourite, offering simple whitewater, rugged riverbanks and a great day learning and honing moving water skills, making this the perfect Scottish whitewater taster.

The Lowdown

DIFFICULTY
Grade 2 rapids.

DISTANCE 11.km, A to B.

DIRECTIONS Park at the Old Bridge Inn at Aviemore (pop in to let them know, and make a reservation for post-paddle food and drink while you're there). You'll need to arrange a shuttle back to the car park from the end point, the road bridge at the village of Boat of Garten.

HAZARDS

CRAFT

	LOCATION	GRID REFERENCE	POST CODE	WHAT3WORDS
START	Old Bridge Inn, Aviemore	NH895117	PH22 1PU	denoting.beans.routines
FINISH	Garten Bridge, Boat of Garten	NH946191	PH24 3BG	blunt.easygoing.rungs

ABOVE Get off grid and explore the wilds of the Highlands on the River Spey.

BACKGROUND The River Spey is renowned for being one of Britain's best whitewater touring rivers, as well as the water source for some of Scotland's tastiest Highland malt whiskies. It starts in the Monadhliath Mountains and flows north east to Spey Bay for 158km, with islands for camping, a wildlife safari and plenty of challenging rapids. The start is in Aviemore, the adventure capital of the Highlands.

ROUTE Launch from the beach area at the bottom of the Old Bridge Inn car park. Be

In lower flows, in summer for example, the channels are more obvious as sand and gravel bars are revealed. About 250m after the first S-bend you'll reach a left-hand bend that snakes back around to straighten out. After these two features the river straightens out for over a kilometre, with a few easy-to-contend-with gravel bars and riffles. The river then enters a much gentler S-bend, with woodland pine on the right side, about 1.5km after the last river bends as you skirt the northern end of Aviemore.

The next 3km are a gorgeous stretch of classic touring river with bends, riffles and much to feel happy in life about. The river then bends sharp left at Auchgourish, where sand martins make homes in the sandy cliffs above. Kincardine Church is set back from the river and once around the bend there's a small island, which is perfect for a brew or a quick snack (reminder to leave no trace). We've often shared this spot with customers landing on the back of the island.

Just over a kilometre later the river snakes right around another bend and reverts back to gentle meanders towards Boat of Garten village. Small lanes follow the river's winding course on either bank, but getting access would be a mission. Just over a kilometre later and the river straightens again to reveal the concrete road bridge of Boat of Garten, with a 700m paddle to the get out.

Exit the river on the left side and be warned: it can be slippery, as one of our chief instructors found out, to his embarrassment. Once on the river you can paddle 50m upstream to the old wooden bridge as a gentle warm-up and to practise your skills. The river narrows slightly downstream as it funnels between the banks and bushes on the left and right.

A mere 200m from the start and the river heads into a fairly tight right-hand S-bend with solid, rocky banks for flood defence, making the paddling line and eddies a little bit more demanding. As you enter the S-bend, turn or set the angle of your craft away from the outside edge of the bend and change as you go around the other side of the turn to avoid scraping the side.

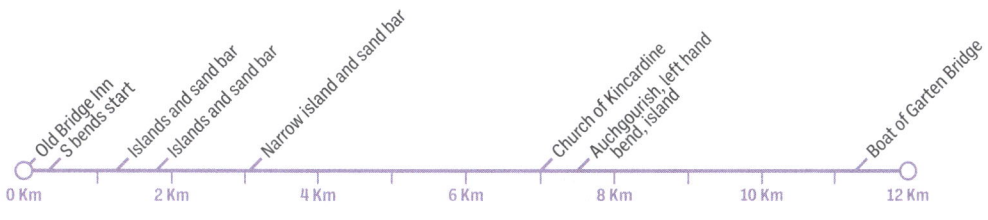

prepared to carry and scramble your craft up through the kissing gate to the road. The road here is wide enough to park your vehicle and allow loading without creating a major obstacle to traffic.

Depending on your experience and pace this is a great day paddle or half day if you simply put your head down and paddle hard. You can shuttle back using the slower and more picturesque B970 or opt for the A9 to return sooner.

EXTEND THE TRIP You can paddle the Spey as a multiday trip by extending the route to Grantown-on-Spey or opt for a longer Spey descent from Loch Insh down to Spey Bay. You could also combine all three Spey day trips (Route 40 on page 259 and Route 42 on page 268) covered in this book! Go big and paddle from Loch Oich to Spey Bay.

A SLICE OF HISTORY Ruthven Barracks stands high on the plateau near Kingussie, and is stunning at night when floodlit, showcasing its former glory. Ruthven is where the Highland army gathered in 1746 after the brutal battle of Culloden. The Jacobite uprising ended when they disbanded. Ruthven is derived from the Gaelic name *Ruadhainn*, meaning 'red place'.

OUR RICH ADVENTURE The River Spey featured in Canoe Trail's Best of Scotland trips for over a decade, as it truly is the pinnacle of whitewater touring by canoe in the UK. Using islands for camping, clients were able to explore the river and learn a whole range of whitewater skills – not always easy to achieve at the same time.

We first paddled from Aviemore to Boat of Garten during a winter spent exploring new trips for Canoe Trail clients. We travelled in a 15ft (4.5m) Silver Birch Broadland and carried lots of kit. It was amazing fun, although a wet ride due to the heavy load! Our favourite sections are those we've included in this guidebook, as they offer great rapids, stunning wildlife and a real sense of adventure.

BELOW Following the line of the River Spey from Aviemore.

41 • RIVER SPEY: AVIEMORE TO BOAT OF GARTEN

ABOVE Be prepared for big weather systems and riffle rapids on the River Spey.

CALORIE CREDITS Pack a picnic and enjoy snacks on the riverbank while you watch the waters rush by. Or allow time in your travel plans to stop at The Old Bridge Inn (W: www.oldbridgeinn.co.uk) or fantastic cafés in Aviemore.

WILDLIFE SAFARI Ospreys, otters and kingfishers are waiting to escort you down this beautiful river, and watch the riverbanks for sand martins and swallows flitting around as they hunt insects.

Further afield on the Cairngorm Plateau, which Scottish writer Nan Shepherd brought to life in her 1977 masterpiece *The Living Mountain*, you'll find lots of ground-nesting species, including grouse, ptarmigan and dotterel.

OTHER ATTRACTIONS Visit Culloden, where the Jacobite Rising came to a bloody end in 1745 (W: www.nts.org.uk/visit/places/culloden), or spend time in the Cairngorms National Park, one of Britain's most remote wilderness areas (W: https://cairngorms.co.uk).

In 1952, Mikel Utsi and his wife Dr Ethel Lindgren introduced a reindeer herd to the Cairngorms. A stay in Reindeer Cottage is a real treat (W: www.cairngormreindeer.co.uk).

THE SHARED ECONOMY Check out Canoe Trail's Best of Scotland expedition for a week of paddling in the Scottish Highlands (W: www.canoetrail.co.uk).

WHERE'S THE MAGIC?

Every twist and turn of this watery paradise is magical. Sand martins and kingfishers flit around the riverbanks and ospreys dive to catch unsuspecting salmon in their talons. The sunsets and early morning mists on this stretch of Scottish wilderness are a wonder to behold.

42 RIVER SPEY: ADVIE TO CARRON BRIDGE

This section of the River Spey offers mesmerising whitewater and endless adventure. You'll paddle rapid after rapid, including the iconic 'Washing Machine' (Blacksboat Rapids) and Knockando (the Scottish Slalom Training Site), which really get your heart racing. The great news is these rapids are achievable for most paddlers with some experience, with rapids followed by slower pools in most cases.

The Lowdown

DIFFICULTY
Bigger whitewater requiring good boat control: Grade 2 rapids.

DISTANCE 18km, A to B.

DIRECTIONS Put in near Advie Bridge (avoid blocking roads or causing an obstruction for fishing ghillies). The shuttle down to the finish, Carron Bridge, is 45 minutes there and back, or ~32km following the Whisky Trail (see below), depending on your route. Park in the village hall car park to avoid blocking residents' driveways. The drive itself is mesmerising, giving you a sense of the fall on the river and the paddling adventure ahead.

HAZARDS

CRAFT

	LOCATION	GRID REFERENCE	POST CODE	WHAT3WORDS
PARKING	Village hall	NJ221413	AB38 7QP	fencing.changes.conquests
START	Advie Bridge	NJ120353	PH26 3PW	times.collects.portfolio
THE 'WASHING MACHINE' (BLACKSBOAT)	Grade 2 can be portaged	NJ179378	AB37 9BQ	paddlers.anyone.plan
KNOCKANDO RAPIDS	Grade 2	NJ189413	AB38 7RP	motored.hatch.launch
FINISH	Carron Bridge	NJ224412	AB38 7QP	fidgeting.hilltop.familiar

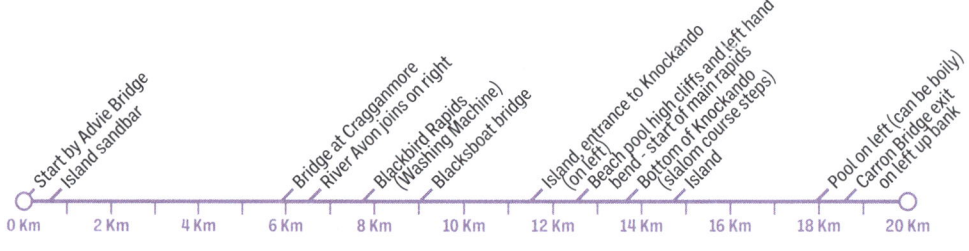

42 • RIVER SPEY: ADVIE TO CARRON BRIDGE

LEFT Dianne and Aaron Buckingham running the Washing Machine (the Blacksboat Rapids).

BACKGROUND The River Spey attracts paddlers from around the globe with its promise of solid Grade 2 rapids offering a more serious challenge. The 'Washing Machine' constricts the flow through two gravel bars with a continuous drop, making a big, bouncy wave train. Knockando, part of the Scottish canoe slalom training facilities, is a more challenging rapid, with more lines and eddies to test the aspiring paddler.

ROUTE Unload by Advie Bridge and walk through the gate and under the bridge to launch your craft. Be aware, the little footbridge can be slippery. While the shuttle is taking place you can get on and practise ferry gliding and surfing on the small wave upstream of the bridge. Once ready to head off the river bends round to the right and is bubbly, with slight riffles to warm up your paddling strokes.

Practise setting your angles to be able to move left and right across the flow on the smaller stuff, which is useful for later on during the trip. Around 700m from the start the river passes the first islands of this section and then bears left, with more gravel bars and islands another 700m further on. The river continues to switch left to right with more gentle bends, and 2km on, it straightens for another kilometre towards Cragganmore.

The river bends right and then straightens again for another kilometre where you'll pass under the Ballindalloch Viaduct, a lattice girder wrought iron railway bridge, now a cycle track. The river bends round to the

ABOVE Ferry gliding across the Washing Machine.

ABOVE A tea break and a breather below the Knockando Rapids.

left-hand side on a wide loop and is joined by the River Avon, which you will have seen on the shuttle to the end. A kilometre on from this and the anticipation and excitement will start to build as you approach the famous 'Washing Machine' (Blacksboat Rapids).

A small fish pool rock jetty appears on the right bank, providing a place to stop and survey the rapid before paddling on. There are benches on the bank here, and you can walk down the right and on to the gravel beach adjacent to the rapid. The Spey heads down and through a 15–20m channel, dropping several metres and producing a great wave train about 50m long, depending on conditions. You can set up throwlines or a rescue canoe below the wave train, but the great thing is that there are limited consequences if you do capsize and need to swim. Entering the rapid and taking a 'point and shoot' approach through the middle, with a 'just keep paddling' mentality, is usually satisfactory. A 'dryer line' is on the right of the main wave train, which reduces the amount of water you might take on board in a canoe or extreme hydration in a kayak.

A kilometre after the rapid is a concrete road bridge (B9138) and shortly after that is a bigger island, which is often used for camping or a brew. Take the left channel here and break out at the bottom of the island if stopping.

The next section offers slower, winding bends for a couple of kilometres as you approach Knockando. The entrance to the rapids is guarded by a large island and the left channel is the best, with a few holes and waves to contend with. As the flows around the island converge the river turns left and loops back on itself. There's a sandy beach on the left bank and a lawn and fishing hut, also on the left. The gravel bank on the right is a good place to empty any water from canoes and grab a breather.

The converging flows below the island create a small, bouncy wave train and the large pool below, opposite the lawned bank, is a large back eddy. Take a moment to enjoy this special place, surrounded by Scots pines and craggy banks. We often use this section as a coaching venue for practising breaking in and out.

After gathering your thoughts it's time to enter the main section of Knockando, around the bend. Aim for the centre channel to the right of the first island and you'll pass between the island and a gravel bar. The river bends round a complete U-shape, so set your angle to move to the right and you'll follow the downstream 'V' between the second, smaller island on the left and the bottom of the gravel bar. As you pass the bottom of the last and third island the river continues to sweep around to the right and then straightens. Be aware that there's a slight sting in the tail with a small hole (whitewater feature) in some water conditions at the bottom of the rapid.

On the left side of Knockando is a get out and steps for the Scottish Canoe Association training venue at the old station car park at Tamdhu. There's a changing area and a toilet on site.

Once past Knockando the river is straight for the next kilometre and then heads into a long left-hand bend. Around 200m past the bend is an island and the main flow goes to the right of it. There are some rocks here and a simple, straight rapid to contend with. Several hundred metres past the island the river bends round to the right in another long turn with a few riffles and waves.

ABOVE The island at Advie Bridge on the River Spey.

The river straightens out for the last couple of kilometres up to Carron Bridge, with a few more waves and a gentle flow to enjoy. This section always seems to take a little bit longer to the finish than you imagine. As you see the banks rise in height with tall pines there is one final bend at the bridge. This is a great place to capture some beautiful photos of craft and tall trees on this special river. The river is a bit boily here, with some big eddies, and as you round this final corner the high span of Carron Bridge comes into view. Paddle under the bridge and get out below the steep bank on river left. Note, there are a few hidden rocks just under the bridge to avoid. The portage and carry up the bank will use up your last bit of energy. Be sure to minimise any disruption to the fishing lodges, ghillies and driveways as you load adjacent to the bridge.

EXTEND THE TRIP Follow the river onwards towards Spey Bay, with more rapids and quaint Spey-side villages and towns such as Charlestown of Aberlour, Boat o' Brig, Fochabers and Garmouth on Spey Bay. You can also stitch together the different day trips covered in this book to capture the majority of the river, from Loch Insh to Bridge of Carron and beyond, and there are lots of islands for blissful camping on the lower sections of the Spey.

A SLICE OF HISTORY There are several beautiful old bridges on this stretch of the river.

The Advie Bridge was built in 1922 and has an unusual concrete span construction. As you head down to the bridge to put in, you'll pass the Advie War Memorial, which is worth a visit.

BELOW Rich and Alan Cooper getting big air on the Washing Machine.

The Old Bridge of Avon spans the River Avon (pronounced 'awn' in Gaelic) near the confluence with the River Spey and is guarded by Ballindalloch Castle. You will see it on the shuttle as the new road passes close by. There is a plaque on the south side of the new bridge showing the level of the river during the 1829 flood known as the Muckle Spate, when the waters rose by 7m.

ABOVE Ash and Amy below the Washing Machine.

Constructed between 1862 and 1863 for Strathspey Railway, Carron Bridge spans an impressive 50m and was the last cast iron bridge to be built in Scotland.

OUR RICH ADVENTURE The River Spey is one of our favourite playgrounds to share with clients wanting to perfect their whitewater skills. We also coach relative novice paddlers. Canoe Trail's original week-long Best of Scotland trip and Duke of Edinburgh expeditions built towards paddling the Grade 2 rapids on this section of the river and have seen many customers surpass their paddling expectations.

CALORIE CREDITS There are no eateries or paddle by cafés so pack a picnic, a flask of tea, some cake and plenty of snacks for the riverbanks. If you're camping on one of the islands, prepare for cooking over a camping stove or campfire.

> **WHERE'S THE MAGIC?**
>
> Surfing the 'Washing Machine' or nailing a tight breakout on one of the Spey's many rapids is simply joyous.

WILDLIFE SAFARI Ospreys, kingfishers, red deer, Sika deer and ptarmigan are common place. As you head towards Spey Bay, keep your eyes peeled for dolphins on the coast. Whales are also occasional visitors, along with golden eagles.

OTHER ATTRACTIONS Visit the WDC Scottish Dolphin Centre at Spey Bay to find out more about one of the smartest mammals on the planet and a frequent visitor to these waters, with over 190 dolphins living in the Moray Firth alone (W: https://dolphin centre.whales.org).

The Malt Whisky Trail takes you to nine wonderful distilleries and other locations in malt whisky country, where you can sample whiskies made from the famous waters of the river you've just paddled (W: https://maltwhiskytrail.com).

THE SHARED ECONOMY Check out Canoe Trail's original Best of Scotland expedition or River Spey Trip for Duke of Edinburgh groups for a week of paddling in the Scottish Highlands (W: www.canoetrail.co.uk).

43 AIGAS GORGE AND RIVER BEAULY

Make sure you bring your fedora for this Indiana Jones-style trip down Britain's answer to the Grand Canyon. Paddle through thousands of years of ancient history, enjoying the wild and untouched landscape of River Beauly and this Highland valley before returning to the modern world at the imposing Aigas Dam.

The Lowdown

DIFFICULTY
Simple rapids, a faster gorge section and committing portage up to the road.

DISTANCE 11.6km, A to B.

DIRECTIONS Park near Struy Bridge (technically the River Farrar) and run the shuttle down to the car park or layby near the dam. Be careful of traffic if walking or cycling. Local taxi companies are used to doing the shuttle, which takes about 10 minutes (allow time for them to get to you from their base).

HAZARDS

CRAFT

	LOCATION	GRID REFERENCE	POST CODE	WHAT3WORDS
PARKING/START	Struy Bridge	NH401 403	IV4 7JS	dampen.handover.jammy
RIVER CONFLUENCE	Confluence of Rivers Glass and Farrar	NH407399	IV4 7JR	fish.shipwreck.shepherds
START OF AIGAS GORGE AT ISLAND	Eileaan Aigasa	NH463414	IV4 7AG	roadblock.deadline.rattler
FINISH	Aigas Dam	NH473 436	IV4 7AG	shoulders.quench.newly

BACKGROUND Nestled in the foothills above Inverness, the Aigas Gorge is one of the most photographed paddles in Scotland. The journey starts 11.6km upstream at Struy Bridge, or you can extend your range further up the River Glas. The ultimate destination is the Aigas Gorge and, shortly after, the Aigas Dam, where you'll end your paddle.

Note, there are a number of sensitive wildlife areas on this trip and paddlers should practise responsible access and follow the Scottish Marine Wildlife Watching Code.

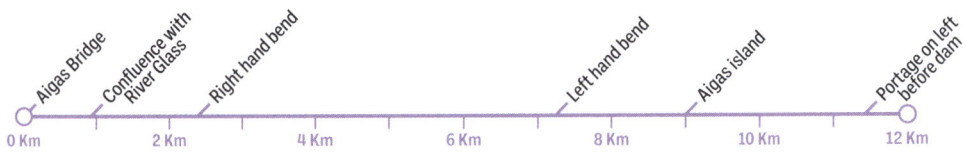

ABOVE Canoes tied up for a lunch stop on the Beauly River.

A SLICE OF HISTORY Bronze Age settlements in the Aigas valley and Beauly area date back an incredible 4,000 years to c. 2000 BC. As you explore the valley and gorge, you sense the eyes of our ancestors peering down on you. The Aigas Dam itself is part of a bigger Highlands electricity generation system that was constructed in 1962.

ROUTE We recommend launching slightly upstream from Struy Bridge giving you time to line up your craft to paddle through the centre of the arches.

> **SUP'ERS NOTE**
>
> It's possible to launch from the small eddy directly at the bridge, but it will put less experienced paddlers under pressure unless you flip your board over or have a retractable fin.

You can break out below the bridge in smaller ribbon eddies on some shallow mini islands in the centre of the flow if you need to regroup. The water here is at its fastest flow. As you re-join you will feel it slow down and begin its meandering wind across the river valley. The route itself is guarded by trees flanking the river on either bank offering vivid colours through most of the seasons. Technically you are paddling on the River Farrar at this point and about 800m downstream is the confluence with the River Glass in the Strathglass valley where the combined flows become the Beauly. Just before the marriage of flows the river bends

ABOVE Paddling through the gorge makes for a truly breath-taking experience.

to the left to negotiate a small island and then sharp left as the Glass joins. This is a great location to practise ferry gliding and breaking in and out using the main eddy on river left at the bend.

Further down the long straight ahead of you is another shallow island, and the main flow kinks left at this point. Around 2.5km from the start the river bends sharp right and flows down through the large river valley with sweeping bends, small islands and sandy beaches, all of which offer good picnic spots. The winding river course generally follows the A831 down the valley.

After 9km you'll reach the Eilean Aigas island, which guards the gorge. Like a scene from an Indiana Jones movie, you'll pick the left channel (river left) to float through the high escarpments above you. It is possible in some conditions to paddle back up through the 350m-wide narrow section of the gorge for a second visit from the bottom using the narrow side eddies to help you.

At the bottom of the gorge is a small island and deep water caused by the dam. You can paddle around to the bottom of the right hand flow, which is shallower and faster flowing. Paddling upstream to the small bridge can be a workout. Towering above you is the replica of a 19th-century hunting lodge. While you're

ABOVE Passing Aigas bridge.

still drawing your breath, from the high cliffs of the gorge the remainder of the paddle has plenty of trees clinging to rocky escarpments and buttresses, and you'll paddle the last 1.75km (1 mile) to the dam. We've been treated to ospreys fishing here on many occasions.

Portage on the LHS before the dam, signalling the end of your 11.6km paddle (don't approach the dam; it has automated sluices that could be dangerous). Exiting the river on the left bank, there's a steep and often slippery climb to the tarmac road and car park at the top.

MY RICH ADVENTURE We've been paddling the Aigas Gorge and Beauly river for many years at different levels with friends and clients who enjoy its unique beauty and paddling pedigree. Like a good magician, it leaves the reveal until near the end. Put simply, it never gets boring. Our trips have included playing and working our way back up the gorge on both sides, eddy-hopping and surfing in waves and small rapids. Writing this, we can't wait to head back to Beauly and paddle it again.

CALORIE CREDITS No watering holes or food stops en route – grab food in Inverness or on the Black Isle while travelling. We always take a decent packed lunch with hot flasks and snacks. No need to slum it!

> **WHERE'S THE MAGIC?**
>
> There's magic around every corner on this trip, whether it's the breathtaking scenery of the gorge, ospreys circling overhead or the occasional sighting of a Highland cow or deer.

RIGHT The view from your canoe through Aigas Gorge.

WILDLIFE SAFARI There's plenty of bird life, the highlight, if you're lucky, being ospreys fishing below the gorge and migrating salmon or trout pushing uphill.

OTHER ATTRACTIONS It's a long journey into the heart of the Highlands, so why not enjoy some of the other activities on offer in the region too? Scotland's ultimate road trip, the North Coast 500, starts and finishes at Inverness Castle (W: www.northcoast500.com). The Aigas Field Centre has been offering wildlife study programmes and holidays for over 40 years from the beautiful Aigas House (W: www.aigas.co.uk). Visit Loch Ness, or paddle on the Moray Firth, where you might spot bottlenose dolphins (see Route 45, page 288).

THE SHARED ECONOMY Several providers offer paddling trips on the Beauly, including Explore Highland (W: www.explorehighland.com) and Canoe Trail on the Best of Scotland trip (W: www.canoetrail.co.uk).

44 THE GREAT GLEN

This is the biggest trip we've included in the book. Build up to it with regular paddling to curb the aches and pains of 4–5 days' medium effort, and your reward will be majestic Highland scenery, history and wildlife. You don't want to rush this trip, but consider scheduling it for spring or autumn to avoid the otherwise ubiquitous midges. Paddling across Scotland will be a trip of the lifetime as you traverse canals and mighty lochs, including Loch Ness.

The Lowdown

DIFFICULTY
A challenging paddle, with long lochs and potentially stormy waters. Check the weather and make realistic plans.

DISTANCE 100km, slightly less if you start at the top of the Neptune's Staircase locks although you can break it into stages.

DIRECTIONS The shuttle is a long one at 100km and ~1.5hr on single-lane carriageways. Check the Great Glen Canoe Trail website for updates and more information (W: http://greatglencanoetrail.info). For harbour access, you are required to obtain permission 24hrs in advance from the Inverness Harbour Master (T: 01463 715715). The canal office is by Muirtown Locks (T: 01463 725500).

HAZARDS

CRAFT
*craft choice will be dictated by conditions and experience.

BACKGROUND There is something bewitching about the Great Glen, the valley that links the lochs nestled between parallel mountain ranges. Its scale and huge vistas, which take an age to reach, are so reminiscent of the Canadian wilderness, with boreal forests aplenty. The Great Glen is host to many lochs, including the most famous of them all, Loch Ness, with its monster and castles.

The Great Glen bisects the Highlands with Fort William in the south and Inverness at the northern end.

SUP'ERS NOTE
There's no wild camping allowed on the canal sections of this route.

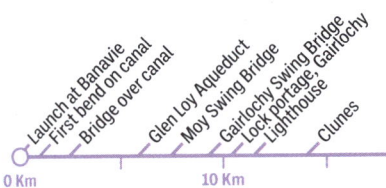

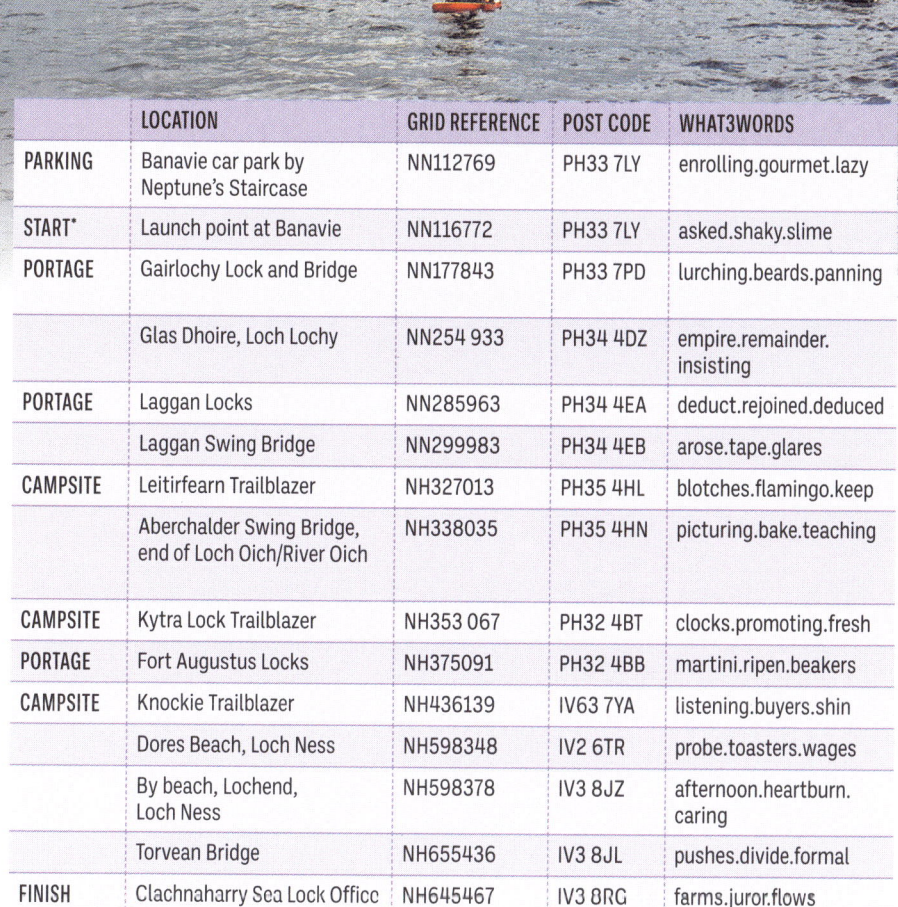

	LOCATION	GRID REFERENCE	POST CODE	WHAT3WORDS
PARKING	Banavie car park by Neptune's Staircase	NN112769	PH33 7LY	enrolling.gourmet.lazy
START*	Launch point at Banavie	NN116772	PH33 7LY	asked.shaky.slime
PORTAGE	Gairlochy Lock and Bridge	NN177843	PH33 7PD	lurching.beards.panning
	Glas Dhoire, Loch Lochy	NN254 933	PH34 4DZ	empire.remainder.insisting
PORTAGE	Laggan Locks	NN285963	PH34 4EA	deduct.rejoined.deduced
	Laggan Swing Bridge	NN299983	PH34 4EB	arose.tape.glares
CAMPSITE	Leitirfearn Trailblazer	NH327013	PH35 4HL	blotches.flamingo.keep
	Aberchalder Swing Bridge, end of Loch Oich/River Oich	NH338035	PH35 4HN	picturing.bake.teaching
CAMPSITE	Kytra Lock Trailblazer	NH353 067	PH32 4BT	clocks.promoting.fresh
PORTAGE	Fort Augustus Locks	NH375091	PH32 4BB	martini.ripen.beakers
CAMPSITE	Knockie Trailblazer	NH436139	IV63 7YA	listening.buyers.shin
	Dores Beach, Loch Ness	NH598348	IV2 6TR	probe.toasters.wages
	By beach, Lochend, Loch Ness	NH598378	IV3 8JZ	afternoon.heartburn.caring
	Torvean Bridge	NH655436	IV3 8JL	pushes.divide.formal
FINISH	Clachnaharry Sea Lock Office	NH645467	IV3 8RG	farms.juror.flows

* If prevailing conditions are from the north, do the trip in reverse, from Inverness to Fort William.

ABOVE SUP'ing the Great Glen Canoe Trail.

LEFT Foxy on the foreshore at a Trailblazer rest site.

OPPOSITE Rich tackling the River Oich (Grade 2).

A SLICE OF HISTORY

In 1620, a Highland prophet called the Brahan Seer predicted that fully rigged ships would sail across Scotland but it wasn't until the 18th century that engineers started realising that vision. William Frazer commented in 1793 that nature had completed half the work, with the lochs left from glaciers thousands of years earlier. The Caledonian Canal as it become known was opened in 1822; it was some feat of engineering for the time.

RIGHT Paddling even a small section of the Great Glen could still make for a long paddle, so look for good spots to take a break.

ROUTE
Assuming the prevailing winds are running south to north, head to Banavie, which will see you paddle from Fort William to Inverness. Unload near the top jetty. To avoid portaging Neptune's Staircase start elsewhere, near the sea lock or on Loch Linnhe if you're maximising your trip.

At the top there's a turning place near the Canal & River Trust toilets and facilities, but the quay is busy so try not to block the route. A 20m walk sees you onto a gang plank down to a floating pontoon and launching on the canal section, where you'll see an enticing backdrop of surrounding hills and treelined watery corridors. As you would expect with a canal that links bodies of water, the passage winds north-east with small bends and a straight course where possible.

The River Lochy tracks the same course as the canal - north-east to south-west, but with plenty more twists and turns. After 500m of paddling the canal bends gently left and then continues a winding course, with the Great Glen Way between the canal and river, so expect to see walkers and cyclists taking an interest in your adventure.

After 2.1km you'll pass a small bridge, and just over 3km on, you'll reach the River Loy Aqueduct, where the canal crosses the river. After another 1.6km you reach the Loy swing bridge, which spans the canal.

Another swing bridge, Gairlochy greets you 2km on. The lock here is usually 'bank error in your favour' and you can pass straight through. Around 200m on you'll reach the lock access to Loch Lochy. For years we have portaged inconveniently on the right-hand side over the rock boulders at the water's edge, hauling canoes up to the track that runs by the canal facilities (with a toilet and water) over a 200m carry. There is, however, a more convenient and shorter portage on the left-hand bank, which is lower, tucks under the pine trees and launches in the small bay on the loch.

Loch Lochy is a tough place to be if conditions are against you. Once on to the loch by the portage, you round the corner

ABOVE Stone balancing on the loch shores.

and a few hundred metres later you'll realise you're partly sheltered behind a breakwater wall with a lighthouse on top.

The loch is 16km long and opens up after the small lighthouse with a sheltered bay to the left with rocky beaches and tree cover at Clunes, or on the opposite side of the bay, depending on conditions. Note, we have avoided providing exact locations for wild camping to prevent overuse and erosion, but there's informal camping at Glas-Dhoire with a Trailblazer Rest Site.

To find a suitable campsite near Clunes means a 3–4km paddle from the portage point or paddling on past Invergloy. Wherever you camp, morning mists and still reflections over the loch make your first brew world class. The paddle along Loch Lochy provides a loch end view in good visibility, giving the illusion of a lack of progress when paddling. Trust your strokes and just keep paddling to reach the headland at Kilfinnan. Follow the water around the corner to the left and you'll see the moorings and cube accommodation pods of Laggan Locks. It's a welcome sight.

Paddle around the back of the moorings to the left of the lock and you'll find a small beach and path there to portage to the top level of the lock to re-access the waterway. It's a picture-postcard location and we enjoyed stunning rainbows over the canal last time we paddled it. This next section of the Caledonian Canal is one of our favourites, as in autumn the Laggan Avenue offers spectacular colours. Stop in at the Eagle Barge Inn (W: https://eaglebargeinn.weebly.com) for refreshments, but beware: it's so cosy you won't want to leave.

Once back on the water, you'll paddle a few straight sections, just over 2.5km to Loch Oich and its idyllic campsite. Keep an eye out for signs to the Great Glen Hostel if you fancy four walls and one of the best hostels in the UK for friendly service.

ABOVE The team nearing the end of their journey across Scotland on Loch Ness.

ABOVE Sam kayaking across Loch Ness near Drumnadrochit.

We've used it as a base on several other trips in the Highlands. At Laggan, paddle under the swing bridge and the main A82 road, and on to Loch Oich.

The loch is 5km of glorious off-grid Highland alchemy with a stunning campsite, islands and an enticing nature. The last trip we did we managed to get a picture on the loch one morning of our canoes, with the Fingal holiday barge passing and an RAF Hercules flyby. Three in one: result! The loch has an hourglass-type shape, contracting and expanding in width as you head north. A kilometre up the loch on the left is the Well of The Seven Heads café and takeaway (T: 01809 501246), a favourite haunt of paddlers.

Invergarry Castle is 2.8km from the Laggan swing bridge, and 500m on from there is a small, finger-like island in the middle of the loch. Another 800m along the right shore is the gorgeous wild campsite at Leiterfearn, which is organised with large meadows and compost loos, so can accommodate a number of groups. Take time to explore, as General Wade's Military Road (W: https://scotways.com/ken/military-roads) runs behind the campsite and this is also a great place to wild swim on the trail.

The top of the loch is 2.5km away and worth a stop-off to inspect the suspension bridge over the River Oich and enjoy the whitewater flow heading below your feet. The Oich is a lovely, bouncy Grade 2 whitewater river but with some rocky rapids, so best to avoid it laden with camping kit unless you're an experienced whitewater paddler. If you're paddling it you can shoot the weir on the left shore following the main flow, which is the left face with a bouncy wave train to access it. If you're unsure of the levels then portage on to the river.

Staying on the canal, you'll pass the Aberchalder Swing Bridge and then another lock 600m further on. Portage the lock and re-join the canal in good spirits. The canal opens up from rigid steel-piled and stone edges to wider, more open sections with marshy banks that seem more appealing to nature and larger, forested areas. After 2.5km the first patch of wider open water appears on the right side and this style continues after you pass Kytra Lock, 500m ahead. Kytra has a wild campsite (designated Great Glen campsite on the right bank as you approach Kytra from the south). There are spots along the left bank towpath where you can see the bubbling whitewater of the River Oich below. The canal gentle winds on for a little over 3.5km until you reach the top of the Fort Augustus flight of locks, which descend or ascend through the town, depending on your direction of travel. Fort Augustus is a change of pace, with shops and places to eat, so top up your energy levels and refill water here. There's a supermarket at the garage, a fish and chip shop, which seems strangely magnetic to paddlers, and other assorted restaurants and pubs.

The portage is a long one around the locks and across the road. You can either launch from the floating pontoons, if there's space, or you'll need to carry further to the end by the toilets to the small beach on Loch Ness at the end of Oich Road. Depending on where you get on, it's between 500 and 800m, so a trolley and barrels or dry bags with rucksack straps become invaluable.

BELOW Rafting up at Dores to sail to Lochend on Loch Ness.

RIGHT Sailing to lunch at a Trailblazer rest site.

Loch Ness (see Route 45, page 288) contains more water than all the lakes in England and Wales combined. Picking a side to stay close to can be useful if the conditions are at all unfriendly, as the loch is up to 2.7km wide at points along its length and there are very few sheltered landing and camp spots (plan accordingly). We have paddled the loch in flat calm to Force 6, when it behaves like a sea with huge waves. It is worth remembering that Fort Augustus with winds from the south may look calm, but once you're out in it or the wind picks up things can change fast. Check the forecast on several locations to be confident it's right for you on the day.

Safety briefing over, it's time to head north in one of the most iconic places you'll ever paddle. There are several different communities on the loch: Invermoriston (8.7km), Alltsigh (3.6km), Foyers (3.9km), Drumnadroichit (11.2km), Dores (5.8km) and Lochend (3.8km) (distances given are between each location as opposed to cumulative). We would definitely recommend visiting Castle Urquhart near Drumnadroichit (see page 295) and Dores Beach, if conditions allow.

Note, we haven't specified wild camping locations as there are only a couple of formal spots with compost toilets and some lean-to shelters (one at Foyers and the other at Knockie, away from the water's edge).

Loch Ness eventually narrows to Lochend, where the shores are clad in the dark green woods of Aldourie, and after a couple of kilometres you'll see the walls of Aldourie Castle, set back in the trees. Lochend is 500m on from this with a pebble beach and the Bona Lighthouse on the right-hand end. The beach is a good place for a paddling pitstop to take in your journey and just how far you've travelled.

Once you reach Loch Dochfort, nestled between Loch Ness and the canal or river system, things calm quickly as the water is sheltered. The loch is short, at 2.2km, and a hidden gem with old wooden freighters and tiny islets adding to the ambience.

From here we'll describe the route via the canal, but you can change to the River Ness if preferred (see Route 45, page 288). After a couple of kilometres you'll reach the weirs leading down to the river and just over a kilometre on you'll reach Dochgarroch Lock. You're on the homeward straight, with a few bends, as you paddle into the outskirts of Inverness. After 5.5km you'll reach Torvean Park on your left and the Inverness sports centre and rugby club, with swimming pool and other facilities. You know you're in the right place as the Torvean swing bridge is dead ahead.

The final section from Torvean to the sea is just under 5km. The A82 road bridge

ABOVE Rainbows over Laggan Locks near the Eagle Barge Inn.

is almost immediately next. Muirtown Locks are 2km from the bridge, which is close to the canal office for return of keys or advice. Just past there is another lock, the penultimate lock before the final one at Clachnaharry Sea Lock.

Give yourself a big pat on the back. You've paddled across a country, no doubt braved four seasons in one day and enjoyed time to rewild yourself. Enjoy the moment and don't forget to allow time to relax and recover before the long drive home.

EXTEND THE TRIP
Start further west on the mighty Loch Linnhe, either close to the Corpach Sea Lock, further along the loch where it narrows at the Corran Ferry, or westward near Ballachulish. Wherever you start, you can exit around by the Caledonian Canal Sea Lock onto the Moray Firth and explore the open body of water to the north of Inverness.

CALORIE CREDITS
We've mentioned the Eagle Barge Inn above, but lochside pub The Dores Inn has also been one of our favourite haunts for 25 years. They do a great range of food and hot drinks and, of course, stronger beverages (W: www.thedoresinn.co.uk).

At the end of the Great Glen Canoe Trail is the multi award-winning Clachnaharry Inn, assuring a warm and hospitable welcome along with great roasts (W: www.clachnaharryinn.co.uk).

OTHER ATTRACTIONS
Visit the breathtaking Lost Valley (Coire Gabhail) in Glen Coe, where allegedly the MacDonalds hid their rustled cattle from English troops. We've crossed the engineer's bridge to access the hidden valley many times over the years. You'll ascend the shoulder of the mountain to find the valley nestled below three mighty Munros.

Or visit the sombre battlefield at Culloden Moor, where the Jacobite Rising of 1745 came to a brutal end in one of the most tragic battles in British history. There's also an immersive visitor centre, museum and shop (W: www.nts.org.uk/visit/places/culloden).

Britain's highest mountain, the mighty Ben Nevis, is not too far from Fort William. Gondolas make access a little easier. As with paddling, check the forecast and conditions before heading up.

Stop at the Red Squirrel Campsite on Glencoe Road, winner of Campsite of the Year 2022 and run by our good friend and former rugby team mate Matt MacLeod and his family (W: https://redsquirrelcampsite.co.uk). The campsite at Foyers, Loch Ness Shores Camping and Caravanning Club site, has more facilities.

If you fancy four walls, the lovely Great Glen Hostel, perfect for outdoor types, is around an hour from Inverness (W: www.greatglenhostel.com).

THE SHARED ECONOMY

Check out Canoe Trail's Great Glen Canoe Expedition, which featured in *The Times* (W: www.canoetrail.co.uk). Or visit Explore Highland (W: www.explorehighland.com), which is run by Donald MacPherson, author of *Great Glen Canoe Trail*, and offers bespoke paddle trips and coaching.

ABOVE Calum sailing across one of the lochs on his Duke of Edinburgh expedition.

BELOW Early morning mists over Loch Oich.

45 LOCH NESS & RIVER NESS

Loch Ness is one of the most famous sections of water in the world, with a vista along its length rivalling parts of the Canadian wilderness. Although adjacent to the Fort William–Inverness road, it truly feels off-grid. Combine this with the Ness, a classic whitewater river with simple rapids and weirs, and you have a fantastic beginner's route for learning to paddle whitewater in Grade 1 and short Grade 2 sections.

The Lowdown

DIFFICULTY
A relatively simple loch and whitewater paddle, assuming fair weather conditions.

DISTANCE Loch and river paddle: ~15km (can take longer if a head wind is blowing from the south).

DIRECTIONS The shuttle from Dores Beach back to the car park at the sports grounds and leisure centre in Inverness is 15km and takes ~20 minutes each way.

HAZARDS

CRAFT
*craft choice dictated by conditions and experience; SUPs recommended on the loch only

	LOCATION	GRID REFERENCE	POST CODE	WHAT3WORDS
START (1) OR CIRCULAR	Dores Beach car park (be sure to spend some money)	NH598348	IV2 6TR	probe.toasters.wages
START (2 - IF STORMY ON LOCH)	By beach, Lochend	NH598378	IV3 8JZ	afternoon.heartburn.caring
FINISH OR CIRCULAR	Inverness sports ground	NH664440	IV3 5SQ	spits.wins.bared

BELOW Jason and Ian from Woodland Ways paddling on a calm Loch Ness.

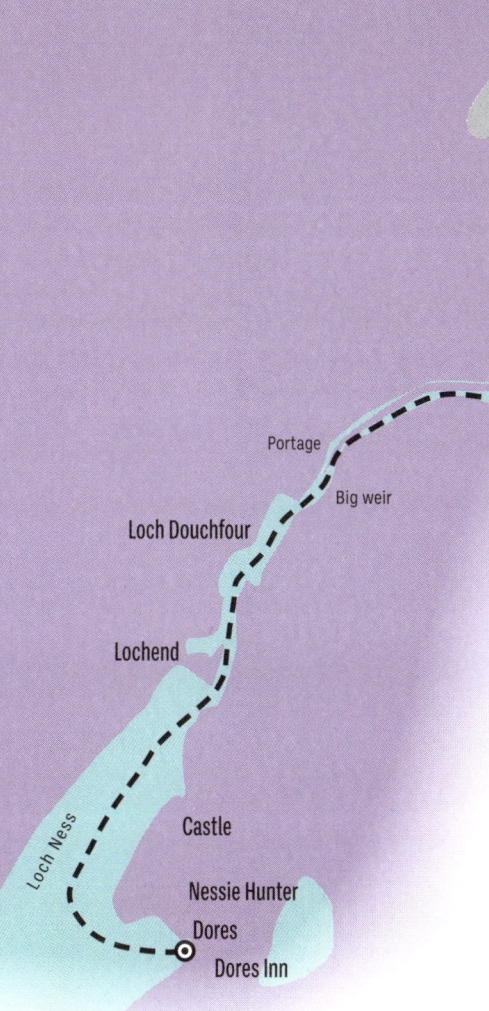

BACKGROUND
Loch Ness conjures up images of deep and secretive waters, Nessie and the Great Glen ridges above. The River Ness is less well known but equally spectacular for providing a bubbly conveyor belt of simple rapids and waves down into Inverness city.

Loch Ness is 37km in length and contains more water than all the lakes in England and Wales combined. At its deepest, it is 229m.

A SLICE OF HISTORY
The Caledonian Canal is part of a rich tapestry of history in this region. It has secured safe passage for freighters and cargo ships across Scotland since 1822. Fifteen minutes from Inverness, the well-preserved Bronze Age cemetery complex Clava Cairns is an incredible example of the historic culture and architecture of the Scottish Highlands. This part of Scotland is also crisscrossed with sites linked to the 1745 Jacobite rising, including the defeat at Culloden Moor.

The impressive Urquhart Castle stands watch over the banks of Loch Ness and, during the 1300s, featured prominently in the Scottish fight for independence. In July 1966, Brenda Sherratt became the first person to swim the length of the loch, in 31 hours and 27 minutes.

ROUTE
Launch from the beach at Dores next to the Loch Ness Monster hunter, Steve. If conditions are windy or waves lumpy, the start is a committing paddle – try to launch earlier in the day when winds are generally calmer. Usually even in calm conditions small waves hit the beach, so set an angle into the waves and push off.

On Loch Ness you often need to paddle a course slightly into the wind and waves to make a more comfortable ride. Head towards Urquhart Castle and turn downwind to Lochend in the north (paddle ~1.4km in a westerly direction). If the forecast is anything less than calm conditions, consider launching from the end of Loch Ness (we have paddled here in force 6 conditions with huge breaking waves hitting the beach – not for beginners or novice paddlers, as launching was like the start of a bobsleigh run).

Turning north, you'll usually have a slight following wind and small waves that gently assist and push you to the end of the loch. The shores are clad in the dark green woods of the Aldourie Estate Woodlands and after a couple of kilometres you'll see the walls of Aldourie Castle, set back in the trees. Lochend is ~500m past this with a pebble beach and the small but important Bona Lighthouse on the right. It is worth stopping on the beach for a snack or a brew, but more importantly to take in this magical and sometimes moody place.

Once you reach Loch Dochfort between Loch Ness and the canal or river system things calm quickly as the water is sheltered. At just 2.2km, Loch Dochfort is short by comparison and a hidden gem – you wouldn't register it as separate to Loch Ness unless someone told you. There are various small boats and several wooden freighter wrecks on the loch, while tiny islets add to the ambience.

Once you reach the weir on the right side drop down onto the River Ness. Paddle the right-hand end, taking great care to avoid the sluices (far right). If you're less confident with the weir, paddle past and portage over the grassy banks to avoid the short whitewater drop.

> **SUP'ERS NOTE**
>
> Be sure you can handle the conditions; Loch Ness behaves like a sea and can have metre-high waves with its 40km fetch. Check the river levels on RiverApp (W: www.riverapp.net/en) before you leave.

ABOVE Jason and Willow tackle the rapids on River Ness.

Once onto the river it drifts left, with the main flow on river right at the outside of the bend as you pass the grassy bank (300m long) between the canal and the river. It then drops towards an island about 800m downstream. You can go either side of the island but decide early, as it is shallow here so the flow pushes you quickly one way or the other at the upstream end.

The island is 250m long and often there are ghillies and anglers in row boats fishing this stretch of the river. The river slowly bends to the right and 700m downstream is a second island for you to navigate. It then bends sharp left and 250m downstream is a shallow fish weir made of rocks - the best channel here is river left with the main flow

ABOVE Deep blue skies paddling to Loch Dochfour.

(I watched one of our clients flip their boat further right along the weir edge).

600m downstream is a second diagonal fish weir adjacent to one of the most beautiful larger fishing lodges you'll see - the lawns look like they're ready for Wimbledon or St Andrew's 18th! The main flow exits across the weir pool with a simple, bouncy wave train on the left side, where there is a gap in the weir at downstream end. As you approach, aim to paddle straight down the main flow, which is a small, bouncy wave train.

The river bends round to the left and just under a kilometre downstream is our

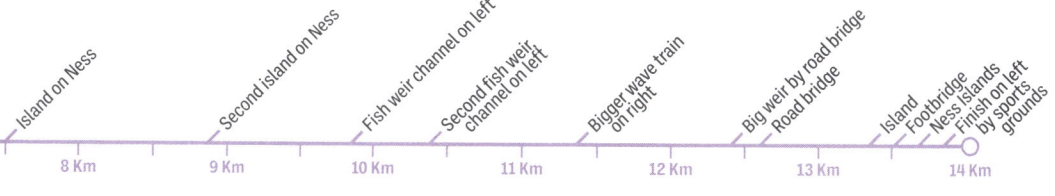

favourite wave train and small rapid on the River Ness. The weir again only extends part of the way across the river, leaving a fast, bouncy wave train on the right side. It is a simple point and shoot wave, but do be aware that the waves are bigger than they look, so maybe take some speed off, or your bow paddler will get a wet ride.

The river runs adjacent to another Highland fishing lodge here, Ness Side Estate, so swimming may be visible to anyone out for a stroll. It's fast here, so swim to the right side, which may take a little while. It's possible to portage the fish weir on the left side but set your line earlier, much further upstream.

The river continues to wind left and then right over the next kilometre until you reach a bigger drop

ABOVE Portaging on the second big weir just before the road bridge at Inverness.

weir next to the A8082 road bridge (Holm Mills), where you do need to get the right paddling line or portage it on the right side. As before, the paddling line is at the top end and right side of the weir, right in the corner next to the old sluice channels. Further along the weir there are bigger flows and

ABOVE Jason and Willow sat below the weir.

ABOVE Starting from the beach at Dores on another glorious sunny day.

lines, but beware they have large boulders in them, which can mean a cheeky capsize and swim. The portage around the weir is far right on the bank and a tricky track, as it's overgrown and a bit of a scramble.

Around 200m after the weir, take the right-hand arch of a new-looking concrete road bridge. If you did want to return to where you started this is the last place you can portage back onto the canal from the left bank, with a 150m carry.

You're now close to the end and the get-out for this paddle. The river kicks around to the right and 800m downstream is the first of a string of islands, where you want to follow the main flow to the left.

You can get out on the left-hand side, just before the small suspension bridge (General's Well on the Great Glen Way), which is adjacent to the sports ground with an ice rink, rugby grounds and leisure centre. It is a scramble up the bank to the road and parking. We used it for years, but prefer now to continue for about 600m, weaving through the Ness Islands to the beach by the fisherman's car park.

Around 200m after the bridge the main flow kicks right between two of the larger islands and you need to paddle through the middle of the small downstream 'V' or tongue of water. The river turns gently left here as you arrive at the beach for your get-out. Pier Ness Viewpoint is a good landmark for landing.

EXTEND THE TRIP Consider paddling the entire Great Glen Canoe Trail (96km), from Fort William to Inverness (note: if prevailing winds are north to south, paddle it in the other direction). This is of course a much larger undertaking, taking 4–5 days (see Route 44, page 278).

You can also extend your trip by paddling the River Ness to the sea. It's 3.5km to the Beauly Firth (turn left when you reach the sea) or Moray Firth (turn right when you reach the sea). Exit around by the Caledonian Canal Lock or on the foreshore by the Caledonian Sea Lock, which is 2km along the coastline.

Finally, you could portage back onto the canal at the A8082 road bridge (Holm Mills) on the outskirts of Inverness and paddle back to Loch Ness and the start on the canal. It's just over 8km to Bona Lighthouse, including the need to portage the Dochgarroch Lock.

OUR RICH ADVENTURE Our first trip traversing Loch Ness was in 1993 or thereabouts. A group of 6 of us drove overnight to Scotland to paddle the Caledonian Canal (Great Glen Canoe Trail). Our silver-coloured canoes were mistaken for the humps of a certain monster, drawing comment in the local papers and causing much amusement. We also took the opportunity to storm Urquhart Castle from the water, much to the surprise of the tourists!

Since then we've led groups and paddled the route on numerous occasions as part of the Spare Seat Scotland for *National Geographic Kids* magazine, starting out at sea and through the Corryvreckan Whirlpool, reaching Oban and navigating Loch Linnhe and then the entire Great Glen.

More recently we have paddled with Canoe Trail customers sharing the lochs, canal and rivers of this route. We have also dodged TV crews filming the Nessie Hunter, Steve Feltham, as we paddled off from Dores Beach. On one trip our Channel-swimming friend, world record holder Sam Mould, took to the water for an icy dip off Lochend.

CALORIE CREDITS Lochside pub The Dores Inn has been one of our favourite haunts for 25 years. They do a great range of food and hot drinks and, of course, stronger beverages (W: www.thedoresinn.co.uk). Pack snacks for the rest of the paddle, until you reach Inverness where you can reward yourself with fish and chips, tea and cake and any number of culinary delights (but mind the gulls!).

WILDLIFE SAFARI There around 200 bottlenose dolphins living in the Beauly and Moray Firth bays if you paddle onto the open water. On my first trip we had dolphins following our silver canoes.

There is a huge wildlife ecosystem surrounding Loch Ness. Fish and good grazing support a diverse range of species including golden eagles, osprey, black

ABOVE Rich and Tom running the first weir (on the right hand side, near the sluice).

ABOVE A more relaxing paddle on Loch Ness.

grouse and ptarmigan. You may see red deer, pine martens, otters and red squirrels, so do keep your eyes peeled. And, of course, don't forget to keep an eye out for Nessie...

> **WHERE'S THE MAGIC?**
>
> This route is a taster of all that is good about paddling in the Highlands. The slightly foreboding, moody nature of Loch Ness combines with the more light-hearted characteristics of the River Ness and will leave you wanting more.

OTHER ATTRACTIONS Guarding the northern banks of Loch Ness near Drumnadrochit, Urquhart is one of the largest castles in Scotland and has witnessed some of the most dramatic events in Scottish history (W: www.historicenvironment.scot/visit-a-place/places/urquhart-castle).

Visit the sombre battlefield at Culloden Moor, where the Jacobite Rising of 1745 came to a brutal end in one of the most tragic battles in British history. There's also an immersive visitor centre, museum and shop (W: www.nts.org.uk/visit/places/culloden).

For something a little different, spend time with alpacas, from simple meet and greet sessions to alpaca treks on the shores of Loch Ness (W: www.lochnessalpacas.co.uk).

With its old bridges, castle, cathedral and Fort George, Inverness has a rare charm. Make time to enjoy the history and stories woven into the fabric of this unique city. The lovely Great Glen Hostel, perfect for outdoor types, is around an hour from Inverness (W: www.greatglenhostel.com).

THE SHARED ECONOMY Check out Canoe Trail's Great Glen Canoe Expedition, which featured in *The Times* (W: www.canoetrail.co.uk).

Visit Explore Highland (W: www.explorehighland.com), which is run by Donald MacPherson, author of *Great Glen Canoe Trail*, and offers bespoke paddle trips and coaching.

WALES

46 LLYN PADARN

Llyn Padarn is a hidden gem nestled in the Welsh mountains near Llanberis in the Snowdonia national park (now officially known by its Welsh name, Eryri). Padarn is a beautiful and accessible ribbon lake offering simple paddling, unparalleled for its majestic backdrops and vistas. It is home to a wide array of outdoor activity providers, and is especially popular with climbers. There are plenty of good eateries to refuel after a day on the water or hill.

The Lowdown

DIFFICULTY
A beautiful and accessible and short river paddle.

DISTANCE The Llyn Padarn circular route is a 7km paddle. You can opt to portage and paddle on Llyn Peris, which will add some calorie credits, a short carry and another 4km to your paddle distance. You can also explore a short section of the Afon Rhythallt, again adding a couple of kilometres.

DIRECTIONS Park at the car park near DMM and Climb Snowdon for access straight onto the water (there are also public toilets close by). It's a 30–50m carry to launch and you can choose whether to paddle the perimeter of the lake clockwise or counter-clockwise, or whether to head to Llyn Peris or the River (Afon) Rhythallt to the north (check water levels in summer) and explore north out and back for a kilometre or so, adding 2km to your trip.

HAZARDS

CRAFT

	LOCATION	GRID REFERENCE	POST CODE	WHAT3WORDS
PARKING/START/FINISH (1)	Launch site, south bank, Llyn Padarn	SH573609	LL55 4EL	shepherds.train.ivory
ENTRANCE TO AFFON RHYTHALLT	Start of river	SH559623	LL55 3NP	hers.cluttered.interest
EXIT TOWARDS LLYN PERIS	Spur down to Dinorwig	SH583602	LL55 4TY	elder.fetches.sped

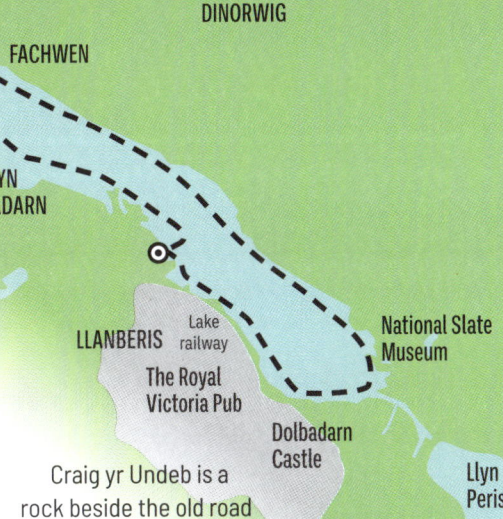

BACKGROUND
At 3.2km long, Llyn Padarn should be a must-do on any paddler's bucket list. The lake is both compact and accessible, allowing you to explore and enjoy its perimeter while marvelling at one of Wales's most wild and rugged locations.

A SLICE OF HISTORY
Llyn Padarn is named after Padarn, a 6th-century saint who has a church dedicated to him in the nearby town of Llanberis.

There is Dolbadarn Castle located on the river spur down to Dinorwig Power Station, which overlooks the lakes and was a defence for the ancient kingdom of Gwynedd. It is believed to have been built by Llywelyn ap Iorwerth (Llywelyn the Great) in the late 12th or early 13th century. It is a short walk, free to visit and worth the effort with unique views.

Craig yr Undeb is a rock beside the old road on the shore of the lake and means the 'Rock of the Union'. It was a frequent meeting place for quarrymen and other workers in Victorian times. Quarrymen weren't allowed to hold public or union meetings or raise union funds at quarries but it was allowed at other

ABOVE The beach at Llyn Padarn is a good place to launch for beginners.

locations including in chapels. During one strike in 1885–86 the Dinorwig quarrymen held meetings here at Craig yr Undeb with up to 6,000 attendees.

Llyn Padarn was also the venue for the rowing events during the 1958 British Empire and Commonwealth Games, which was held in Cardiff.

ROUTE Park at the car park on the south bank, less than a stone's throw from the water's edge. Once onto the water we paddled clockwise, but you can of course choose your own route and plans. Heading left there is a small peninsula with various inlets and crannies for about 400m and then the lake widens out again. The tree-lined bank then runs for about a kilometre following the A4086 road. Ahead of you the lowland rises up with the rocky hill that is Craig yr Undeb and the lake begins to narrow. This area is used for bouldering and rock climbing, so keep your eyes peeled for fellow outdoor enthusiasts.

It's about 400m to the bridge, Pont Pen-y-Llyn, at the head of the lake and the start of the River Rhythallt. When your inner explorer is satisfied, turn around and head back to Llyn Padarn. The north shore has fewer features and does not have road access. About 2.5km down the lake is Cei yr Undeb rock and Cei Llydan station on the steam railway. From here a bay cuts in for about half a kilometre and then straightens

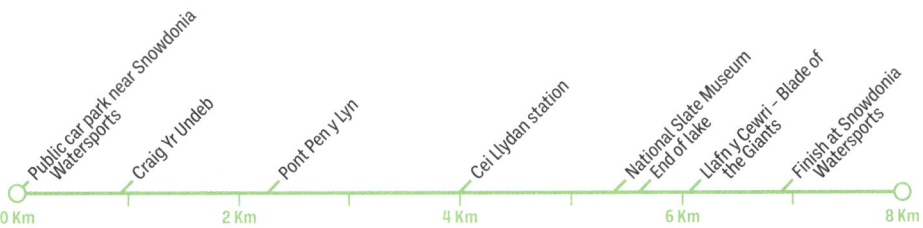
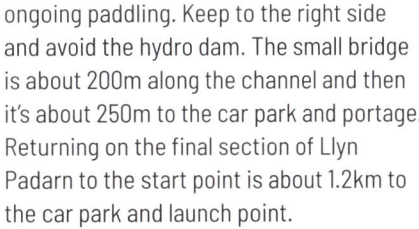

as you approach the Llanberis Quarryman's Hospital and then the National Slate Museum.

This end of the lake is wider but also narrows to a rounded end by the museum, old spoil piles and lagoon ponds. It's a further 400m to the end. The lake narrows again and there's a small waterway leading out to the Dinorwig hydro power plant and potential portage on to Llyn Peris and ongoing paddling. Keep to the right side and avoid the hydro dam. The small bridge is about 200m along the channel and then it's about 250m to the car park and portage. Returning on the final section of Llyn Padarn to the start point is about 1.2km to the car park and launch point.

Padarn really does offer so much in the space of a short paddle. Enjoy exploring!

EXTEND THE ROUTE Head north for some river time, leaving the Padarn for the Afon Rhythallt passing under Pont-y-Llyn. There are actually two bridges on the river here about 100m apart and the river is narrow, with tree-lined banks. Be aware in low levels it can be shallow with rocks and gravel beaches. Around 500m along, the river widens into the small but perfectly formed Llyn Bogelyn. You'll need to judge the water levels to see how far you can go (check from the bridge you might drive over on your way there). The river continues north towards the village of Llanrug, but access is not easy.

You can extend the trip further by paddling south on to Llyn Peris, an example of a moraine-dammed lake, meaning the meltwater was not able to leave after a natural dam formed. Llyn Peris is 1.8km long, adding further stunning paddling in this beautiful mountainous location. If you're accessing Llyn Peris then avoid the hydro plant and paddle to the Dolbadarn Castle car park.

LEFT SUP legend Louise Royale on Llyn Padarn.

OUR RICH ADVENTURE We've spent a great deal of our life heading to this mountainous part of the world and enjoying all it has to offer, from climbing Snowdonian summits to paddling the lakes and rivers of this beautiful region. Both Ash and Rich have enjoyed paddling this small glacial ribbon lake and it is included in Canoe Trail's Best of Wales trips. As a family, Rich and his brother Matt spent many happy days hiking up mountains and camping in all weathers here.

The Blue Peris Mountain Centre, which is just a few miles away from here, offers leader training and outdoor activities to cater for many different interests. It's an incredible centre that Rich visited three times as a student, helping to build his love of and skills for tackling wild and rugged places.

CALORIE CREDITS Pete's Eats is famous among the outdoor climbing and walking community here. It serves great food and a hot beverage after a day on the water or in the hills (W: https://petes-eats.co.uk).

At the north end of Padarn is the Snowdon Inn, with its lovely bakehouse and campsite (W: https://www.thesnowdoninn.co.uk). Other great cafés around Padarn include Caffi'r Ffowntan (T: 01286 871906) in Llanberis and Lone Tree Café (T: 01286 879001) on the southern shores at the eastern end.

WILDLIFE SAFARI Padarn Country Park and Coed Allt Wen, a sessile oak woodland, are located on the northern shore and the lake and woodland are designated SSSIs.

OTHER ATTRACTIONS Visit the National Slate Museum, a living museum housed in the industrial workshops that once serviced the nearby Dinorwic slate quarry (W: https://museum.wales/slate). Or why not hitch a ride on the Llanberis Lake Railway (W: www.lake-railway.co.uk)?

If you're up for something a bit more invigorating, check out Ropeworks Active, an outdoor adventure activities and high ropes centre based in Llanberis (W: https://ropeworksactive.co.uk).

There are plenty of campsites and B&Bs around Llanberis, offering great places to rest your head after a day on the water or in the mountains. We like Camping In Llanberis (W: www.campinginllanberis.com), which offers camping, glamping, yurts and a touch of home comforts.

And, of course, Snowdon and the rest of the Snowdonia National Park are just around the corner, offering world-class hiking in breathtaking scenery.

THE SHARED ECONOMY Visit Snowdonia Watersports for SUP hire, single and tandem kayaks and supported open water swimming (W: www.snowdoniawatersports.com).

You can book in for coaching or group sessions for paddling, coasteering, gorge scrambles and a range of other activities at Boulder Adventures (W: www.boulderadventures.co.uk).

> **WHERE'S THE MAGIC?**
>
> Welsh mountains calling you, Llyn Padarn's mystical waters and a community of people converging to enjoy the great outdoors – this is what the best paddling locations are made of. All of this is on the doorstep of Llanberis, one of Britain's outdoor capitals, and in the shadow of Snowdon (Yr Wyddfa in Welsh), the tallest mountain in Wales at 1,085m.

OPPOSITE SUP ninja Darren admires the kind of dramatic view you'll get on this paddle.

47 RIVER CONWY

North Wales is the land of epic landscapes, fantastic beaches, enchanted castles and meandering rivers, and there can't be many trips offering such a wide range of beautiful sights as the River Conwy. From its picturesque start in Llanrwst to its fairy tale ending at Conwy Castle, a UNESCO World Heritage Site, this is one paddle you won't want to miss. You can paddle A to B or time the tides to paddle out and back from Conwy Castle and Harbour or Beacons Car Park.

The Lowdown

DIFFICULTY
A lovely paddle with a short section of exciting rapids. Make sure you get the tide times right.

DISTANCE Llanrwst to Conwy Castle with estuary meandering: ~21km or use the tide from Conwy out and back from the same start and finish point.

DIRECTIONS We parked at the small tea shop in Llanrwst and organised a taxi shuttle to drop the command vehicle to Conwy, some 20km away, which takes about 25 minutes depending on traffic.

Note: you'll need to time your trip to allow for the tidal section at the end to avoid an absolute slog against the tide and any wind.

HAZARDS
*near the end of route

CRAFT

	LOCATION	GRID REFERENCE	POST CODE	WHAT3WORDS
START	Llanrwst Bridge, Tu Hwnt I'r Bont tea rooms	SH798614	LL26 0PL	adopting.satin.onion
TIDAL RANGE	Trefriw	SH781638	LL27 0JT	usages.foresight.husky
POTENTIAL START	Tal-y-Cafn	SH785718	LL28 5RJ	mindset.envy.asked
RAPIDS	Tal-y-Cafn	SH783709	LL28 5RR	windows.daydream.conspire
CONWY CASTLE	By railway bridge	SH784774	LL32 8BD	compiled.precluded.brownish
FINISH	Slipway near road	SH785773	LL32 8UB	happening.homes.silent
FINISH (2) - BEACONS CAR PARK	Slipway at mouth of estuary	SH774789	LL32 8GJ	documents.arrived.modifies

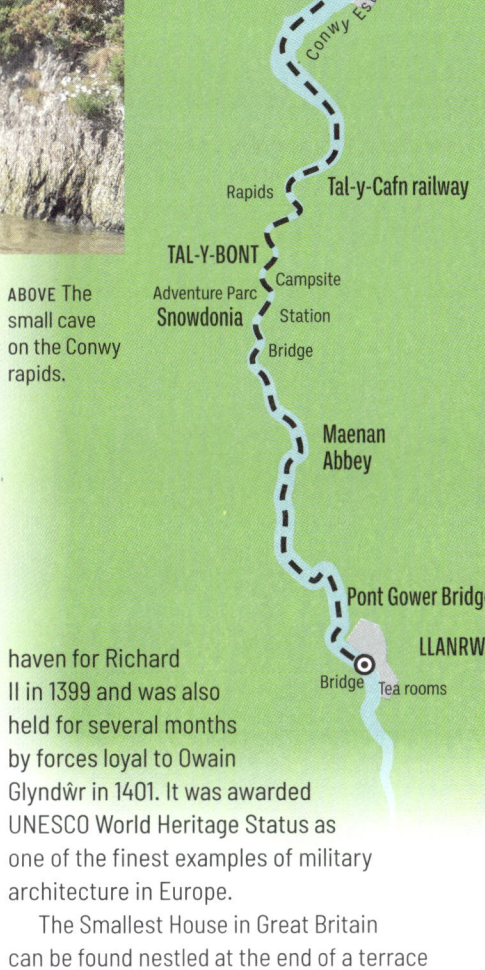

BACKGROUND North Wales is an adventure playground of world-class stature, with mountains, sea kayaking, castles and history to keep you busy. The River Conwy is a mesmeric set of riffles and gentle rapids from Llanrwst or starting downstream at Tal-y-Cafn Bridge on river left. The UNESCO World Heritage Site at the castle and walls is worth a visit just on its own before you add in some of the walks, paddling, nature reserves and so much to do around the area. The name 'Conwy' derives from the old Welsh words *cyn* ('chief') and *gwy* ('water') and the river flows over 55km from the source to the sea.

A SLICE OF HISTORY Conwy Castle is a walled 700-year-old fortress overlooking the ancient port town. The castle and town walls were built by King Edward I and his architect Master James of St George in just four years between 1283 and 1287. It has an impressive history including withstanding the siege of Madog ap Llywelyn in the winter of 1294–95, acting as a temporary

ABOVE The small cave on the Conwy rapids.

haven for Richard II in 1399 and was also held for several months by forces loyal to Owain Glyndŵr in 1401. It was awarded UNESCO World Heritage Status as one of the finest examples of military architecture in Europe.

The Smallest House in Great Britain can be found nestled at the end of a terrace of ancient houses on Conwy's quayside. It is just 1.8m wide by 3.1m high. It was last inhabited by 6ft 3" (1.9m) fisherman Robert Jones.

ABOVE Starting out at Llanrwst.

The stunning river crossing and tea room at Llanrwst Bridge was constructed by Inigo Jones in 1636. It is recorded that Richard Wynn of Gwydir acted as Treasurer to the Queen and paid Jones and the aptly named master mason Nicholas Stone, from whom Wynn also commissioned a plaque for Llanrwst church in 1634.

ROUTE Launch just downstream of the Pont Fawr (Inigo Jones Bridge) in Llanrwst down the bank from the café on the grassy riverbank. You are immediately enjoying gravel bars and short sections of Grade 1 riffles. Do check the river levels and tides, or you're guaranteed a tough scrape and tide against you later on.

The river runs pretty straight and true for the first 700m before turning 90 degrees to the right and passing under Pont Gower, 250m around the bend. The river bends to the left in 250m as you leave Llanrwst behind you. A kilometre further on, the river enters a left-hand S-bend, doubling back on itself.

Half a kilometre later the river passes through gravel bars and receives a small flow from a ditch-size tributary, and then bends right and heads north. You're not far from the B5106 on the left bank and you're within walking distance of the Princes Arms Hotel. The river winds gently north at slow speed with shallow bars for the next couple of kilometres. As you get level with the rural settlement of Maenan, the river dog legs right slightly before returning to its northerly course.

After about 1.2km of winding paddling you'll pass under a small bridge close to

Dolgarrog railway station. Shortly after the bridge are some larger sand bar islands, where the main flow is on the right side of the river. Just over 1.4km downstream the river bends right as you pass behind Adventure Parc Snowdonia's surf venue.

Afon Porth-llwyd joins the River Conwy and together they thread past various sand bars and braids as they flow north, carrying you closer to the Conwy estuary. A couple of kilometres after the Afon Roe has joined, the features change, with a short and more meaty rapid. This almost comes as a bit of a surprise, as you're now entering actual whitewater after slow-moving riffles. If it helps you to identify it on the map, you're just short of the small settlement Tal-y-Cafn. The rapid is just over 100m long and the main channel is two-thirds of the way across the river to the right side. The left side has a smaller channel between a rock shelf and there is a small cave tucked away if you look back.

A kilometre past the rapid you'll paddle under the B5279 road bridge close to the Tal-y-Cafn railway station. This is a potential launch site for a paddle if you want to shorten the distance or as mentioned above change to an out and back slingshot paddle with the tides from the Castle or from Beacons Car Park. In summary there are plenty of ways to enjoy the Conwy.

The river bends slowly left and widens here, as its characteristics become more estuary then river. About 2.5km downstream the river estuary bends right and opens further and is almost 400m wide at this point. Don't forget, as the tide ebbs much of this is mud flat and not ideal for us as paddlers. At lower tide conditions the mud flats become a predominant feature and potential barrier to your paddling trip, with S-bends and winding flows. On our trip the wind had picked up and was hampering progress along with a flooding tide. The fun and jokes began to dry up quickly. Waiting to see Conwy Castle with its impressive defensive position became our all-consuming thought (are we nearly there yet?!).

ABOVE Launch at the Tal-y-Cafn Bridge for a shorter paddle.

About 2km on and finally the left-hand bank recedes to reveal the town and castle. As the estuary bend heads left it's still another 2km paddle to reach the castle and railway that passes in front. It's worth hugging the left-hand bank to cut the corner and potentially shelter from any head winds.

Once at the castle, a UNESCO World Heritage Site, your joy at arriving here becomes euphoric. Take time to paddle around the castle, topping up your holiday photo albums and to see the harbour and different viewpoints of the defences. Despite the raw anticipation of regal fanfares announcing our arrival at the castle, none were forthcoming. Oh well, perhaps next time.

EXTEND THE TRIP You can paddle onwards from the Castle to the mouth of the estuary just past Conwy Marina Village, landing on the shore to access Beacons Car Park on the left bank. It is about 2km past the castle and you can explore further around the bay closer to Deganwy and Great Orme Head. The mood of the water changes in this last section with lots of boat moorings. Do be careful when the tide is running fast as there is a risk of being broached in front of the buoys and boats.

OUR RICH ADVENTURE This paddle is one of our favourites, with lots of wildlife, small rapids, winding estuaries and, of course, a massive walled town and castle to top it all off. It had long been on our wish list, as our friend and former Royal Marine Roger Palin had been stationed there running adventure training courses from Llanrwst.

We did the shuttle, availing ourselves of the café's tea and cakes at Llanrwst Bridge before heading off. We enjoyed some beautiful riffles and Grade 1 rapids along the route, as well as plenty of small gravel bars. We also stopped to let the dogs have a stretch on one of the mini beaches in the middle of the river and with the light and

BELOW The pipeline bridge over the river.

shallows managed to act out a scene where it literally looked as if Ash was walking on water!

We pushed off for a fantastic adventure on the small rapids, tidal estuaries and then a massive head wind sting in the tail. The rapids near Ty'-n-groes appeared like a figment of the imagination, after having enjoyed flat water paddling for miles. On a more recent paddle we explored the little cave on river left and rapids were submerged with the tide in. After then, strong winds and an incoming tide began to reduce our headway, meaning that rounding the last mud flat to see the castle was a euphoric moment. There is a lovely nature reserve opposite the castle on the foreshore, which we can also wholeheartedly recommend.

CALORIE CREDITS The 15th-century Tu Hwnt I'r Bont tea rooms is right at the start of your day's paddle and offers great cake and refreshments while you complete the shuttle (W: www.tuhwntirbont.co.uk), but we also recommend taking a picnic and snacks, otherwise you'll need to forage along the route as there are no pub or café options. Once you reach the castle and city walls you are assured of choices galore, with many lovely cafés, restaurants and pubs.

WILDLIFE SAFARI Mergansers, kingfishers and lots of wading birds lined the route to keep us occupied. Out in the harbour, there were more cormorants on the rigging lines, as well as gulls queueing for ice creams!

> **WHERE'S THE MAGIC?**
>
> Robust castle walls surrounding an iconic castle nestled on the Conwy estuary make for one of the most incredible finishes of any paddle we've completed, and that includes finales at Tower Bridge, Loch Ness and even the Statue of Liberty. The small rapid section adds a little excitement to the trip, too.

ABOVE Rich and Foxy on the sands of the Conwy Estuary with the castle in sight.

OTHER ATTRACTIONS Visit Adventure Parc Snowdonia, an artificial surf wave and an engineering masterpiece. There's also an excellent aquapark and indoor climbing facilities (W: www.adventureparcsnowdonia.com). Meandering around Conwy Town, grabbing fresh fish and exploring the town walls is a brilliant way to enjoy a few hours' downtime. It's literally a maze of ancient walls, arches and narrow passages (W: www.visitconwy.org.uk/towns-and-villages/conwy).

Visit the world's smallest house (183cm wide x 310cm high), according to the Guinness Book of Records, which is set on the Conwy quay and was home to Robert Jones, who was 6ft 3in (1.9m).

If you're visiting the area, then it's worth making a detour to see the impressive Menai Straights. Be aware that paddling it requires serious tidal planning and experience, but you can hire a local guide.

Finally, you have some of Britain's finest walking within striking distance, with Swallow Falls in Betws-y-Coed Forest, Llanberis Pass and its many routes and, of course, Snowdon itself.

THE SHARED ECONOMY About 40 minutes away is the lovely Snowdonia Watersports, offering single and double kayak hire, SUPs and open water swimming (W: www.snowdoniawatersports.com).

48 RIVER DEE: LLANGOLLEN CANAL AND THE PONTCYSYLLTE AQUEDUCT

At 110km long, the River Dee (Afon Dyfrdwy) is a Welsh giant that runs through North Wales and into England. It remains one of my favourite rivers of all time, offering a Plan A, B and C of various options depending on levels and conditions, while the Llangollen Canal ensures a literal natural high as you paddle over the Pontcysyllte Aqueduct. The Dee loop from river to canal can be paddled throughout the year.

The Lowdown

DIFFICULTY
A lively whitewater paddle with simple rapids, compact loop with some technical rapids and a breath-taking aqueduct across the sky.

DISTANCE
Coed-Y-Glyn Log Cabins to Llangollen Pavilion: 12km.
Dee Loop, Mile End Mill onto Canal, Chain Link rapids back to Mile End Mill: 5.2km.
Llangollen Pavilion to Pontcysyllte Aqueduct/Aqueduct Inn: 10km.

DIRECTIONS
If you're doing the first route in the list above, you'll find a car park just off the A452. For the second route, paddle the Llangollen Loop starting at Mile End Mill or the car park at Horseshoe Falls. For the third local Dee paddle from the Horseshoe Falls car park or the car park at the Llangollen Pavilion.

RESTRICTIONS AND ACCESS
Paddling is allowed if the water level is at least 3ft (0.9m) on the Coed-Y-Glyn gauge at 8am, at any time of the year.
Between 1 April and 30 August, paddling is allowed on Wednesdays and Saturdays irrespective of water height.
In all cases, launching is between 10am and 12.30pm and downstream of Groeslwyd by 1.30pm.
Source: Welsh Dee Partnership

HAZARDS

CRAFT

BELOW The Llangollen Canal next to the Pavilion car park.

WALES

BACKGROUND The River Dee is simply extraordinary and is constantly changing, from directed flows and eddies to boiling masses of whitewater. It has many fantastic rapids and iconic locations, such as the deep valleys it winds through, to the incredible Pontcysyllte Aqueduct and canal system. It seamlessly blends natural world wonders with engineering feats and offers so many different experiences, you'll return to paddle it for years to come. The Dee Valley is a destination to stay for a few days and unwind in an adventure paradise.

A SLICE OF HISTORY The Pontcysyllte Aqueduct was designed by Thomas Telford and William Jessop and completed in 1805 spanning the Dee Valley. It was constructed by John Simpson, a stonemason, and William Hazledine, an ironmaster. A pioneering and bold civil engineering solution, it employed a cast iron trough suspended 38m above the river with supported iron arched ribs. The entire structure was supported on 18 hollowed masonry pillars and was recognised as a UNESCO World Heritage Site in 2009.

The first Llangollen chain bridge was built in 1818 by the fabulously named Exuperius Pickering. It was built to transport materials such as coal, lime and stone from the canals across the Dee Valley to meet the London to Holyhead Road built by Telford. The new bridge was more direct and avoided the Llangollen toll bridge downstream allowing him to transport coal from his Acrefair mines using the canal and onwards to Corwen.

ABOVE Kayaking over the Pontcysyllte Aqueduct.

The Cistercian abbey Valle Crucis (known in Welsh as both Abaty Glyn Egwestl and Abaty Glyn y Groes), was built in 1201 by the Prince of Powys Fadog and is located in Llantysilio in Denbighshire.

Castell Dinas Brân was built in the 13th century by Gruffydd Maelor II, a prince of Powys Fadog. It was built on the site of an earlier Iron Age hillfort, but is now just ruins. It was perched above the campsite we used for our group trips tucked in the valley hill folds called Wern Isaf Farm. You can walk up to the castle in about 30 minutes from the campsite. *Dinas Brân* has been variously translated as the 'crow's fortress' and was known as Crow Castle to the English.

	LOCATION	GRID REFERENCE	POST CODE	WHAT3WORDS
START (1)	Coed-Y-Glyn Log Cabins	SJ152429	LL20 7YY	issuer.standards.loss
START / FINISH	Weir at Horsehoe Falls	SJ195433	LL20 8BS	global.showcases.spaceship
SERPENTS TAIL	Rapid Grade 3(4) Portage on left	SJ200433	LL20 8BH	buying.booster.wished
FINISH (1)/START (2)	Car park at Llangollen Pavilion	SJ210426	LL20 8SS	proved.sentences.graced
ALTERNATIVE START (3)	T and R Llangollen Mile End Mill	SJ207428	LL20 8AG	directors.gracing.divides
RIVER EXIT TO TUNNEL	Portage under railway to Llangollen Pavilion	SJ210423	LL20 8SY	misted.validated.captures
FINISH (2)	Pontcysyllte Aqueduct Trevor Basin	SJ270420	LL20 7TY	rams.utensil.framework

ABOVE On the Dee loop of the Llangollen Canal, heading up to Horseshoe Falls.

ROUTE Head upstream on the old coach road, the A5, and turn right at Nant y Pandy to cross the River Dee. Pre-arrange to launch from Coed-Y-Glyn Log Cabins on the Dee and you are immediately onto one of the best deep valley paddles in the UK, through treelined bends that appear to drop off the edge of the world, reminiscent of paddling in the Canadian boreal forests.

The river flows quickly, so once you break into the blue highway you're off downstream. Around 300m from the launch point the river sweeps left and shows you its true colours with bubbling rapids, though nothing too complicated. Another 800m downstream it bends right with similar purpose and more enjoyable whitewater moments. After the river has carved its arc it straightens for 1.5km.

The river valley is stunning here, with high hills flanking your low road. The next few kilometres are geological masterpieces carved through the millennia, where the river loops are so pronounced they feel like they want to touch each other. As you start the left-hand bend there are several more meaty rapids with a general clear channel down the centre of the river.

At 9.5km you'll round the final right-hand bend before Horseshoe Falls. Don't worry: it's not like a Tarzan film or Niagara Falls, where it will suck you over the edge, but you do need to be far left of the river, by the bank. Exit at the Horsehoe Falls car park or join the canal and chose whether to paddle to Pontcysyllte Aqueduct or exit at the Pavilion Car Park.

Below the falls is great whitewater down to the mill, including the much loved Serpent's Tail which is included in the Dee Loop.

The Dee Loop

Starting this paddle from the conveniently located Mile End Mill, you can chose to park, pay and play at T and R Outdoors. You can turn left in the car park and walk up 50 or so metres to the slipway and paddle the chutes. There are various small rapids in front of the Mill and you can paddle and loop this smaller section around a 150m in length around rock slabs and an island. In the centre of the river are several islands which divert the flows and create great eddies and features to play on.

Heading downstream the main flow bears left and curves around a large island on the left side. 550m downstream from the start the river bears left and there is a tunnel under the railway allowing access to the road (river left). This is 200m below the end of the island river left. Carry your craft up to the A452, Abbey Road, turn left, portage to the Pavilion car park, which is 150m along the road and 300m to the canal to resume your paddle.

Relax and kick back exploring the canal, upstream against the minimal flow up to the Chainbridge Hotel, which is 2.85km to Horseshoe Falls. Look out for the horse-drawn tourist canal barge (don't worry, you can squeeze in between the edge and the barge). At the head of canal by the falls you switch back to the river and scramble down the bank above the Chainbridge Hotel. If kayak is your mode of travel there is a great kayak 'seal launch' ramp. Once on the water the main flow is left side as you pass under the arches of the King's Bridge Viaduct.

The flow squeezes left side and runs alongside the hotel with some bubbly Grade 2 rapids lasting about 50m. It slows with some pools for about 100m before the river narrows to the entrance to the Serpent's Tail. You can land on the left side where there are lots of slab rocks allowing you to portage or run the Grade 3 narrow rapid (check the levels). The river drops several metres as it narrows into the gorge and bends to the left and accelerates into the narrowest section, which is only about 3-4m wide. It straightens and then squeezes out through a constriction with a rock making the river not much wider than your canoe or kayak. Scout it first as this can be a pin risk so ensure you have safety set up with throwlines and experienced people or walk around the rapid.

After Serpent's the river returns to a more solid set of Grade 2 rapids with flat fast sections. It kinks a little right and then left with simple features. The river curves round a right hand bend next to the

ABOVE The mighty Dee is a lovely Grade 2 river for paddling.

RIGHT Rich navigating some riffles above Horseshoe Falls.

OPPOSITE A good place to launch or stop in the section between the cabins and Horseshoe Falls.

Llangollen Motor Museum and runs through a weir and short rapid with easy lines but a few rocks in low water. Around the bend there are some small riffles before you paddle under the railway bridge. 150m on and you will see a slab rock across the river with the main channel in lower water on the left side. The channel squeezes around the outside of the bend and you need to steer right of the channel as a rock blocks the centre. Effectively it's a right angle turn on the river left.

Cross to river right and paddle down the right side of the island in the centre of the river 100m below the slab rocks. At the bottom of the island (about 70m) the river kicks left with a simple riffle rapid which can be shallow in low flows. The end slipway is in sight on river right before the river bends left. Loop done you can exit to the car park or paddle down for the next 150m or so and still make the car park.

The Canal Section

The river joins the canal to the left of Horseshoe Falls and there is a small building and indents into the bank, where you can exit the river. You'll need to portage around the bank and field through the wooden gates, where you cross over the canal to join on the right bank as you look ahead. It's ~150m carry around to the canal, and what a contrast! This is now very much a yin yang paddle, and you move from rapids and whitewater to leisurely, serene paddling on the canal, but still with so much to see. The mighty Dee is on your right, still falling down the valley and gorge-like rock buttresses towards Llangollen. You can in places hop onto the towpath and look down to see waves, old bridges and the town as you circumnavigate it.

Around 150m along the canal you'll pass under the first of many bridges. Be aware that the horse-drawn barge operates along here, with glass windows giving passengers a viewing gallery of your paddle. Don't forget to strike a pose and smile!

Just past the bridge you'll paddle past the Chainbridge Hotel and the bridge of the same name. Below the water wrestles through narrower gaps, folding over on itself in angry turmoil. The canal, which has hewn rock outcrops from time to time and wooded areas providing welcome shade, moves slowly forward, never seemingly in a hurry towards its hidden destination. It is the definition of relaxation as the gentle flow is with you and every one of your paddle strokes. About 1km on you'll pass the

LEFT Kayakers dropping over the left hand side of Horseshoe Falls in safe conditions (low flow).

BELOW Paddling along the Llangollen Canal.

Llangollen Motor Museum on the right as the canal bends a gentle rightwards arc.

The canal straightens and continues for another kilometre until you reach Llangollen Pavilion, providing an option to get out and end your trip or split it over two days. There's a small red brick-style bridge and signs on the footpath to signify your exit, and a car park and short carry to load/unload your craft. Another 300m from the Pavilion, on the left of the canal, is Llangollen Basin, a significant fleet of larger boats. Shortly after, you'll arrive at the horse-drawn canal boat centre with a wharf and bridge over the canal.

Below you in the town is Llangollen Bridge, rapids (which are a serious undertaking) and the railway station. The canal remains straight for another kilometre and then begins to curve left and then back to the right before passing under a small road bridge. The canal straightens again, following the natural contours, and then runs parallel to the A539 before dipping under the bigger road bridge after 500m (you are now 14.9km from the start).

There's just 500m of straight paddling to reach The Sun Trevor pub, which we've used to access the canal many times before while, of course, availing ourselves of their services. You'll pass under another bridge on the canal, which is close to two campsites, the Ty Canol Caravan Park and Bryn Howel Caravan Park, close to the next bridge. They are both set back a short distance from the canal. The canal curves around an arc south and then back to the north, passing several small bridges for the next 1.5km before noticeably widening.

Are we nearly there yet? Yes, the aqueduct is not far now, with Bridge 33W the next landmark, which crosses the Offa's Dyke Path. From here you are reaching the dog leg of the Trevor Basin and a right-hand bend over the Dee on to the Pontcysyllte Aqueduct, the world famous 'stream in the sky'.

Explore Trevor Basin, where you can reward yourself with a drink of choice at the Telford Inn or the Pontcysyllte Tea Rooms as well as explore the visitor centre. Then, turn right and head across the aqueduct. It's super exciting. The last time we paddled it the wind was blowing a hooley, and it felt a little bit intimidating, but get those once-in-a-lifetime photos and enjoy the experience up, down and around as you pass over the Dee far below. Be aware, standing on paddleboards across the aqueduct is now (quite obviously) forbidden.

Once across, you'll reach the canal on the other side and trees and houses return to view. All that remains is to paddle 500m to the left-hand turn by the lift bridge and depart the water near the Aqueduct Inn, conveniently located on the A5 old coach road. No fist-pumping necessary, but this really does feel like a true paddling adventure.

EXTEND THE TRIP Paddle from below Llangollen on the Dee to complete the double of paddling both over and under

ABOVE Foxy on guard whilst going under one of the many bridges over the Llangollen Canal.

the aqueduct. This section of whitewater is fantastic and we've paddled it multiple times over the years.

Launch near Mill Street and access the river below Town Falls and the weir, and head downstream for another exciting Dee paddle. The river tracks the canal route so it's possible to return on the canal, but of course the portage up onto the canal can be a serious mission. At 7.3km downstream, after various bends and small rapids, you'll reach Trevor Rocks by the old Pontcysyllte Bridge. Turning the corner you'll pass the towering pillars of the Pontcysyllte Aqueduct, which offers a great photo opportunity.

There are small islands, moorhens and coots as well as a second impressive structure as you reach the Traphont Cefn Mawr Viaduct, which is a Grade II-listed railway bridge 2km on from the aqueduct. Much of the route is gorgeous treelined paddling with heavily wooded areas. The river loops and bends here like a writhing mythical beast as you split your time between England and Wales on the border. The River Ceiriog joins on the right bank and you'll push north for a stretch.

After some more bends and about 20.5km from the start you'll reach a weir, which needs to be portaged, and the good news is you're not far from the get-out. Portage on the left bank and you're now 500m from the riverside pub, the Boat Inn, next to St Hilary's Church in Erbistock. This is a delightful paddle, but allow some time as it's 21.5km to the finish.

OUR RICH ADVENTURE The mighty Afon Dyfrdwy is one of our favourite rivers and it feels like a second home. We've attended many leadership and coaching courses here with some of the best in the business, including Leo Hoare and Chris Charleston of Getafix and Ray Goodwin Coaching.

On a different trip we approached Horseshoe Falls in spate and needed to portage on to the canal. A young leader signalled for us to paddle down to the smallest eddy in flood, with him already

BELOW Ash canoeing over the Pontcysyllte Aqueduct.

in situ. We politely declined and exited safely upstream.

On our last Canoe Trail Best of Wales trip we braved the Dee Loop in canoes and kayaks, starting at T and R at Mile End Mill, playing on the friendly rapids and chutes there. The charming rapids were a great place to share and coach whitewater skills with our customers. We portaged onto the canal up to the Horseshoe Falls and ran the river, mostly the right way up back to the Mill via the Chainbridge Hotel rapids and the Serpent's Tail.

CALORIE CREDITS The Sun Trevor pub and restaurant in Llangollen became a second home to us during our training. It has views over the valley and good access to the water (W: www.suntrevor.co.uk).

Pontcysyllte Chapel Tearooms (W: www.pontcysylltechapeltearoom.com) – we filled up on tea, cake and much, much more. Located in the old converted chapel it is an obvious place to refuel.

We rewarded ourselves for our huge act of bravery battling the aqueduct in strong winds at The Telford (T: 01978 820469).

The Aqueduct Inn is another great watering hole, located at one of the potential exits on this route (W: www.facebook.com/TheAqueductInn/).

ABOVE Extend your route and paddle under the Pontcysyllte Aqueduct too.

WILDLIFE SAFARI The river is keenly fished for trout and salmon so be respectful of other users. Lapwing, otters, kingfishers and herons all share the waterways. Unlike many of the rivers we paddle, we've probably seen less wildlife here, as we're usually concentrating on the rapids and scenery.

OTHER ATTRACTIONS Check in to the lovely Dee-side cabins at Coed-Y-Glyn for a paddling holiday (W: www.coedyglyn-logcabins.co.uk).

Find out more about the Aqueduct and its UNESCO World Heritage Site status on the Canal & River Trust website (W: https://canalrivertrust.org.uk/places-to-visit/pontcysyllte-aqueduct-world-heritage-site).

Visit Chirk Castle, a medieval fortress and former Welsh stronghold (W: www.nationaltrust.org.uk/visit/wales/chirk-castle).

> **WHERE'S THE MAGIC?**
>
> Paddling both under and over the Pontcysyllte Aqueduct spanning the Dee is always something a bit special. Make sure you take time to breathe it all in. The whitewater sections of the Afon Dee bring paddlers from across Britain to enjoy the rolling valley hills, adventure playground and exhilarating rapids. The Dee Loop and Serpent's Tail rapids are bucket list trips.

ABOVE Stunning views from the top of the Pontcysyllte Aqueduct.

Mitchell's Fold Stone Circle is hidden away and despite visiting this region for decades, we always missed it – until now (W: www.english-heritage.org.uk/visit/places/mitchells-fold-stone-circle/).

Walk the Offa's Dyke Path, a national trail spanning 285km along the England–Wales border and built by King Offa in the 8th century (W: www.nationaltrail.co.uk/en_GB/trails/offas-dyke-path/trail-information).

THE SHARED ECONOMY

As you would expect for this natural adventure playground, there are many outfitters to choose from. Canoe Trail's Best of Wales trip includes paddling on the Dee and the Llangollen Canal (W: www.canoetrail.co.uk). Or you can drop in to TNR Outdoors, where you can play on a fantastic stretch of the Dee as well as check out their other activities including axe throwing and trips further afield (W: www.tnroutdoors.co.uk).

Stand Up Paddle Board UK (W: www.standuppaddleboarduk.com), run by the lovely and impressive Anthony and Lianne Ing, offers SUP courses, whitewater rafting and archery, while Ty Nant Outdoors offer trips across the aqueduct (W: https://tynantoutdoors.com).

For those more serious about paddling, you can book coaching and Paddle UK courses with Leo and the team at Getafix (www.getafix.com), or visit Ray Goodwin for one-to-one coaching (W: www.raygoodwin.com).

49 LAKE BALA (LLYN TEGID) AND THE HEAD OF THE RIVER DEE (AFON DYFRDWY)

This beautiful lake nestled in the mountains of Gwynedd is one of our favourite places to paddle in Wales, with its unique location launching the mighty Dee on its way with short moving water sections against the backdrop of a large mountainous landscape. Bala is set in the Snowdonia National Park (officially now known by its Welsh name, Eryri), which is the capital of outdoor activities for all of Wales, so it's worth putting on the out-of-office replies and setting your phone to silent to really make the most of your time in this mountain wilderness.

The Lowdown

DIFFICULTY
A beautiful and accessible lake and short river paddle.

DISTANCE 12km around the circumference of the lake, with option to add 2–3km at the southern end and ~1.5km at the northern end of Afon Dyfrdwy.

DIRECTIONS Park by Bala Adventure and Watersports Centre, ensuring you pay-and-display. From there you can head on to the water from the beach shallows at the southern end. If there is a strong prevailing wind, consider launching further along the lake near Llangower station on the south bank and head out from there.

HAZARDS

CRAFT

	LOCATION	GRID REFERENCE	POST CODE	WHAT3WORDS
PARKING/START	Bala Adventure and Watersports Centre	SH922354	LL23 7SN	evenly.watching.somewhere

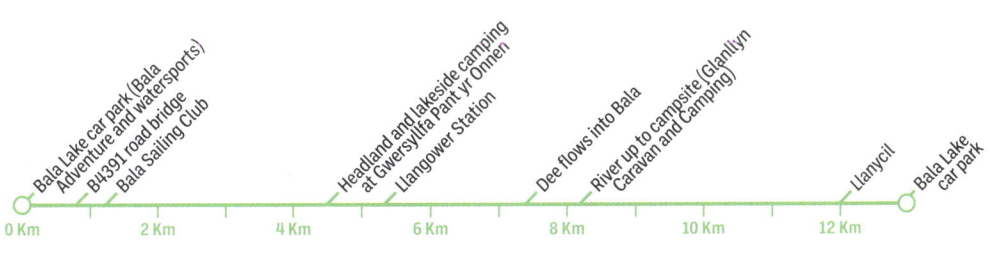

ABOVE Getting ready for some SUP fun in windy conditions.

BACKGROUND Llyn Tegid is a large freshwater glacial lake in Gwynedd, with shallow shores of pebble beaches and grassy banks. The lake is home to a wide array of watersports including paddling and sailing and is served by the small railway. The River Dee, which has its source on the slopes of Dduallt in the mountains of Snowdonia, feeds the 6km long and 0.8km wide lake.

A SLICE OF HISTORY Bala was formed in an ancient glacial valley at the end of the last Ice Age along the fault line between Bala and Tal-y-Llyn. The receding Dee valley glacier left a recessional moraine, like a dam, creating a lake where the market town lies.

Bala is situated at the head of Llyn Tegid in south Snowdonia and has been instrumental in Welsh history and culture. It gave its name to Bala, Ontario, Canada in 1868 and they have more recently become twin towns.

Bala is believed to have been the administrative centre of the commote of Tryweryn, and was fortified in the 1200s, when Prince Llywelyn ap Iorwerth drove out Elis ap Madog, Lord of Penllyn. It was granted a charter, permission to create a mayor role and became a Norman borough in 1310.

In 1974, a little more random was residents reporting seeing random lights streaking across the sky prompting theories that a UFO crashed in the Berwyn Mountains. According to experts, this was a bolide meteor shower and minor earthquake, registering 4-5 on the Richter scale, creating the phenomenon.

ROUTE Park on the large hard standing in front of Bala Adventure and Watersports Centre, unload, and walk the short distance to the lake shore. The beach area shallows can result in short waves if windy and care should be taken to avoid an impromptu dip. If conditions dictate or you need shelter, stay close to the shore. On flat, calm days you can paddle around to your heart's content, zigging and zagging to lakeside locations as you wish.

Heading left in a clockwise direction, skirt along the shoreline with grassy banks and shallows. About 500m later you'll pass Bala Rugby Club (Clwb Rygbi Y Bala). A further 250m on and you'll reach the entrance and outlet for Afon Dyfrdwy (the River Dee), which passes under the B4391 road bridge. Rounding the corner to head south-west you are now adjacent to the Bala Lake Railway. There's a station here and the Pen Y Bont campsite if you're planning on staying in the area for a few days.

It's a couple of hundred metres from Afon Dyfrdwy to Bala Sailing Club, where the paddle becomes a little more remote and tranquil as you leave the town and facilities behind. The B4403 runs along the southern shore so there is some access if needed, albeit it's a fair carry from the water's edge. This section is about 1km across to the other shore so make crossings if wind and waves allow.

You'll follow the shoreline for about 3km, enjoying the peace and quiet of Llyn Tegid, before reaching a headland where it narrows slightly for about another kilometre of paddling. The beautiful Pant Yr Onnen campsite is located here. After the headland there's a small bay, about half a kilometre long, as you approach the end of the lake. It juts out again with a much smaller outcrop, giving you another 500m of paddling around the feature before you push into the further reaches of Bala for another 500m.

You now need to turn right again and navigate the lake end. As you skirt the bays it's about 500m to the inlet of Afon Dyfrdwy, offering the chance to paddle a little bit of its narrow headwaters. It's about 2km upstream to the confluence of Afon Dyfrdwy with Afon Lliw.

Back on the lake, continue clockwise and you'll reach the large bay with the Glan-llyn Outdoor Centre tucked away in the corner. It's 500m across the larger bay if you cut the corner.

Your paddling route follows the gentle undulations of the lake shore and the main road, the A494. Half a kilometre later and the lake widens and heads in a more northerly direction for a few hundred metres opposite the Pant Yr Onnen campsite.

The lake now runs north-east for about 3km, all the way back to the Bala Adventure and Watersports centre. About a kilometre into your return leg the land juts out slightly before a small bay. About 1.7km later you'll reach the Byd Mary Jones World (W: www.bydmaryjonesworld.org.uk), set on the banks of the lake in an old church. You are now just a kilometre from your start point and refreshments.

If the prevailing wind is in your favour, you may well enjoy sailing or running with the wind, downwind back to the centre from the head of the lake.

EXTEND THE TRIP Paddle down a short section (about 800m) of Afon Dyfrdwy towards the sluices on the top section of the mighty river, which bends left and right in gentle curves. To access the river here, paddle under the B4391 bridge and go with the flow. Around 600m downstream there's an inlet from a weir, providing some bubbles and flow where the Afon Trweryn joins.

At the other end of the lake you can paddle a couple of kilometres down the other part of the Dee feeding the lake. You'll need to check the water levels, as

BELOW Coaching on Llyn Tegid on Canoe Trail's Best of Wales trip.

there are gravel bars and small rapids to contend with.

You could also check out Route 48, page 309, which guides you down another section of this stunning river.

OUR RICH ADVENTURE We have enjoyed many a day out on Llyn Tegid during Paddle UK courses with 'Uncle' Ray Goodwin, author of *Canoeing*, and Getafix coaching. Whatever the weather, good, bad or indifferent, it has left us feeling inspired and enthused to simply paddle more. In particular, paddling the southern shore feels a little more remote and secluded.

On one trip we were blasted around the lake by strong winds while practising a range of traditional skills, from sailing to lining and tracking just to make progress upwind. Stopping to grab a brew and a snack break in changeable conditions really does boost your morale on stormy days.

More recently we spent time with our Open Water SUP leader provider (Paddle UK tutor), practising skills and drills. The short section of the river at the lake mouth also offers a fantastic place to play and practise gentle moving water skills on this slow-moving piece of water.

CALORIE CREDITS The Loch Café next to the car park is fantastic for a wide range of excellent snacks, ice cream and a strong brew (T: 01678 520226). Or head into the bustling market town of Bala, where you can enjoy a range of local pubs, cafés and hostelries of all shapes and sizes.

WILDLIFE SAFARI The rare gwyniad fish is native to the lake, while there is a huge range of wildlife in the Bala & Penllyn area, including otters, badgers, foxes, squirrels, red kites and buzzards.

> **WHERE'S THE MAGIC?**
>
> Lynn Tegid is a deeply spiritual place best explored by paddle, slowly, one stroke at a time. It has a rugged and dignified feel to it, while it never quite seems to reveal all of itself, leaving a sense of mystery and excitement for subsequent visits. Despite my many trips to the lake, I still don't feel I know all of it.

OTHER ATTRACTIONS There is so much to do in the region, voted fourth in the world by Lonely Planet for their Top Ten Regions (W: https://visitbala.org.uk). You could also book into Canolfan Tryweryn, the National White Water Centre for Wales (W: www.nationalwhitewatercentre.co.uk) on the dam-controlled River Tryweryn for a session of white-knuckle whitewater rafting or canyoning, only 8km from Bala.

After you're done exploring this mountain wilderness, pull up a chair and relax at Pant Yr Onnen, a lakeside campsite on the shores of Llyn Tegid (W: www.pantyronnencampsite.co.uk).

THE SHARED ECONOMY Bala Adventure and Watersports Centre offers a wide range of activities including canoeing, kayaking, sailing, windsurfing and SUPs. They are an RYA accredited centre and hold an AALA licence (W: www.balawatersports.com).

Canoe Trail offers a Best of Wales paddling trip, which includes Lynn Tegid (W: www.canoetrail.co.uk/canoe-camp/expeditions/paddle-bow).

BELOW This paddle takes you into Eryri (Snowdonia), the capital of outdoor activities for all of Wales.

50 RIVER USK (AFON WYSG)

Chase rainbows through lush green Welsh valleys on this solid whitewater paddle. This is a must-paddle on the 'bucket list' of brilliant grade 2 whitewater in the UK, with bouncy rapids and beautiful scenery. The canal offers a chance for calmer paddling and a potential return loop. Note: ensure you read the seasonal access restrictions, which only allow paddling October to March. Take time to enjoy Brecon's curiosity shops and culture as well as head up to the Brecon Beacons for some additional fresh air miles.

The Lowdown

DIFFICULTY -
A challenging whitewater journey with Grade 2 rapids.

DISTANCE The Promenade, Brecon to Talybont-on-Usk Bridge, A to B: 13.5km.

DIRECTIONS Drive to The Promenade put in at the end of Fenni Fach Road. Park in the car park there and paddle across the river well above the weir to land on the opposite bank. You may need to ferry glide to achieve this so if you haven't perfected that skill, stop, and save this trip for another day. You can either portage on the left bank to access near the bowling green or our preference is to paddle across for the shorter portage on river right, re-joining the river where the River Tarell (Afon Tarell) tributary meets the Usk. It's a 12km shuttle back from Talybont-on-Usk, taking 13 minutes or so by road.

HAZARDS

CRAFT

	LOCATION	GRID REFERENCE	POST CODE	WHAT3WORDS
PARKING/START	Launch site at the Fenni Fach Car Park	SO036289	LD3 9LL	connects.demotion.badge
PORTAGE POINT	At weir; re-join at tributary	SO037289	LD3 8EG	squashes.barmaid.smiling
	Rapids and broken weir	SO084269	LD3 7SL	comment.overlooks.flags
FINISH	Talybont Bridge (right bank before bridge)	SO122233	LD3 7YP	specifies.shrimp.tutorial

BACKGROUND The River Usk offers an adventurous paddle with plenty of rapids and moving water sections whether in canoe or kayak. It is well known in the paddling community as a place to hone whitewater skills and cut your teeth on faster water.

SUP'ERS NOTE

Sensitive access arrangements apply to the River Usk and these must be followed to prevent future restrictions on the wider paddling and fishing communities. The river can only be paddled between 18 October and 2 March inclusive. Check the Wye & Usk Foundation website for up-to-date information (W: www.wyeuskfoundation.org).

A SLICE OF HISTORY

The Tretower Court and Castle lies within the Brecon Beacons National Park. The massive circular tower castle was so striking that the site became known as Tretower or 'the place of the tower'. Originally built over two centuries, from 1100, it became a Welsh stronghold, the tower being four storeys high with walls up to 2.7m thick.

Brecon town has historic defences with four gatehouses and ten semi-circular bastions built from cobble by Humphrey de Bohun after 1240. Welsh prince Owain Glyndwr rebelled against the English in the 1400s. The royal government improved the fortifications to protect Brecon in the event of a Welsh attack during these turbulent times.

ROUTE Launch from the Brecon Promenade and paddle across to the other bank above the weir. You need to be able to ferry glide and paddle across flow to stay away from the weir. Land and portage around the weir, re-joining below and where the River Tarell joins, in about 150m. Once back on the river

BELOW Bridges over the River Usk in higher flows.

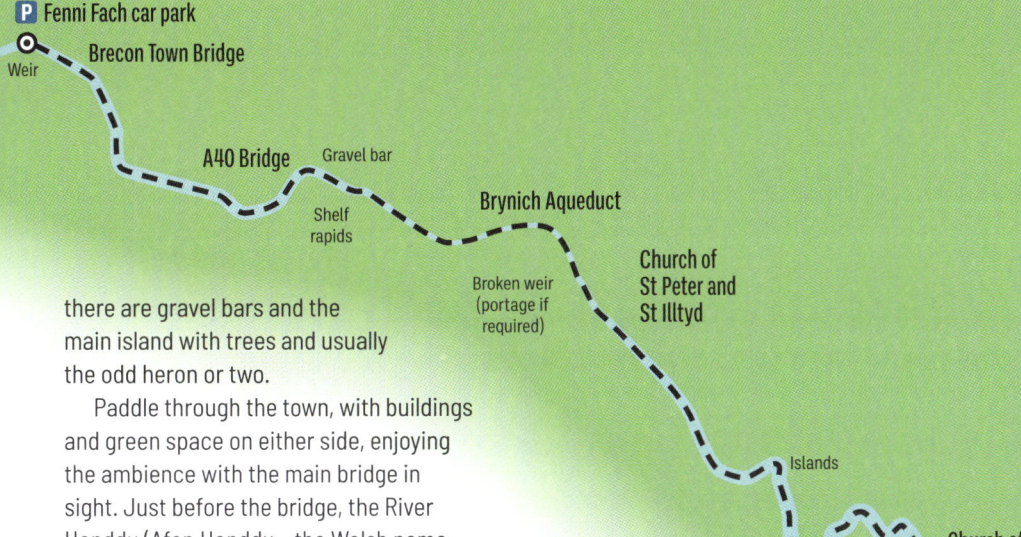

there are gravel bars and the main island with trees and usually the odd heron or two.

Paddle through the town, with buildings and green space on either side, enjoying the ambience with the main bridge in sight. Just before the bridge, the River Honddu (Afon Honddu – the Welsh name means 'mouth of the Honddu') meets on the left bank. Pass under the arches of the impressive looking bridge and you feel a real sense of freedom. Gravel bars and small islets with willow and other foliage decorate the way.

Green fields reveal the rural nature of this beautiful river and after about 800m of fairly straight passage the river swings left with a right-angle bend. It roughly runs parallel to the A40 dual carriageway with some gentle twists and turns. After around 3km with smaller rapids and small waves, the river passes under the A40. There are some larger gravel bars just ahead and, depending on levels, the river kicks left around them or may allow you to bisect the island. Follow the main flow and the riffle rapids.

The rapids begin to change a little as they are massaged by laterally running slab rock, creating some waves and slight drops which are great fun. The Usk bends gently left and you'll see the B4558 road bridge adjacent to the Brynich Lock. About 200m after the bridge is the Brynich Aqueduct and then a series of smaller, fun whitewater sections with obvious channels and downstream 'V's to follow.

About 1.5km downstream you'll reach an old rock weir across the Usk, which was hard to spot in the flood conditions we were enjoying. The farm buildings on the left bank are a good landmark. We portaged this for safe passage on the left bank through the farm. It's a reasonable carry but a good chance to stretch your legs. About 500m downstream you'll pass the Peterstone Court Country House & Spa, but don't get

ABOVE Rich and Craig on the River Usk on a winter's day.

ABOVE The broken weir rapid that may be portaged around.

distracted from your mission and abandon ship! Just past the spa is the Church of St Peter and St Illtyd, which serves as another good landmark. The river calms at this point and runs south-east for 1.5km until reaching a sharper left-hand bend with oxbow-type characteristics and sand bars, islands and channels depending on the levels. It sweeps right around on to itself before heading south for about 500m. The next section is a series of wild switchback loops with multiple channels at lower levels. Follow the main flow where possible and keep an eye out ahead for trees blocking channels (strainers), which can be dangerous.

The river completes a giant S-shaped course, snaking past islets, trees and island channels while heading to follow the A40 again. More bucking and bronking from the river follows to bring it back on to a straight courses as it winds and waves its way along, following the main road. Eventually it calms and runs parallel to the dual carriageway as it heads towards the bridge at Talybont-on-Usk. You'll see St Ffraid's Church and the bridge. Exit on the right bank before the bridge and carry to the gate across the field. Shuttle back to Brecon and kick back for a few days in this spectacular area.

EXTEND THE TRIP You can paddle the upper stretches of the Usk from Sennybridge down to Brecon, which is a more committing paddle and requires significantly more experience, as there are several more technical drops and narrow, rocky elements. They can be portaged but it's a more serious undertaking at Grade 2/3.

Plan a second day of paddling using the Monmouthshire and Brecon Canal, which mirrors the route of the Usk. You can of course opt for out-and-back trips on the canal to the aqueduct or further on to Tallybont-on-Usk, or head out A to B and arrange a shuttle.

OUR RICH ADVENTURE The River Usk is one of the last rivers I paddled for this book and a recent addition to my collection after a lifetime of paddling. We arrived in Brecon with the river in spate and unloaded under the arc of a radiant and colourful rainbow, having stayed in cabins with a crew of paddlers who were eager to explore a number of local rivers.

Once on the river we were straight into continuous rapids and setting accurate courses to avoid sand bars and trees. The river was fast and vast, as levels meant some features were washed out and hidden below the bubbling, whirling, fast-flowing torrent. One of the larger rapids was simply huge and although we could see a line to paddle it we didn't have anyone experienced with safety with us, and the consequences of a swim or a pin seemed near fatal. We shelved the plan to paddle it and portaged around, happy with our decision. The river continued to excite and challenge in equal measure from start to the end. We left smiling, promising to return.

CALORIE CREDITS Head eastwards to the Three Horseshoes Inn at Groesffordd, which has even featured in *Vogue* magazine (W: http://threehorseshoesgroesffordd.com), while the Star Inn in Talybont is very accommodating and includes a store, a café and a post office on the canal side (W: www.talybontstores.co.uk/). Finally, The Old Ford Inn is on your shuttle route (W: www.theoldfordinn.com).

WILDLIFE SAFARI Kingfishers, herons, deer... it was a busy day for spotting wildlife, despite the heavy rain we had experienced over the previous days.

> **WHERE'S THE MAGIC?**
>
> The Usk is known as one of the classic Welsh whitewater rivers, with tumbling rapids along much of its stretch. Don't be put off by the access restrictions; simply paddle carefully and look forward to discovering this beautiful river for yourself.

BELOW Heading further down the River Usk.

OTHER ATTRACTIONS Brecon itself is one of those towns that punches well above its weight. It holds an annual jazz festival, which has been running for 40 years, while there are stunning views from the hills around the town. And, of course, this is the Brecon Beacons National Park, which became the first International Dark Sky Reserve in Wales in 2012. The visitor centre and tea rooms in the park are particularly inviting (W: www.breconbeacons.org/business/attraction-brecon-beacons-national-park-visitor-centre).

Further south, but likely on your route to the Usk, is the impressive Clydach Gorge near Abergavenny, where you can rock hop around the cascading river and gorge.

Just minutes away is the National Showcaves Centre with a dinosaur park, shire horse centre and three giant caverns (W: www.showcavesbookings.co.uk). Or visit the Llangorse Multi Activity Centre, which has climbing, horse riding, archery, accommodation and more (W: www.activityuk.com).

If you're looking for a place to stay, check into Rhydywernen Farm Camping Site in Brecon, which you can book through Pitchup. Or stay at Talybont Farm Camping, which is a working farm with good facilities close to the river and canal (W: www.talybontfarmcamping.co.uk). Gilestone in Talybont-on-Usk offers a wide range of options, from glamping with hot tubs to camping and a Georgian farmhouse for rent (W: www.gilestone.co.uk). And there's always the YHA in Talybont-on-Usk, so you can enjoy a base camp with four walls.

THE SHARED ECONOMY Find your inner adventurer with Adventure Britain, which is located in the Brecon Beacons and offers watersports, canyoning and plenty more to get your heart racing (W: www.adventurebritain.com).

Visit the Boat House Near Fenni Fach car park where you can book pedalos and other craft (T: 01874 622995).

ABOVE This can be quite a challenging paddle, especially with high flows.

ABOUT US

RICH

I moved 13 times by the time I was 13, following Dad's work as an engineer, but in doing so I developed a love of the sea, rugged hills and mountains, and rivers. I was born a water baby by all accounts so it was no surprise that when we settled in Bedford some 40 years ago I joined Viking Kayak Club. Bedford is a river town. The River Great Ouse is the heart of the place.

Learning to kayak at Viking with the late great Copper Harper, who ran the youth service, we were immersed in paddling by a people who simply loved our sport. It has been our great privilege to 'pay it forward', passing on skills and a passion for paddling to thousands of others.

In 2009 I created The Big 5 Kayak Challenge, which involved me tackling several particularly challenging paddles for charity. This included my first Channel crossing to France, paddling the length of the River Thames in 33 hours, paddling from Land's End to the Isles of Scilly, paddling all the way around the Isle of Wight and also paddling 1,000 miles by sea kayak from Vancouver to Alaska. I was hooked and have now completed over 14,500 miles' worth of adventures (not all of them with my paddle!), from skiing in the Yukon winter (minus 50 degrees...) to cycling the Sahara (over 40 degrees) by fat bike.

There have been plenty more incredible paddling adventures too, including canoeing the Yukon River, sea kayaking Scotland to Ireland, paddling from Niagara Falls to the Statue of Liberty with the New York Spare Seat Expedition, and London to Marrakech by bike and kayak.

During the last decade I have embraced the Paddle UK pathway to qualifications, becoming an Advanced Canoe Leader, Moderate Water Endorsed Coach, Sea Kayak Leader, guide and now a provider of leader and instructor qualifications through Canoe Trail. I am a Fellow of the Royal Geographical Society for my human powered adventures and an inspirational speaker.

Ash and I developed Canoe Trail, which means the rivers (along with lochs and the sea) are our office as well as our playground. Leading trips for our customers is the best kind of remote working.

ASH

I grew up in a sleepy Bedfordshire village on the Greensand Ridge called Clophill, where I fell in love with horses. I was lucky enough to start riding and went to university, where I eventually completed a Masters in Human and Equine Biology. Holidays were always camping or by the sea and I loved nothing more than swimming and surfing.

Years later Rich and I met and paddling adventures, the great outdoors and horses (we have three shires and a cob) remain a core focus of our lives. In between I worked at one of the Queen's horse yards, working with horses that needed more training. Experience grafting outdoors has given me a head start transferring skills to paddling, but having good balance has helped too!

Rich and I also run a multi award winning social enterprise called www.inspiredlife.org, which has engaged over 47,000 people with well-being resources and was a London 2012 Project.

I've quickly developed a love for big paddling adventures to wild places in the likes of Wales, Scotland and Canada. I qualified as a Level 2 coach and completed Canoe Leader training, white water safety and rescue courses, SUP qualifications, developing theories and skills in parallel.

Much of my apprenticeship was on the trail, in remote locations, paddling big rapids that are far off the beaten track. To this day I remain in love with the wilder, more rugged places, enjoying hills and dales, wild swimming, and paddling our more remote waters.

ACKNOWLEDGEMENTS

Thanks so much to many coaches and friends at Viking Kayak Club such as Mike, Geoff Tilford, Revo, Aaron and Dean Buckingham, Marc Nicolson, Aisling and so many other stalwarts who are the lifeblood of sports clubs. You have really helped me to maintain a Peter Pan paddling existence.

A huge mention must go to Copper Harper and his family, who inspired a generation of outdoor types at Newgale, and Peter Wathan, our sports teacher who persevered with us reprobates, presumably seeing something in the rough diamonds. They all saved me from self-destruction and gave me the start I loved in paddling.

Since then so many friends have joined me on expeditions, including Olly Jay (Active4season) who has been a mentor and expedition buddy and saved my bacon on many occasions. Thanks also to a wider group of paddling legends including: Roger Palin (general paddling buddy), Ben Campbell (paddling machine), Ray Goodwin (Canoe Leader training), Rob Campbell, who introduced me to racing canoes (and has won the DW in C1 three times), Nick Cunliffe (sea kayak leader training), Ken Hughes (Moderate Water and Advanced Canoe Leader training and assessment), Leo Hoare and Chris Charleston of Get A Fix training (Core Coach Level 2 assessment).

Thanks a million to paddlers from the highest levels of our sport for providing us with inspiration every day and who we can call friends, including James 'Pringle' Bebbington (former British and World Freestyle Champion), Helen Reeves (Olympic Bronze Medalist), Etienne Stott and Tim Baillie (Olympic Champions, London 2012), James Reeves (former World Freestyle Champion) and Chris Harvey (former world surf kayak champion). Not forgetting so many other incredible paddlers we have spent time with, including the late Bren Orton, Dr Tim Brabants, several GB Rafting teams over the years and many more lifelong paddlers.

Thanks also to long suffering friends, Tuffin, Billy, Cody and others, and of course my brother Matt for joining us on countless paddling adventures.

Thanks to some incredible brands who have supported our dreams over many years including BAM (a bamboo clothing company run by the incredible Dave 'BAMpants' Gordon), Paramo Clothing (the world's first Fair Trade outdoor clothing company), Valley Sea Kayaks, Bending Branches, Aquabound Paddles, MSR Kit, Flint Group, Esquif Canoes, Surly Bikes, Palm Equipment and of course everyone at our own company, Canoe Trail.

Canoe Trail has allowed us to share our love of watersports and adventure with likeminded people, from families to customers embarking on charity challenges, through our adventure school youth programmes to the Duke of Edinburgh Award Scheme. You make our job never feel like work when you bring beaming smiles to the rivers, lakes and sea. Thank you.

We wanted to dedicate our first book to some joyful spirits in our lives, people who have lit up our lives or others around them and in particular Rich's dad Alan, whose smile and love of the outdoors was unfaltering. And Bren Orton, who always inspired and had time for everyone. We miss them.

Finally to our publishing team, we salute you for your vision and patience, provided in equal measure. Putting together a comprehensive paddling guide is never easy but coupled with lockdowns and challenging times this has been tough. Thank you for believing in us.